Higher Creativity for Virtual Teams:
Developing Platforms for Co-Creation

Steven P. MacGregor
IESE Business School, Spain

Teresa Torres-Coronas
University Rovira i Virgili, Spain

INFORMATION SCIENCE REFERENCE

Hershey · New York

Acquisitions Editor:	Kristin Klinger
Development Editor:	Kristin Roth
Senior Managing Editor:	Jennifer Neidig
Managing Editor:	Sara Reed
Assistant Managing Editor:	Sharon Berger
Copy Editor:	Joy Langel
Typesetter:	Jamie Snavely
Cover Design:	Lisa Tosheff
Printed at:	Yurchak Printing Inc.

Published in the United States of America by
Informaion Science Reference (an imprint of IGI Global)
701 E. Chocolate Avenue, Suite 200
Hershey PA 17033
Tel: 717-533-8845
Fax: 717-533-8661
E-mail: cust@igi-pub.com
Web site: http://www.igi-pub.com

and in the United Kingdom by
Information Science Reference (an imprint of IGI Global)
3 Henrietta Street
Covent Garden
London WC2E 8LU
Tel: 44 20 7240 0856
Fax: 44 20 7379 0609
Web site: http://www.eurospanonline.com

Library of Congress Cataloging-in-Publication Data

Higher creativity for virtual teams : developing platforms for co-creation / Steven P. MacGregor and Teresa Torres-Coronas, editors.

p. cm.

 Summary: "This book presents advanced research on the concept of creativity using virtual teams, demonstrating a specific focus and application for virtual teams. It presents tools, processes, and frameworks to advance the overall concept that leveraging ideas from different locations in an organization and within extended networks is based on creativity, which can deliver innovation"--Provided by publisher.

 Includes bibliographical references and index.

 ISBN 978-1-59904-129-2 (hardcover : alk. paper) -- ISBN 978-1-59904-131-5 (ebook : alk. paper)

 1. Virtual work teams. 2. Teams in the workplace. 3. Creative ability in business. I. MacGregor, Steven P. II. Torres-Coronas, Teresa, 1966-

 HD66H545 2007

 658.4'022--dc22

                         2007007265

British Cataloguing in Publication Data
A Cataloguing in Publication record for this book is available from the British Library.

Table of Contents

Section I
Tests: Discovering Insights for Creative Success in Virtual Teams

Section II
Tales: From the Battlefield of Virtual Team Practice

Section III
Tools: Unlocking the Power of Virtual Teams for Creativity

Detailed Table of Contents

Section I
Tests: Discovering Insights for Creative Success in Virtual Teams

Chapter I

Modeling Work Processes and Examining Failure in Virtual Design Organizations /
Steven P. MacGregor 1

Based on two industrial case studies this chapter models the virtual process observed in original and adaptive/variant design environments. Virtual problems or 'failures' are generated and examined using failure modes and effects analysis (FMEA), to develop insight into possible solutions. The suitability of the design field is shown for the study of creativity in virtual teams and the link between design, creativity, and business performance is discussed.

Chapter II

Creativity in Asynchronous Virtual Teams: Putting the Pieces Together / *Rosalie J. Ocker* 26

This chapter explores creativity within the context of asynchronous virtual teams. Using four experiments, Dr. Ocker studies how creative performance is affected by individual team member personality, team composition, and team interaction.

The key resources for development are product developers, but it is questionable whether existing structures are appropriate for the education of such professionals. This chapter describes the European Global Product Realization (E-GPR) course program and reflections from the perspective of participating students and company representatives.

In this chapter the authors conduct an empirical study of the media ensembles employed by 46 industrial teams involved in hi-tech new product development. They find that being above or below average cannot be explained by theories that focus on single media: the creative performance of new product development teams is a function of the media ensembles used.

This chapter presents a model that outlines five building blocks for enhancing and supporting creative work in virtual teams. The five building blocks are—design, climate, resources, norms, protocols, and continual assessment. By building and maintaining each of the five building blocks discussed in this chapter, virtual teams may move to higher levels of creativity and ultimately success.

Section II
Tales: From the Battlefield of Virtual Team Practice

This chapter presents insights from conversations with global team leaders on how to foster creativity in global virtual project teams in the field of product development. It shows how the leaders pay attention to team formation and managing the group dynamics in order to create a climate in which creativity will flourish.

Drawing from experiences in automotive and aerospace development, the authors argue that it is time to radically progress our current understanding of how creativity could be introduced in organizations where factors like legal demands and contractual agreements severely restrict 'outside-the-box' thinking, and where well-known creativity enablers such as trust, shared goals, and shared culture are becoming increasingly difficult to accomplish.

Chapter VIII

This chapter describes, through four case studies, how a typical small and medium size enterprise (SME) achieved successful virtual team working within their organization. A "Strategy for Enabling Creative Virtual Teams" encompassing the processes, methods, and tools developed and implemented within the company to achieve this success is presented. Generic and transferable findings drawn from this study aimed at helping other SMEs, form the conclusion of this chapter.

Chapter IX

In this chapter, a detailed insight is provided into three experiences of virtual teams from companies in the Mondragón Cooperative Corporation. Details are provided regarding the needs and opportunities behind the decision to set up the virtual team, the organizational structure adopted in each case, the dynamics incorporated to achieve higher creativity, and suggested practices that can put the reader on the path toward common drivers for virtual creativity.

This chapter uses examples from the industrial and interaction design sector to examine the challenges of managing customer expectations, explore the membership dynamics of virtual teams, and suggest a new framework for assessing the progress of creative virtual teams—concept maturity. An example from the creative virtual team at Synaptics, the Red Dot Award winning Onyx mobile phone concept, is used to delve deeper into these concepts.

Section III
Tools: Unlocking the Power of Virtual Teams for Creativity

This chapter examines the ways in which currently available software applications can support the creative process in general, and designers, in particular, working in virtual teams. The chapter provides examples of tools, considering their strengths and limitations, and speculates on future directions for software development to support creativity and collaboration within virtual teams.

This chapter provides tools and approaches for being flexible to the inevitable changes in contemporary teamwork as creative teams proceed. These include ways of lowering the cost of change, anticipating change, isolating change, and maintaining options as late as possible. Such tools and approaches will help virtual teams working on highly creative projects to take advantage of their creativity without compromise.

This chapter offers a spatial concept of the way virtual design teams communicate, work, and ultimately design. It is concerned with two problems that face creative teams today: (1) That the design process is carried out through a diverse range of digital media, and (2) That the digital tools used by virtual teams are not designed for virtual team work, which often limits the creative efficiency.

This chapter looks at the way a virtual space may be built and used to facilitate group, team, and individual thinking in developing projects and also shaping practice in organizations where innovation is an important focus. The chapter describes the work being done to produce an interactive networked based 'coinnovation' environment (iCE).

This chapter presents an overview of a virtual design environment (virtual platform) developed as part of the European Commission funded VRShips-ROPAX (VRS) project—where the design of an innovative passenger ship was the overall aim. The main objectives for the development of the virtual platform are described, followed by the discussion of the techniques chosen to address the objectives, and finally a description of a use-case for the platform. The platform may be extended out with ship design to the creative development of any large made to order product.

Foreword

IS "CREATIVE VIRTUAL-TEAMS" AN OXYMORON?

I recommend this book to anyone who would like an answer to the question.

It is not a trivial proposition. A certain preoccupation with things "virtual" may well have a causal relationship to growing concern in the sociotechnical development community (those seeking innovation), that things are not getting better. That, in fact, all this "virtual" communication may well be undermining creative behavior, in part by demanding that more and more attention cycles go to "coordination" rather than substantive creative thought. Others might even argue that by spending more time in "virtual team" scenarios we have less time for personal creative thought.

At the risk of being too academic, please consider the definition of "oxymoron" offered to us by a well-known "virtual encyclopedia," the Wikipedia (2006):

An oxymoron (plural oxymora or, more commonly, oxymorons) (noun) is a figure of speech that combines two normally contradictory terms.

Oxymoron is a Greek term derived from oxy (sharp) and moros (dull). The meaning is "that which is sharp and dull," thereby designating and also exhibiting an opposition between two adjectives, which serve as predicates for one subject.

Oxymorons are a proper subset of the expressions called contradictions in terms. What distinguishes oxymora from other paradoxes and contradictions is that they are used intentionally, for rhetorical effect, and the contradiction is only apparent, as the combination of terms provides a novel expression of some concept, such as "cruel to be kind."

In popular usage, the term oxymoron is sometimes used more loosely, in the sense of a simple contradiction in terms. Often, it is then applied to expressions that, unlike real oxymora, are used in full earnest and without any sense of paradox by many speakers in everyday language. I encourage the reader to see that this book's editors, Steven P. MacGregor and Teresa Torres-Coronas, use "creative virtual teams" in later sense. They and the authors of these collected works seek to empower and afford creative activity in circumstances dominated by the technology of the virtual. To my way of thinking, they strive to make the virtual-teamwork "real."

HOW, IN THE PURSUIT OF CREATIVE BEHAVIOR, CAN "VIRTUAL TEAMS" BE MADE MORE REAL?

I encourage the reader to use the book's extensive introduction to gain an overview of the strategies applied by our authors to make virtual teamwork real. In most cases, the context of the scenario is overwhelming critical to choosing how best to proceed. The reader is advised to first review those papers that appear to address virtual teamwork in circumstances most like those they are encountering in their own work and organizations. There are many insightful examples. And, as is so often the case in design-thinking, it is the context that defines the successful design, not an overarching theory. Therefore, let context be your guide.

Don't leave the book without exploring most of the other cases. They will help you gage the robustness and generality of solutions found and proposed in cases your most identify with.

Speaking for myself, I have been deeply engaged in creative product development and research teamwork for over 30 years. During the past 15 years, those teams have been increasing colocated and distributed globally and institutionally, academic and corporate. At this time, 100% of my engagements are globally distributed new product innovation teams. We use any and all technology available to do real creative teamwork.

The one and only general principal that I can offer to date is that making teammate relationships "real" is the number one functional design requirement. Any manner of physical and/or technical adaptation that furthers this goal is worth exploring. More difficult, is the need to change human behavior, especially social behavior, needed to support cocreative activity. But this is another story, for another time.

You have in your hands an extraordinary opportunity to sample the experiential wisdom of some extraordinarily bright people who have been struggling to empower creativity in virtual team. I know many of them through decades of collaboration and several "virtual teamwork scenarios" we have done together. I can speak comfortably to the fact that they know what they are talking about.

There are important practical consequences for, amongst others, engineering design, innovation management, discovery science, and knowledge management. Going beyond the big effects, there are also everyday implications for creative activity any time, anywhere with anyone.

REFERENCE

Oxymoron. (2006). Retrieved November 20, 2006, from http://en.wikipedia.org/wiki/Oxymoron

Larry Leifer has been a member of the Stanford School of Engineering ME Design faculty since 1976. He teaches a year long master's sequence, me310, "Team-Based Design Innovation with Corporate Partners," the "Design Theory and Methodology Research Forum," and a freshman seminar "Designing the Human Experience: Design Thinking in Theory and Practice." He is the founding director of the Stanford-VA Rehabilitation R&D Center (1978-89), Stanford Center for Design Research (1984), Stanford Learning Lab (1997-2002), and member of the new Hasso Plattner Institute of Design at Stanford (d.school) (2005). Active research projects include: (1) creating collaborative engineering environments for distributed product innovation teams; (2) instrumentation of that environment for design knowledge capture, indexing, reuse and performance assessment; and (3) design-for-wellbeing as socially responsible engineering.

Preface

Virtual teams are gathering increasing pace in industry and academia. In general, practice in both areas has moved beyond early experimentation toward maturity. Perhaps surprising is that such experimentation dates back 20 years with a mature knowledge base evident, at least in the past 10. As editors, our own experiences with virtual teams—as students, teachers, researchers, and practitioners - belie this long lifespan. With maturity comes an expectation of increased performance which, arguably, has not been realized. At the very least, dialogue in the community should encompass value-adding characteristics of the virtual teams approach as opposed to merely addressing challenges and constraints of virtual work. Most work to date has stalled on problems and a mostly defensive, reactive approach to virtual teams. In this book (in Chapter I, although departing from a problem focused stance), we focus on added value—specifically creativity—therefore linking virtual teams to proactive choice. The ultimate aim should be performance levels beyond conventional collocated working practices. In theory, due to the possibility of pooling a large diverse knowledge base, virtual creativity could be greater than collocated creativity. In practice this is often not the case. No longer should virtual teams be considered new or suboptimal methods of working. They now constitute standard practice and the value which they add should be greatly increased.

This is a book for those involved in working with or managing (creative) virtual teams, or indeed anyone involved in the active pursuit of co-creation or innovation in the modern enterprise. There are two factors at play here—first, most, if not all collaborative work these days includes some element of virtual work and second, for innovation in an increasingly demanding environment, creativity, higher creativity is a critical element. Of course, it is not the whole story for innovation but if innovation is the destination, creativity can be viewed as the journey, or at least the first critical steps on that journey.

Higher Creativity for Virtual Teams: Developing Platforms for Co-Creation presents insights gained by leading professionals from the practice, research, and consulting side of the virtual team, design, new product development, and creativity fields. This book should be useful to a variety of constituents who are interested in the interrelationships between virtual working environments and creative performance, including managers who need innovation as a key factor for organizational success, leaders wishing to develop the creativity within their organizations, IT experts, researchers, consultants, and practitioners. Each audience may have different levels of interest in the support tools, practical experiences, and empirical data presented in this book.

So what is a virtual team? On a simple level, it is a team that is separated physically and uses information and communication technologies (ICTs) to connect and complete the team's task. This physical separation is a function of time and place—virtual teams do not occupy the same place at the same time. Further, separation may be a mix of geographical, organizational, or temporal distance while the term *virtual* has become the de facto standard for the community; other terms include distributed, dispersed, and global. Additionally, the term virtual is sometimes used to denote the nonpermanent nature of a team—for us, virtual teams need not be temporary although the virtual space *is* highly dynamic. Little time is spent on definitions and explanations in the remainder of the book, focusing instead on experiences, insights and solutions. We spend just enough on definition and context so as to uncover the true needs of co-creation platforms for real creative performance improvement.

The increased growth of virtual teams practice can be attributed on the main to advances in ICTs and the globalization of industry and markets. Technological advancement has been important, yet development has been facilitated by several other factors that have improved performance, including better work processes and increased understanding and awareness of how to operate in the virtual space. The turbulent environment in which we live and work today provides the operating context for the normalization of virtual teams. The concepts of the extended enterprise and the Open Source movement, among others, show that work can be highly collaborative, potentially large-scale, and without boundaries. The Global Innovation Outlook 2.0 from IBM (2006) envisages the future of the enterprise where boundaries continue to disappear, facilitating fluid, contract knowledge work between people, the majority of whom may not be affiliated to any particular organization. This resonates strongly with classic views on the emergence of knowledge workers (Drucker, 1969). Peter Drucker was the first to envision the pervasiveness of virtual organizations in which the true value of the knowledge worker is exploited. The recent emergence of *open innovation* (Chesborough, 2003), shows that such historical views are in the here and now and impact heavily on business success. The most valuable implementation of this concept to date comes from Procter & Gamble, whose 'Connect & Develop' business model has already reaped significant returns (Huston & Sakkab, 2006). This shows a possible common future in industry—one that is highly collaborative, very large-scale, and without boundaries.

Yet the author of the *open innovation* term has also criticized the virtual team model (Chesborough & Teece, 1996), arguing that it cannot be implemented for each and every business case. This may be partly attributed to the date of publication (and state of virtual work at that time), but also disappointment with the resultant performance levels of most virtual endeavors—suboptimal levels that we believe have persisted to this day. Our vision therefore is to re-ignite the virtual team's movement, which has perhaps suffered in recent years through, among other things, a realization that technology cannot replicate exactly the collocated space.

In this context it is time to analyze how to achieve high levels of creative performance. Only a few researchers have focused on how a virtual team can use creativity to perform better or build a really creative virtual environment. This is despite the fact that, "80 per cent of managers rated creativity as one of the most important elements in corporate success, yet less than 5 per cent of organizations actually put this emphasis into practice" (Walton, 2003, p. 143). Today, it is broadly accepted that the key to organizational success lies in developing intellectual capital and acquiring a new set of thinking: the creativity to produce an idea and the innovation to translate the idea into a novel result (Roffe, 1999). Explaining the meaning of creativity is not straightforward, there are many definitions of the term. So, for the purpose of this book we will understand creativity as the shortest way to search for unconventional wisdom and to produce ideas. This unconventional wisdom through the generation and use of creative knowledge is the key to building sustainable competitive advantage.

Why then should creativity be related to virtual teams? As stated, the virtual team's movement should move away from a defensive stance—problem-centric, to a value-adding one. Although a large body of work exists on virtual teams there is relatively little that deals with creativity. When one considers the opportunities provided by virtual teams, to truly exploit different knowledge sets and diversity, then the pursuit of creativity is well matched to virtual teams. A greater dialogue on creativity is certainly required—and increasingly critical in a world which demands innovation. In this new world, creativity is rapidly emerging as one of the main differentiating factors for success. As such, virtual teams can be hardwired to innovation objectives. Showing the increasing focus on creativity for business success, many top business schools are busily introducing new creative based curricula in response to industry requests for better prepared managers (Nussbaum, Berner, & Brady, 2005). Such a call from industry is partly in response to the difficulties they face in achieving continuous, systematic and sustainable innovation. Recent reports have talked about an 'innovation drought' (Mullaney, 2006) and there is no doubt that innovation is getting harder. Cox (2005) reports on the Innovation Survey from PricewaterhouseCoopers, which states that top innovators generate over 75% of revenue from products not in existence five years ago. He states that the ability to innovate, in turn, depends on the availability and exploitation of creative skills.

The work of Cox was delivered within the context of a recent push on creativity by the UK Government. Recognizing the role of creativity in delivering better business performance the *Cox Review of Creativity in Business* and economics analysis by the Department of Trade & Industry linking creativity, design and business performance (DTI, 2005) were published. Demonstrating commitment to creativity at the very top of Government, the Chancellor of the Exchequer, Gordon Brown notes the challenge as "not just to encourage creative industries, our priority is to encourage all industries to be creative." In this technological age and to take advantage of the distributed knowledge base it is clear that virtual teams will play a key role in helping to deliver the higher creativity necessary for innovation and business performance.

Given such challenges, we aim to help *develop platforms for co-creation*. As shown by policy development of the British Government creativity is viewed as a strategic element for innovative co-creation and increased business performance. What do we mean by co-creation? Co-creation is an existing term, with roots in the business community (von Hippel 1994, 2005; Prahalad & Ramaswamy, 2004). On a basic level therefore, we aim to connect virtual teams to business, or at least have a clearer view on value creation. The 'creation' process is about the design and development of products and services—about innovating in an era of increasing constraints and problems. And of course, in virtual work this creation is not done in isolation but with a large input from internal and external stakeholders—dispersed colleagues, customers, and other collaborators with a wide range of skills and personalities, and from a wide degree of functions and cultures. As an existing term co-creation focuses on the involvement of customers in the innovation process—but we do not restrict our definition in this way. The key for us is that the virtual team process is open and collaborative—which will of course involve customers, but not exclusively, nor for each and every occasion. The virtual platform offers opportunities for innovative work, innovative *co-creation* that is, as noted above, highly collaborative, potentially very large-scale, and without boundaries.

Platforms are not reserved for the tools section of this book, which details three virtual environments in addition to other methods and technology. We have a holistic view of co-creation platforms that includes an understanding of challenges, experiences, and possible solutions. Culture, organization, and the wider ecosystem—indeed elements described in detail from the authors which comprise this book—are important constituents. Platforms are in essence a basis for extending virtual work, of creating powerful networks of highly dispersed, diverse people in highly dynamic structures. This vision will result in highly creative, innovative work, leading to top business performance. This is the future, yet as shown by Procter & Gamble, it is also the present—and so those who wish to form the next generation of business leaders should pay heed to the logic.

Co-creation platforms go hand in hand with creative virtual teams. We aim to exploit the full creative power of virtual teams by managing and optimizing such platforms. The development of more effective virtual platforms will re-ignite the global innovation co-creation movement. Our wish is that this book is a small step towards this—towards true virtual *co*-creativity.

Value and Highlights

There is no quick and easy answer to achieving the higher creativity necessary for innovative co-creation. However, through the 15 chapters of this book several critical insights emerge which will help the reader find an answer for their own context. Several key themes are progressed through three distinct parts of the book, the ABCs of virtual teams and creativity: "Section I: Tests," is the experimental test-bed for uncovering critical insights into virtual teams and creativity. This preliminary section aims to build a thorough understanding of the principles of virtual teams and creativity—in essence detailing a specification for creative virtual teams support. Next, "Section II: Tales" regales experiences from the 'battlefield' of virtual team practice. Industrial cases show the use of virtual teams and current status in leading companies, thereby moving towards a general understanding of how we can improve the virtual creative work of such teams, as well as showcasing best practice for others to implement. Finally, "Section III: Tools" details support in the form of technology, methods and processes, as well as integrated environments which combine elements of each. Three parts, five chapters in each, tied together by the common aim of higher creativity for virtual teams. It is important to promote dialogue between different areas of the virtual community—researchers, practitioners, and teachers—in order to facilitate a holistic approach to adding value through virtual work—one that is at the same time rigorous, practical, and efficient. In this way, different members of the community may help evolve virtual creative performance.

We now note interesting themes, highlighting several chapters. A full chapter by chapter description follows later. We therefore view the content on both a comparative, cross discussion and individual level.

First, it may no longer be appropriate to talk about 'virtual' and 'nonvirtual' teams. Roger Leenders, Jan Kratzer, and Jo van Engelen (Chapter IV) state that all teams are now virtual and it is the *degree* of their virtuality which distinguishes different teams and work designs. Indeed, Margaret Oertig and Thomas Buergi (Chapter VI) state that the majority of virtual team leaders interviewed for their research—senior level managers with years of experience, "have no experience of project management in a colocated team". So, if all teams are virtual to some extent, should the aim be to replicate the colocated space? Leenders et al., in their investigation of the right "media ensembles" that lead to higher creativity stress the importance of media richness, believing that for complex creative work, face-to-face interaction, or at least the richest communication media available (thereby replicating face-to-face interaction) is essential. Several other authors concur on this point, although through experimentation Rosalie Ocker (Chapter II) showed that asynchronous teams were at no performance disadvantage as compared to synchronous teams. She uses several of these previous experiments to uncover further insights into asynchronous creative work, highlighting, for example, the importance of team composition and personality.

Communication modes are but one area of the overall environment to encourage higher creativity. The role of leadership is highlighted by Oertig and Buergi (Chapter VI) who discuss that effective virtual leaders have to know when to encourage new ideas and when to inject realism into the process, acknowledging that virtual teams can sometimes lose sight of the project constraints and overall objective. Higher creativity is therefore also important in the context of new workable solutions as well as radical ideas. This is highlighted by Andreas Larsson, Tobias Larsson, Nicklas Bylund, and Ola Isakson (Chapter VII) who discuss the role of creativity for "*streamlined*" product development (mature, accelerated development with a focus on cost reduction while maintaining or increasing performance), highlighting several creative dilemmas, including trust and information sharing. This contrasts with the 'fuzzy front end' focus examined in detail by John Feland (Chapter X) and shows that virtual teams are pervasive at all stages of the co-creation process, and that creativity has a role to play in different types of industry.

Realism and control may also be related to the pressures that virtual teams often operate under. The impact of time and stress on the performance of virtual teams, and creative output in particular, is discussed in several chapters. Most of the industrial tales (including Larsson et al., Chapter VII, and Javier Fínez, Chapter IX) state that time pressure has a positive effect on creative output. This is mostly anecdotal and is contrasted with the academic based experimentation by Ocker (Chapter II) which found the exact opposite—she highlights and confirms research by Amabile, Hadley, and Kramer (2002) which states that creativity is reduced when individuals feel time-pressured to complete the task. Yet creative tension has been noted in several places as being a prerequisite for successful innovation. With apologies to our Swiss authors it is perhaps worth recalling the famous (yet factually incorrect) line from Orson Welles in *The Third Man* regarding the respective creative outputs of Italy and Switzerland during their periods of war and peace. In comparing da Vinci with the cuckoo clock we can perhaps conclude that in practice, at least some element of stress and tension is good for creativity.

Knowing when to encourage and control creativity can be related to patterns of divergent and convergent work, a common feature of best practice design. The rationale for using design as a lens to examine creativity in virtual teams is discussed by Steven MacGregor in Chapter I. Design allows a view of 'extreme virtual teams'—the most challenging type of work for virtual teams, because of the large diversity of knowledge bases, cultures, and complexity that usually comprise the design function. If we can make these work the hypothesis is that we can show how all types of virtual teams can strive for higher creativity. In total, six chapters focus on the role of design—in various guises—Chapters I, X, XI, XIII, XIV and XV. A new product development (NPD) focus further complements this co-creative core in another six chapters (Chapters III, IV, VI, VII, IX, and XII).

Arguably, the more conventional view of creativity for virtual teams focuses on the conceptual stage of co-creation where radical ideas can be generated. Several authors allude to concepts of 'experimentation' and 'playfulness' in the virtual space. Larsson et al. (Chapter VII) detail that the present industrial 'battleground' may convert to the 'playground', as a result of higher levels of trust, and in agreement with the disappearance of boundaries as detailed in the IBM GIO 2.0 noted earlier (IBM, 2006). Feland (Chapter X) refers to the *"sandbox"* of virtual teamwork, detailing a very successful case—the prototype development of the Onyx mobile phone concept at Synaptics Inc.

The success of the Onyx project can be partly attributed to the process frameworks used by manager Feland during the project. Concept maturity and an understanding of technical, business, and human level progression helped the virtual team to maintain a high awareness of progress. Such mental models help to measure creative evolution in the virtual space, the importance of which is first discussed in Chapter I by MacGregor. Effective platforms for co-creation therefore rely on effective processes and structures. Fínez (Chapter IX) details the organizational structures used by three successful companies in the Mondragón Corporation. Developing an examination of types of creativity presented above, he highlights the switch in focus between incremental and radical creativity. Through the description of several forms of mature, successful virtual structures, for example the use of stable virtual teams and project virtual teams in MCC graphics, we can at last see the virtual teams model as a value-adding complement to conventional team structures such as heavyweight, lightweight, and tiger teams.

Other process frameworks are detailed by Avril Thomson, William Ion, and Angela Stone (Chapter VIII) who detail a strategy for virtual teams in SMEs. Such a roadmap approach is perhaps essential for smaller enterprises that often, as shown in the chapter, have to deal with day-to-day 'firefighting' pressures at the expense of virtual team performance and creativity. Thomas Leerberg (Chapter XIII) shows how a view of supplemental and substituted processes results in technology more fit for virtual team purpose while Jill Nemiro (Chapter V) sums up the fundamental building blocks that should be considered for creative virtual teams, in one way, a basic specification for the platforms we aim to develop.

Technology of course plays a central role in virtual teams, and used correctly with the right processes and structures, can contribute greatly to creativity. Julian Malins, Stuart Watt, Aggelos Liapis, and Chris McKillop (Chapter XI) provide a guide for those engaged in the design process to the main proprietary tools that can contribute to success. Even for those out with the design field, identified tools for tasks such as idea generation, collaboration, and knowledge management may provide significant value. Clues as to the necessary role of technology for virtual creativity can be derived from the three very different virtual environments which constitute the final three chapters of the book. Leerberg (Chapter XIII) and particularly Terry Rosenberg and Mike Waller (Chapter XIV) focus on less complex design and the pursuit of radical new ideas for creativity. In contrast, Ian Whitfield, Alex Duffy, Alistair Conway, Zuchao Wu, and Jo Meehan (Chapter XV) focus on the engineering design of a large, technically complex product (ship design). It follows that the necessary support in each environment to facilitate creativity will be very different. Technology support for Leerberg, Rosenberg, and Waller takes on the role of a medium to improve communication and creative development between members of the virtual team, while Whitfield et al. exploit technology as an "intelligent assistant", using the power of technology to manage complexity and perhaps free up 'cognitive space' for creativity, a concept introduced by MacGregor in Chapter I. Further, depending on the specific type of design different needs may be satisfied by each of the environments. Whereas Whitfield et al. admit that due to "tool management limitations ..., it was not possible to provide any additional information ... regarding the rationale for undertaking the activity." Rosenberg and Waller show that rationale traceability will be a key feature of their iCE environment. In the section "Leaving Traces" they show how *innovation trajectories* may be recorded during the course of co-creation.

Yet tools for creative success should not focus on the development of technology. Effective methods are also required as shown in the flexibility framework detailed by Preston Smith in Chapter XII. How virtual teams cope with change is of course important, and an area that they have been traditionally poor in coping with. Innovation is about change and Smith details methods that virtual teams may use to cope with the inherent change in creative work. His flexibility framework details eight methods, influenced by fields including agile and lean development, and design.

Creativity-based management aimed at fostering virtual team creativity must also better manage similar environmental variables. This will help to enhance employees' internal drive to perceive every project as a new creative challenge. Nemiro (Chapter V) identifies several key elements that influence creativity in virtual teams and therefore result in effectiveness and high levels of performance. In a virtual team, creativity is highest where the design is appropriate, the climate is supportive of creativity, the resources are sufficient, the proper norms and protocols are agreed on and adhered to, and the team takes the time to assess and to learn from its assessments.

Finally, how to measure creativity is a common theme. Teams ought to have an idea of overall progression regarding the final objective. Various authors use notions of performance, quality (Ocker, Chapter II), and satisfaction (Thomson, Chapter VIII), either using outside evaluators or asking the virtual team members themselves (Leensberg et al., Chapter IV). In both cases, there is an agreement about the measurement of creative performance through "the expert subjective point of view"; a perspective broadly accepted in the literature. The value of higher creativity may also be linked to the learning process, whether it is situated in an academic project or executive education (Roman Žavbi, Jože Tavčar, and Jouke Verlinden, Chapter III). This chapter together with that by Leenders (Chapter XIII) perhaps show the next generation of virtual academic projects, moving beyond a simple evaluation of learning functionality (which dates back over 20 years) to a test-bed for truly preparing students for the real world after their studies. As shown in Chapter III the virtual space offers opportunities for all in an age where the learning process does not stop after university. The lessons learned by Žavbi et al. are also being exploited to train present members of industrial teams, a real need as identified by several authors in the book, including Nemiro (Chapter V).

Detailed Description of Content

The characteristics of each section of the book add value: "Section I: Tests" involves the participation of over 100 teams involved in either industrial or academic virtual creative work. "Section II: Tales" is a detailed description of virtual creative work in eight companies, seven of which are leaders in their field while four are large multinationals and four SMEs. The sectors of automotive, aeronautical, domestic electrical appliances, industrial design, mechanical and electrical engineering design consultancy, design and print graphics, and plastics manufacturing, comprise these rich experiences. Finally, "Section III: Tools" prescribes a wide range of technologies, methods and integrated environments which have either been used extensively in practice or tested on virtual creative teams in academia. The content in each part may either facilitate direct implementation or generate ideas, either for practice or research. Higher Creativity for Virtual Teams: Developing Platforms for Co-Creation is comprised of the following 15 chapters:

In the first chapter, "Modeling Work Processes and Examining Failure in Virtual Design Organizations," Steven P. MacGregor examines virtual work and 'failure' in the oil and gas and fast moving consumer goods sectors. Based on two case studies originally conducted to develop process support for virtual (distributed) design, he models the virtual process observed in the original and adaptive/variant design environments that characterize each sector. These models are used to generate a list of virtual problems or 'failures' which are subsequently examined using the engineering-based techniques 5W2H and Failure Modes and Effects Analysis (FMEA) to develop insight into virtual team problems and possible solutions. The suitability of the design field is shown for the study of creativity in virtual teams and the link between design, creativity and business performance discussed. In many cases, if support is provided to solve virtual team problems not directly associated with creativity then team members may free up time and energy to focus on the increased 'cognitive capacity' required for higher creativity.

Rosalie J. Ocker, in her chapter, "Creativity in Asynchronous Virtual Teams: Putting the Pieces Together," presents four studies conducted to explore creativity in asynchronous virtual teams. Following the input-process-output model developed by Hackman (1987), Ocker investigated different aspects related to team's creativity. Her analysis highlights the importance of team members, in terms of personality, as well as the composition of individuals into teams, in influencing team interaction and the resulting level of team creativity. One relevant finding from her research is that "the findings from the studies of asynchronous virtual teams are consistent with those of traditional teams. Thus, it appears that the body of research on creativity in face-to-face teams applies to asynchronous virtual teams." This statement gives rise to the conclusion that maybe there are no meaningful differences between the factors that affect creativity in traditional environments and those that affect creativity in virtual contexts.

In Chapter III, "Educating Future Product Developers in Virtual Collaboration: Five Years of the E-GPR Course," Roman Žavbi, Jože Tavčar, and Jouke Verlinden describe the European Global Product Realization (E-GPR) course program and reflections from the perspective of participating students and company representatives.

The E-GPR course tries to bring the reality of the virtual enterprise into the classroom through international and cross-disciplinary virtual teams, thereby raising awareness in the students of the principles of global product realization in virtual enterprises. Žavbi, Tavčar, and Verlinden show us an exceptional 'learning- by- doing' experience designed to develop knowledge about the new distributed organizational world and the new professional skills required.

In "Media Ensembles and New Product Team Creativity: A Tree-Based Exploration," the main argument presented by Roger Th. A.J. Leenders, Jan Kratzer, and Jo M.L. Van Engelen (Chapter IV) is that creative teams are not characterized by their use of one particular mode of communication, but rather by the combination of the modes they use. In this chapter the authors attempt to explain why the creativity of some teams is above average, whereas others perform below the average. The results show that being above or below average cannot be explained by theories that focus on single media: the creative performance of NPD teams is a function of the media ensembles used. Some ensembles afford much higher probabilities for above-average creativity than others. These findings enrich theories of media choice and may provide managers with some ideas of how team creativity can be managed.

In the fifth and final chapter of Section I, "The Buildings Blocks for Creativity in Virtual Teams," Jill Nemiro reviews the relevant literature, including prominent models of virtual team performance, and factors necessary for creativity in teams in general. The main aim of this chapter is to present a model that outlines five building blocks for enhancing and supporting creative work in virtual teams: design, climate, resources, norms and protocols, and continual assessment. By building and maintaining each of the five building blocks discussed in this chapter, virtual teams may move to higher levels of creativity and ultimately success. Lastly, an integrative model is proposed which links the five building blocks back to the earlier discussed models of virtual team performance.

"Section II: Tales," begins with Margaret Oertig and Thomas Buergi's chapter, "Fostering Creativity in Global Virtual Teams: Conversations with Team Leaders." Oertig and Buergi present insights from conversations with global team leaders on how to foster creativity in global virtual project teams in the field of product development. Conversations show how the leaders pay attention to team formation and managing the group dynamics in order to create a climate in which creativity will flourish. Three major themes (the leadership challenge, virtual aspects of communication, and developing trust) and four subthemes (managing the task, people, language, and cultural issues) are identified as key factors that affect the project management task.

Next, Andreas Larsson, Tobias Larsson, Nicklas Bylund, and Ola Isaksson present the fascinating 'battlefield' of auto and aero engine development in "Rethinking Virtual Teams for Streamlined Development." They focus on people and teams that might not usually describe their own work to be of a primarily 'creative' nature, and that currently work under circumstances where traditional approaches for enhancing creativity might no longer be applicable. Drawing from experiences in Volvo Aero and Auto Corporation, they argue that it is time to radically progress our current understanding of how creativity could be introduced in organizations. Virtual teams (and organizations) that are able to build the foundation for creativity in natural, seamless, and effortless ways, will be way ahead of the competition.

In Chapter VIII, Avril Thomson, Angela Stone, and William Ion detail the results of case studies in a UK based SME in "Enabling Creative Virtual Teams in SMEs." It is a medium sized company contribution to the *tales* section yet it also complements the tools and methods of the book through the presentation of a strategy for supporting the creative potential of virtual teams within distributed design projects. It is not uncommon for SMEs to have tools and working practice imposed on them by collaborating multinationals to meet the requirements of the multinational. SMEs however, need to develop their own working practices to support effective, virtual team design within their own organization or extended design team. This chapter describes, through a series of four case studies, how a typical SME achieved successful virtual team working within their organization. Generic and transferable findings drawn from this two year study aimed at helping other SMEs, form the conclusion of this chapter.

Javier Fínez then writes a chapter about "Virtual Teams and Creativity in the Mondragón Cooperative Corporation." A detailed insight is provided of three experiences of virtual teams built into MCC (Mondragón Cooperative Corporation) cooperatives, companies in the domestic electrical appliances, plastics manufacturing, and design print and graphics sectors. Each company is a market leader and forms part of MCC, the largest industrial cooperative in the world, based in the Basque Country in the North of Spain. Detailed for each case is an overview of the company's activity, before going into greater depth regarding the needs and opportunities behind the decision to set up a virtual team, the organizational structure adopted in each case, the dynamics incorporated to achieve higher creativity, and suggestions for some practices that can put the reader on the path towards common drivers for virtual creativity.

A growing number of enterprises are building virtual teams to assist in crafting new opportunities in the fuzzy front end of the innovation process. John Feland, in the 10th and final chapter of Section II, "Virtual Teams in Practice: Tales from the Battlefront of the Fuzzy Front End of the Innovation Process," uses examples from industry to examine the challenges of managing customer expectations, explore the membership dynamics of virtual teams, and suggest a new framework for assessing the progress of creative virtual teams, concept maturity. An example from the creative virtual team at Synaptics, the Red Dot award-winning Onyx mobile phone concept, is used to delve deeper into these concepts. Finally, trends for the diffusion of creative virtual teams as well as potential challenges in bringing such teams into your organization are investigated.

"Section III: Tools" starts with "Tools and Technology to Support Creativity in Virtual Teams" by Stuart Watt, Julian Malins, Aggelos Liapis, and Chris McKillop. The authors examine the ways in which currently available software applications can support the creative process in general, and designers, in particular, working in virtual teams. It follows the main stages in the design process, examining how existing software can support the creative process. Emerging innovations for each stage of the design process are also presented. The chapter provides examples of tools, considering their strengths and limitations, and speculates on future directions for software development to support creativity and collaboration within virtual teams.

"Enhancing Flexibility in Dispersed Product Development Teams," a chapter by Preston G. Smith, is devoted to exploring the paradox between dispersed (virtual) teams that are easiest to manage when they can execute their plans without change and the changes required to be creative. To address this, the author introduces the notion of flexibility in dispersed teams showing how one can enhance the flexibility of a team to deal effectively with change. If the team is dispersed, the complications of dealing with changes in plans magnify. This chapter provides tools and approaches for being flexible to such changes as creative teams proceed. These include ways of lowering the cost of change, anticipating change, isolating change, and maintaining options as late as possible.

The final three chapters of the tools section, and of the book, detail three very different virtual environments for virtual team work. In Chapter XIII, "A Spatial Environment for Design Dialogue," Thomas Leerberg offers a spatial concept of the way virtual design team work. He is concerned with two problems that face creative teams today: (1) that the design process is carried out through a diverse range of poorly integrated digital media and (2) that the digital tools used by virtual teams are not designed for virtual team work, which often limits the creative efficiency. The chapter argues that space has a structure and that we can use that structure to navigate and place information in space and thereby create a design space with the virtuality and creativity of an open 'reflection-in-action.' Further, it argues that we have to develop concepts of team setting, team solving, substituted process paths, and supplemented process paths to expand our understanding of these issues. These concepts are demonstrated through two constructions for virtual teams: virtual platform and topos.

Terry Rosenberg and Mike Waller, in their chapter entitled "iCE: Interactive Co-Innovation Environment," point out the way a virtual space may be built and used to facilitate group, team and individual thinking in developing projects and also shaping practice in organizations where innovation is an important focus. The chapter describes the work being done to produce an interactive networked based 'co-innovation' environment (iCE); where members of an organization, individually and variously, may contribute their thoughts to help innovate—developing 'prospects'—for the organization's projects.

Finally, in Chapter XV, "A Virtual Environment to Support the Distributed Design of Large Made-to-Order Products," Robert Ian Whitfield, Alex Duffy, Alastair Conway, Zhichao Wu, and Joane Meehan, present a virtual environment for ship design which can be generalized to any large made to order products. An overview of the virtual environment developed as part of the European Commission funded VRShips-ROPAX (VRS) project is presented. The main objectives for the development of the virtual platform are described, followed by the discussion of the techniques chosen to address the objectives, and finally a description of a use-case for the platform. Whilst the focus of the VRS virtual platform was to facilitate the design of ROPAX (roll-on passengers and cargo) vessels, the components within the platform are entirely generic and may be applied to the distributed design of any type of vessel, or other complex made-to-order products.

FINAL NOTE

Finally, we must note that the development of this book—like many academic and industrial endeavors these days—was a virtual collaborative project that required high levels of creativity. The numbers are interesting but perhaps not 'extreme': 38 people (two editors, three publishers, 33 authors), 22 different locations, and nine native languages—united by English, complemented by a healthy dose of Spanish. Tame by some of today's standards but nonetheless very challenging. We hope that you enjoy the results of our own creative virtual efforts as you aim to increase creativity in your own virtual teams. Enjoy the learning and don't forget to share your knowledge, impressions and interests in this creative field with all of us!

REFERENCES

Amabile, T. M., Hadley, C. N., & Kramer, S. J. (2002). Creativity under the gun. *Harvard Business Review, 80*(8), 52-61.

Chesborough, H. (2003). *Open innovation: The new imperative for creating and profiting from technology.* Boston: Harvard Business School Press.

Chesborough, H. W., & Teece, D. J. (1996). Organizing for innovation: When is virtual virtuous? *Harvard Business Review, 74*(1), 65-73.

Cox, G. (2005). *Cox review of creativity in business: Building on the UK's strengths.* Retrieved November 15, 2006, from http://www.hm-treasury.gov.uk/cox

Drucker, P. (1969, reprint 1992). *The age of discontinuity: Guidelines to our changing society.* Somerset, NJ: Transaction Publishers.

DTI. (2005, November). Economics paper No. 15. Creativity, design and business performance. Department of Trade & Industry, UK.

Hackman, J. R. (1987). The design of work teams. In J. Lorsch (Ed.), *Handbook of organizational behavior* (pp. 315-342). Englewood Cliffs, NJ: Prentice Hall.

Hippel, von E. (1994). *The sources of innovation.* New York: Oxford University Press.

Hippel, von E. (2005). *Democratizing innovation.* Boston: The MIT Press.

Huston, L., & Sakkab, N. (2006). Connect and develop: Inside Procter & Gamble's new model for innovation. Harvard Business Review, 84(3), 58-66.

IBM. (2006). *Global Innovation Outlook 2.0 (GIO_2.0).* Retrieved July 27, 2006, http://domino.research.ibm.com/comm/www_innovate.nsf/pages/world.gio.html

Mullaney, T. J. (2006, October 9). Is there an innovation drought? *Business Week.* Retrieved November 15, 2006, from http://www.businessweek.com/bwdaily/dnflash/content/oct2006/db20061009_449256.htm

Nussbaum, B., Berner, R., & Brady, D. (2005, August 1) *Tomorrow's B-school? It might be a D-school*, in get creative! *Business Week*. Retrieved November 15, 2006, from http://www.businessweek.com/magazine/content/05_31/b3945418.htm

Prahalad, C. K., & Ramaswamy, V. (2004). *The future of competition: Co-creating unique value with customers*. Boston: Harvard Business School Press.

Roffe, I. (1999). Innovation and creativity in organizations: A review of the implications for training and development. *Journal of European Industrial Training, 23*(4/5), 224-237.

Walton, A. P. (2003). The impact of interpersonal factors on creativity. *International Journal of Entrepreneurial Behaviour & Research, 9*(4), 146-162.

Acknowledgment

With gratitude, love, and respect we thank the following people without whom the book would not have come to fruition. To our publisher, IGI Global, who supported this project and, particularly Kristin Roth and Meg Stocking who provided constant support during a challenging process. To Larry Leifer for agreeing to pen the foreword, allowing us to take advantage of his years of experience and insight in the field. A special note of thanks also to our contributors who were so kind as to share their expertise in a reviewing role, showing their commitment to producing a high quality book as opposed to merely focusing on their own chapters. To all those working to expand and enhance scientific knowledge in the field of virtual teams and creativity, and who have contributed—and continue to do so—to the development of guidelines to achieve more efficient and effective management. And last but not least, (from Steven) to Pamela for her continual support. I hope to reverse that role as you re-start your own creative journey soon. And (from Teresa) to my creative sons, Arnau and Jordi, who have made my life a fascinating journey.

Steven P. MacGregor, Girona, Spain
Teresa Torres-Coronas, Tarragona, Spain
November 2006

Section I
Tests: Discovering Insights for Creative Success in Virtual Teams

Chapter I
Modeling Work Processes and Examining Failure in Virtual Design Organizations

Steven P. MacGregor
IESE Business School, Spain

ABSTRACT

Based on two case studies originally conducted to develop process support for virtual (distributed) design, this chapter models the virtual process observed in two industrial sectors characterized by original design and adaptive/variant design activity, thereby requiring different types of creativity. These models are used to generate a list of virtual problems or 'failures' which are subsequently examined using the engineering based techniques 5W2H and failure modes and effects analysis (FMEA) to develop insight into virtual team problems and possible solutions. The suitability of the design field is shown for the study of creativity in virtual teams and the link between design, creativity and business performance discussed. In many cases, if support is provided to solve virtual team problems not directly associated with creativity then team members may free up time and energy to focus on the increased 'cognitive capacity' required for higher creativity.

INTRODUCTION

This chapter advances research first conducted on mapping the virtual (distributed[1]) design space (MacGregor, 2002a, 2002c) for the development of appropriate virtual team support. The study context was two large multinational companies involved in the design and development of products, with sites in the UK, but with very different client and product development, or co-creation focus. One is an engineering design organization from the oil and gas sector involved primarily in adaptive and variant design. The other is involved in product design within the fast moving consumer goods (FMCG) sector and is characterized by higher levels of original design. The differences in this experimental test-bed allow a comparison of how virtual work is characterized across different types of design activity as well as the corresponding requirements or pressures associated with creativity.

An understanding of the virtual design workspace, established through the two cases, is developed through an examination of failure. Failure in this context is defined as some form of suboptimal virtual work which may result in the cessation of collaboration and affect overall performance, satisfaction and ultimately, creativity. Requirements are specified in response to the challenges and failures highlighted.

Design provides a fitting experimental test-bed for virtual teams and creativity. The suitability of design and its fit with creativity, virtual work, and business performance is discussed in the next section. This is followed by a description of the research methodology used in the cases. Next, various models are presented which aim to describe the virtual work in each organization. The section, "Summary of Virtual Problems" constitutes the failure focus of the chapter, developing a process failure modes and effects analysis (FMEA) which examines the severity, occurrence and remedial action associated with virtual work. Finally, the main useful output of the FMEA and implications for creativity are discussed briefly in the conclusion.

Virtual Work, Creativity, and Design

A note on the applicability of using the design field as an experimental test-bed for creativity is useful. Many of the chapters in this book are focused on the design and/or new product development fields. These areas, especially in the context of virtual work, can be grouped under the general activities of co-creation. Bessant, Whyte, and Neely (2005) link design to innovation by stating that: "Design is the purposive application of

creativity to all the activities necessary to bring ideas into use either as product (service) or process innovations." But how, exactly does design fit with creativity? First, it is important to note the increasing attention to creativity in general for increased business performance. In a world of increasing demands, challenges, and competition, the most innovative companies and next generation leaders will be those who sustain high levels of creativity inside the enterprise and across their networks. The Department of Trade and Industry (DTI) of the UK Government recently released an economics paper on 'Creativity, Design and Business Performance' (DTI, 2005). They define creativity as "the production of new ideas that are fit for a particular business purpose" and design as a "structured creative process." It could be argued that for creativity to be successful in the highly pressurized environment of virtual teams, a structure for creativity is required, which may therefore be met by design. Of course, the very essence of creativity demands that it be allowed flexibility and freedom, and not be constrained—and best practice design strikes the right balance between chaos and control. Iterative experimentation and cycles of convergence and divergence that are required for creativity are also established features of good design.

The DTI specify that creativity and design, used effectively, are important competitive tools for firms. They detail the work of Swann and Birke (2005) showing the link between design, creativity, innovation, and productivity. Creativity is shown as the root of business performance with design an important delivery mechanism to transition creativity into innovation and, ultimately, productivity and business performance (Figure 1).

To fully understand these relationships one must understand the nature and characteristics of design. Design, like innovation does not just concern products. Tether (2005) details the many and varied roles and applications of design, from artistic painting through interior design and

Figure 1. Linking creativity and design to business performance (Adapted from Swann & Birke, 2005, who note that elements of design are included in research and development [R&D])

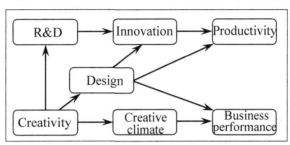

architecture, to engineering component design. Each has a balance regarding emotion, rationality, function, and expression—and can therefore be applied to the arts, science, and R&D. In most cases however, and certainly for the context of this chapter and book, design is a team-based process and highly social activity (Bucciarelli, 1984) which relies on the input of people from different backgrounds and therefore different perspectives on the design need. Communication and collaboration play a crucial part in reconciling these perspectives to achieve an optimum solution which satisfies all team members and most importantly the customer. Social interaction is therefore at the core of design work. Studies from Tang (1991) have detailed the nature of design further, within the context of shared drawing activity. The importance of gesturing in design activity is emphasized. If such actions are required for design success, virtual design is made ever more difficult as gesturing is impossible in many virtual scenarios.

Further, the nature of the thing being designed stipulates the type of design activity (Pahl & Beitz, 1996):

- **Original design:** New and creative solutions for new or old tasks; the distinguishing factor is that it involves a new solution principle.
- **Variant design:** Function and solution principle remain the same; only sizes, materials

or arrangement of existing solution changed. Also known as "same as except."

- **Adaptive design:** Known solution adapted to a new or changed task; the solution principle typically remains the same but original design of parts, components or assemblies are generally required.

It follows therefore that more creativity, a higher creative load in essence, is present or required in original design activity—new solution principles will require higher creativity than merely the adaptation or reapplication of existing ones. In theory, therefore, it will be harder to do virtual work in original design environments than in variant/adaptive environments. In the product design domain Pugh (1990) discusses the decrease in original design at a product level over the years, detailing that innovation becomes more pervasive at the subsystem and component level as well in manufacturing processes. This shows that although original design may not exist at the overall product level, it can at the subsystem and component level result in higher complexity and a high creative load also. In general, adaptive and variant design environments are characterized by high degrees of complexity. As such, the exact type of co-creation being undertaken should have different effects on the problems and challenges encountered in virtual work and support required.

Design is therefore a highly diverse, social activity. Its success depends in part, on the effectiveness of collaboration and communication channels between members of the design team. The diversity of activity together with ever challenging customer requirements leads to teams greater in size and complexity with higher levels of knowledge requirements. This, in turn, leads to a low probability of teams being in the same physical space. Since team structure depends on the nature of the thing being designed and specific customer requirements, virtual design occurs across a range of scales—from teams being separated by different floors in a building to different countries and different time-zones. Virtual colleagues may be external or internal to one's own organization, relationships may be temporary or permanent and work may be tackled synchronously or in a 'hand-off' fashion. Such variables show the importance of context in virtual design and the challenges in supporting it.

Design may therefore be viewed as an 'extreme' virtual context which deals with the concept of creativity at its very core. The design context may therefore provide an appropriate experimental test-bed in this book to investigate creativity in virtual teams and the pursuit of higher creativity. Not all chapters are centered on design—there is a balance in the book as detailed in the introduction—but where design is the focus of activity there is a hope that nondesigners may still read with interest and take on the lessons which apply to virtual teams and creativity in general.

RESEARCH METHOD

Two four month studies of virtual design were carried out sequentially in UK industry. The summary approach is presented in Table 1. Semistructured interviews were used to discover the main case issues and represented the first means of data collection. Questionnaires charted current activities and perceptions of the case participants and daily diaries sampled virtual activity over time. These were augmented by direct observation and documentation analysis. Further, two iterations of each of these methods were employed. This facilitated investigation of a breadth of issues, after which some midcase analysis ensued. The goals of the case study were then re-aligned in accordance with this analysis and the study completed. The core team of around 10-12 in each company took part in all the methods while discussions took place with others, usually at the managerial level, throughout the investigation period.

The research group in each case was diverse and either involved in the design process or some level of virtual creative work. Record sheets were completed for significant events, interactions or studies in order to produce a detailed, fully traceable case base. A more complete discussion on the research methodology used can be found in (MacGregor, 2002b).

Generalizing findings from cases and ensuring validity is a common problem. The overall research methodology and strength of conclusions were validated through a five month research tour of North America, strategically placed after initial analysis of the case base. This tour included several small industrial studies with companies such as Microsoft, Sun Microsystems, and IDEO, which helped to shape the accuracy of the descriptive base. Leading academics in three top North American Universities were also used to bridge the development from description to prescription. As a final measure, all development completed to the end of the tour was validated during several repeat visits to the original case companies in the UK, just prior to final reporting.

As stated above, multiple methods were used to investigate different facets of virtual design activity as well as help with the triangulation of data. The investigation of different time-spans was also facilitated. Interviews allowed the investigation of historical experiences while the questionnaires sampled current perceptions. The daily diaries helped to detail contemporary

Table 1. Size of the main case study database

	Size of data set	
Method	**Case 1**	**Case 2**
Semi-structured interviews *(main case issues)*	40, 12 hours	46, 13 hours
Questionnaires *(current activities, perceptions)*	24	18
Daily diaries *(sampling virtual activity)*	174 days data, 87% response	35 days data, < 25% response
Augmented by direct observation, interpretation, company documentation, and system analysis		

virtual activity, with findings compared to the other methods to ensure validity and flag issues for further examination.

The Industrial Context

The two main case companies were the oil and gas company ABB Vetco Gray and the consumer goods multinational Lever Fabergé. A short profile of these companies now follows.

ABB Vetco Gray (ABB VG) are world-wide market leaders in the production of pressure control and drilling equipment for the oil and gas industry. The main case study site was in Aberdeen, Scotland and based within R&D. Aberdeen is the head office of the Eastern region of ABB VG, a region which includes the UK, Europe, Africa, and Russia. Work is widely distributed. With regional headquarters in Aberdeen, Houston, and Singapore, many challenges within the virtual domain are present, including a high level of separation, different time-zones and cultures, and the need to integrate knowledge, information, and data. ABB VG also has engineering, manufacturing, and sales operations in 59 locations and 24 countries around the world. Work is also technically complex. The design of engineering pressure control and deep sea drilling equipment adds another challenging dimension to the company's distribution. This

necessitates the optimal use of knowledge, to ensure that meaning is transferred efficiently between dispersed colleagues.

Lever Faberge (Lever), formally Lever Bros. and part of the Unilever group were the second case company. They are worldwide market leaders in several categories within the fast moving consumer goods (FMCG) market and manufacture products including toothpastes and soaps. The case study site was Port Sunlight near Liverpool, England and is the Packaging Design and Technology Center within the Home and Personal Care Europe (HPCE) division. Lever is widely distributed and also culturally diverse with design operations in South East Asia and South America as well as North America and Europe. HPCE includes 19 factories, 8 Innovation Centers (IC), (of which Port Sunlight is the head IC) and 20 local companies in 33 countries. The majority of the designers in Port Sunlight work in a 'cross-category' role which means they are involved in different product categories such as oral hygiene and household cleaning. They field requests from various categories in different locations, and as such, give insight into work proceeding at different locations. Virtual challenges exist with respect to transferring design intent and creative thought.

Multilevel Virtual Process Analysis

Table 2 shows a three step approach to the overall body of research that is one of description and prescription with part of the description the focus of this chapter. Firstly, the existing processes are observed and described, and then any perceived failures are mapped to the existing processes. This then leads to the prescription of a process for supporting virtual design (MacGregor, 2002c).

The process findings are presented on three levels (as shown in Table 3): microprocesses detail the day-to-day working practices of designers in a virtual environment; macro-processes detail longer-term work patterns within the context of a project; and preached processes detail company processes which designers are expected to follow. An examination of these levels should indicate the suitability or otherwise of company policy and provide clues as to what types of processes might be implemented to improve virtual work. An important point to make is that certain areas of a designer's work are open to change whereas other areas are part of natural human behavior and therefore very difficult to change. Both areas should be acknowledged and catered for in any implemented process.

Modeling the Virtual Process

Microprocesses: Adaptive/Variant Design Environment

Observations of the working processes of ABB VG showed the importance of switching or changing between different types of work in a virtual design project. The main work types were simple information exchange/searching and collaborative design. Information exchange is defined as interaction with any virtual colleague internal or external to the organization that may be involved on a component level but has no interest in the overall system. For example, a subsupplier who provides a specification for a component that may be used in the final design. Collaborative design is distinguished from information exchange by the fact that, although the collaborators may exchange information, they have a common interest in developing the design. The engineers were found to go through a cyclic process of long periods of simple information exchange and short intense periods of collaborative design. These interactions were found to occur in a ratio of approximately 5:1. Information exchange was characterized by asynchronous interaction, primarily through e-

Table 2. Multilevel analysis approach

Phase	Step	Definition
Descriptive	(describing) PROCESS	Existing multilevel processes (Table 3) within industrial case studies
Descriptive	(describing) FAILURE	Failures/problems arising from processes above
Prescriptive	(prescribing) PROCESS	New processes to help counteract failure modes identified above

Table 3. Process definitions

Level	Definition
Micro	day-to-day working practices of designers in a virtual environment
Macro	longer-term working practices evident from designers work, usually within the context of tackling a project
Preached	on a macro level but different from above as designers rarely replicate exactly what is considered policy from the company. Academic processes from the design field are also considered

mail and often included low levels of problems (with the notable exception of external collaboration which was fraught with difficulty, especially concerning remote availability). Collaborative design was usually conducted in a synchronous fashion using any tools at the engineers' disposal. It was characterized by a much higher level of difficulty, including unachievable design details and miscommunication of specifications. Distribution appears to exacerbate problems found in both information exchange and collaborative design in a collocated environment.

At the micro level, the process of collaborative design can be represented simply as a black box process where a period of collaborative design transforms some information into a new set of ideally useful, information. It was observed that a critical mass of information is needed before collaborative design can commence (a detailed analysis of this phenomenon through the information interactions of the team at ABB VG can be found in MacGregor, 2001). In some circumstances the collaborative design phase is initiated, due to time constraints, before the critical mass of information has been reached. This usually gives rise to a greater number of problems. The information produced by a period of collaborative design is then used as input for another period of collaborative design, shown by the continual process modeled at the bottom of Figure 2. It was evident from the case study that some level of common understanding and individual work is required before collaborative phases can commence.

Another micropattern discovered in the adaptive/variant design environment, outlined in Figure 3, centered on basic information exchange with little or no virtual collaborative design. The first stage in this work pattern is the discussion of a work problem or need. This is usually carried out synchronously and centers on some abstract representation of the problem/need. At this stage the designers only possess mental models of the work in question. Through discussion, the abstract representations become more concrete and information exchange becomes asynchronous. Finally, some level of synchronous review and discussion takes place in order to clarify or develop the representation.

Finally, the design process existed on a microlevel within each design stage (Figure 4). For example, the concept design stage in ABB VG virtual projects contained iterations of specification, conceptualizing, detailing, and evaluating. This pattern repeated within all stages of the design process.

Figure 2. IE/CD model

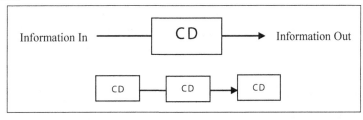

Figure 3. Basic IE model

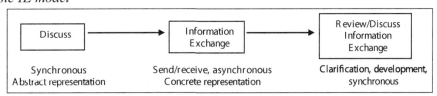

Figure 4. Microprocess iteration

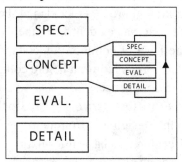

Microprocesses: Original Design Environment

Although each of the above microprocesses was discovered initially in the variant/adaptive design environment, the same general patterns were observed in the original design environment of Lever but with a few key differences. Firstly, a very low amount of virtual, collaborative design took place. Although it was observed that a critical mass of information was required before collaborative design could take place, the design sessions were often collocated rather than virtual. Collaborators would often travel or key individuals were collocated for the duration of the project. It is assumed that due to the decreased complexity of the product being designed in Lever, the possibility of having all necessary interactions in a small, collocated team is greater. Also current technologies do not make it easy to transfer creative, innovative design work between distributed individuals and collocated sessions are more

effective in progressing design activities such as brainstorming and generating concepts. This is especially true of the early design phases. The original design environment required more iterations and a greater percentage of the time actually spent designing. However, much of this design was done on an individual basis and then shared—there was very little synchronous, co-operative design. The observed microprocess is shown in Figure 5, which is, in essence, a combination of the processes shown in Figures 2 and 3.

Another defining feature was the continual need for feedback from physical models (see Figure 6). These were used at all stages of the design process and were valuable in a knowledge transfer sense but were time-consuming in a virtual environment due to the need for conventional mail, while the electronic transfer of virtual models did not prove as informative.

As the designers in Lever work frequently with physical models, they encounter difficulty when operating in the virtual domain as they are forced to work with virtual or mental models only. Few of the ABB VG engineers work on a daily basis with physical models (the design of large scale, highly complex products mean that only scale models are produced very occasionally) and so work relatively trouble-free using virtual and mental representations. Figure 7 shows the different development paths for each environment. Studies have shown design work to proceed faster in a collocated setting when dealing with concrete models over abstract ones (Eris, 2002).

Figure 5. Original design process

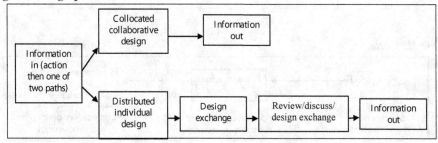

Figure 6. Representation stages

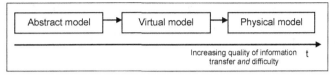

Figure 7. Development paths in the physical and virtual domain

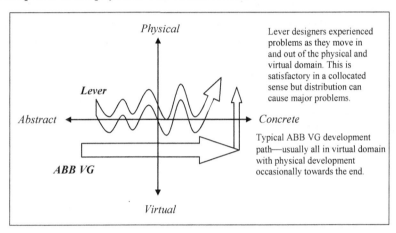

In a virtual setting, concrete models are less open to ambiguity than abstract models. A joint view of concreteness and type of representation should therefore be considered when aiming to support virtual work. Depending on the stage and context of the process physical, virtual, concrete or abstract models may be desirable.

Microprocess Issues

Observation in ABB VG indicated a high level of problems in the collaborative design phase. This may also be the case in collocated design—when collaborating, individual work is open to question more immediately by the rest of the team. However, some of the problems were exacerbated by virtual factors. Many were related to information—having timely transfer and a critical mass necessary for collaboration. All could be linked to the need for having a greater awareness of people and their activities at different locations. Problems are detailed later in Table 4.

Macro-Processes: Adaptive/Variant Design Environment

Figure 8 models the observed virtual design process on a general level and is linked closely with the IE/CD micro pattern shown in Figure 2. The collaborative design (CD) 'stream' is ongoing in terms of the design being continually progressed while information exchange (IE) 'threads' exist. These pursue matters external to the main design development and often include others external to the core design team, but are nevertheless very important to overall development. For example, the electrical connection details from a subsupplier and the name of a person from a sister company who worked on similar projects in the past—real examples encountered in the examination of virtual processes at ABB VG. The main CD stream included work with a Norwegian design partner and the IE threads supplier collaboration and informal consultation with other parts of ABB VG.

However, the CD stream rarely proves trouble-free. Frequent bottlenecks appear at stages of the main CD stream and sometimes only open up when output from one of the IE threads feeds back into the stream. In a virtual environment there is increased potential for these bottlenecks to cause disruption due to the increased delay in information transfer. Engineers stated the importance of the right levels of constraints and resources at the beginning of the stream. Virtual design process management should therefore strategically view the role of IE threads so that the main CD stream progresses in a timely and efficient manner.

Figure 9 shows the virtual design process and product structure in ABB VG. The process starts with a design need and a perceived solution to that need. In many instances, this early stage of the design process is collocated. The overall perceived solution is then split into subsystems. These parts of the solution are then tackled by virtual teams according to resources and expertise. Few problems are realized within these teams, partly due to work methods being the same, but problems arise when attempting to integrate these subsystems to form the overall solution.

The physical subsystems shown in Figure 10 can also be considered as 'chunks' of knowledge distributed between different locations and members of the design team. The overriding factor is the need to achieve sufficient integration of these disparate elements of the final design. One other possible measure of solving these problems is to optimize the interfaces between subsystems before optimizing the content of those subsystems. However, Figure 9 illustrates some of the problems when dealing with this. Often stages 2 and 3 of

Figure 8. Stream/thread model

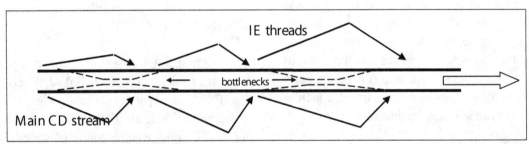

Figure 9. Subsystem model

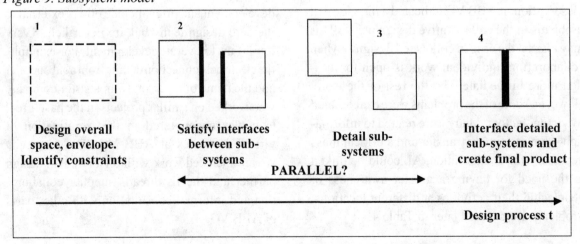

the process have to be conducted in parallel due to the different needs of virtual collaborators. These 'interface' problems also exist in collocated design but are exacerbated by distribution.

One possible solution to the interface problem as communicated in the ABB VG sample case is to spend more time on a joint specification and set out a very accurate solution envelope. However in practice, due to time constraints, the envelope is usually defined quickly and briefly after which accuracy is achieved through iterations.

Macro Processes: Original Design Environment

As with the microprocesses, general patterns observed in the original design environment were similar to the variant/adaptive design environment. The CD stream/IE thread model (Figure 8) also applies to this environment. However it was observed that collaborations out with the core design team/organization were more efficient than those within the company. This increased efficiency appeared to be due to good relationships which were evident with external suppliers, and can be partly attributed to the lower complexity in product and therefore supply chain. Furthermore, this efficiency emphasizes the importance of relationships and trust in virtual work. Difficulties encountered in the CD stream were attributed to the broad discipline base, each with a different

perspective on the work and slightly different goals. The subsystem model of Figure 9 was also applicable but there were fewer subsystems due to decreased product complexity. Furthermore, a broader discipline base is evident here resulting in a greater variety of inputs and different disciplines or organizations at each of the locations. The dynamic subsystem model of Figure 10 was also representative but on a smaller scale. The typical number of interfaces in the original design environment product was two or three but with variant/adaptive environment products the number of interfaces could be as high as 100.

Macro Process Issues

The stream/thread model again emphasizes the importance of the timeliness and quality of information transfer when faced with the prospect of bottlenecks in the main design stream. Further, it highlights the importance of the extended design team. Problems are evident with external collaborators in the variant/adaptive design environment with its associated complex supply chain. Although previous designs may be re-used, areas of these extended collaborations may be new, and open to difficulty, partly due to the high volatility of staff movement in today's marketplace. Ensuring common goals is a necessity within the extended design team. Conversely, more problems were evident in the main design

Figure 10. Dynamic subsystems model

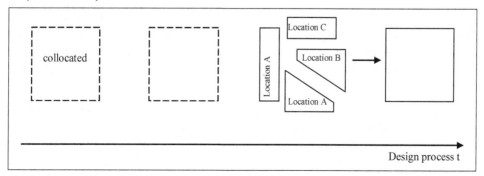

stream within the original design environment; problems were evident due to the presence of different disciplines and their varying perspectives on the design. Figure 9 highlights the importance of virtual subsystems in a product and their integration and interactions. Collaborators need a clearer idea of the virtual space and how that fits with the product. The original design environment is less complex and is less troubled by such challenges but they remain relevant partly due to the diversity of disciplines involved, resulting in difficult interactions. The dynamic subsystem model (Figure 10) takes the distribution/product structure theme further. Again, there is less of an issue in the original design environment but the importance of interfaces on physical, information, and 'virtual space' levels cannot be underestimated.

Preached Processes

Preached (standard) processes within each company were rarely followed. These included Pugh's model of total design (Pugh, 1990) within ABB VG and a three-stage process funnel of idea/feasibility/capability in Lever. General patterns are used but behavior is contingent on the project context, including time pressures. These processes and nearly all other published models of design fail to explicitly consider the impact of design being conducted by team members who are geographically or temporally dispersed. Some may argue that it is not possible to prescribe a process of design which can be different for each new case, and that the design process emerges or evolves in each project. However, for virtual work it is necessary to have at least some support in place. Previous design processes, including those preached within the cases take a 'task-oriented' view. These can be useful but respondents in the case stated that they "do their own thing" based on their own training, judgment, and immediate needs.

Summary of Virtual Problems

A focused examination on virtual 'failure' now follows, complimenting the issues highlighted in the modeling section. There are three main stages. Firstly, a list of all problems encountered in the industrial studies is presented. A short section then follows which discusses some of the content and attempts to classify it. Finally, an FMEA exercise is then completed in order to develop a deeper understanding of virtual problems. In summary this section attempts to define the problems encountered in more detail, examining the what, where, how, when, and why of failure modes in virtual work.

Database of Failure Modes

The cases detailed characteristics and issues which form the basis of the failure focus. The main characteristics of virtual activity included the concept of switching behavior where virtual designers switch between different work focus and activities, including information exchange and collaborative design, synchronous and asynchronous work, and individual and co-operative work. Furthermore, product structure was shown to be important including the effects of subsystems and interfaces on the physical and knowledge levels.

Other areas of the research detailed the need for augmenting understanding of the people domain and human behavior in virtual settings. Taking the view of the research as a whole, relevant issues include:

- The need for sufficient, quality and timely information to enable virtual work
- The difficulty encountered in transferring creative design work, particularly during the early stages of the process
- The need for adequate product representation
- Problems encountered in reconstituting product subsystems

- Problems encountered in duplication of effort
- The effects of relationships, number of interfaces, team interaction, and discipline on virtual work

These issues helped to form the list of virtual problems shown in Table 4. In total, 47 problems are included, divided into six categories. Each category is also matched to the type of problem according to a simple classification of people, product, process, and tools used to segment the virtual workspace during the initial stages of the research:

- Information and data (people, product, process)
- Signal transfer (people, process)
- Process/task work (process)
- People/teamwork (people)
- Culture (people)
- Systems/technology (tools)

Table 4. Summary of virtual problems found in the cases

A Information and Data	Compatibility of legacy data/current information	ID1
	Not knowing who to contact for information/data	ID2
	Not knowing where to look for information/data	ID3
	Insufficient information/data	ID4
	Too much information/data	ID5
	Timeliness of information transfer (including time zone issues)	ID6
	Inability to access information/data	ID7
	Poor distribution of information/data	ID8
B Signal Transfer	Virtual colleague misinterpreting actions	ST9
	Virtual colleague making incorrect assumptions	ST10
	Misunderstanding during design work	ST11
	Ambiguous information	ST12
	Difficulty in visualization/transfer of meaning	ST13
	Not understanding the reasoning behind decisions	ST14
C Process/ task-work	Too many team members managing information	PT15
	Too many people managing the process	PT16
	Poor visibility, unaware of work going on at other sites/previous work	PT17
	Duplication of effort	PT18
	Lack of ownership/autonomy	PT19
	Insufficient resources (e.g. tools, people)	PT20
	Unachievable design detail	PT21
	Disagreement in design	PT22
	Incompatibility of subsystems/interfaces	PT23
	Lack of physical representation	PT24

continued on next page

Table 4. continued

D People/ teamwork	Virtual colleague unavailable	PE25
	Inaccessibility of virtual colleague	PE26
	Unexplained design decision by virtual colleague	PE27
	Compromising between virtual team members requirements	PE28
	Quality of virtual work/lack of competence/experience at virtual location	PE29
	Lack of response/noncommunication	PE30
	Not being informed of all decisions	PE31
	Vague communication of requirements/actions	PE32
	Lack of trust/poor relationship with virtual colleague	PE33
	Colleagues without a full grasp of the issues, insufficient context	PE34
	Inconsistent point of contact at virtual location	PE35
	Inability to identify as part of a team	PE36
	Unrealistic expectations of work	PE37
E Culture	Different work processes/techniques	CU38
	Different perceptions of criteria/phenomena	CU39
	Language difficulties/conflict	CU40
	Different terminology/nomenclature	CU41
F Systems/ technology	Inconsistent systems/resources at dist. locations	SY42
	Lack of system/tool functionality	SY43
	Inappropriate use of systems/technology	SY44
	System/tool breakdown	SY45
	Too much reliance on tools	SY46
	Poor infrastructure at virtual sites	SY47

Each listed problem was found in both cases although their severity and occurrence varied. Although many problem types are similar, the small distinctions drawn are valid. For example, although not knowing who to contact for information and not knowing where to look for information result in the same information deficiency, they can be solved by different means. Furthermore, many of the failure modes may be linked through a cause and effect relationship which is evident in the completed FMEA matrix. Typical failure modes for each case are now summarized.

Within the ABB VG case, problems resulted due to the complexity of the product and the creation of specialists within the company who worked on their own discrete work packages. This resulted in a low awareness of other locations work and conditions, leading to conflict, misinterpretation, and technical language differences. The preponderance of design re-use also placed high demands on finding the right information at the right time although company systems aided in this task.

Lever designers also encountered problems with low awareness, partly due to the paucity of communication tools. This also led to problems regarding team relationships, particularly with other disciplines and the communication of early phase design intent. Finally, the lack of touch and physical engagement was one of the major problems in Lever virtual design work.

The timeliness of information was one of the most important factors in both cases. Virtual work is often halted until information is received or, potentially worse, incorrect assumptions are made to the detriment of the process. The competence of personnel was also found to be crucial in both cases while low awareness of virtual projects also led to duplication of effort.

Anecdotal Evidence

Sample anecdotes from each case help describe each problem and category. Each one illustrates a problem listed in Table 4:

- **Section A. Information and data:**
  - **Lever sample—Problem ID1:** Incompatibility of legacy data/current information: Value improvement projects (VIPs) are carried out on existing products to modernize a product, save money, or take advantage of recent advances in manufacture or design. However, some VIP projects have not been completed due to the incompatibility of legacy data from the original product. There is a high turnover in design modeling and drafting systems.
  - **ABB VG sample—Problem ID8:** Poor distribution of information/data: "I was waiting on drawings of the template design to fit onto my own subsystem but they actually sent them to the bid engineer and did not copy them to me—he was off, so the day was wasted."
- **Section B. Signal transfer:**
  - **Lever sample—Problem ST9:** Virtual colleague misinterpreting actions: When creative designer SM found some design material relevant to a project in Italy she sent it via PowerPoint to her colleague. However, the Italian col-

league was upset at what she thought was an attempt by SM to force her way into the project and tell her what to do. SM bemoaned the fact there was no background communication support to enable less intrusive transfer of information.
  - **ABB VG sample—Problem ST13:** Difficulty in visualization/transfer of meaning: "Had difficulty in describing the test procedures we required to the factory over the telephone so had to go over in person and show what was needed."
- **Section C. Process/teamwork:**
  - **Lever sample—Problem PT17:** Poor visibility, unaware of work going on at other sites/previous work: "The South American design office scaled a 10-year old 750ml bottle from Canada down to make a new 500ml bottle. In fact, the 750ml bottle had previously been scaled up from a 500ml European bottle!"
  - **ABB VG sample—Problem PT18:** Duplication of effort: A collocated brainstorming meeting of engineers from the regional headquarters began with an engineer from Aberdeen describing the problems he has encountered in an unresolved project. A Houston-based engineer then shouts that his team encountered and solved the same problem the previous year.
- **Section D. People/teamwork:**
  - **Lever sample—Problem PE35:** Inconsistent point of contact at virtual location: Due to the high turnover of staff and huge comparative size of the Marketing department, the design office fail to build relationships with Marketers, leading to project conflicts.
  - **ABB VG sample—Problem PE29:** Quality of virtual work/lack of competence/experience at virtual location:

Analysis engineer, SK encountered several problems and unexplained results in an analysis job completed by an external consultant. Although competent in 'pure' thermodynamics the consultant was unaware of some applied factors when products go 'sub-sea'.

- **Section E. Culture:**
  - ° **Lever sample—Problem CU40:** Language difficulties/conflict: Subtle language differences are sometimes encountered with colleagues from the US and can go unnoticed due to the belief that both parties are speaking the same language.
  - ° **ABB VG sample—Problem CU41:** Different terminology/nomenclature: "The use of abbreviations between the 'sister' companies varies, the complexity of the discussion of the equipment was very detailed and confusing, considering I am not familiar with their equipment, and two of them were Norwegian—say no more!"
- **Section F. Systems/technology:**
  - ° **Lever sample—Problem SY46:** Too much reliance on tools: KK found frequent communication problems and breakdown in a project which relied extensively on the use of video-conferencing. They found it to be "gimmicky and providing no time for understanding complex spoken information."
  - ° **ABB VG sample—Problem SY42:** Lack of consistent systems, resources at different locations: Colleagues at the Brazil branch feel isolated and sometimes reluctant to communicate due to not having the same information and knowledge management systems used by their sister companies.

Classification

The Nature of Problems

Only some of the problem types listed are caused solely by virtual work (around 30%) with the rest present in conventional, collocated work but exacerbated by the virtual setting. However, this 30-70 split correspond to problem type. When examining the actual number of problems, there is an increase in the percentage share of problems created solely due to virtual work.

Another factor is the maturity of organization. Problems which exist in some industrial environments may not be present in others due to differences in the sophistication of tools and/or processes. Although relatively simple tools were used in both environments a low percentage of problem types were associated with tools. Furthermore, both case sites were successful multinationals with relatively advanced work processes. It is therefore believed that many of the problem types listed in Table 4 would be relevant in most case environments.

Preliminary Classification

Regarding the classification of people, product, process, and tools noted above, most problem types are evident within people, followed by process and then tools. Product is inherent in these groups. Further, many people problems can be attributed indirectly to a lack of process support. This is confirmed in the questionnaire findings of the research where respondents defined problems as being "people based" and "centered on the process".

Mapping the exact number of problems to design activity proves difficult. Although case respondents felt original design projects presented most problems a higher amount of actual problems is encountered during variant and adaptive design due to higher frequency. Additionally, the high level of resource allocation associated with original projects ensures they proceed relatively smoothly compared with some less supported adaptive and variant design projects. Certain features within the design activity account for specific problem types. For example, a higher degree of multidisciplinary, which is evident in some original projects, can lead to problems regarding different working languages.

A useful classification of problems used to partly describe the problem type database is provided by Gutwin and Greenberg (2000) who discuss the task work (the task and reason for the virtual work) and teamwork (the work of working together). This classification also ties in with the design and collaboration distinction drawn in MacGregor (2002a), confirming that the teamwork has to be successful for the task work to stand any chance of success. This also specifies the need for communication/collaboration processes to improve virtual design work.

Table 5. Virtual problem classification

Type of classification	Details
Activity classification *What?*	• Review, especially, synchronous, of complex information was difficult with such complexity open to interpretation. • This is also true of early stage design where more uncertainty results in conflicting assumptions and actions by different members of the design team. • Collaborative Design (CD) more problematic than simple Information Exchange (IE). This is usually due to the required compromise between conflicting requirements whereas IE merely fulfils a need for information. • Since IE represents the bulk of virtual work more actual problems and problem types are associated with this activity. • CD problems map to those that exist within collocated work but are exacerbated by distribution while most IE problems are caused specifically by distribution. Typical IE problems include being aware of information and getting the right information at the right time.
Process classification *When?*	• Most problems evident towards the end of the design process and particularly detail design. Partly attributed to the fact that detail design acts as a detection mechanism for problems although the integration of disparate interfaces at this stage is perhaps a clearer indicator. • The front end of the process includes a high level of uncertainty but most activities are collocated so virtual problems are minimal. • Other stages of the design process stated as proving troublesome include the specification stage (in ABB VG) and tooling (Lever).
Collaborator classification *Who?*	• Both cases provided different characteristics with ABB VG engineers enjoying fewer problems with those inside the organization and Lever designers working well with subsuppliers and less well with internal marketing colleagues. • Both successful collaborations can be characterized by consistent points of contacts, long-term relationships and a common language which leads to trust and efficient communication. • Collaborator classification also depends on location.
Location classification *Where?*	• On a geographic level more problems are generally encountered as distance increases. This is due to a variety of factors: • There is usually less collaboration with distant colleagues due to less awareness and time-zone difficulties, leading to weaker relationships. • Cultural differences, more likely with increased distribution, usually add to existing pressures. However, the same cultural effects can result in distant collaboration being more successful than collaboration in close proximity. • With respect to product location, most problems are encountered at the interfaces where subsystems are required to come together. • With respect to design specification, performance proved most problematic followed by materials. • Process location has already been discussed above citing people and process as being most problematic. This is confirmed in the questionnaires where process support, process planning and people communication are cited as being most problematic.

What, When, Who, Where, and Why

Table 5 further classifies virtual problems using a what, when, who, where, and why framework, based on a common engineering problem analysis technique—5W2H.

Why? Shared Understanding and Awareness

On a general level, most problems can be attributed to a lack of shared understanding between virtual colleagues. This can be linked to team identity which calls for a common goal and shared understanding, as most respondents viewed themselves as being individuals with a job to do rather than a member of a team. This calls for additional communication process support. It is believed that a lack of shared understanding results from low levels of awareness – of work, of information, and of people and their circumstances, which constitute many of the problems identified in virtual work. Communication process support should therefore aim to increase an understanding of the different elements of awareness and eventually, higher levels of it. Ideally, this will lead to an increased shared understanding, greater team cohesion, and fewer virtual failures. In essence, the remainder of the why?—examining the root cause and associated effects of virtual team problems—is completed in the FMEA exercise.

FMEA

Failure modes and effects analysis (FMEA) predicts what failures might occur in a product or process, what the effect of such failures might be on its functional operation, and what steps might be taken to prevent failure and effect on the function. The FMEA method is traditionally used for products and manufacturing processes but in this case is used for the virtual communication process, with the effect on the virtual team measured.

The identification and classification of failure modes presented above fulfills an important need in the understanding of virtual design practice and process support needs. FMEA develops these needs to detail the cause and effect or propagation of failures in the design process. The specific value of the FMEA method is in identifying the necessary characteristics and eventual suitability of prescription method to address the most serious problems and/or the greatest population of problems.

However, there are limitations of the FMEA method. There is an inherent subjectivity in completing the analysis which is increased through individual completion by the author (as opposed to the normal team-based effort). This should therefore be acknowledged when viewing the results. However, the real value of the method is not in the ratings and RPN results (FMEA rates Severity, Occurrence, and Detection of failures which are multiplied to produce the Risk Priority Number – RPN) but in the process of completing the analysis and becoming more familiar with the content and characteristics of the failures. It facilitates a higher level of understanding of virtual challenges from the models presented earlier in the chapter. Of particular value is the text-based description of cause and effect and the recommended actions which form the basis of prescriptive actions.

The problems listed in Table 4 were used as input to the FMEA. Many similar failure modes were combined which may have similar effects and profiles. Additionally, the systems/technology section of the database has been omitted for two reasons. Firstly, relatively few problems and problem types exist within the tools domain and secondly, prescriptive development in the original research focused on the people and process domain. This results in a reduction of 47 to 29. The severity, occurrence, and detection ratings are shown in Table 6 and the completed FMEA is shown over the next few pages in Table 7.

Table 6. FMEA rating table

Rating	Severity Rating Scale	Occurrence Rating Scale	Detection Rating Scale
	Description		
10	Dangerously high: Failure could result in project cessation	Very high: Failure is almost inevitable	Absolute uncertainty
9	Extremely high		Very remote
8	Very High	High: Repeated failures	Remote
7	High		Very low
6	Moderate: Failure results in a noticeable drop in team performance	Moderate: Occasional failures	Low
5	Low		Moderate
4	Very Low		Moderately high
3	Minor	Low: Relatively few failures	High
2	Very Minor		Very high
1	None: Failure would not be noticeable to the team and would not affect team performance	Remote: Failure is unlikely	Almost certain

CONCLUSION

Focusing on Failure

The FMEA has developed a set of recommended actions (subsequently developed in the D4D process (MacGregor, 2002)). Many of these actions have the aim of increasing awareness of the virtual workspace, and include:

- Clearer management understanding and strategy for virtual work
- Virtual training: How to communicate and design at distance
- Resource allocation: Responsibility for actions clear to complete team
- Interaction design: Transparent people network with value-adding interactions between collaborators
- Creation of virtual agents/champions

The modeling section identified issues which fed into the FMEA. Specifically, models regarding interaction, expertise, and the product, form the basics of supporting structures for the D4D method. The FMEA can be used to increase an awareness of typical virtual failures and the means by which they may be addressed. As noted above the value of the FMEA method is not in producing RPN numbers but in the process of completion, specifically the detailing and contextualization of the communication failures. An understanding of the cause and effect of problems will improve virtual communication through increasing team awareness of how failures can occur and what to do to minimize them. A partially completed matrix should be consulted by the management or virtual project team. Potential failure modes and cause and effect details should be examined, with a decision made on which ones are relevant within the given context. The team should then complete the sections on current process controls and recommended actions while the RPN numbers may also be completed to increase the level of context. New organizational support in the form of these actions is the other main output of the FMEA together with an increase in team awareness of the virtual communication process.

The FMEA shows that there are few current process controls for the problem types listed. Many

Table 7. Process FMEA matrix

Process category	Potential Failure Mode	Potential Effects of Failure	SEV	Potential Causes/ mechanisms of failure	OCC	Current process controls	DET	RPN	Recommended actions
Information and Data	Incompatibility of data/information	Unable to re-use data/information	6	Different systems/tools	5	Supplier evaluation and applied IT policy	2	60	Increase awareness of re-use needs and spend more time on improving usability of information at end of project
	Unable to find/source information	Gaps in understanding/available facts leading to possibility of incorrect assumptions	8	Poor storage of information/data. Low process support. Poor integration of resources.	7	None	2	112	Increase awareness of who knows what, relevant information sources and training.
	Insufficient information	Gaps in understanding/available facts leading to possibility of incorrect assumptions	8	Reluctance to share information (lack of trust). Poor distribution of information.	7	Information repositories. Brainstorming meetings	2	112	Incentive schemes to enable sharing. Greater awareness of virtual team and specific needs.
	Too much information	Knowledge 'swamp'—using wrong information or using information the wrong way	4	Poor storage and classification of information/data	4	Information systems controller/ IT officer	2	32	Implement consistent approach in storage and classification. Increase awareness in virtual practice.
	Timeliness of information transfer	Gaps in understanding/available facts leading to possibility of incorrect assumptions. Delay in project.	8	Poor relationships. Conflicting priorities. Unrealistic expectations of work.	9	Process phase gates.	3	216	Increase incentive for knowledge sharing. Increase or relate common objectives. Increase awareness of colleague workloads.
Signal Transfer	Misunderstanding/ misinterpretation of actions/work	Breakdown in communication/ relationship. Delay in project. Error in design work.	7	Low awareness of colleague's background and experience. Poor technological support. Poor communication style.	9	None/Design review	4	252	Increase in tools support. Increase in awareness of virtual colleague. Training.
	Making incorrect assumptions	Error in design work. Delay in project.	6	Incomplete or ambiguous information.	7	None	5	210	Process checks after virtual interaction. Training.
	Ambiguous information	Need for clarification and delay in work. Possibility of making incorrect assumptions.	5	Incomplete information. Lack of competence, poor communication style.	7	None	4	140	Template/checklist for information documentation/ sharing. Training.
	Difficulty in visualization/ transfer in meaning	Need for collocated interaction and delay in progress. Misunderstanding, incorrect assumptions.	6	Complexity of task. Lack of competence/ experience. Poor communication style.	6	Software visualization tools.	3	108	Asynchronous interaction for complex work. Training.
	Not understanding reasoning behind decisions	Inefficient design re-use. Duplication of error. Lack of understanding.	6	Incomplete documentation. Poor communication style.	8	None.	2	96	Project completion template. Training. Increase awareness of available expertise.

continued on following page

Table 7. continued

Process category	Potential Failure Mode	Potential Effects of Failure	S E V	Potential Causes/ mechanisms of failure	O C C	Current process controls	D E T	R P N	Recommended actions
Process/ task work	Too many members managing process/ information	Conflict. Duplication of effort. Design error. Inconsistent information.	7	Poor process control/ resource allocation/ management.	5	None/Project planning	2	70	Clear management strategy. Transparent team member roles. Communal controlled supported systems.
	Unaware of previous work/other sites	Duplication of effort. Unrealistic expectations of work. Sub-optimal design work.	7	Poor integration of resources and storage of information.	8	Collocated meetings. Intranet.	6	336	Virtual site contacts. Creation of transparent people network.
	Duplication of effort	Wasted resources. Low morale. Project delay.	7	Unaware of previous work. Unclear role allocation.	6	None	5	210	Identification of common goal and similar job function teams followed by increase in knowledge transfer.
	Lack of ownership/ autonomy	Low motivation. Project delay. Poor quality.	7	Poor management strategy. Inability to identify as part of a team.	6	None	3	126	Checks for virtual competence. Incentive schemes.
	Insufficient resources	Low motivation. Project delay. Poor quality.	8	Poor understanding of needs. Lack of investment.	5	None	2	80	Initiate improvement/needs meeting within communities of practice.
	Conflict in design work	Breakdown in relationships. Project delay. Poor quality.	5	Low awareness of colleagues work and circumstances.	8	Design review/ collocated meetings	2	80	Increase awareness of virtual teams needs and problems. Collocated meetings at strategic points.
	Incompatibility of sub-systems/interfaces (especially product level)	Project delay, poor quality. Design 'turbulence' and strain on relationships.	8	Organization of virtual sub-groups.	9	Detail design, Design review/ collocated meetings	2	144	Increase awareness of virtual teams needs and problems.
	Insufficient representation	Poor visualization. Poor understanding of consequence of actions.	6	Poor tool support. Geographic separation.	8	None	2	96	Strategic collocated meetings.

continued on following page

21

Table 7. continued

Process category	Potential Failure Mode	Potential Effects of Failure	S E V	Potential Causes/ mechanisms of failure	O C C	Current process controls	D E T	R P N	Recommended actions
People/teamwork	Unavailability of colleague	Gaps in knowledge/ understanding. Possibility of incorrect assumptions. Project delay.	6	Conflicting objectives/job functions. Different work processes.	9	Activity diaries	2	108	Increase awareness of colleagues work processes team needs and alternative means of fulfilling needs.
	Not being informed of/unexplained design decisions	Reduced understanding. Breakdown in trust. Low motivation.	7	Low levels of trust, perception of competence/ unimportance/ Irrelevance.	6	Team meetings	3	126	Awareness of team needs. Use of shared workspace.
	Poor quality of virtual work/ insufficient understanding	Poor quality of work. Project delay. Breakdown in relationships and communication.	8	Unrealistic expectations of work. Insufficient training. Low awareness of experience.	8	None	3	192	Competence checks. Training. Understanding checklist.
	Lack of response/non-communication	Breakdown in relationships. Gaps in knowledge/ understanding.	7	Heavy workload. Poor relationship.	6	None	1	42	Provide incentives. Increase awareness of colleagues work. Create information 'gurus'.
	Vague communication of requirements/actions	Misinterpretation. Gaps in knowledge/ understanding.	5	Language difficulties. Poor communication style.	6	None	2	60	Training. Template for information exchange.
	Lack of trust/poor relationship with virtual colleague	Poor quality of work or project failure.	9	Social conflict. Conflicting objectives. Low awareness of colleague's background.	5	None/team design	3	135	Collocated meeting at start of project. Consistent point of contact. Agreed agenda and work practices.
	Inconsistent point of contact at virtual location	Lack of trust/poor relationship with virtual colleague.	8	Different scales of collaborating parties. Unavailability of colleague. Low perception of worth.	7	None	2	112	Consistent point of contact supported by technology systems.
	Inability to identify as part of a team	Low motivation. Low amount of knowledge transfer/information sharing	7	Lack of common goal. Low awareness of other team members.	6	Collocated meetings	4	168	Incentives. Collocated meetings. Increase awareness of other member's activities and share experiences.
	Unrealistic expectations of work	Conflict. Poor project estimation and delay.	6	Differing scales of collaborator. Low awareness of experience.	7	None	3	126	Increase awareness of experience, competence and workload/objectives.

continued on following page

Table 7. continued

Process category	Potential Failure Mode	Potential Effects of Failure	S E V	Potential Causes/ mechanisms of failure	O C C	Current process controls	D E T	R P N	Recommended actions
Culture	Different work processes/techniques	Project conflict. Unavailability. Misunderstanding.	7	Different cultures/ backgrounds/ job functions.	9	Intranet	2	126	Increase general awareness of collaborators practice. Swap team members between locations.
	Different perceptions of criteria/phenomena	Different evaluation of work. Conflicting decisions.	6	Different cultures/ backgrounds/ job functions.	7	None	4	168	Create location profiles. Swap team members between locations.
	Different working languages/ terminology	Misunderstanding. Need for confirmation. Project delay.	6	Different cultures/ backgrounds/ job functions.	8	Glossary of terms	3	144	Swap team members between locations.

of the problems are not explicitly considered or catered for. In many cases the effects of virtual problems are acknowledged but it is important to understand the root of the problem and the fact that distribution can often be the cause. According to the RPN results, the highest failure modes are:

1. Unaware of previous work/other sites
2. Misunderstanding/misinterpretation of actions/work
3. Timeliness of information transfer

Although the RPN scores are limited in value due to subjectivity discussed, they confirm the need for higher levels of awareness in virtual design. Problem 2 involves low levels of awareness of the task at hand and/or collaborators backgrounds while problem 3 may involve a low level of awareness of collaborators information needs. Most of the other failures examined in the FMEA can be linked to a shortfall in either people or product awareness, also developed in the resultant D4D method.

Re-Visiting Creative Needs for Design Activity

In design work the type of design activity affects the level of creativity. Original design naturally involves higher levels of creativity through the search for a new solution principle, as opposed to the adaptation or re-application of existing solutions for adaptive and variant design. For those out with the design field but engaged in virtual work it is important to consider that different virtual team endeavors will involve varying levels of creativity—as such, the original, variant, and adaptive design distinction studied here may be used as a frame of reference. In most industries today variant and adaptive design accounts for the vast majority of work. Furthermore, as shown in the Lever case, when original design is pursued, it is often deemed of such high importance that it

is collocated and benefits from a high level of resources. With these factors in mind most problems are found in adaptive and variant design. Higher creativity is still required in such work, yet it is more incremental in nature and often associated with high levels of complexity (new solutions are often required at the subsystem and process levels). Two approaches to higher creativity therefore exist—tackling creativity directly, or better managing complexity and other associated virtual problems to free up time, energy or 'cognitive space' to better focus on virtual creative work.

The cases highlighted several factors important for higher creativity. Creative work needs a critical mass of information and so basic information management should be addressed to ensure the right amount of knowledge transfer between virtual team members. Complexity of the product is important and also leads to complexity of collaborations—essentially the virtual supply chain. When this is simpler, better relationships can be built which leads to higher creativity. Product representation was also shown to be important in both cases. An understanding of how virtual team members usually work—with abstract, virtual or physical models—is important, and whether virtual team members can work effectively with mental models. Creative solutions also have to be realistic and workable—which often involves a high degree of complexity and technical expertise. The progress of rapid prototyping, 3D printers, and Haptic interfaces will help visualization and the transfer of understanding between virtual team members, yet comfort in dealing with dynamic mental models will help the virtual creative process.

In many cases, if support is provided to solve virtual team problems not directly associated to creativity—many of which have been detailed here—then team members will free up time and energy to focus on the increased 'cognitive capacity' required for higher creativity.

REFERENCES

Bessant, J., Whyte, J., & Neely, A. (2005). *DTI Think Piece Management of creativity and design within the firm.* Advanced Institute for Management (AIM) and Imperial College.

Bucciarelli, L. (1984). Reflective practices in engineering design. *Design Studies, 5*(3), 185-190.

Cox, G. (2005). *Cox review of creativity in business: Building on the UK's strengths.* Retrieved November 15, 2006, from http://www.hm-treasury.gov.uk/cox

DTI. (2005, November). Economics paper No. 15. Creativity, design and business performance. Department of Trade & Industry, UK.

Eris, O. (2002). *Perceiving, comprehending and measuring design activity through the questions asked while designing.* Doctoral dissertation, Center for Design Research, Stanford University, CA.

Gutwin, C., & Greenberg, S. (2000, June). The mechanics of collaboration: developing low cost usability evaluation methods for shared workspaces. In *Proceedings of the IEEE 9th International Workshop on Enabling Technologies: Infrastructure for Collaborative Enterprises (WET-ICE '00), NIST,* Gaithersburg, MD.

MacGregor, S. P., Thomson, A. I., & Juster, N. P. (2001, September). Information sharing within a virtual, collaborative design process: a case study. In Proceedings of the ASME Design Engineering Technical Conferences, Pittsburgh, PA.

MacGregor, S. P. (2002a). New perspectives for virtual design support. *Journal of Design Research, 2*(2). Retrieved November 15, 2006, from http://jdr.tudelft.nl/articles/issue2002.02/article2.html

MacGregor, S. P. (2002b). The case study method for detailed industrial descriptions: experiences examining distributed design. In *Proceedings of the International Workshop on the Role of Empirical Studies in Understanding and Supporting Engineering Design Work, NIST,* Gaithersburg, MD.

MacGregor, S. P. (2002c). *Describing and supporting the virtual workspace: Towards a prescriptive process for design teams.* (Doctoral dissertation, DMEM, University of Strathclyde, Glasgow, UK). Retrieved November 15, 2006, from http://www.design4distribution.com

Pahl, G., & Beitz, W. (1996). *Engineering design—A systematic approach.* London, Springer-Verlag.

Pugh, S. (1990). *Total design: Integrated methods for successful product engineering.* Wokingham, UK: Addison-Wesley.

Swann, P., & Birke, D. (2005). *How do creativity and design enhance business performance? A framework for interpreting the evidence.* DTI Think Piece, University of Nottingham Business School.

Tang, J. C. (1991). Findings from observational studies of collaborative work. *International Journal of Man-Machine Studies, 34*(2), 143-160.

Tether, B. S. (2005). *The role of design in business performance.* DTI Think Piece, CRIC, University of Manchester.

ENDNOTE

[1] The original research used the term *distributed* in place of *virtual*, which more accurately described the research context. Smith (this volume) makes the argument for the term *dispersed* in place of virtual. For the sake of consistency, *virtual design* replaces the term *distributed design* in this chapter.

Chapter II
Creativity in Asynchronous Virtual Teams:
Putting the Pieces Together

Rosalie J. Ocker
The Pennsylvania State University, USA

ABSTRACT

Three related experiments, involving nearly 100 teams and 400 graduate students, found that virtual teams communicating strictly asynchronously produced significantly more creative results than did teams that engaged in some amount of synchronous communication (i.e., face-to-face or synchronous electronic communication). Using these experiments, four studies are conducted to explore creativity in the asynchronous virtual teams—each from a different aspect. Study one investigates individual team member personality, study two investigates team composition, while studies three and four investigate facets of team interaction. This chapter presents key findings from each study and synthesizes results across them. The analysis highlights the importance of team members, in terms of personality, as well as the composition of teams, in influencing interaction and the resultant creativity on a team level.

INTRODUCTION

Three related experiments, involving nearly 100 teams and 400 graduate students, investigated creativity in virtual teams (Ocker, 1995, 2001; Ocker et al., 1996; 1998; Ocker & Fjermestad, 1998). In each experiment, teams worked for approximately two weeks to determine the high-level requirements and design for a computerized

post office (Goel, 1989; Olson et al., 1993). The means of communication, in essence, the way in which teams collaborated to complete their work—was manipulated in these experiments. Some teams interacted only electronically via either asynchronous or synchronous computer conferencing, while other teams used a combination of asynchronous communication interspersed with face-to-face (FtF) meetings. Still other teams collaborated via a series of traditional FtF meetings without any electronic communication, to provide a base-line for comparison.

Interestingly, and seemingly a paradox to many, is the consistent finding across experiments that teams in the asynchronous computer-mediated communication (CMC) condition—those teams without any FtF or synchronous electronic communication—produced significantly more creative results than teams in the other communication conditions. To explore this finding in more depth, four additional studies were conducted, each using a subset of asynchronous virtual teams from the aforementioned experiments. Each study was designed to explore creativity from a different aspect. Study one investigated individual team member personality. Study two focused on team composition. Studies three and four investigated the facets of team interaction. This chapter presents key findings from each study and synthesizes results across studies, to put together the pieces of asynchronous virtual team creativity.

The remainder of this chapter is organized as follows. The chapter proceeds with an overview of experimental design and methods of the ex-

Table 1. Comparison of experiments 1, 2, and 3

	Experiment 1 (extended)[1] (Ocker et al., 1996, 1998)	Experiment 2 (Ocker & Fjermestad, 1998)	Experiment 3 (Ocker, 2001)
Communication modalities	asynchronous, synchronous, hybrid (asynch. & FtF), FtF	asynchronous, hybrid (asynch. & FtF)	asynchronous, hybrid (asynch. & FtF)
Length	14 days	same	17 days
Subjects	predominantly CIS and IS graduate students from mid-Atlantic university	same	MBA and MSIS grad. students from a different mid-Atlantic university
Computer conferencing system	EIES2	Web-EIES (EIES2 base with a web user interface)	First Class
Training task	entertainment for Dutch Visitors	same	same
Training procedures	detailed script of procedures developed and followed	similar (modifications made to reflect web interface)	similar (modifications made to reflect First Class interface)
Experimental task	Automated Post Office	Computerized Post Office	same
Experimental procedures	detailed script of procedures developed and followed	same	similar (minor modifications made to reflect 17 day experiment length)
Measures	multiple surveys; panel of judges rated creativity	same	objective measure of creativity; Adjective Check List added to surveys

periments from which the four studies are drawn. Following that, the four studies of creativity in asynchronous virtual teams are presented. Background, method, analysis and results, and summary of findings are included for each study. The chapter culminates with a synthesis of findings across studies, conclusions, and suggestions for future research.

OVERVIEW OF EXPERIMENTAL DESIGN AND METHODS

Table 1 provides a comparison of the three experiments, which form the foundation for the studies. Although not identical, the experimental design and methods are quite similar.

- **Communication modalities:** Experiment one[1] included four communication conditions: asynchronous CMC, synchronous CMC, hybrid (combination of asynchronous CMC and FtF meetings), and FtF. Experiments two and three included asynchronous CMC and hybrid conditions.
- **Task:** The Automated Post Office (APO) (Goel, 1989) was the task used in experiment one. Teams were required to reach consensus on the initial requirements of the APO and to submit these requirements in a formal report at the end of the experiment; each team produced a single report. The report was to cover the functionality of the APO along with implementation considerations, and was also to contain a description of the user interface design. This is a modification of the task used by Olson et al. (1993), with added emphasis on the design of the user interface. Olson et al. (1993), characterize this as a complex task incorporating aspects of planning, creativity, decision-making, and cognitive conflict (McGrath, 1984). Experiments two and three employed the same basic APO task, but with several minor changes

(e.g. the requirement to discuss maintenance of equipment was dropped; the request for a cost/benefit analysis was modified to a request for a discussion of advantages and disadvantages). This task is referred to as the Computerized Post Office (CPO).

- **Subjects:** Subjects in experiments one and two were graduate students drawn predominantly from the CIS and IS programs at the same mid-Atlantic university. Subjects in experiment three consisted of MBA and M.S.I.S. graduate students in a different mid-Atlantic university. For their participation, all subjects received course credit. Team size was typically between 4-6 persons. All teams had a zero-history of working together.
- **Length:** Experiments one and two were 14 days in length. Experiment three lasted for 17 days.
- **Technology and facilitation:** In experiments one and two, teams used the proprietary computer-conferencing system called EIES, albeit different versions. EIES2 had a command driven user interface while Web-EIES had a GUI interface. Teams in experiment three used the FirstClass, a commercially developed computer conferencing system, also with a GUI interface. The feature set of these systems, as instantiated in these experiments, was largely the same. That is, the level one (Poole & DeSanctis, 1992), 'vanilla,' purely computer conferencing version was used in all experiments. Thus, subjects could compose, reply, and thread through conferencing comments.
- **Training:** In all experiments, individuals were trained on the mechanics of the computer conferencing system using the same practice problem, called Entertainment for Dutch Visitors (Olson et al., 1993). In an effort to ensure consistency across training sessions and experiments, trainers followed the same basic script. Only slight modifica-

tions to the training materials, regarding the mechanics of the user interface, were required across experiments.

- **Procedures:** Procedures were the same for asynchronous virtual teams across experiments. These teams were not given any process or structure to follow. They were simply told that, by the end of the experimental period, their team report had to be submitted on-line via their computer conference. Thus, each team determined the content and layout of the formal report, although the APO/CPO task delineated certain aspects that should be addressed.

Each team exchanged only *asynchronous* electronic comments within its own computer conference. All members were explicitly instructed to communicate solely within their respective conferences. It was suggested to subjects that they try to communicate with their team on a daily basis. All conferences were minimally facilitated; the facilitator's role was that of a technical assistant, helping teams with equipment problems and answering questions of a technical nature.

Teams in experiments one and two had a leader who volunteered for the role at the end of the training session. This person was tasked with

ensuring that his/her team submitted a formal report at the end of the two-week experimental time period. In the third experiment, no leadership functions were explicitly designated.

- **Measures:** Multiple survey instruments were administered to collect data on participant demographics as well as various aspects of team dynamics. A personality measure was added in experiment three. A panel of judges rated the creativity of team solutions as well as the quality of team solutions in experiments one and two. An objective measure of team creativity was utilized in experiment three while team quality was rated by judges. In all instances, judges consisted of professors and doctoral candidates in IS, all with academic and/or professional experience in software design.

FOUR STUDIES OF CREATIVITY IN ASYNCHRONOUS VIRTUAL TEAMS

The principal model used to organize and analyze the inter-related components that affect teams is the well-known input-process-output model espoused by Hackman (1987). According to the

Figure 1. The four studies in terms of the input-process-output model

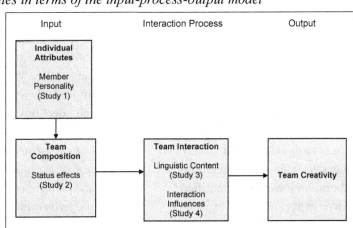

model, a variety of inputs combine to influence intra-team processes, which then impact team outputs. Inputs include the individual, which pertains to team member attributes (e.g. personality), as well as team composition (the individual members that comprise the team). Process refers to the interaction process between team members, and includes aspects that influence interpersonal team member behavior, such as communication mode. Team outputs are the results of the team effort, such as the creativity of the team's work product.

The studies on virtual team creativity are labeled one to four, to indicate a logical progression from the standpoint of the input-process-output model. However, these numbers are not indicative of the sequence in which the studies were conducted—quite the contrary. Study three preceded study four, which led to study two, which was followed by study one. However, the purpose of this chapter is to put together the pieces of virtual creativity. Therefore, the studies will be presented according to their logical sequence, rather than their chronological order.

INPUT

Individual Creativity

An individual's level of creativity is a function of cognitive abilities and personality traits. A substantial body of research has focused on the divergent production of ideas as the dominant cognitive link to creativity. Divergent thinking progresses away from a problem in a variety of different directions and involves breaking down barriers and restrictions on thoughts. Convergent thinking, on the other hand, involves progression towards a single answer (Thompson, 2003). The cognitive processes of fluency, flexibility, originality, and elaboration have been identified as essential to the divergent production of ideas

(Guilford, 1984). Personality traits associated with creativity include independent thought and judgment, autonomy, persistence, self-confidence, intellectual honesty and an internal locus of control (e.g., Barron & Harrington, 1981; Amabile, 1988; Woodman & Schoenfeldt, 1989).

Task-related aspects also influence creativity. The level of an individual's intrinsic motivation towards the task impacts creativity (Barron & Harrington, 1981; Amabile, 1983). Rewards may adversely affect intrinsic motivation, as effort is given toward fulfilling reward requirements as opposed to the heuristic aspects of the creative task (Amabile, 1979). Furthermore, an individual's interest and creativity is reduced when a strategy for approaching and solving the task is imposed (Amabile, 1983). Creativity is also reduced when individuals feel time-pressured to complete the task (Amabile et al., 2002). Domain-relevant knowledge and skills impact creativity (Amabile, 1988). Although previous experience can induce a 'functional fixedness' which inhibits an individual from forming a creative solution, some level of knowledge of the task domain is typically required to produce a creative solution of high quality.

STUDY 1: PERSONALITY FACETS

Study one focuses on the impact of individual personality facets on team creativity and attempts to determine whether differences in terms of the level of team creativity versus the quality of the team deliverable are predicted by individual member personality.

A positivist study was conducted to investigate the research questions:

- *Do individual member personalities predict virtual team creativity?*
- *Do individual member personalities predict virtual team quality?*

Background

Personality traits distinguish individuals from each other, and are persistent across time and situations. It is readily accepted that there are five broad factors or dimensions of personality traits (Costa & McCrae, 1992; Goldberg, 1993) which are continuous, rather than discrete. An individual therefore will fall somewhere along the continuum of a given dimension.

The five dimensions are extraversion, openness, agreeableness, conscientiousness, and negative emotionalism (also known as neuroticism). Extraversion encompasses an individual's tendency for sociability and interactivity as opposed to solitude and seclusion. Openness encompasses an individual's tendency for abstract or original ideas versus tangible facts. Agreeableness encompasses an individual's tendency for cooperative versus competitive interaction with others. Conscientiousness encompasses an individual's tendency for convergent, task-oriented versus divergent, process-oriented work styles. Finally, negative emotionalism encompasses how an individual responds to stress, from a wide-range of emotions to a narrow range of emotions.

The five dimensions are broad in context. To more precisely measure the particular attributes subsumed within these broad domains, personality facets were developed. Each of the five factors has multiple facets associated with it. Each facet includes a common 'portion' attributable to the factor, as well as a portion attributable to that particular facet. McCrae and Costa (1992) developed six 8-item facet scales for each dimension. As a means of assessing the discriminant validity of the facet scales, they related each scale to various items from the adjective check list (ACL) (Gough & Heilbrun, 1983). Twenty-six of these "ACL-defined" facets achieved discriminant validity and are depicted in Table 2.

Method

- **Data set:** The data set consisted of 47 participants from the ten teams comprising the asynchronous communication condition in experiment three.
- **Personality measure:** The adjective check list (ACL) (Gough & Heilbrun, 1983) was used to assess participant personality. The ACL is comprised of 300 descriptor words. An individual checks the words that are self-descriptive (there is no limit to the number of words that one can check). The ACL was administered to each participant at the end of experiment three.
- **Measure of team creativity:** To ascertain the degree of creativity of teams' CPO design, a process that resulted in an objective measure of creativity was developed (Ocker, 2005). Using each team's report deliverable, a list of the unique ideas was compiled with regard to services contained in the team's CPO design. The unique list of services from each team was merged into one combined list of unique services and duplicate services were eliminated.

Based on this list, the number of *original* ideas for each team was counted. Statistically, original ideas are unique ideas generated by less than 5% of a given sample (Thompson, 2003). As there were 47 subjects participating in the experiment, an idea was considered original if it occurred once or twice. Because teams generated different length reports and team size varied between four and five participants, *percentages* (rather than the actual count of ideas) were deemed to be a more accurate way to objectively measure creativity. Thus, using the total number of unique ideas within each team's report as the denominator, the percentage of original ideas was calculated.[2]

- **Measure of team quality:** Two expert judges measured the quality of each team's solution as contained in the report deliverable. Judges rated various aspects of the report content, including the feasibility of the solution (i.e., realistic or unrealistic), as well as the clarity of the written presentation and the completeness of report (as per the task description). Judges also rated the overall quality of each team's solution.

Table 2. ACL personality facet scales

Negative emotionalism	
Anxiety	anxious, fearful, worrying, tense, nervous, -confident, -optimistic
Depression	worrying, -contented, -confident, -self-confident, pessimistic, moody, anxious
Self- Consciousness	shy, -self-confident, timid, -confident, defensive, inhibited, anxious
Vulnerability	–clear-thinking, -self-confident, -confident, anxious, -efficient, -alert, careless
Extraversion	
Warmth	friendly, warm, sociable, cheerful, -aloof, affectionate, outgoing
Gregariousness	sociable, outgoing, pleasure-seeking, -aloof, talkative, spontaneous, -withdrawn
Assertiveness	aggressive, -shy, assertive, self-confident, forceful, enthusiastic, confident
Activity	energetic, hurried, quick, determined, enthusiastic, aggressive, active
Excitement Seeking	pleasure-seeking, daring, adventurous, charming, handsome, spunky, clever
Positive Emotions	enthusiastic, humorous, praising, spontaneous, pleasure-seeking, optimistic, jolly
Openness	
Fantasy	dreamy, imaginative, humorous, mischievous, idealistic, artistic, complicated
Aesthetics	imaginative, artistic, original, enthusiastic, inventive, idealistic, versatile
Feelings	excitable, spontaneous, insightful, imaginative, affectionate, talkative, outgoing
Actions	interests wide, imaginative, adventurous, optimistic, -mild, talkative, versatile
Ideas	idealistic, interests wide, inventive, curious, original, imaginative, insightful
Values	– conservative, unconventional, -cautious, flirtatious
Agreeableness	
Trust	forgiving, trusting, -suspicious, -wary,,- pessimistic, peaceable, -hard-hearted
Straightforwardness	– complicated, -demanding, -clever, -flirtatious, -charming, -shrewd, -autocratic
Compliance	– stubborn, -demanding, -headstrong, -impatient, -intolerant, -outspoken, -hard-hearted
Modesty	– show-off, -clever, - assertive, -argumentative, -self-confident, -aggressive, -idealistic
Conscientiousness	
Competence	efficient, self-confident, thorough, resourceful, confident, -confused, intelligent
Order	organized, thorough, efficient, precise, methodical, -absent-minded, -careless
Dutifulness	– defensive, -distractible, -careless, -lazy, thorough, -absent-minded, -fault-finding
Achievement Striving	thorough, ambitious, industrious, enterprising, determined, confident, persistent
Self-discipline	organized, -lazy, efficient, -absent-minded, energetic, thorough, industrious
Deliberation	– hasty, -impulsive, -careless, -impatient, -immature, thorough, -moody

Analysis and Results

Team Creativity and Quality:

The results of the assessment of team creativity (based on original ideas) and quality (overall) are shown in Table 3. Three teams—A7, A8, and A10—topped the creativity rankings with over 20% of their ideas falling into the original category. However, A10's solution was judged to be unrealistic. In terms of overall quality, A3 and A5 were judged highest with scores of 98% and 95%, respectively.

Personality Dimensions and Facets:

Based on responses to the ACL, participant scores were calculated for each of the five personality dimensions as well as 26 facets. The facets were calculated based on the facet adjectives contained in Table 2. That is, for each adjective that a participant selected, a point was added or subtracted to the facet score, according to the sign of the adjective. The five factors were calculated by summing the facet scores associated with each factor.

Regression Analysis

Testing for a Group Effect

The data for this study have a multilevel structure since participants are nested within teams and there are variables describing participants (personality traits) and variables describing teams (creativity and quality). Because members inter-

Table 3. Team creativity and quality scores

Team	A1	A2	A3	A4	A5	A6	A7	A8	A9	A10
Total Unique Ideas	35	37	41	40	44	15	49	36	34	37
Original	6	6	4	7	6	0	18	9	4	8
% Original	0.17	0.16	0.10	0.18	0.14	0.00	0.37	0.25	0.12	0.22
Overall Quality (Out of 100%)	93	85	98	75	95	75	85	85	90	93[a]
[a] unrealistic solution										

Table 4. Factor regression model for creativity and quality

Creativity Factors						
Model	**Sum of Squares**	**df**	**Mean Square**	**F**	**Sig.**	**Adj. R Square**
Regression	507.63	5	101.53	1.25	0.31	0.03
Residual	3002.78	37	81.15			
Total	3510.41	42				
Quality Factors						
Model	**Sum of Squares**	**df**	**Mean Square**	**F**	**Sig.**	**Adj. R Square**
Regression	43573	5	87.15	1.5	0.21	0.06
Residual	2144.96	37	57.97			
Total	2580.7	42				

acted with one another in teams, there is a lack of independence and the potential for a team or group effect (Gallivan & Bebunan-Fich, 2005). To test for a group effect, a dummy variable was created for each team. A series of regression analyses were conducted where the dependent variable was the personality factor or facet, with the teams constituting the independent variables. No between team significant differences were found for any personality factor or facet, indicating that a group level effect was not evident. Thus, an analysis at the individual member level was permissible.

Exploring the Effect of Member Personality

Two sets of regression analyses were conducted to explore the impact of member personality on the creativity and quality of team reports. First, the five personality dimensions were regressed on each dependent variable (percent original ideas were used for creativity). The results, as contained in Table 4 indicate that none of the five broad factors were predictive of either creativity or quality.

Second, the facet scores were regressed on team creativity, again, using percent original ideas

Table 5. Facet regression model for creativity and quality

Creativity Facets						
Model	Sum of Squares	df	Mean Square	F	Sig.	Adj. R Square
Regression	603.90	26	23.23	1.87	0.10	0.36
Residual	186.22	15	12.42			
Total	790.11	41				
Quality Facets						
Model	Sum of Squares	df	Mean Square	F	Sig.	Adj. R Square
Regression	21722.06	26	835.46	1.88	0.08	0.33
Residual	8899.60	20	444.98			
Total	30621.66	46				

Table 6. Facet regression coefficients for creativity and quality

Creativity			
Facet (dimension)	Std. Beta	T	Sig.
Idea (openness)	1.42	3.26	0.005
Assertive (extraversion)	1.92	2.48	0.03
Achievement striving (conscientiousness)	-0.74	-2.22	0.04
Anxiety (neuroticism)	0.79	2.21	0.04
Quality			
Facet (dimension)	Std. Beta	T	Sig.
Trust (agreeableness)	-0.46	-2.43	0.03
Deliberation (conscientiousness)	0.79	2.53	0.02

and overall quality. Summary statistics for the creativity regression model, as contained in Table 5, show that the model is marginally significant at the .10 level.

As shown in Table 6, four personality facets were found to significantly predict team creativity. (The related personality dimension is indicated in brackets). The idea, assertiveness, and anxiety facets are positively related to creativity while the achievement striving facet is negatively related. Based on the standardized beta coefficients, the assertiveness and idea facets account for more variance than do the achievement and anxiety facets.

Summary statistics for the quality regression model, as contained in Table 5, show that the model is marginally significant at the .08 level. As shown in Table 6, two personality facets were found to significantly predict team quality. (The related personality dimension is indicated in brackets). The deliberation facet is positively related to quality while the trust facet is negatively related. Based on the standardized beta coefficients, deliberation accounts for more variance than does trust.

Summary of Findings

At the factor level, personality did not predict either team creativity or quality. This lack of significance at the factor level is not an unusual finding, given the broad nature of the measures (e.g., Paunonen & Ashton, 2001). Hence, researchers have increasingly turned to personality facets as a more revealing measure of personality differences. In line with other research, the results of the analysis of personality facets were more revealing. Two quite different member profiles emerge from this facet analysis, both of which have face validity.

Different personality facets were predictive of team level creativity and quality. In terms of creativity, we see an individual who is an imaginative and original thinker, who enthusiastically ex-

presses his/her ideas (without being over-bearing), and who is more concerned with ideas than the project grade. Interestingly, each significant facet comes from a different personality dimension (the only dimension not represented it Agreeableness). With regard to quality, the analysis points to an individual that is deliberate, thorough and careful, and not terribly trusting of his or her teammates. That is, this individual is more apt to rely on him or herself to complete the project work rather than rely on other teammates.

TEAM COMPOSITION

Team creativity is influenced by the creativity of the individuals comprising the team. However, it is also influenced by the composition of the team—that is, the arrangement of individuals into teams.

Creativity at the team level is more likely to occur when the composition of the team includes "stimulating colleagues" (Parmeter & Gaber, 1971). Heterogeneous teams comprised of individuals who bring different knowledge, ideas and approaches to problem solving improve teams' creative performance (Hoffman, 1959; Hoffman & Maier, 1961). Diversity in terms of areas of specialization and work responsibilities are especially relevant to enhanced team creativity.

STUDY 2: STATUS EFFECTS OF TEAM COMPOSITION

Dominance was found to be a key inhibitor of virtual team creativity in study four (Ocker, 2005). As a result, a qualitative study was undertaken (Ocker, forthcoming) to explore the research question:

- *How is dominance manifested in virtual teams?*

Background

Dominance within traditional teams is evidenced when a member has undue influence over the team's processes or work product. A dominant team member exhibits behavior that eschews compromise and consensus such that control and compliance are fostered (Callaway, Marriott, & Esser, 1985; Brown & Miller, 2000). Dominant behavior is typically evidenced by forceful, domineering, decisive and authoritative actions (Jackson, 1967).

Dominance often stems from an individual's *status,* which can be broadly defined as *"a position in a social network"* (Sell et al., 1992, p. 47). It involves beliefs about social worth, such that persons of higher status are deemed superior or more valuable than persons of lower status (Sewell, 1992). Although a member's status may have little or no relevance to the team's work, status has an organizing effect on teams—it delineates the 'pecking order' or hierarchy, and thus serves to regulate intra-team interaction. For example, even without expertise commensurate with other team members, higher status individuals are more vocal and tend to control the team discussion (Bales, 1950; Sherif, White & Harvey, 1955; Ridgeway, 1984).

Method

- **Data set:** The data set consisted the eight mixed-sex teams from the asynchronous communication condition in experiment three (the two same-sex teams, A5 and A8, were not included in this study).

Analysis Process

A qualitative analysis of the team transcripts was conducted, as they constitute the entirety of team communication and collaboration. Following the case study method (Yin, 1998), where each team was viewed as a separate case, an interpretive analytical approach was taken in an effort to understand *how* the significant differences were reflected in the context of team communication (Myers, 1997). The analysis process followed the grounded theory method in analyzing team transcripts (Glasser & Strauss, 1967; Strauss & Corbin, 1998). Open coding was conducted as team communication transcripts were read, summarized, re-read, and compared against one another. Each team was treated as a case. Both within-case and cross-case analyses of teams were performed.

Findings

Five teams experienced dominance. In all five teams, the dominant member was the first to contribute a *significant amount* of task-related content and then proceeded to control the content development of CPO services (i.e., the functional requirements). In all cases, the dominant member belonged to the team's majority sex. This result held in teams where males were in the majority as well as those where females were in the majority.

Findings indicate that dominance, as well as its absence, was driven by a combination of a few team member status traits—namely age seniority, work experience seniority, and expertise. Specifically, in four of the five dominated teams, one or more of these status markers belonged to a single person—the dominant member—and was absent in the other members. In the three nondominated teams, these status indicators occurred across multiple members, such that a counter balance was apparent.

INTERACTION PROCESS

Hackman and Morris (1975) propose that the key to understanding team effectiveness is to focus on the interaction process among team members.

The team interaction process is viewed as a mediator of team input-performance relationships and includes all observable interpersonal behavior occurring between two arbitrary points in time (t1 and t2). Hackman and Morris explain:

Thus, if highly cohesive groups (input at t1) perform better on some task (outcome at t2) than less-cohesive groups, it should be possible to explain the performance difference by examining the difference between the interaction processes of the high and the low cohesive groups. That is, the 'reason' for obtained input-performance relationships always is available - albeit sometimes well-hidden—in the interaction process itself; by appropriate analysis of the interaction process it should be possible to develop a rather complete understanding of input-output relationships in any performance setting. (1975, p. 50).

Studies three and four consider aspects of team interaction in relation to team creativity.

STUDY 3: LINGUISTIC COMMUNICATION CONTENT

In the initial study of virtual team interaction, a positivist analysis was conducted on high and low creative teams to address the research question:

- *Are highly creative teams distinguishable from less creative teams, in terms of linguistic content?*

Background

West (1990) proposes that creative teams operate in an environment of participative safety and foster a climate for excellence. Collaboration which occurs in a nonjudgmental and supportive team atmosphere engenders a feeling of interpersonal safety among participants. West reasons that this nonthreatening atmosphere promotes creativity

as members are more likely to risk proposing new ideas.

A climate for excellence refers to a team atmosphere where there is a mutually shared concern for performance excellence pertaining to a vision or outcome. A tolerance for diversity of opinion and constructive conflict are the hallmarks as opposing opinions are not only offered, but also debated and critiqued by team members (King & Anderson, 1990).

Research on asynchronous CMC provides a few corollaries to characteristics of participative safety and a climate for excellence. Regarding participative safety, CMC teams tend to exhibit more uninhibited behavior (e.g. Siegel et al., 1986; George et al., 1990; Dubrovsky, Kiesler & Sethna, 1991) as well as equality of participation by team members (e.g. Hiltz, Johnson & Turoff, 1986; George et al., 1990; Dubrovsky et al., 1991), resulting in more opinion giving and the expression of additional ideas (e.g., Siegel et al., 1986; George et al., 1990). Studies of electronic brainstorming find that computer-mediated teams generate more unique ideas compared to FtF teams and noninteracting teams (e.g. Gallupe et al., 1988, 1991, 1992). Given these findings, it is speculated that highly creative virtual teams will interact in an environment of participative safety. It is hypothesized that, compared to less creative virtual teams:

H1: *Highly creative virtual teams will exhibit increased levels of supportive communication.*

Regarding a climate for excellence, research has found that CMC teams experience greater difficulty in reaching consensus compared to FtF teams (e.g. Hiltz et al., 1986; Gallupe et al., 1988, George et al., 1990). One reason for this finding could be that, since these teams tend to share more diverse opinions (e.g. Hiltz et al., 1986, Siegel et al., 1986), there is an increased likelihood for task-related conflict which is manifested in the critical debate of issues. Therefore, it is speculated that a climate for excellence is prevalent in highly creative virtual teams. Specifically, it is hypothesized that, compared to less creative virtual teams:

H2: *Highly creative virtual teams will exhibit increased levels of critical debate.*

Method

- **Data set:** To investigate the differences between highly creative and less creative asynchronous virtual design teams for the current analysis, a theoretical sampling approach was adopted. The two highest rated and the two lowest rated asynchronous teams were selected from experiments one and two. Thus, the data set consists of a total of eight teams. This polar sampling strategy was employed with the intent of making differences between the high and low teams as 'transparently observable' as possible (Eisenhardt, 1989).
- **Measure of creativity:** The level of creativity contained in each team's design was measured by a panel of three judges. Founded upon her extensive research on creativity,

Table 7. Creativity score for each team based on average of expert judges' ratings

Team	Experiment	Creativity Rating (1-7)
1	3	7
2	3	7
3	2	6.3
4	2	6.3
5	3	5
6	2	3
7	2	2.3
8	3	4.5

Amabile (1983) advocates that a 'product or response is creative to the extent that appropriate observers independently agree it is creative' (p. 359). Furthermore, there is scant agreement on subcategories that are appropriate in rating creativity. Thus, the expert judges were not provided with explicit rating categories for creativity; rather, they were instructed to judge the creativity of each team's report using the general category of "Creativity of Solution."

Analysis and Results

- **Content coding:** In their study of electronic brainstorming groups working on a creative task, Connelly, Jessup and Valacich (1990) devised a coding scheme to capture both supportive and critical comments. Two coders who were blind to hypotheses and the category of the teams (i.e., high vs. low creativity) independently coded each team's transcript, which constituted the totality of team interaction. The coders met weekly to discuss the coding results of each team and to resolve minor discrepancies.

Team Creativity
Table 7 shows the mean score of the judges' ratings for creativity for each team. A t-test analysis showed no significant differences in the expert judges' ratings of creativity *within* the high performing or low performing teams. However, there were significant differences in creativity *between* the high and low performing teams (p = .002). Thus, there were significant differences in creativity between the 'high' and 'low' teams selected for this study.

Hypothesis Testing
As team size varied between five and six members, all numbers presented in the statistical calculations have been normalized by dividing the number of words by the number of members in the respective

team. Thus, the results show the mean number of words communicated for a single team member. ANOVA analyses were conducted to test both hypotheses. Table 8 contains the least square means for all variables while Table 9 contains the ANOVA results.

The first hypothesis predicted that the high creativity teams would exhibit increased levels of supportive communication. Although this occurred, the difference was not significant (88 words/member vs. 36 words/member, $p = .18$), thus hypothesis H1 was not supported. However, support was found for hypothesis H2, as high teams exhibited increased levels of critical debate (107 words/member vs. 31 words/member, $p = .04$).

Summary of Findings

The results of this study indicate that a key differentiator of high and low creative teams was the extent of critical debate. Specifically, high creative teams engaged in significantly more critical debate than did low creative teams. The teams did not, however, differ in the extent of supportive comments. That is, team members were equally nonthreatening and encouraging across the high and low teams.

STUDY 4: INFLUENCES ON CREATIVITY

In a second study of team interaction (Ocker, 2005), a qualitative analysis of virtual teams was undertaken to address the research question:

- *What influences the creative performance of asynchronous virtual teams?*

Background

This study is informed by literature previously reviewed in the prior sections on input and interaction as well as the background section for each of the prior studies.

Method

- **Data set:** All (10) asynchronous teams from experiment three were included in this study.
- **Measure of team creativity:** The measure of creativity used in this study is identical to that of study one, shown in Table 3.

Table 8. Least-square team means

	High Teams	**Low Teams**
Supporting words*	88	35
Critical words*	107	31

*Note: * Figures shown are the average number of words per team member.*

Table 9. ANOVA results

		DF	**Sum of Squares**	**F value**	**Pr > F**
Supporting words	**Model**	1	5449.68	2.3	0.181
	Error	6	14250.4		
Critical words	**Model**	1	11552	6.65	0.042
	Error	6	10427.5		

Analysis and Results

An interpretive analysis of team communication transcripts was conducted. As before, these transcripts constitute the entirety of team communication and collaboration. Open coding at both a macro (e.g., communication related to the project management) and a micro level (e.g. communication pertaining to a specific aspect of the task) was completed which resulted in the identification of nine inhibitors and five enhancers of team creativity, as shown in Table 10.

Inhibitors of Creativity

Inhibitors include member dominance, technical and functional domain knowledge, focus on external reward, time pressure, downward norm setting, structured problem solving approach, technical difficulties, lack of a shared understanding, and nonstimulating team members.

Dominance was the most frequently occurring inhibitor of creativity (five teams). In the heavily dominated teams, a single individual determined almost the entire functionality. In three teams, technical or domain knowledge (i.e. related to the post office) had the effect of reinforcing in-the-box thinking. Two teams put a heavy emphasis on the external reward—the report deliverable—and focused on that at the expense of cultivating potentially creative ideas. Two teams experienced time pressure and resorted to a streamlined approach, which fostered convergent thought. Downward norm setting, where members reduce their performance level to match that of the least productive team member (Camacho, 1995; Thompson, 2003), was evident in four teams. Teams that followed a structured problem solving approach also suffered from reduced creativity. Although some members from various teams experienced intermittent technical problems, one team's ability to communicate was hampered due to a corporate firewall. In two teams, two different conceptualizations of the CPO were pursued in parallel. Although this duality of concepts can spawn creativity as divergent viewpoints are explored, an inability to reach agreement thwarted their efforts to elaborate upon a single cohesive concept. Finally, not everyone is creative. One team had a preponderance of members who were not original thinkers.

Table 10. Inhibitors of creativity (Source: Ocker, 2005)

Inhibitors	A1	A2	A3	A4	A5	A6	A7	A8	A9	A10
					Team					
Dominant member	Serious	Serious	Some						Serious	Some
Domain knowledge		Some	Serious			Serious				
External reward	Some		Some							
Time pressure	Serious								Serious	
Downward norm setting				Serious		Serious		Some	Serious	
Structured approach				Serious						Some
Technical problems					Serious					Serious
Lack of shared understanding	Serious									Serious
Nonstimulating colleagues					Serious					

Enhancers of Creativity

Enhancers include stimulating colleagues, a variety of social influences, setting the example for creativity, collaborating on problem definition and requirements, and surfacing and reducing equivocality.

Two teams, A7 and A8, were exceptionally creative. They were both composed of stimulating team members. While various members of other teams encouraged their teammates to be creative and think out of the box, they did so without actually providing any ideas. However, in the highly creative teams, one or more members contributed creative ideas very early in the project. Additionally, members did not fall into routines of interaction, such as habitual agreement or disagreement. Rather, individuals contributed varied responses, depending on the issue. These teams collaborated—multiple members were involved in defining the concept and requirements—they pooled their efforts and collaborated on these important activities, rather than providing critical feedback on the work of a single team member.

Finally, these teams surfaced and then reduced equivocality—they converged through a process of coming to terms with divergent perspectives.

Summary of Findings

All teams other than A7 and A8 exhibited at least two inhibitors. While in some cases, the existence of one inhibitor no doubt influenced the occurrence of another inhibitor (e.g. time pressure and dominance), this was not always the case. Thus, consistent clusters of inhibiters were not found across teams—each team had its own unique combination of inhibitors.

Two teams were exceptionally creative. Much of their success can be attributed to avoidance of the inhibitors that thwarted the creativity of the other teams. However, their creativity was enhanced by the confluence of several things that worked in their favor. Overall, the inhibitors and enhancers cut across individual, team composition and team interaction components to influence the creative performance of the teams.

Figure 2. Impacts on asynchronous virtual team creativity

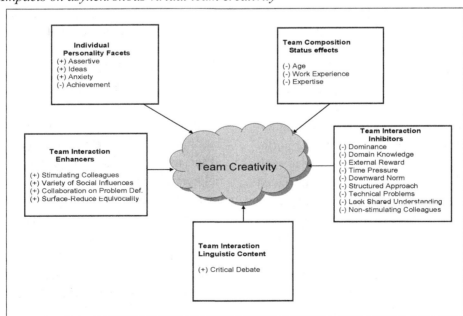

OUTPUT

Although three experiments with a relatively large number of teams and participants provided the basis for the studies, the actual number of participants included in the four studies was more limited. Furthermore, participants in experiment three were utilized in three of the four studies. Participants were graduate students, and although the majority had several years of professional work experience, they were functioning in an academic context. Additionally, if different measures of creativity were used, it is possible that the results of the three foundation experiments could change. Although the experimental design and methods across experiments, including the features of the computer conferencing systems, were essentially the same, to aid comparison across studies, due to these limitations, the generalizability of findings should be made judiciously.

SYNTHESIS OF FINDINGS ACROSS STUDIES

Figure 2 depicts the impacts on asynchronous virtual team creativity based on the findings from the four studies. Aspects that were found to enhance creativity are preceded with a (+) and those that inhibited creativity are preceded with a (-).

The impact of personality is evident in many enhancers and inhibitors of creativity. Those teams populated with stimulating colleagues—with members who were more curious and imaginative (idea facet/openness factor) than the norm, were at an advantage—they were seeded with creativity. When members were more intrigued by the task itself—the conceptualization of the CPO—than with producing a polished report deliverable, creativity was fostered. Thus, members who were intrinsically rather than extrinsically motivated by the CPO task enhanced their team's creativity.

Teams where multiple members exhibited self-confidence and assertiveness (assertive facet/extravert factor) were linked to creativity. Where critical debate thrived, as opposed to mere polite acquiescence, creativity was encouraged. Teams that struggled through a period of uncertainty to define their concept of a CPO explored various alternatives as they worked to reach a shared understanding. These teams experienced a variety of social influences (i.e., majority, minority and normative influence) as they interacted.

However, assertiveness without debate was the downfall of some teams, as one or two members dominated team interaction and the resulting solution. Convergent rather than divergent thinking permeated these teams. Thus, in teams where the composition was unbalanced in terms of member status—namely age, work experience, and/or domain expertise—participation was skewed, unanimity of opinion prevailed based on the dominant member, and creativity was thwarted.

Beyond the mix of effects of member personality, team composition, and team interaction, some teams experienced several constraints that impeded creativity. Time pressure reduced discussion, paving the way for dominance and a streamlined approach to the problem. An ill-fitting structured problem solving approach, not surprisingly, impeded creativity.

Opposing Results: Creativity vs. Quality

Results from study one indicate that a different set of personality facets were tied to the quality of the team deliverable. Persons that exhibited deliberate behavior and who were not particularly trusting of their colleagues enhanced the quality of their team's work product. These results help to explain a general finding across experiments that teams highest in creativity were not the same teams that were highest in quality. Indeed, looking across the three experiments, of the top two creative teams in each study, only one of the six teams was also rated in the top echelon in terms of quality.

Although the output of the creative teams—their report deliverable—contained ideas that were creative 'gems,' in many cases, these were like 'diamonds in the rough.' One had to get passed the unpolished look of the report and focus on ideas. Indeed, some of the deliverables, when compared to teams that produced polished, professional looking reports, appeared quite lacking at first glance—as though teams were unmotivated and perhaps merely going through the motions. However, upon further investigation, the value in terms of original ideas became apparent. Truly, the difference in deliverables between the high quality and high creativity teams was quite evident. And the fact that personality differences were evident between high creativity and high quality teams is quite telling. Teams with deliberate, thorough members (deliberate facet/conscientious factor) who did not trust that their teammates would do the work (trust facet/agreeableness factor) were more apt to produce high quality, polished deliverables, seemingly at the expense of creativity. Those teams with original thinkers (idea facet/openness factor) who were not particularly thorough or determined (achievement striving facet/conscientiousness) fared better in terms of creativity. It is impossible to tell whether, given more time, the creative teams would have produced higher quality deliverables. What is certain is that, given a time delimited context (i.e., 14 or 17 days), teams were rarely able to produce both a high quality and creative work product.

CONCLUSION

From the series of studies on creativity in asynchronous virtual teams, we are able to see how the separate studies combine to paint a picture of creativity in teams working within the context of the studies. That is, teams of graduate students collaborating via an asynchronous computer conferencing system over about a two-week time frame to determine the high-level requirements and design for a computerized post office.

The findings from this research stream demonstrate the power of individuals, in terms of their personality, to influence team creativity. Also highlighted is the influence on team interaction and the accomplishment of work that the *composition* of these individuals into teams had on team outcome. Status-balanced teams were an important foundation of team creativity. There were teams that were highly interactive—that engaged in active debate. However, dynamic interaction, by itself, was not a sufficient condition for creativity. Stimulating individuals were a necessary ingredient in the mix. In their absence, critical debate of inconsequential topics could take on the character of one-upmanship.

The good news is that the mix of individuals in terms of team composition can be controlled. It is the purview of management. Yet, how to compose teams to get the intended results (e.g., a creative solution) remains a topic that is in need of research, although some research on team level personality is being conducted (e.g., Halfhill et al., 2005).

So in the end, what have we learned? The four studies show that there are identifiable 'reasons' why asynchronous virtual teams are creative—or not. These pertain to team member personalities, the status effects that occurred as a result of team composition, and how these influenced the interaction processes of teams as they worked on the CPO. No doubt there are more reasons that were not uncovered by these studies. However, these findings show that we can expect asynchronous virtual teams to be creative—it should not come as a surprise that these teams are quite capable of producing an innovative solution. These studies provide insights into how and why teams with members who are 'not here now' are creative. They also indicate what impedes creativity in these teams.

The findings from the studies of asynchronous virtual teams are consistent with those of traditional teams. Thus, it appears that the body of research on creativity in face-to-face teams applies to asynchronous virtual teams. However, this chapter did not address *why* asynchronous virtual teams, in each of the foundation experiments, were significantly more creative than teams where some form of synchronous interaction took place (i.e., FtF or CMC). That remains an intriguing and open question for future research to address.

ACKNOWLEDGMENT

This work is partially supported by grants from the National Science Foundation (NSF 9015236; CISE—ITO 9732354); the opinions expressed are those of the author and may not reflect those of the NSF. I would like to thank all those involved in this research, especially Jerry Fjermestad, Starr Roxanne Hiltz, Murray Turoff and the students whose participation in the experiments made this research possible.

REFERENCES

Amabile, T. M. (1979). Effects of external evaluation on artistic creativity. *Journal of Personality and Social Psychology, 37*, 221-233.

Amabile, T. M. (1983). The social psychology of creativity: A componential conceptualization. *Journal of Personality and Social Psychology, 45*(2), 357-376.

Amabile, T. M. (1988). Within you, without you: The social psychology of creativity and beyond. In B. M. S. L. L. Cummings (Eds.), *Research in organizational behavior* (pp. 123-167). Greenwich, CT: JAI Press.

Amabile, T. M., Hadley, C. N., & Kramer, S. J. (2002, August). Creativity under the gun. *Harvard Business Review*, 52-61.

Bales, R. F. (1950). *Interaction process analysis: A method for the study of small groups.* Chicago: The University of Chicago Press.

Barron, F. B., & Harrington, D. M. (1981). Creativity, intelligence, and personality. *Annual Review of Psychology, 32*, 439-476.

Brown, T. M., & Miller, C. E. (2000). Communication networks in task-performing groups: Effects of task complexity, time pressure, and interpersonal dominance. *Small Group Research, 31*(2), 131-157.

Callaway, M. R., Marriott, R. G., & Esser, J. K. (1985). Effects of dominance on group decision-making: Towards a stress-reduction explanation of groupthink. *Journal of Personality and Social Psychology, 49*, 949-952.

Camacho, L. J. (1995). The role of social anxiousness in group brainstorming. *Journal of Personality and Social Psychology, 68*(6), 1071-1080.

Connelly, T., Jessup, L. M., & Valacich, J. S. (1990). Effects of anonymity and evaluative tone on idea generation in computer-mediated groups. *Management Science, 36*(6), 689-702.

Costa, P. T., Jr., & McCrae, R. R. (1992). Normal personality assessment in clinical practice: The NEO Personality Inventory. *Psychological Assessment, 4*, 5-13.

Dubrovsky, V. J., Kiesler, S., & Sethna, B. N. (1991). The equalization phenomena: Status effects in computer-mediated and face-to-face decision making groups. *Journal of Human-Computer Interaction, 6*, 119-146.

Eisenhardt, K. M. (1989). Building Theories from Case Study Research. *Academy of Management Review, 14*(4), 432-550.

Gallivan, M. J., & Benbunan-Fich, R. (2005). A framework for analyzing levels of analysis issues in studies of e-collaboration. *IEEE Transactions on Professional Communication, 48*(1), 87-104.

Gallupe, R. B., Bastianutti, L. M., & Cooper, W. H. (1991). Unblocking brainstorms. *Journal of Applied Psychology, 76*(1), 137-142.

Gallupe, R. B., Dennis, A. R., Cooper, W. H., Valacich, J. S., Bastianutti, L. M., & Nunamaker, J. F. (1992). Electronic brainstorming and group size. *Academy of Management Journal, 35*, 350-369.

Gallupe, R. B., DeSanctis, G., & Dickson, G. W. (1988). Computer-based support for group problem-finding: An experimental investigation. *MIS Quarterly, 12*(2), 277-296.

George, J. F., Easton, G. K., Nunamaker, J. F., & Northcraft, G. B. (1990). A study of collaborative group work with and without computer-based support. *Information Systems Research, 1*(4), 394-415.

Glaser, B. & Strauss, A. (1967). *Discovery of grounded theory.* Chicago: Aldine.

Goel, V. P. (1989). Motivating the notion of generic design within information-processing theory: The design problem space. *AI Magazine, 10*(1), 18-35.

Goldberg, L. R. (1993). The structure of personality. *American Psychologist, 48*, 26-34.

Gough, H. G., & Heilbrun, A. B. (1983). *The adjective check list manual.* Palo Alto, CA: Consulting Psychologists Press Inc.

Guilford, J. P. (1984). Varieties of divergent production. *Journal of Creative Behavior, 18*(1), 1-10.

Hackman, J. R. (1987). The design of work teams. In J. Lorsch (Ed.), *Handbook of organizational behavior* (pp. 315-342). Englewood Cliffs, NJ: Prentice Hall.

Hackman, J. R., & Morris, C. G. (1975). Group tasks, group interaction processes, and group performance effectiveness, a review and proposed integration. In L. Berkowitz (Ed.), *Advances in experimental social psychology* (pp. 47-99). New York: Academic Press.

Halfhill, T., Sundstrom, E., Lahner, J., Calderone, W., & Nielsen, T. M. (2005). Group personality composition and group effectiveness: An integrative review of empirical research. *Small Group Research, 36*(1), 83-105.

Hiltz, S. R., Johnson, K., & Turoff, M. (1986). Experiments in group decision making, 1: Communications process and outcome in face-to-face vs. computerized conferences. *Human Communication Research, 13*(2), 225-252.

Hoffman, L. R. (1959). Homogeneity of member personality and its effect on group problem-solving. *Journal of Abnormal Social Psychology, 58*, 27-32.

Hoffman, L. R., & Maier, N. R. F. (1961). Quality and acceptance of problem solutions by members of homogeneous and heterogeneous groups. *Journal of Abnormal Social Psychology, 62*, 401-407.

Jackson, D. N. (1967). *Personality research form manual.* Goshen, NY: Research Psychologists Press.

King N., & Anderson, N. (1990). Innovation in working groups. In M. A. West & J. L. Farr, (Eds.), *Innovation and creativity at work: Psychological and organizational strategies* (pp. 81-100). Chichester, UK: Wiley & Sons.

McCrae, R. R., & Costa, P. T., Jr. (1992). Discriminant validity of NEO-PIR facet scales, *Educational and Psychological Measurement, 52*, 229-237.

McGrath, J. E. (1984). *Groups, interaction and performance.* Englewood Cliffs, NJ: Prentice-Hall.

Myers, M. D. (1997, June). Qualitative research in information systems, *MIS Quarterly, 22*(2), 241-242.

MISQ Discovery, archival version, Retrieved June 1997, from http://www.misq.org/discovery/MISQD_isworld/

MISQ Discovery, updated version as of March 24, 2006.

Ocker, R. J. (1995). *Requirements definition using a distributed asynchronous group support system: Experimental results on quality, creativity and satisfaction.* Unpublished doctoral dissertation, Rutgers University, NJ.

Ocker, R. J. (2001, January). The relationship between interaction, group development, and outcome: A study of virtual communication. In *Proceedings of the Thirty-Fourth Hawaii International Conference on System Sciences (HICSS 34)*, HI (CD ROM). IEEE Computer Society.

Ocker, R. J. (2005). Influences on creativity in asynchronous virtual teams: A qualitative analysis of experimental teams. *IEEE Transactions on Professional Communication, 48*(1), 22-39.

Ocker, R. J. (forthcoming). A balancing act: The interplay of status effects on dominance in virtual teams.

Ocker, R. J., & Fjermestad, J. (1998, January). Web-based computer-mediated communication: An experimental investigation comparing three communication modes for determining software requirements. In *Proceedings of the Thirty-First Hawaii International Conference on System Sciences, (HICSS 31)* (CD ROM). IEEE Computer Society.

Ocker, R. J., Fjermestad, J., Hiltz, S. R., & Johnson, K. (1998). Effects of four modes of group communication on the outcomes of software requirements determination, *Journal of Management Information Systems, 15*(1), 99-118.

Ocker, R. J., Hiltz, S. R., Turoff M., & Fjermestad, J. (1996). The effects of distributed group support and process structuring on software requirements

development teams, *Journal of Management Information Systems, 12*(3), 127-154.

Olson, J. S., Olson, G. M., Storrosten, M., & Carter, M. (1993). Groupwork close up: A comparison of the group design process with and without a simple group editor. *ACM Transactions on Office Information Systems, 11*, 321-348.

Parmeter, S. M., & Gaber, J. D. (1971, November). Creative scientists rate creativity factors. *Research Management*, 65-70.

Paunonen, S. V., & Ashton, M. C. (2001). Big five factors and facets and the prediction of behavior. *Journal of Personality and Social Psychology, 81*(3), 524-539.

Poole, M. S., & DeSanctis, G. (1992). Microlevel structuration in computer-supported group decision making. *Human Communication Research, 19*(1), 5-49.

Ridgeway, C. L. (1984). Dominance, performance and status in groups: A theoretical analysis. In E. Lawler (Ed.), *Advances in group processes: Theory and research* (Vol. 1, pp. 59-93). Greenwich, CT: JAI Press.

Sell, J., Lovaglia, M. J., Mannix, E. A., Samuelson, C. D., & Wilson, R. K. (1992). Investigating conflict, power, and status within and among groups. *Small Group Research, 35*(1), 44-72.

Sewell, W. H., Jr. (1992). A theory of structure: Duality, agency, and transformation. *American Journal of Sociology, 98*, 129.

Sherif, M., White, B. J., & Harvey, O. J. (1955). Status in experimentally produced groups. *American Journal of Sociology, 66*, 370-379.

Siegel, J., Dubrovsky, V., Kiesler, S., & McGuire, T. (1986). Group processes in computer-mediated communication. *Organizational Behavior & Human Decision Processes, 37*, 157-187.

Strauss, A., & Corbin, J. (1998). *Basics of qualitative research: Techniques and procedures for developing grounded theory* (2nd ed.). Thousand Oaks, CA: Sage Publications.

Thompson, L. (2003). Improving the creativity of organizational work groups. *Academy of Management Executive, 17*(1), 96-109.

West, M. A. (1990). The social psychology of innovation in groups. In M. A. West & J. L. Farr (Eds.), *Innovation and creativity at work: Psychological and organizational strategies* (pp. 309-333). Chichester, UK: Wiley & Sons.

Woodman, R., & Schoenfeldt, L. F. (1989). Individual differences in creativity: An interactionist perspective. In J. A. Glover & C. R. Reynolds, (Eds.), *Handbook of Creativity* (pp. 77-92). New York: Plenum Press.

Yin, R. K. (1998). An abridged version of case study research: Design and method. *Handbook of applied social research methods* (pp. 229-260). Sage.

ENDNOTES

[1] Experiment one includes the original FtF and asynchronous conditions reported in Ocker et al. (1996) as well as the synchronous CMC and hybrid conditions reported in Ocker et al. (1998).

[2] Other categories of ideas were determined (i.e., rare, pervasive and common) and are presented in Ocker (2005).

Chapter III
Educating Future Product Developers in Virtual Collaboration:
Five Years of the E-GPR Course

Roman Žavbi
University of Ljubljana, Slovenia

Jože Tavčar
Iskra Medanizmi d.d, Slovenia

Jouke Verlinden
Delft University of Technology, The Netherlands

ABSTRACT

Integrated product development is a set of complex activities and its level of difficulty is additionally increased by the ever-changing business environment, primarily by functional associating of geographically dispersed human resources. The key resources for development are product developers, but it is questionable whether the existing systems are appropriate for the education of such professionals. The chapter describes the European Global Product Realization (E-GPR) course program and reflections from the perspective of participating students and company representatives. To investigate the long-term effects of the course, a survey was conducted on all present and former students, and company representatives. Students, lecturers, instructors, and company representatives all have high praise for the course, believing the acquired knowledge and experience to be invaluable for future members of product development teams.

INTRODUCTION

The world is in the middle of the globalization process that, among other things, forces companies into acquisitions and mergers, strategic alliances of various governance structures, and forming of cross-functional teams. This leads to the merging of geographically, organizationally, and culturally heterogeneous human resources, including product developers (Žavbi & Tavčar, 2005).

Research has confirmed that development of innovative and competitive products and the use of information technologies will have a crucial influence on production in the future; only the sale of such products will enable long-term success in the global market (Hundal, 1995; Beitz & Helbig, 1997). The development of such products requires appropriately trained product developers who posses a broad spectrum of professional abilities (e.g. customer-oriented thinking, methods for systematic product development, application of information technology and communication tools, international team interaction). Another characteristic of product development is the high share of tacit knowledge, especially during the conceptualization phase.

Tacit knowledge is personal, hard to formalize (it is often not able to be formalized) and highly context specific, and as such difficult to transfer or share; for example, experience, intuitions, insights, and hunches are of tacit nature. Spender suggested that tacit knowledge could be understood best as knowledge that has not yet been abstracted from practice (Spender, 1996). Another kind of knowledge is explicit knowledge, which can be expressed, for example, in scientific equations, specifications, and blueprints. This type of knowledge can be transferred between individuals formally and systematically (Nonaka & Konno, 1998).

The constraints on engineering problem-solving today are increasingly not technical, but rather lie on the societal and human side of engineering practice (Grimson, 2002). As an example, Beitz

and Helbig (1997) found large deficiencies in the fields of group interaction skills and ability to translate thoughts into action.

In addition, integrated product development requires cooperation of all stakeholders in the product life cycle during the early phases of development, especially during product design (e.g. Andreasen & Hein, 2000). More and more of these stakeholders are becoming organizationally, geographically, and culturally dispersed (the automotive industry is a typical example, e.g. May & Carter 2001; Segrestin, 2005).

Market and organizational changes, the integrated product development process, and available information and communication technologies (ICT), thus present a number of challenges for future product developers, including:

- Working with a global customer base
- Work in cross-functional teams
- Work in multidisciplinary teams
- Work in multinational teams
- Work in geographically dispersed teams
- Selection and application of appropriate ICTs
- Developing communication skills
- Learning to apply and further improve engineering knowledge and skills
- Transfer of tacit knowledge

However, it is questionable whether existing conventional systems for educating product developers are adequate for the highly changeable business environment which industry is facing, and to address the high knowledge tacitness of the product development process.

The chapter is structured as follows: First, "Nonconventional Educational Programs" presents three generations of educational programs. "E-GPR Course" then presents the course, its outline, projects, and the communication equipment used. The "Evolution of Task and Prototype Complexity" within the course is described next. "E-GPR Course and Creativity from the Participating Students' Perspective" describes various influences on the creativity within teams and is followed by "Reflections on the E-GPR Course and Creativity from Company Representatives' Perspective." In the section "Virtual Training Course for Product Development Team Members from Industry," the authors propose a customized course to suit the needs of working professionals. Finally, a conclusion section summarizes main findings, and reflections and experiences of the participating students, lecturers, instructors, and working professionals from the participating organizations.

NONCONVENTIONAL EDUCATIONAL PROGRAMS

Three generations of educational programs can be described, which are based on nonconventional academic arrangements and advanced ICT infrastructure (Figure 1).

First generation approaches were dedicated to the realization of the virtual university. Bodendorf and Swain (2001) explained this concept as an

electronic representation of the features of a real university based on networked hardware, distributed software, and knowledge infrastructure: courses and study programs are converted into electronic format, dedicated interactive course material is developed and put on the Internet, tuition is available in the form of asynchronous and synchronous communication, academic and administrative support services are electronically simulated, and so forth. The basic purpose of a virtual university is to offer education, which is flexible in time, place, content, and pace. A vital strategy, e-learning, was adopted to achieve the paradigm shift required (Soyjaudah & Jahmeerbacus, 2000). The various computer-network and videoconferencing-based engineering courses essentially focused on the inclusion of the available results of information and communication technologies in engineering courses in order to explore the opportunities and to gain experience (Chu, Urbanik, Yip, & Cheung, 1999). Irandoust and Sjöberg (2001) considered the challenges of internationalization. They found that creation of an international culture on campus and the involvement of an international dimension in all activities ought to concern university management. Graduates should be able to develop the various elements of competence, such as skills mixed with attitudes and a global perspective, the ability to adapt technology to different needs, networking, communication and professional behaviour, entrepreneurship, and attitudes and capacity for lifelong learning (Sclater, Grierson, Ion, & MacGregor, 2001). Andersen (2001) gave details about a typical, one semester-long course that was offered to international students from 14 countries to develop technical as well as personal competencies. This course assumed that designers must learn to appreciate the requirements of marketing, work within the bounds of available technology, and that collaboration and cooperation are vital activities of every designer.

Second-generation approaches introduced various organizational frameworks such as

Figure 1. The scope of videoconferencing-based engineering courses (Source: Horváth, Duhovnik & Xirouchakis, 2003, p. 85)

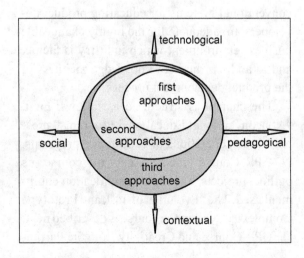

extended or multiprofessional classroom, project-based virtual workshops, and academia-led virtual companies (Marchman, 1998). A virtual enterprise is a temporary alliance of autonomous, diverse and possibly geographically dispersed organizations (e.g. universities, laboratories, companies) that come together to share skills and resources in order to better respond to business opportunities (educational challenges in our case), and whose cooperation is supported by ICTs (Cardoso & Oliviera, 2005). For example, Volpentesta, Frega, and Muzzupappa (2001) reported on a one semester-long educational experience using the virtual enterprise organization model. Students with different backgrounds formed a laboratory class and were then divided into multidisciplinary teams that played different roles while they were collaborating in the Web-based virtual enterprise (VE). They were also busy with virtual prototyping of products of average complexity. Gibson (2001) confirmed that a project-based pedagogy permits the brighter students to extend themselves towards their full potential; beyond what is possible with formally taught courses. Practice-oriented international courses teach the students how to 'survive' in a different culture, to put the already acquired knowledge and skills into practice, and to broaden technical knowledge and skills (Rompelman & de Vries, 2002).

Third-generation approaches extend the contextual scope by integrating advanced educational concepts with ICTs, to achieve the best possible results and to create a pro-innovation attitude in the education of engineering students. Essentially, this was the main motivation to initiate and organize the international education course called European Global Product Realization (E-GPR).

The specific aim of the E-GPR organizational team (Table 1) was to raise awareness in the students of the principles of global product realization in virtual enterprises (VEs) (Horváth et al., 2001). Generally, VEs and virtual teams within them are supposed to provide many advantages over traditional settings, including the ability to bridge time and space (e.g. "follow-the-sun" product development), better utilization of distributed human resources without physical relocation of employees, ability to hire the best people regardless of their location, and organizational flexibility (e.g. Biggs, 2000; Lipnack & Stamps, 2000; Paul, Seetharaman, Samarah, & Mykytyna, 2004). All these should result in realization of high-quality products at reduced costs (Barlett & Ghoshal, 2000).

A VE typically nurtures a culture of innovation together with capturing and harnessing skills and expertise. From a layout point of view, a VE is a holistic combination of functional components, which provides a dynamic framework for the organization and operation of the enterprise. As a result of the dynamic framework and flexible foundational technologies, a VE is able to respond promptly to new opportunities and problems. It is safe to predict that the concept of VE and the realization of products in a global context will proliferate in the near future. As an illustration,

Table 1. Organizational team of the E-GPR course

Member	Institution	Educational Program	Time period
1	Delft University of Technology, the Netherlands	Industrial Design	2002-present
2	Swiss Federal Institute of Technology, Lausanne, Switzerland	Microengineering and Communication systems	2002-present
3	University of Ljubljana, Slovenia	Mechanical Engineering	2002-present
4	City University, London, United Kingdom	Electrical Engineering	2004-present
5	University of Zagreb, Croatia	Mechanical Engineering	2004-present

in a study dating from 2000 (Biggs, 2000), the Gartner group predicted that by 2004, more than 60% of the professional workforce in the Global 2000 Company would work in virtual teams. For this reason, the operating principles of VEs have been borrowed to formulate the concept of the academic VE. This is believed to be one possible answer to the educational challenges.

On the other hand, we have to be aware of the fact that many companies have tried to develop products using virtual teams, with greater or smaller degrees of success (e.g., May & Carter, 2001; IJsendoorf, 2002). In the same study from 2000, the Gartner group predicted that by 2003, 50% of virtual teams would fail to meet either strategic or operational objectives due to their inability to manage a distributed workforce. This is not surprising, since we are just beginning to understand what fundamental factors drive the success and failure of virtual teams (Kanawattanachaia & Yoob, 2002).

The purpose of this chapter is mainly to present the E-GPR course, evolution of the complexity of tasks and prototypes, effects of the E-GPR set-up on creativity, and experiences of students and industrial partners who took part in the E-GPR course over the past 5 years.

E-GPR COURSE

The new educational concept is to shift the responsibility of learning to the students, with the instructors playing the supporting role of advisors and establishing the framework, objectives, and the boundaries of the course/project. For these reasons, the theoretical and methodological framework of the E-GPR course rests on the following three hypotheses (the framework and concepts described in this section are drawn from the report on E-GPR found in (Horváth, Xirouchakis, Duhovnik, & Wiersma, 2003), where details on the course can also be found):

- Opening the conventional educational institution towards an academic virtual enterprise
- Consideration of the university students as evolving young professionals, acting as academic knowledge producers and facing practical engineering problems
- Putting creative problem-solving and disciplinary research in the position of the 'engine' behind academic learning and teaching

Students were supposed to take part actively in the knowledge exploration and utilization process and to evolve into creative professionals who:

- Co-operate in goal-driven learning of the subject materials and in developing the skills of problem-solving, collaboration and coordination
- Solve real-life engineering problems in communities of practice by using the most advanced technologies
- Learn the principles of remote collaboration, knowledge brokerage, capacity acquisition/outsourcing and providing services
- Transfer their results and experiences directly to industry, and publish in international journals and proceedings

This position formulates both intellectual and professional requirements for learners (Green & Kennedy, 2001). Among the intellectual requirements, perhaps the most important one is self-driven enquiry that is propelled through learning-by-doing, and by the reflection of creation. Engineering students must be able to find, mine, and synthesize information from various knowledge sources. In addition, the ability to exploit various (external) knowledge sources is a critical ingredient of innovative capabilities (Cohen & Liventhal, 1990). Integration of information is also important for forming comprehensive views involving technical, economic, social, and environmental aspects since integrated product development should consider viewpoints of all stakeholders. The request for system-oriented integral thinking appears as an intellectual requirement that enables them to generate multiple alternative solutions for complex real-life problems.

At the very least, they must stay abreast of changes of professional practice; and, as Johnston (2001) spells out, cultural diversity is a fact of professional life: "Engineers are being employed in ever greater numbers by multinational and transnational corporations and are routinely working across national and cultural boundaries" (p. 78). It gives rise to the need to understand cultural differences and, at the same time, of having enough knowledge to stimulate, communicate, negotiate, and persuade across all kinds of cultural boundaries. It makes the students prepared for working effectively in multidisciplinary teams in virtual, physical, and hybrid collaborative environments.

Course Outline

The E-GPR educational institutions designed an educational course comprised of lectures on specialized topics and project team work supported by selected companies. The course concludes with a one-week closing workshop and presentation of functioning partial or complete prototypes that have been produced by virtual teams. In this last week, all students meet face to face for the first time.

The lectures and project work take place twice a week (formally, four academic hours per week). Communication is conducted in English. Via lectures, students are provided with a systematic insight into basic knowledge and given concrete examples of global products. Academic lectures, cases from industry and project work are interwoven throughout the semester, in which the lectures act as navigated learning elements for the project work. For example, an interactive workshop on creative thinking (covering creative

problem solving, mind mapping, brainstorming) is provided prior to the project's idea generation phase. The specific features of products intended for the global market, their classification into categories (Ulrich & Eppinger, 2000), and so forth, are presented. The concept of a virtual enterprise is introduced also, along with the specifics of work in such enterprises. The presentation of successful companies (two per country) lasts 90 minutes. In addition to the technical presentation of the products and their global level marketing, the company organization and strategy is discussed. Each company presentation is followed by an in-depth lecture.

The curriculum is prepared in such a manner as to constitute a well-rounded package (see Figure 2). Image materials for the lectures are accessible at the project home page a week before each lecture. The students are thus able to prepare for the lectures in advance and participate in them more actively during Q&A sessions. All lectures are recorded and the tapes/DVD's are available on the server as files in RealPlayer™ format (Žavbi & Tavčar, 2005).

Projects

The organizers of the E-GPR course strive to develop the type of project work that would most realistically reflect the circumstances, activities, and tasks of professional product development teams. The reason there is such a large emphasis on realism is that we desire to show the students (i.e., future members of product development teams) the challenges that professional product development teams are faced with every day. The project work is very intensive and plays the central role for the students. Intensity of effort is one of the characteristics of successful product development and also important for later retrieval of product development knowledge: the more material is processed—the more effort used, the more processing makes use of associations between the items to be learned and knowledge already in the

Figure 2. Layout of the E-GPR course in 2004 spring semester (Source: Horváth, Wiersma, Duhovnik, & Stroud, 2004, p. 513)

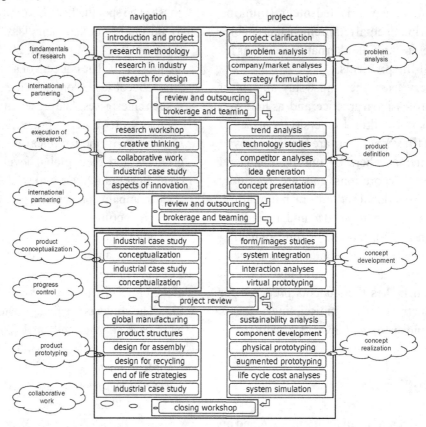

memory—the better will be the later retrieval of the item (Cohen & Levinthal, 1990). The set of tasks (i.e., products to be developed) is drawn up by the representatives of the participating companies (Table 2). Each virtual development team is composed of students from all the five (three in the first three years) participating universities.

A virtual team can be defined as a multinational and multidisciplinary team whose members are geographically and organizationally disperse. Their collaboration is made possible via the use of IT&T technologies. Team members usually do not have a common history, and the probability of them cooperating again when the current project is over is also small. E-GPR teams, on the other hand, are characterized by the fact that parts of teams composed of students from individual

universities have had a common history, as they have already cooperated during their studies.

Complete teams are formed during the so called brokerage process, which is conducted via a video-conference. On the basis of video-conference presentations of the partial teams, the questions and answers that follow and their preferences, as well as the assistance of moderators (i.e., participating lecturers), students form complete teams. At the intermediary review sessions, each team presents their work (analysis, concepts, or detailed product proposal). Feedback is given by other teams, clients, and company representatives. The latter collaborate closely with student teams during the entire process of product development—via their requirements, knowledge, and comments—they contribute to realism of the context in which project work is performed. Choice of a team leader and distribution of tasks within the teams are also left to team members—it is anticipated that a team leader would appear during work (emergent leadership). Teams are also allowed to choose the methods, time and frequency of communicating, as well as other details concerning the presentation of final results (e.g., type and number of prototypes). The schedule of intermediary presentations, time-table of the closing workshop, and presentation of final results, however, are predetermined (Žavbi & Tavčar, 2005).

Product development within the E-GPR course comprises activities such as:

- Concept development, for example, identification of lead users, collection of customer needs, identification of competitive products, synthesis of concepts (Figure 3).
- Feasibility study of concepts and building and testing of experimental prototypes (Figure 4).

- Detail design, for example, choice of materials, definition of part geometry (Figure 5), assigning of tolerances.
- Prototyping, generating of virtual and physical prototypes (Figure 6).

Figure 3. A concept of a cargo carrier (E-GPR academic year 2006)

Table 2. E-GPR participants

Year	Univ. participants	#students	Core company	Educational focus
2002	UoL, EPFL, DUT	29	LIV Postojna, Slovenia De Vlamboog BV, the Netherlands	Redesigning and prototyping of consumer durables for global market.
2003	UoL, EPFL, DUT	38	De Vlamboog BV, the Netherlands	Conceptualization and prototyping a future product for the core company.
2004	UoL, EPFL, UoZ, DUT	47	De Vlamboog BV, the Netherlands	Combining operational research and product conceptualization.
2004 pilot	EPFL, UoZ, CUoL, DUT	16	FEI company, the Netherlands	Conceptualization and prototyping of a collaborative virtual laboratory.
2005	UoL, EPFL, UoZ, CUoL, DUT	41	AVIDOR, Swizerland	Human- and environment centered product development.
2006	UoL, EPFL, UoZ, CUoL, DUT	51	Niko, Slovenia	Conceptualization and prototyping a product to a new market for the core company.

Note: EPFL—Ecole Polytechnique Federale Lausanne, Switzerland; UoL—University of Ljubljana, Slovenia; UoZ—University of Zagreb, Croatia; DUT—Delft University of Technology, The Netherlands; CUoL—City University of London, England

Figure 4. Experimental power supply and control unit (E-GPR academic year 2003)

Figure 5. Embodiment design of vacuum cleaner (left) and finite element analysis (right, E-GPR academic year 2003)

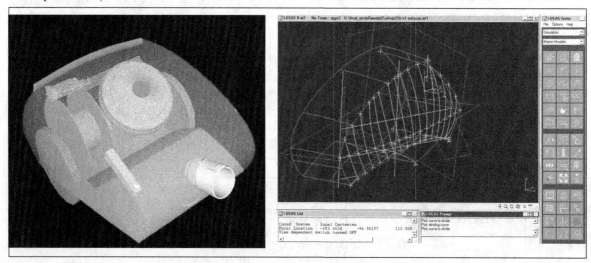

Naturally, all activities can not be performed (e.g., extensive testing of prototypes) within the available E-GPR course timeframe, but we nevertheless believe that we have enabled students to apply their knowledge and acquire the experience important for product development.

E-GPR enables tacit knowledge transfer between students, and students and instructors via cross-functional virtual teams engaged in project work (learning by doing), supported by a coaching system. Knowledge transfer is also facilitated via ad-hoc based team member interaction with other team members, instructors, and working professionals from participating companies.

These modes give opportunity to individual knowledge transfers, which are believed to be a successful way to transfer tacit knowledge in organizations (internally) and among collaborating

Figure 6. A prototype of vineyard spraying machine (E-GPR academic year 2004/2005)

organizations (Inkpen & Dinur, 1998; Nonaka & Konno, 1998; Ylinenpää & Nilsson, 2000).

Employed Communication Equipment

Aside from regular digital communication facilities like electronic mail and chatrooms, media rooms in Ljubljana, Delft, and Lausanne (and later London and Zagreb) were appropriately equipped and have created a joint virtual classroom. The most important of all components is the video-conferencing system (compatible with H.323 and H.320 protocols) consisting of a smart camera that follows the speaker, digital projectors and/or TV screens, additional video camera, microphones, amplifier, speakers, a video-conferencing multi-point server, and IP-based connections (during the first year three ISDN lines were used simultaneously, which was relatively costly).

The lecture rooms have to be set up at each location in such a way as to let the students have the best view on the screens and to allow the lecturers to keep contact with both the local audience and the remote ones. Digital projectors are used to display the local and remote presentations. Computers for projection of slides are visible on the Internet (via IP number) and are interconnected using Microsoft NetMeeting. A TV or another digital projector serves to show all the audience at the five locations simultaneously. Typically, two video cameras are used. One is the smart camera, pointed at the audience, and the second one is a portable video camera for viewing the local lecturer. The video system contains a video recorder and a DVD recorder for recording purposes.

EVOLUTION OF TASK AND PROTOTYPE COMPLEXITY

The first E-GPR course (academic year 2001/2002) was a challenging undertaking for all participants; organizers, instructors, students, and industrial professionals. Everyone had to face the new model for educating future product developers, new telecommunication technologies and equipment, different time schedules and so forth. It follows therefore that the first products to be developed/re-designed were relatively low in complexity and technical content. Later, when the organizers and instructors gained more experience and skills, the focus was more on sophistication of the products/prototypes to be developed.

The E-GPR course has been constantly developing and improving over the last five years. One of the indicators is the increase in prototype complexity (Table 3), which was confirmed by the company representatives' answers. During the initial years teams of students were focused primarily on the appearance of the products. One of the reasons is that design is a very important factor for product aesthetics. The increased complexity has been achieved through greater involvement of the companies, larger, more multidisciplinary teams, and better management. As well as increased complexity these elements helped to increase opportunities for higher creativity.

Coffee makers, vacuum cleaners, and some of the respiratory units were not working functional prototypes; the focus was on appearance and only some of the functions were implemented. Besides the physical prototype, the product platform was realized only in the form of 3D models and a graphical presentation. Larger scale input (knowledge, financial support) from the company in 2005 clearly impacted on the students' work. Students were more motivated, which in turn stimulated creativity. Working prototypes had a higher level of function implementation and therefore higher practical value for the company.

Products have different types of complexity (definition from Tavčar & Duhovnik, 2005):

- Complex products are from the construction point of view, for example, a camera mechanism.
- Simple products in mass production are often very complicated from the technological point of view (e.g., electric bulb).
- Adaptation of products to customers often results in a vast number of variants, which are difficult to manage (household appliances).
- Complex products are also composed of a vast number of different elements.

The E-GPR course does not include the whole product's life-cycle, therefore complexity is focused on prototypes only.

The period of one semester proved to be appropriate for the execution of the E-GPR seminar according to several criteria. There should be an agreement on the timetable and program between all five universities. In such a period, there is too little time to develop a complex product, especially if market research is performed. If one wanted to increase the level of difficulty and the usefulness of project results for companies, the course would have to be extended to two semesters. In this case, more concrete results could be expected, so company investments could also be greater, for example, for support and production of prototypes.

Sources of creativity are new working principles (i.e., physical laws), topology, materials, and geometry. The product type largely determines the sources of creativity. For example, a vacuum cleaner and a coffee maker are mature products and it is difficult to invent new working principles in one semester. A deep knowledge and overview of existing solutions is necessary before real work can start. On the other hand, industrial design creativity or topology redesign requires a shorter warm-up time. This is an explanation why the E-GPR projects are successful from the industrial design (vacuum cleaner) and topology creativity (spraying machines) points of view. In the present course (2006), product realization requires advanced mechanical design. A short project duration can be compensated with more intensive support from the company.

During the past 5 years, project teams have been multidisciplinary and international as specified in Table 1. This has proved to be an important source of creativity. Multidisciplinary teams also contributed to the product complexity. Since 2003, the participants from the EPFL have been oriented towards microengineering, which has contributed

Table 3. Level of complexity during the years

Year and product	Construction complexity	Prototype-appearance	Prototype-implementation of functions	Number of parts	Total complexity
2002 – Vacuum cleaner	3	4	3	2	**12**
2003 – Respiratory unit for welders	3	4	2	3	**12**
2004 – Protection mask for welders	4	4	3	3	**14**
2004 pilot – Collaborative virtual environment for Electron Microscopes	5	4	2	3	**14**
2005 - Vineyard spraying machines	5	4	5	3	**17**
2006 - Universal Carriage	5	4*	5*	5	**19**

*Note: * project is not finished yet; year 2005/2006*

to the growth of product complexity, introducing the development of advanced microelectronic components. Knowledge about industrial design, mechanical engineering and microelectronic was supplementary and the students could split the tasks easier (as observed by staff).

The product development activity during the course is executed in a purely virtual environment. Students meet face to face in the final week to prepare the presentation and finish the prototype—the virtual environment has been a barrier regarding the sophistication of the prototypes. Students prepare subassemblies at different locations and then come together to assemble them. An important factor therefore for prototype sophistication is the level of support and available equipment at the closing workshop.

E-GPR COURSE AND CREATIVITY FROM THE PARTICIPATING STUDENTS' PERSPECTIVE

In previous publications, the organizers of the e-GPR course have reflected on the key experiences of both students and educators (Horváth et al., 2001; Horváth, Duhovnik, & Xirouckakis,

2003; Horváth, Wiersma et. al., 2004; Horváth, Xirouchakis et. al., 2004; Žavbi & Tavčar 2005; Tavčar, Žavbi, Verlinden, & Duhovnik, 2005). The main sources of information were personal communication and some focused student questionnaires. For example, Horváth, Xirouchakis et al. (2004) identified mixed views on the additional overhead of such a cross-academic venture and positive effects of the closing workshop and the concept of the academic virtual enterprise. However, we have little or no knowledge on the long-term effects of the course or on its creative aspects.

To investigate these elements, a survey was conducted on all present and former students. A questionnaire was sent to each by electronic mail. It was divided in four subsections (1) personal information, (2) personal assessment of the course, (3) the team result and creative activities, (4) other elements that might have influenced creativity.

As the course is generally taken by senior students (equivalent with the first year of a master's program) it was challenging to track down past participants, as many have graduated and abandoned their university email accounts. Furthermore, some crucial enrollment information was lost for the first two years, which could only be partially reconstructed by retrieving printed email correspondence. As shown in the histogram below (Figure 7), the final response is well divided over the years, with an exception of 2003. Furthermore, all nationalities are represented: 11 Slovene, 10 Swiss, 9 Dutch, 6 Croatian, and 2 British.

Team Result and Creative Activities

Overall, the respondents were very satisfied with their end result, and claim that the end result provided a solution to the company's problem. The judgment of the design outcome is summarized in Figure 8 (on a 5-point scale, 5 = excellent).

There is a more mixed view on the level of innovation. This indicator could be interpreted as a level of creativity of the proposed solution— whether the design included novel principles or novel applications. This judgment differs per year, as depicted in Figure 9. It is unanimously high 2002 and 2005, while both 2004 series get a more neutral response with a larger variation. For the

organization De Vlamboog (acting as a client in 2002, 2003, and 2004), the first assignment was more redesign with later ones more focused on future products and technologies. The students' response seems to contradict the impressions by staff and client; we have no explanation on this phenomenon. The 2005 case (Avidor) required technological innovations and functional prototypes, which seem to positively influence the judgment of the innovation level.

In the questionnaire, the respondents could specify which creative tasks went well and which were more challenging for the team. Both open questions were answered with similar activities, which we coded as:

- **Conceptualization:** Creating product concepts
- **(Technical) problem solving:** Finding (technical) principles that solve particular problems

Figure 7. E-GPR student questionnaire response

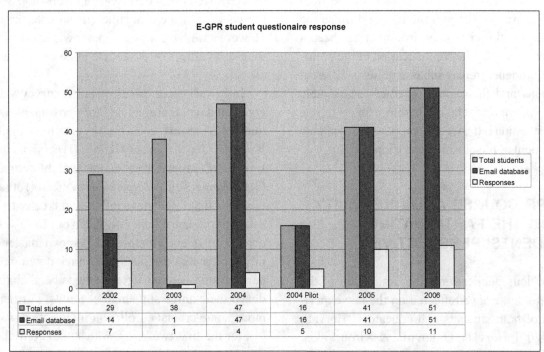

E-GPR student questionaire response

	2002	2003	2004	2004 Pilot	2005	2006
Total students	29	38	47	16	41	51
Email database	14	1	47	16	41	51
Responses	7	1	4	5	10	11

Figure 8. Judgment of the end result on a 5-point scale, 5 = excellent (in % of the respondents)

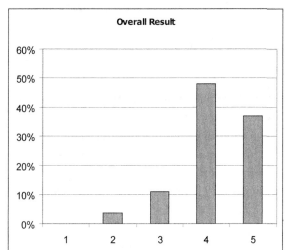 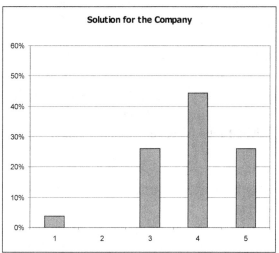

Figure 9. Annual average and standard deviation of the level of innovation of the end result

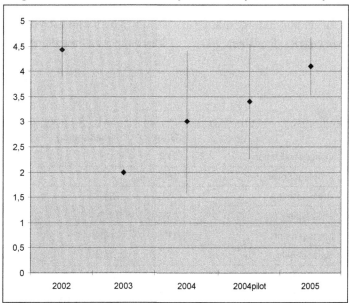

- **Brainstorming:** Associative treatment of a particular topic in the team
- **Prototyping:** Creating physical prototypes
- **Management:** Time management, team coordination
- **Embodiment:** Detailing and harmonizing the design of both the outside shape of the product and its internal structure

- **Communication:** Various electronic forms of information exchange

In essence, all of these are considered as important elements in creative collaboration. They can be split into general tasks and responsibilities that run throughout the project (Brainstorming Management, Communication) and processes that are specific to particular phases of design (problem solving, conceptualization, embodiment, prototyping). Team management is considered to be the most challenging (to be discussed further in the next section), followed by Embodiment, Prototyping and Conceptualization. When aggregated, many activities appear in both "good" and "challenging" categories as shown in Table 4. The exceptions are Problem Solving (only positive), Embodiment & Communication (both only negative).

Aspects that Influence Team Creativity

When asked about the elements that limited team creativity, the respondents report (1) time pressure, (2) differences in skills and knowledge, and (3) limited communication facilities.

Time pressure can be explained in many ways—the course has very strict deadlines, ex-

pected quality level is high, and a consistent, high level of effort is required to harmonize team vision. Individual differences in skills and knowledge are also influential, as expected in teamwork. It is unclear to which extent these differences are due to the fact that participants vary in disciplines or by culture/nationalities. Differences in attitudes will be discussed later in the chapter. Problems with communication are paramount while the virtual setting strongly increases the need for communication, as for example with videoconferencing. This also comes from uncertainty on whether the other team members have read messages, and if not, why not; the existence of technical problems or rather a lack of interest; whether or not the messages are interpreted correctly, and so forth. Furthermore, engineering and formgiving concepts are difficult to share due to limited channels of communication. Creative blockage as a result of the design assignment

Table 4. Creative tasks that went well or were considered to be more challenging (in % of respondents)

	Good	Challenging
Conceptualization	21%	11%
Problem Solving	18%	-
Brainstorming	16%	5%
Prototyping	13%	11%
Management	11%	18%
Embodiment	-	11%
Communication	-	5%

Table 5. Aspects that limited team creativity (response percentage)

% of respondents	Limitation
58%	Time pressure
50%	Individual differences in skills and knowledge
47%	Limited communication facilities
37%	The company, the assignment
18%	Cultural differences
16%	Lack of skills
5%	Intensive use of computer tools

and the related company is identified solely by participants of the current project (2006); this most likely relates to the natural process that such constraints are viewed differently in retrospect, when the project is over.

These top three limitations of team creativity persist each year (time pressure was mentioned by 100 % respondents from 2002). Cultural differences and lack of skills only seem to be significant in 2002 and 2004 pilot (both situations in which new locations were introduced). A similar fluctuation was found in attitudes (discussed below).

The respondents also rated the influence of several course elements, summarized in Figure 10. The most stimulating are the closing workshop and intermediary team meetings. According to the respondents, the most useful feedback at the intermediary reviews is given by their own team and the company representatives (58% and 45% of the respondents), while the mentors and other teams are less influential (at 39% and 34%). At the closing workshop, the response from the company and other teams is valued most, yet the mentors and the own team are also influential (respectively 52%, 52%, 48%, and 44%).

Although other course ingredients are rated fairly neutral, lectures by videoconferencing are generally found to be limiting the creative process. This part of the course is one of the most passive parts. Staff members have confirmed that the lecture content is often already known by students from at least one location, which decreases the added value of the lectures. Although lectures are taped and can be viewed by the E-GPR intranet, this does not happen often due to the fact that navigation within the presentations and retrieval of interesting fragments is difficult.

Influence of Diversity

As the participants of the academic virtual enterprise differ in many aspects, we asked about the diversity in the team and how this influenced creativity. The results are summarized in Table 6. The level of participation refers to the limited availability of many students due to differing university rosters and, to a certain degree, to the level of commitment of the individual (mentioned three times). Many students report a degree of shyness to the international team and to the way

Figure 10. Course aspects that influence creativity (average with standard deviation)

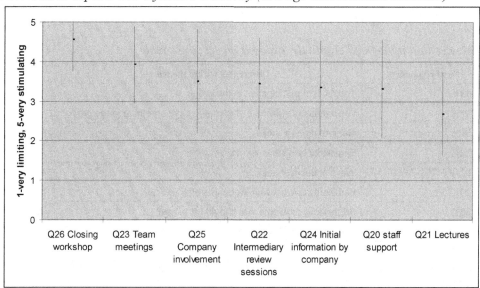

of communicating—they are reluctant to speak up while others are more extroverted. This might also be influenced by some difficulties to express oneself in English as a second language. The diversity in disciplines is viewed as a positive effect in quickly generating new ideas for a multitude of product aspects, although some students report difficulties in brainstorming.

Over the years, these influences change. For example, differences in familiarity with team working and openness for discussion become more influential over the years; respectively from 20% to 40%, and from 0% to 45%. The inclination towards communication technology was high in 2002 (60%), but has decreased over the years (18% in 2006). Since 2005, students have fully adopted MSN messenger and Webcam-based discussions and are moving away from the Polycom videoconferencing system that is still a scarce resource at the universities. Interestingly, competition and the need for definite answers are both reported to highly influence creativity when new locations are introduced (2002 and 2004 pilot). Although students are always new to the course, familiarity between the staff members and the respective curricula/disciplines seems to smooth these two elements.

Impact and Lessons Learned

As we already heard in personal communication over the years, students are very positive about the opportunity to work in a virtual academic enterprise. From respondents that finished the course, 33% consider it to be the most valuable course they have attended, while another 55% judge the course to be useful. Three students were less positive about the course and stated the course was not different from other courses in their curriculum. Designing in multidisciplinary teams and using videoconferencing and related equipment are considered to be the most valuable lessons learned (55% of the respondents put these in their top 3), followed by English language (47%) and learning from other cultures, problem solving/creativity, and prototype building (each 37%). There were no significant differences in learning elements between the years or a correlation to the overall judgment of the course. However, the learning goals differ per locations, as indicated in Figure 11 (unfortunately, no British response could be included as these were still involved in the 2006 course).

Some of these differences can be explained on the basis that the students will welcome additions to their local curriculum. For example, the Dutch

Table 6. Differences that influenced creativity, ordered on response rate

% of respondents	Differences within the team
53%	The level of participation in the group
47%	Willingness of individual students to say something in the group
34%	Generating new ideas
32%	Familiarity to work in teams
32%	Ways of decision making
26%	Familiarity to work with Webcams etc
26%	Addressing problems that should be solved
26%	The need for definite answers
26%	Openness for discussion
21%	Competition between students

have finished an extensive prototyping design project prior to this course, while they haven't yet experienced real contact with industry. In contrast, Slovenian students exclusively attend individual design assignments before entering the E-GPR course, while they have had intensive contact with companies.

REFLECTIONS ON E-GPR COURSE AND CREATIVITY FROM COMPANY REPRESENTATIVES' PERSPECTIVE

This subsection is written from the perspective of the company representatives. In a constant search for new market opportunities and development potential, companies strongly support the E-GPR course. Both short-term benefits and major advantages for the future are expected.

Companies have been impressed by the results of the students, primarily by the originality and level of elaboration of the prototypes, given the available time to develop them.

Students are open and receptive to new ideas and can adopt them within a relatively short time as standard work methods. Companies always show a genuine interest in courses that provide students with considerable general level experience during their education, learning by trial and error is still inexpensive, while the long-term process of acquiring specialized knowledge and skills still remains to be performed within the company.

Company activities are complex; as a rule they can be managed only by teamwork, while university studies have traditionally been more individualistic. The personal experiences of teamwork, trust and working in mixed development teams are very important elements of effective

Figure 11. Learning goals across locations

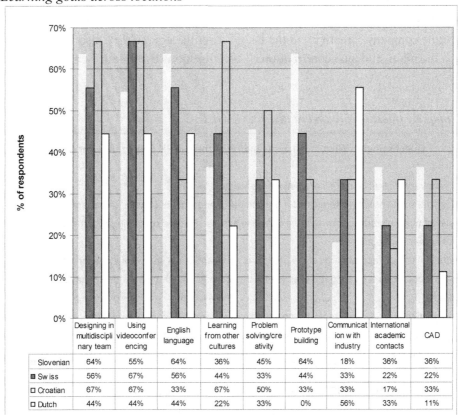

	Designing in multidisciplinary team	Using videoconferencing	English language	Learning from other cultures	Problem solving/creativity	Prototype building	Communication with industry	International academic contacts	CAD
Slovenian	64%	55%	64%	36%	45%	64%	18%	36%	36%
■ Swiss	56%	67%	56%	44%	33%	44%	33%	22%	22%
□ Croatian	67%	67%	33%	67%	50%	33%	33%	17%	33%
□ Dutch	44%	44%	44%	22%	33%	0%	56%	33%	11%

participation in regular company operations. Based on personal experience with this type of work, one also becomes better informed on what can be expected from for example, industrial designers and the ways to achieve consensus.

A questionnaire on creativity and the use of technical solutions for companies was handed out to company representatives who had prepared a project definition (Figure 12). Since 2002, five different companies have been involved and all companies (100 %) returned the answers. All the questions are listed below. The level of agreement was assessed from 1 to 5 (with the exception of question I, Figure 13).

Representatives unanimously agree that students have generated innovative technical solutions that are interesting for the companies. The prototypes were also useful and companies learned something from them. However, a higher sophistication of the prototypes does not necessarily mean a higher contribution to the company. Companies also agree that the industrial design (appearance) of the product was novel and provided inspiration for the company. Creativity in the E-GPR course is the main students' contribution.

Companies have expressed the opinion, however, that the project results do not bear significant practical value. The concepts cannot be directly transferred to production and the second phase of the project, embodiment and detail design, is of the highest importance for the company. Furthermore, students did not make a significant contribution to marketing information with the companies keen to learn more about the end-user needs in various countries. Time limitation forces students to go straight to the conceptual phase of product development.

There are different opinions concerning communication with, and guidance of, the student teams. Some company representatives would like to have a more active role in project execution. It follows that more proactive involvement would mean bigger influence on students' work projects, but this isn't always possible. The company representatives have their everyday obligations and therefore only participate in video conferences in most cases three to four times during the course and always attend the final workshop. Throughout the course they also answered the students' questions by e-mail.

Figure 12. Company questionaire on creativity of E-GPR

Questionnaire: What is the contribution of the E-GPR course for your company?

A)   There were very innovative technical solutions (conceptual level).

B)   The technical solutions were interesting for the company, and were subject to further analyses.

C)   Sophistication of the prototypes is high, the company has also learned something from them and it is a good starting point for further development.

D)   The industrial design (appearance) of the product is novel and it is a source of ideas for the company.

E)   The E-GPR course was a very good exercise for the students, but the results do not have   practical value for the company.

F)   The contribution of the E-GPR project is new marketing information (customer needs ...) on the designed product.

G)   Company had sufficient opportunity to communicate with the student teams and guide them.

H)   The company had sufficient opportunity to communicate with the staff members to have an influence on the project goals.

I)   How could we improve the E-GPR course to make final results more useful for the supporting company?

Figure 13. Results of questionnaire from company representatives

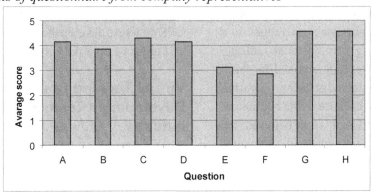

The last question was: *How could we improve the E-GPR course to make final results more useful for the supporting company?*

Companies are attempting to prepare as much information as possible about the product's functions, manufacturing technology, customers' needs and marketing, to 'bootstrap' the student's projects. There are always limitations in this knowledge transfer to students. A realistic project definition in the first phase is a prerequisite for guiding students in the right direction and for useful results at the end. To enable this, students should pay more attention to market research in order to better understand customers' needs. Some possible improvements include visiting the company during the starting period of the project and a longer duration of the project. Communication between students and company representative should be also intensified with regular meetings once a week suggested as being optimum. However, this would not necessarily increase the level of creativity as more information often means more constraints and limitations. But guided students could focus their attention on more directly applicable solutions. In 2006, the Niko company representative intends to meet the students frequently in an attempt to positively influence the outcome.

The following problem appeared as a result of low influence by the representative in 2002.

Once students discovered that it would be difficult for them to express their creativity at the desired target price, they requested that this limitation be cancelled. By doing so, they tailored the initial requirements to their needs, which naturally is a clear deviation from real circumstances. During project execution, students also experienced difficulties in decision making. A clearer definition of the role of the project supervisor from the company would eliminate these dilemmas and ensure that the project runs in accordance with the company's expectations and objectives. Furthermore, it would also contribute to a greater degree of realism. More active cooperation also requires more company time. This is acceptable, provided that all conditions are met to achieve good project results. The above is in line with the latest trends in engineering design methods. The author of the dynamic development model (Ottosson, 2004) claims that for innovative products and new designs it is not possible to take everything into account at the time of project definition. Project objectives need to be dynamically adjusted throughout execution because of new findings (see Smith's presentation of flexibility methods in Section III of this book which addresses this phenomenon in detail).

New ideas and the rights to them through intellectual property contracts (students are recognized as authors but the company retains all business rights) also helps to justify the time and costs committed by the companies. At other universities that run similar courses, legal regulation of cooperation with companies is arranged in a comparable manner (e.g. Cardozo et al., 2002).

So far, company presentations and in-depth lectures have been conducted at the participating universities, primarily because of the equipment in lecture rooms. However, it is now believed that these activities should take place in companies in order to reduce traveling for industry as well as give students insight into the company and its products. For some time, companies have desired to introduce video-conferencing as a means of communication for their activities with customers and suppliers. Purchasing of equipment is not the problem; it is rather that people need to master and accept this type of communication. The E-GPR course therefore plays a double role; it serves both as a demonstration of an effective use of such equipment as well as transferring the necessary skills to companies.

The E-GPR course is regarded as an opportunity for closer cooperation between the university and the company. Students are able to gain valuable work experience in experimental mode without daily fire-fighting while companies ensure a flow of fresh ideas and young talent into the business—student projects may lead to graduate level engagements, placements, and job offers. Cooperation through such projects is also a good way for the company and its potential new employees to get to know each other. Furthermore, companies normally develop only those projects in which adequate business results are expected with limited risks. In cooperation with faculties, though, more daring projects can be executed, because the costs are significantly lower.

International teams' structure and the use of advanced ITCs stimulate students to produce creative work in E-GPR. The lack of time to learn new tools allied to work overload often means that the opposite holds in industrial practice. Engineers in industry have experience in virtual teams, which is nonetheless normally less intensive, using

mostly e-mail and telephone. Industrialists may therefore take training modules similar to the E-GPR course to develop their skills in virtual teams and improve creativity in the workplace.

Virtual Training Course for Product Development Team Members from Industry

Based on the experiences gained during the last 5 years we have conceived a program for an industrial module which aims to develop the skills necessary for virtual product development and increase creativity in the workplace. This will be promoted to industry at each of the partner institutions. The course program consists of the following four steps:

- **Setting up of communication equipment:** A distributed physical location is preferred for course execution. Course participants do not always have required video conferencing equipment and so are invited to visit one of the E-GPR video-conference rooms for consultation and viewing of the initial E-GPR lecture and students at work.

- **Lectures on specific requirements for effective work in virtual product development teams:** The second phase of the course consists of a set of lectures on specifics of the work in the virtual environment. The main message from these lectures is the experiences from the E-GPR course. Nine necessary steps for effective work in virtual product development teams are summarized in Table 7. Successful work also requires certain special skills, as shown in Table 8.

- **Learning by doing:** Course participants are split into project teams of around five members. Each group works on a small project and is supported by mentor from the course staff. The amount of work is about 10 hours per person and the project group typically has 5 days to finish. They can work on the

Table 7. Requirements for work in global teams

A	**Preparations for the virtual development project** Activities before the beginning of project execution which are the prerequisite of successful work. The goals should be set clearly, adequately trained individuals should be selected, and the necessary infrastructure for communication and work should be provided.
B	**Project management** Virtual development work requires careful planning and monitoring. In a virtual environment, a competent leader is especially indispensable during the initial phase (Lurey & Raisinghani, 2001; Smith & Blanck, 2002).
C	**Presentation and understanding of goals** Work in virtual teams requires a clear understanding of goals (Lurey & Raisinghani, 2001).
D	**Determination of methods of working and communicating within the team** A communication timetable and rules have to be agreed on between team members. More complex tasks require more intense communication (Leenders, van Engelen & Kratzer, 2003).
E	**Legal regulation of relationships within the virtual team** A clear legal regulation of relationships is the prerequisite for an open dialogue and close collaboration (Hoffner, Field, Grefen & Ludwing, 2001).
F	**Training of team members** In addition to technical knowledge required to use the communications equipment, special features of work in a virtual team also need to be taken into account, for example, regular responses, which are important for building trust. Each virtual team member must be independent and must show initiative. Training in the use of unified software in the entire team (e.g. 3D modeler).
G	**Familiarization of project team members and building of trust** A personal relationship and trust among team members are very important for a creative dialogue and effective cooperation (Kasper-Fuehrer & Ashkanasy, 2001). Via active management and training, it is necessary to ensure that this relationship and trust are built from the beginning and then maintained (Jarvenpaa & Leidner, 1998).
H	**Project work** Current monitoring of project execution and adaptability are important. For effective project execution, work needs to be divided into well-rounded wholes. Reliable and quick data exchange on project work should be ensured. Project documentation is accessible to all members.
I	**Project conclusion** It is necessary to ensure that the project is completed and that crucial team members remain accessible for any subsequent supplements.

project from their company, home or one of the E-GPR video conference rooms.

- **Final workshop—discussion on project work in distributed environment:** The last part of the course starts with short project presentation to all participants. Personal experiences of participants are discussed in a round table format.

CONCLUSION

Students, product developers of the future, need to be appropriately educated, so that they will be up to the challenges encountered during the development of competitive products. They also need to face the ever-changing business environment in which they will work, which is characterized by the proliferation of multinational teams and geographical dispersion. The E-GPR is therefore conducted in as realistic circumstances as possible and with real topics. We believe realism to be the essential strength of the course.

International and cross-disciplinary aspects stimulate creativity and team work, which is crucial for professional engineers and designers. Each year, the E-GPR organizers need to refine the complexity of the assignment, the client, communication technology, and mentoring strategy. In the academic environment, three main challenges to creativity are (1) differences in the level of participation and commitment, (2) communica-

Table 8. Specification of skills required for effective communication and work in virtual product development teams (Source: Tavčar et al., 2005)

Team member skills	❑ Willingness to cooperate and work for common project goals
	❑ Effective communication in a virtual team (trust building)
	❑ Initiative and ability to find information and make decisions
	❑ Mastery of a common spoken and written language (English)
	❑ Mastery of a common technical language (similar background is an advantage in communication)
	❑ Personal experience of working in a virtual team (communication skills, organization of work, etc.)
	❑ Working with the communications software
	❑ Ability to use the computer in all phases of design (CAD sketches can be transferred to other users without scanning)
	❑ Specialized knowledge (compatible with other team members)
Managing skills	❑ The project leader should be well versed in virtual team management (distribution of tasks, trust building, monitoring of progress, motivation of team members)
	❑ Management of a joint server on which all project and product data are stored
	❑ Operation of the communications equipment (technician)

tion skills and attitudes, and (3) familiarity to work in teams. By providing navigated learning, each of these should receive careful attention. In contrast to many virtual teams which meet in person at the beginning of a project, here, face to face meetings are only orchestrated at the end. Although this situation is mainly driven by cost constraints, the resulting momentum at the closing workshop is intense and allows the teams to compensate for mistakes.

The lower performance of some teams was due to the fact that the accepted tasks were not always distributed among individual team members. The tasks were accepted by parts of teams of an individual university, and not by individual team members. Too often, this allowed some members to expect tasks to be done by others. The reason for this lies in inadequate team management, which is in accordance with the findings of (for example) Olson, Olson, and Meader (1995) that distributed working requires more of a group management and coordination overhead than standard face-to-face meetings. In designing the E-GPR course, it was assumed that team members would select the team leader among themselves. For this reason, each team was assigned an instructor at the beginning, who was supposed to passively monitor the team's progress. In Ljubljana, this shortcoming of

project management has been eliminated in recent projects; the instructors now play a more active role, which has yielded good results so far. The observation that managed teams are more efficient than self-directed virtual teams is also reported in literature (e.g. Piccoli & Ives, 2000).

An important part of the course was also showing the students the broad range of possibilities associated with virtual team work and ICTs. Video-conferencing was used most; in our opinion it considerably compensated for lack of classic face-to-face communication. Another important realization is that messages should be communicated in writing, primarily technically adequate sketches and equations. Such communication reduces the possibility of misunderstandings and lack of clarity, and thus facilitates the dissemination of information. This has an effect on both the quality of discussions and decision-making. In general, quality of communication is one of crucial elements for successful and creative functioning of virtual teams.

Given time constraints in industry the best time to develop virtual team working skills is in university through industrial collaborations. Individuals who have acquired the necessary knowledge and personal experience in working in global teams will be more successful in the global environment. The E-GPR course has been constantly developing and improving over the last five years. The number of institutions and disciplines has grown, the complexity of prototypes increased. Improvements have been achieved through closer involvement of the companies, more disciplines, larger teams, and improved project leadership. Students, lecturers, instructors and company representatives all have high praise for the course, believing the acquired knowledge and experience to be invaluable for future members of product development teams.

The E-GPR course will continue in the coming years but it is unlikely that the number of involved universities will increase given associated organizational challenges. It is more realistic to split universities into two or more groups of three or four. The advance of broadband technologies may also extend the model from University based project work to anywhere type study.

Finally, we believe that the E-GPR course could serve as a method of continuing executive education: company members (engineers, designers, etc.) can be enrolled in the course and participate in it as team members. In this way, it would be possible to educate engineers from companies which intend to conduct more virtual team work and need to achieve creative co-creation.

ACKNOWLEDGMENT

We would like to thank all organizers and participants of the E-GPR course, in particular professors Dr. Imre Horváth and Dr. Jože Duhovnik. Furthermore, we would like acknowledge the contribution of Dr. Tomaž Kolšek and Ernest van Breemen in helping us to contact all students and clients of the course.

REFERENCES

Andersen, A. (2001). Implementation of engineering product design using international student teamwork—to comply with future needs. *European Journal of Engineering Education, 26*, 179-186.

Andreasen, M. M., & Hein, L. (2000). *Integrated product development* (reprint). Lyngby: Institute for Product Development, Technical University of Denmark.

Barlett, C.A., & Ghoshal, S. (2000). *Transnational management: Text, cases and readings in cross-border management*. Boston: McGraw-Hill.

Beitz, W., & Helbig, D. (1997, August). The future of education for product developers. In *Proceedings of the 11th International Conference on Engineering Design*, Tampere, Finland (pp. 493-498).

Biggs, M. (2000, September). Assessing risks today will leave corporate leaders well-prepared for the future of work. *InfoWorld*, Retrieved November 3, 2006, from http://www.infoworld.com/

Bodendorf, F., & Swain, P. H., (2001). Virtual universities in engineering education. *International Journal of Engineering Education, 17*, 102-107.

Cardoso, H. L., & Oliveira, E. (2005). Virtual enterprise normative framework within electronic institutions. In M. P. Gleizes, A. Omicini, & F. Zambonelli (Eds.), *Engineering societies in the agents world V* (pp. 14-32). Springer.

Cardozo, R. N., Durfee, W. K., Ardichvili, A., Adams, C., Erdman, A. G., Hoey, M., et al. (2002). Perspective: Experiential education in new product design and business development. *The Journal of Product Innovation Management, 19*(1), 4-17.

Chu, K. C., Urbanik, N., Yip, S. Y., & Cheung, T. W. (1999). The benefit of virtual teaching to engineering education. *International Journal of Engineering Education, 15*, 334-338.

Cohen, W.M., & Levinthal, D. A. (1990). A new perspective on learning and innovation. *Administrative Science Quarterly, 35*(1), 128-152.

Gibson, I. S. (2001). Group project work in engineering design-learning goals and their assessment. *International Journal of Engineering Education, 17*, 261-266.

Green, G., & Kennedy, P. (2001). Redefining engineering education—The reflective practice of product engineering. *International Journal of Engineering Education, 17*, 3-9.

Grimson, J. (2002). Re-engineering the curriculum for the 21st century. *European Journal of Engineering Education, 27*(1), 31-37.

Hoffner, Y., Field, S., Grefen, P., Ludwig; H. (2001). Contract Driven Creation And Operation Of Virtual Enterprises. *Computer Networks—The International Journal of Computer and Telecommunications Networking*; *37*(2), 111-136.

Horváth, I., Duhovnik, J., & Xirouckakis, P. (2003). Learning the methods and the skills of global product realization in an academic virtual enterprise. *European Journal of Engineering Education, 28*(1), 83-102.

Horváth, I., van Breemen, E., Dutta, D., Yip-Hoi, D., Kim, J., & Lee, K. (2001, September). Education for global product realization on a global scale. In *Proceedings of DETC01/ASME01 Design Engineering Technical Conferences*, Pittsburg, PA (pp. 1-11).

Horváth, I., Wiersma, M., Duhovnik, J, & Stroud, I. (2004). Navigated active learning in an international scientific academic virtual enterprise. *European Journal of Engineering Education, 29*(4), 505-519.

Horváth, I., Xirouchakis, P. Duhovnik, J., & Wiersma, M. (2004). Reflections of teaching global product realization in academic virtual enterprise. In *Proceedings of DETC04/ASME04 Design Engineering Technical Conferences and Computers and Information in Engineering Conference* (pp. 1-10). New York: ASME.

Hundal, M. S. (1995, August). Engineering design education in the USA: Issues and challenges. In *Proceedings of the 10th International Conference on Engineering Design*, Praha, Czech Republic (pp. 318-323).

IJsendoorf, H. (2002). Application of computer aided systems, PD&E Automotive, E-GPR industrial case study, quote from a class discussion.

Inkpen, A. C., & Dinur, A. (1998). Knowledge management processes and international joint ventures. *Organization Science, 9*(4), 454-468.

Irandoust, S., & Sjöberg, J. (2001). International dimensions: a challenge for European engineering education. *European Journal of Engineering Education, 26*, 69-75.

Jarvenpaa, S. L., & Leidner, D. E. (1998). Communication and trust in global virtual teams. *Journal of Computer-Mediated Communication, 3*(4). Retrieved November 15, from http://www.ascusc.org/jcmc/vol3/issue4/jarvenpaa.html

Johnston, S. F. (2001). Towards culturally inclusive global engineering? *European Journal of Engineering Education, 26*(1), 77-89.

Kanawattanachaia, P., & Yoob, Y. (2002). Dynamic nature of trust in virtual teams. *Journal of Strategic Information Systems, 11*(3/4), 187-213.

Kasper-Fuehrer, E. C., & Ashkanasy, N. M. (2001) Communicating trustworthiness and building trust in virtual organizations. *Journal of Management Studies, 27*, 235-254.

Leenders, R. Th. A. J, van Engelen, J. M. L., & Kratzer, J. (2003). Virtuality, communication, and new product team creativity: A social network perspective. *Journal of Engineering and Technology Management, 20*(1/2), 69-92.

Lipnack, J., & Stamps, J. (2000). *Virtual teams: People working across boundaries with technology* (2nd ed.). New York: John Wiley.

Lurey, J. M., & Raisinghani, M. S. (2001). An empirical study of best practices in virtual teams. *Information & Management, 38*(8), 523-544

Marchman, J. F. III. (1998). Multinational, multidisciplinary, vertically integrated team experience in aircraft design. *International Journal of Engineering Education, 14*, 328-34.

May, A., & Carter, C. (2001). A case study of virtual team working in the European automotive industry. *International Journal of Industrial Ergonomics, 27*(3), 171-186.

Nonaka, I., & Konno, N. (1998). The concept of "Ba": Building a foundation for knowledge creation. *California Management Review, 40*(3), 40-54.

Olson, J. S., Olson, G. M., & Meader, D. K. (1995, May). What mix of video and audio is useful for small groups doing remote real-time design work? In *Proceedings of the Conference on Human Factors in Computing Systems*, Denver, CO (pp. 362-368).

Ottosson, S. (2004). Dynamic product development (DPD). *Technovation, 24*(3), 207-217.

Paul, S., Seetharaman, P., Samarah, I., & Mykytyna, P. P. (2004). Impact of heterogeneity and collaborative conflict management style on the performance of synchronous global virtual teams. *Information and Management, 41*(3), 303-321.

Piccoli, G., & Ives, B. (2000). Virtual teams: Managerial behavior control's impact on team effectiveness. In *Proceedings of the 21st International Conference on Information Systems* (pp. 575-580).

Rompelman, O., & de Vries, J. (2002). Practical training and internships in engineering education: Educational goals and assessment. *European Journal of Engineering Education, 27*, 173-180.

Sclater, N., Grierson, H., Ion, W. J., & MacGregor, S. P. (2001). Online collaborative design projects: overcoming barriers to communication. *International Journal of Engineering Education, 17*, 189-196.

Segrestin, B. (2005). Partnering to explore: The Renault-Nissan Alliance as a forerunner of new cooperative patterns. *Research Policy, 34*, 657-672.

Smith, P. G., & Blanck, E. (2002). From experience: Leading dispersed teams. *The Journal of Product Innovation Management, 19*(4), 294-304.

Soyjaudah, K. M. S., & Jahmeerbacus, M. I. (2000). A new digital communication course enhanced by PC-based design projects. *International Journal of Engineering Education, 16*, 553-559.

Spender, J.C. (1996). Organizational knowledge, learning, and memory: Three concepts in search of a theory. *Journal of Organizational Change, 9*, 63-78.

Tavčar, J., & Duhovnik, J. (2005). Engineering change management in individual and mass production. *Robotics and Computer-Integrated Manufacturing, 21*(3), 205-215.

Tavčar, J., Žavbi, R. Verlinden, J. & Duhovnik, J. (2005). Skills for effective communication and work in global product development teams. *Journal of Engineering Design, 16*(6), 557-576.

Ulrich, K. T., & Eppinger, S. D. (2000). *Product design and development* (2nd ed.). Boston: Irwin/McGraw-Hill.

Volpentesta, A., Frega, N., & Muzzupappa, M. (2001). Models and methodology for simulating virtual enterprises in educational environment. *European Journal of Engineering Education, 26*, 391-405.

Ylinenpää, H., & Nilsson, N. (2000, June). Knowledge transfer and organizational competence building: a case study of two knowledge-intensive firms. In *Proceedings of the 5ᵗʰ Conference on Competence Management*, Helsinki, Finland (pp. 1-17).

Žavbi, R., & Duhovnik, J. (2001). Model of conceptual design phase and its applications in the design of mechanical drive units. In C. T. Leondes (ur.). *The design of manufacturing systems, Vol. 5. Computer aided design, engineering and manufacturing* (pp. 1-38). Boca Raton [etc.]: CRC Press.

Žavbi, R., & Tavčar, J. (2005). Preparing undergraduate students for work in virtual product development teams. *Computers & Education, 44*(4), 357-376.

Chapter IV
Media Ensembles and New Product Team Creativity:
A Tree–Based Exploration

Roger Th.A.J. Leenders
University of Groningen, The Netherlands

Jan Kratzer
University of Groningen, The Netherlands

Jo M.L. Van Engelen
University of Groningen, The Netherlands

ABSTRACT

New product development (NPD) project members are increasingly dispersed across the globe. As a result, traditional face-to-face communication is often substituted and supplemented by more "virtual" media. A common concern is whether NPD teams that frequently use virtual media can be truly creative. In this chapter we attempt to explain why the creativity of some teams is above average, whereas others perform below the average. By using classification trees, we conduct an empirical study of the media ensembles employed by 46 teams involved in hi-tech NPD. We find that being above or below average cannot be explained by theories that focus on single media: the creative performance of NPD teams is a function of the media ensembles used. Some ensembles afford much higher probabilities for above-average creativity than others. These findings enrich theories of media choice and may provide managers with some ideas of how team creativity can be managed.

INTRODUCTION

Creativity is an essential part of organizational life. The development of new products, answers to customer complaints, response to actions of competitors, dealing with changes in govern-ment regulations, creating collaboration with partners in the industry: all nonroutine activity involves some process of creativity. New product development (NPD) may be the epitome of "non-routineness": by definition it involves the search for output that does not exist yet and arriving at that output often involves knowledge, technology, and procedures that have to be created along the way. Add to this competing goals, unstable environments, long time horizons, incompleteness of operational specifications, and unclear applicability of past experience (Pasmore, 1997) and the need for creativity is unmistakable.

Modern NPD activity is pervasively organized through teams (Griffin, 1997; Van Engelen, Kiewiet, & Terlouw, 2001). Whereas over the last two decades 'teams' have become part of NPD managerial vocabulary, 'virtual teams,' within and across organizations, are a more recent phenomenon (Andres, 2002). A concern that has been raised is whether it is possible for virtual NPD teams to develop truly creative new products and solutions. Research in this area is scarce—the few existing articles include Leenders, Kratzer, and Van Engelen (2003, 2004), Martins, Gilson, and Maynard (2004), Nemiro (2000, 2002) and chapters in this volume.

In this chapter we will study one aspect of this issue: how the technology used by NPD team members in their mutual communication affects the creativity of their teams. Communication between members of NPD teams is the means through which information and knowledge is disseminated and new knowledge is created. Different teams can easily be observed using different mixes—in terms of the communication tools used and the intensity with which each is employed. Since academic research clearly shows that NPD team creativity is largely couched in the team's communication process, it makes sense to expect that differences in use of communication tools may lead to differences in team level creativity. In addition, not much is known about the extent to which the findings regarding "traditional" teams are valid in the case of more "virtual" NPD teams. Since virtuality involves the use of "virtual" media such as internet and video conferencing—adding to replacing face-to-face interaction—the palette of media that are at the disposal of NPD teams is changing. Given that NPD teams are becoming increasingly dispersed, gaining knowledge relating virtuality to NPD team creativity is of increasing importance.

In this chapter we will argue that the effect of media choice on the creative performance of NPD teams can best be understood by considering the combinations of media used by the team, rather than considering which medium is in primary use. What makes one team more creative than another is not explained by the frequency of use of one particular medium. Rather, the explanation is in the way various communication media are used in a consistent media ensemble. Given the scarcity of research in the area of team creativity and virtuality, we will report on an exploratory study of communication media use in NPD teams.

The remainder of the chapter is organized into four sections. First, we will discuss the concept of virtuality and argue that teams vary in their level of virtuality. Second, we will discuss the extant literature on media choice and media use and develop our main argument: creative teams are not characterized by their use of one particular mode of communication, but rather by the combination of the modes they use. Third, we will present our exploratory study of media use in NPD teams. The dependent variable is whether or not a team's creativity is above-average and the search is for combinations of media that explain whether the creativity of a team is above or below the average. For the analysis we employ a classification tree approach, a statistical technique that is uniquely suited for our research task. Finally, we provide a discussion of our findings and fruitful future research.

NPD TEAM COMMUNICATION AND CREATIVITY

There are several reasons why modern NPD activity is typically organized through teams working within project structures. First, the development of new products often involves the concerted input of professionals with various areas and levels of expertise. New product development may involve the need for knowledge about issues of procurement, production, marketing, service, legal issues, organization strategy, and so forth. New products may also involve in-depth knowledge of specific technical issues; for example many engineers with widely different specializations may be involved in the development of a new engine or a household item such as a refrigerator or an electric shaver. These teams are put together for a good reason: they are required when nobody alone possesses all of the required knowledge, skill, time, influence, and oversight to develop the new product alone. While the strength of a new product team is in combining, integrating, and organizing varied sets of knowledge, this is also its weakness. If the communication between team members does not flow smoothly, the innovative performance of the team will likely falter; the creation of a team establishes increased need for coordination and management.

The core product developed by NPD teams is knowledge, and teams create knowledge through interaction. Through effective communication, and building on the knowledge of other people in the team, team members exchange information and create new knowledge and insight (DeMeyer, 1985; Csikszentmihalyi & Sawyer, 1995; Sethia, 1995; Moenaert, Caeldries, Lievens, & Wauters, 2000). To achieve innovation there must be ideas and these initially appear from among individuals in the team. Developing, refining, testing, and in the end implementing these ideas further rests on cooperation among the team members (Gupta, Ray, & Wilemon, 1985; Agrell & Gustafson, 1996). Communication can therefore be considered as the vessel by which a team manages knowledge and information. In order for the team to be creative and devise novel and useable solutions to technical and commercial problems, cross-fertilization of ideas is essential; this happens through interaction between team members (Mumford & Gustafson, 1988; West, 1990b). In

a team context in which underlying assumptions are challenged, ideas and practices are monitored and appraised, and opposing opinions are encouraged and explored, it is likely that a larger number of more innovative ideas will be generated and given fair evaluation. Through consultation and interaction, team members are likely to anticipate and prevent potential weaknesses in technical and marketing solutions—a task which neither could have been performed by any team member in isolation nor would have followed from the simple addition of the individual inputs of team members without communication between them. In other words, the expertise and knowledge that is held by individual team members or that is contained in specialized documents or databases represent the team's repository of current knowledge; the team's communication provides the logistics through which knowledge is accessed, travels between team members, and can be combined into new knowledge and insight (Cross, Parker, Prusak, & Borgatti, 2001). The creative performance of NPD teams thus is a function of the team's communication effectiveness; NPD teams that can not communicate effectively are unlikely to be able to generate novel and feasible solutions to the multifaceted complex problems they are faced with.

VIRTUALITY AND TEAM CREATIVITY

Organizations are progressively increasing the level of virtuality in their NPD activity. Firms increasingly move towards smaller, more numerous, more decentralized units that suit the increasingly complex and information-rich nature of NPD (e.g., Drucker, 1988; Boutellier, Gassman, Macho, & Roux, 1998). The specialized skills and talents required for the development of new products often reside (and develop) locally in pockets of excellence around the company or even around the world. Firms therefore disperse their new product units to access such dispersed knowledge and skill. Internationalization of markets, specialization of skills and knowledge, and the requirement to involve an increasingly large pool of knowledge simultaneously in the NPD process have all pushed firms to rely more and more on virtuality of their NPD teams. These tendencies have existed for a long period of time, but organizing through virtuality requires the availability of supporting technology—which has only become available to meet NPD demands in recent years.

A virtual team is often defined as a team of individuals collaborating in the execution of a specific project while being geographically and often even temporally distributed, possibly anywhere within (and beyond) their parent organization (Martins, Gilson, & Maynard, 2004). Other definitions of virtuality can be found in other chapters of this book. In tandem with the increasing number of virtual teams, the definitions of what constitutes a virtual team have proliferated as well. The majority of definitions build around the notion that virtual teams rely on technology-mediated communication tools while crossing geographical, organizational, or temporal boundaries (Maznevski & Chudoba, 2000; Lurey & Raisinghani, 2001; Montoya-Weiss, Massey, & Song, 2001). In some definitions virtual teams are defined as teams that interact exclusively through electronic media (e.g., Bouas & Arrow, 1996). Some researchers have relaxed this restriction to allow for some face-to-face communication, as long as the majority of interaction occurs through electronic means (e.g., Jarvenpaa & Leidner, 1999; Maznevski & Chudoba, 2000).

Recently, it is increasingly argued that virtual teams in fact do not exist. Instead, virtuality is argued to be a continuum and all teams are more or less virtual (Bell & Kozlowski, 2002; Griffith, Sawyer, & Neale, 2003; Leenders, Kratzer, & Van Engelen, 2003; Martins et al., 2004). This means that the term "virtual team" becomes misleading since it implies a distinction between teams that are virtual and teams that are not. The focus thus

should not be to contrast traditional/face-to-face teams with virtual teams but to consider the *extent* to which a team is virtual (Zigurs, Poole, & DeSanctis, 1988; Griffith & Neale, 2001; Bell & Kozlowski, 2002; Leenders et al., 2003; Kirkman, Rosen, Tesluk, & Gibson, 2004; Leenders et al. 2004). Consequently, recent definitions stress the omnipresence of virtual interactions, pointing out that a purely face-to-face team that does not use any communication technology is rare. Members of most "virtual" NPD teams do meet each other outside of cyberspace every so often. Large and complex NPD projects, in particular can hardly be successfully conducted without at least some level of traditional interaction (Kratzer, Leenders, & Van Engelen, 2006).

If virtuality refers to a continuum rather than a dichotomy, the question becomes what makes a team more or less virtual. Many answers have been given to this question; a full overview is beyond the scope of this chapter. Overviews of the relevant literature are provided by Leenders et al. (2003) and Martins et al. (2004). In Leenders et al. (2003) team virtuality is defined along a three-factor model: member proximity, communication modality, and team task structure. This model attempts to capture the most common factors put forward in the current literature. The first factor, member proximity, addresses the physical distance between the members of the team. The second factor, communication modality, denotes the nature of the medium through which NPD team members engage in their interactions. The third factor is 'team task structure,' a factor that refers to 'the assignment of particular components of the team's collective task to individual team members or subsets of team members.' In concert with the view of virtuality being a continuum, Martins et al. (2004, 808) argue that studies should focus on "team-ness" in concert with "virtual-ness" and move away from simply describing input factors; this encourages a focus on understanding the functioning of virtual teams rather than on simply comparing them to face-to-face teams. If all teams are indeed virtual to some extent, then literature that compares virtual teams with nonvirtual teams can not satisfactorily guide theoretical development in the field. While much of the literature undoubtedly is still useful to the study of virtuality, its claims about the effect of a team being virtual (or not) have to be reconsidered. Within the context of the current article, it moves the focus from the question of whether virtual teams can be innovative to the question of how the level of team virtuality affects its innovative performance. Given the prominence of the effects of communication on the creative performance of NPD teams, in this chapter we address this question by limiting ourselves to studying the effect of communication modality. Although other factors certainly affect NPD team creativity, the effect of the increasing use of new communication technologies on the ability of NPD teams to perform creatively is perhaps currently the least understood.

TEAM COMMUNICATION MODALITY

It follows from the previous arguments that, for the study of how virtuality affects the creativity of NPD teams, it is essential to study the team's communication process. In this chapter we study how the use of various communication modes affects NPD team creativity.

Several theories exist about the use of various modes of communication and their effects. These theories can be divided into two groups: those that consider the use of one particular medium and those that consider the use of multiple media in combination.

Media choice theory is one of the main theories emphasizing single media; the proliferation of communication media means that individuals are presented with problems of media choice for communication. Most media choice research emphasizes *sender preferences*, such as preferences relating to the affordances of various media

(Short, Williams, & Chudoba, 1976). For example, some people prefer e-mail because it provides a memory of past interactions, while others find the directness of phone communication desirable. In an ethnographic study of media use in the workplace, Nardi, Whittaker and Schwarz (2002) showed that media choice was in fact dependent on both *recipient preference* and the *development history of interaction*. This made media choice a far more complex activity than a simple matter of individual evaluation of the affordances of media. Media richness theory (Daft & Lengel, 1986) assesses the extent to which media allow exchanges of information with rapid feedback, in "languages" such as body language or mathematical notation, and in audio or visual modes. "Rich" media, such as video, allow ample information transfer while "lean" media like text, allow little. Social presence theory (Short et al., 1976) analyzes how well media provide information about the "presence" of others, including facial expression, tone of voice, and attributes such as goals and attitudes. For the purpose of this chapter, these theories are strongly related. Walther and Parks (2002) and Whittaker (2003) summarize these theories by stating that they are ultimately concerned with the "bandwidth" of the media: how rich is the information that travels through them. Various other theories exist that consider the choice for particular media, such as the Symbolic Interaction perspective of Trevino, Lengel, and Daft (1987) and Walther's social information processing theory (Walther, 1992). All "bandwidth" theories start from the assumption that individuals will choose the particular medium that is most suited for their purpose.

Although these theories differ in the particular purpose and the definition of what makes a medium suited, they all eventually arrive at an optimal choice for communication. For example, according to media richness theory different media can be ranked from rich to lean, with the richest medium providing the highest capacity for immediate feedback and number of cues and channels, personalization and language variety. Daft and Lengel (1986) proposed that face-to-face communication is the richest medium, followed by telephone and written text. In a related study, Zmud, Lind, and Young (1990) produced similar findings, but included electronic mail and fax in their study; these were considered leaner than paper-based communication. According to Schenkel (2004) face-to-face communication is only slightly richer than telephone communication, but email trails far behind in richness.

Given the highly complex tasks that NPD teams need to solve, media richness theory would predict that face-to-face interaction should be the prevalent communication mode. In concert with this argument, Allen (1977) has argued that, to exchange information engineers and technologists have to talk to each other in each other's presence. The engineer can of course read about new technologies, specific market conditions, or competitive developments. However, to be able to understand and digest this information the engineer also needs the context of the information. Rich media allow experts to explain their issues to other experts or, perhaps even more relevant, to those with less knowledge in that particular area of expertise. In addition, the multidisciplinary character of many NPD teams requires media that allow multiple participants to interact simultaneously; a face-to-face meeting is much more effective for such tasks than a long trail of email back and forth. In other words, an important factor is the extent to which media enable synchronous collaboration (Riopelle et al., 2003). Thus, whereas desktop videoconferencing is relatively high in media richness and in synchronicity, e-mail is lower on both dimensions.

An alternative argument, however, is that traditional communication media—face-to-face conversations and meetings—are too formal and too constrained by scheduling and distance to be able to fully support the spontaneous, informal, collaborative communication necessary for NPD work. Computer-mediated interaction—in particular, e-mail—may help overcome these temporal, physical, and formal obstacles (Rice, 1994). Consequently, his argument of departure is that creativity in NPD is best served by electronic interaction rather than by face-to-face interaction. However, Rice's empirical findings were that most forms of interaction were negatively related to performance ratings, including interaction through electronic channels.

A second, smaller stream of theory is concerned with the use of multiple kinds of media and allows for ensembles of media being used. These theories do not assume one type of medium superior to another for a given task, rather the focus is on which media are used and why. One could argue that these theories are of a less prescriptive nature. Main theories in this area are media ecology (McLuhan, 1964; McLuhan & Fiore, 2005) and information ecology (Nardi & O'Day, 1999). Information ecology connects ecological theory with the modern day growing and complex digital informational environment—the information space is viewed as an ecosystem. Ethnographic studies in the workplace by leading information ecologist Bonnie Nardi (Nardi, Whittaker, & Bradner, 2000; Nardi & Whittaker, 2002) yielded results quite different from those suggested by media richness theory and social presence theory. As it turned out, people tended to use a repertoire of media and often did not rely on the medium that presented the ideal level of richness or presence.

Given the complex and multifaceted nature of their creative work we expect NPD teams to use multiple modes of interaction. E-mail may be used to discuss relatively straightforward issues, video conferencing may be used for issues that require richer and synchronous exchange of ideas, and postal mail may be used in situations where the problem is relatively easily explained and direct interaction between team members is unnecessary. In other words, teams vary in terms of the intensity of use across the various modes of interaction. In addition, team members may also use communication modes that are less optimal from a richness point of view, but that have proven their worth in past interactions. Alternatively, teams may be limited in their choice of communication media based on availability of various media at the time at which they are required. Our working hypothesis is that teams with above-average creativity employ different ensembles of media than do teams that perform below the creative average. We expect to find differences in the extent to which each medium of communication is used *in conjunction with* other media, rather than above-average creativity being explained by the use of only one medium. The research question then becomes: *what combinations of media use set apart teams with above-average creativity from the teams that perform below the average on creative performance?*

Unfortunately, literature that assists an analyst in building theoretically grounded hypotheses on which mix of communication modes affords above-average creativity is scant. To be sure, media richness theory and related theories are useful in studying how various modes compare against one another and may provide some guidance in building hypotheses. But this usefulness reduces through the fact that most theories of communication do not address how various modes of communication work together. In addition, current theory also does not address the fact that the problems that NPD teams require creative solutions to are generally highly complex and multifaceted. As a result, we expect that the most creative teams employ an ensemble of communication modes with varying levels of richness, synchronicity, and personality. Given this dearth of useable theory for building sound hypotheses, we will conduct an exploratory analysis of which combinations of communication modes separate teams with above-average creativity from NPD teams with creativity below the average.

EXPLORATORY DATA

NPD Teams

For this analysis we employ data on the use of communication media in 46 NPD teams. All of these teams develop new technology for space and earth research, such as measurement instruments on satellites. The members of each team were *formally* colocated, although in many teams team members actually lived in and worked from different cities or buildings. The sampled teams were located across the globe.

Team members were almost exclusively male. Almost 40% had at least a PhD degree, an additional 48% had a university or polytechnic degree. Most team members had an education in engineering and performed engineering tasks in the team. Twenty percent called himself an astronomer. The main engineering specializations include software engineer (15%), electrical engineer (12%), system engineer (10%), mechanical engineer (10%), and instrument engineer (7%). Some members had two specializations, but most only held one. The age of the team members varied between 24 and 67, with an average age of 42 years.

Although the various teams were all working on different development tasks, the tasks shared important characteristics. All of them were involved in precision engineering, allowing for only exceptionally small tolerances. Many projects involved cryogenic technology and high resolution optics. These projects have in common highly demanding and detailed specifications. Typically, the teams work on developing a very small part of a larger instrument, telescope, or satellite. Such a large task is strongly decomposed into components. Since every single component requires a very high level of technical expertise, two components that will end up adjacent to each other in the telescope may require very different kinds of expertise and skill. As a result, the development of each component is assigned to a separate team. The team then devotes all of its attention to finding ways to meet the requirements. Most of the requirements these teams work with are considered critical and do not allow the team to develop solutions that even marginally deviate from the specifications. Any deviation, regardless of how tiny, has an immediate and pervasive effect on the adjacent component, and thus affects the viability and integrity of the component developed by another team somewhere else in the world.

As a consequence, the teams are strongly output driven. They are free to develop almost any technology, as long as it assists in meeting the extremely strict output specification; a description of the steps taken in such NPD processes is given in Leenders et al. (2007). Regardless of the intense hi-tech nature of the tasks and the detail with which the required output is described, a great amount of creativity is required of these teams. Although the specifications may have been set, in many cases being able to meet them requires devising and developing new technology, new knowledge, new ways of doing things, and improving upon existing knowledge and procedures. These teams truly work on the boundaries of what is currently known and possible and are often required to push

boundaries further. Demands on the creativity of these teams are thus often strong; the work can be characterized as clearly demanding creativity.

Communication Media

Communication in the teams is mainly of a problem-solving nature. Engineers working on finding solutions to technical problems consult other engineers in order to come up with new ideas or create new knowledge. Part of such communication concerns the explanation of the problem at hand; but team members also often share drawings, discuss scale models, computer simulations, calculations, and test versions of the component. Every team member was asked to indicate how frequently he/she would use a particular communication medium: e-mail, Internet, intranet, formal meetings, informal meetings, phone, and teleconferencing. Frequency of use was indicated on a seven point scale, ranging from 1 = very seldom to 7 = very often. The descriptives of the use of these seven media are given in Table 1. From the table it is clear that e-mail is in very frequent use in all of the teams. The least used

Table 1. Means, standard deviations

Variable	Mean	St.dev.	Scale
E-mail	6.83	0.45	
Internet	5.70	1.65	NET
Intranet	4.46	2.08	
Formal meetings	5.16	1.16	FACE
Informal meetings	5.51	1.45	
Phone	5.57	1.42	TELE
Tele conferencing	4.11	2.04	
Newness and originality	5.15	0.92	
Number of solutions developed	4.77	1.07	CREATIVITY
Number of solutions considered	4.93	1.06	
How innovative	5.37	1.12	

Note: n = 167 team members

Table 2. Means, standard deviations, and correlations

Variable	Mean	St.dev.	Min.	Max.	2	3
1. Team creativity	0.52		0	1		
2. Face-to-face use	10.81	1.65	6.50	13.75		
3. Net use	17.07	2.53	10.00	21.00	0.41**	
4. Tele use	9.54	2.21	3.00	14.00	0.03	0.23

*Note: n = 46 teams, ** p < .01*

is teleconferencing, although the high standard deviation shows that a degree of variation exists across the sample.

Since we are interested in the creativity of teams, rather than of individuals, the eventual sample size in the analysis is $n = 46$ teams. For reasons of statistical reliability and computational stability, we reduced the seven communication media into three consistent scales. After performing tests on consistency (reliability), uni-dimensionality, and inter-correlation of items, we calculated three scales: FACE (face-to-face communication), NET (computer-mediated communication), and TELE (telephone-based communication). Table 2 shows descriptive statistics for the three scales. The FACE scale captures the extent to which members in a team involve in formal and/or informal face-to-face meetings. Since it is the addition of the two separate items, each running from 1 to 7, the FACE scale runs from 2 to 14. The average score is 10.8, which implies that formal and informal face-to-face interactions are quite frequent in these teams. This is also obvious from the scores of the individual items (5.16 and 5.51). The higher the score on FACE, the more the members of the team employ the medium of face-to-face interaction.

The scale NET captures the team's intensity of using computer-mediated interaction tools: email, Internet, and intranet. E-mail, in particular, is used extensively by all teams, while intranet is the least prominent among the three. Given its large standard deviation, there is large variation in the use of intranet among the various teams. As a whole, the scale also shows quite a bit of variation between the NPD teams in the frequency of use of computer-mediated interaction. The coefficient of variation—which standardizes the standard deviation according to the mean of the scale—is almost equal to that of face-to-face use. Teams thus have comparable variation in the use of FACE or NET.

The final scale, TELE, has even more variation among the teams. This scale captures the use of telephone-based interaction, and collapses the use of telephone and teleconferencing. Teleconferencing is on average the least popular interaction tool of all seven, but has a very high variation. As a whole, the variation in use of tele-based interaction is considerably larger than the variation in NET or FACE (taking into account differences in the means of the scales). Figure 1 shows the box-and-whiskers plot for the three scales. For easy comparison, in the figure we centered the scales around zero. A value of 0 thus refers to the average value of that communication medium across the teams. From the figure it is clear that there is more variation in electronic and telephone-based media than there is in face-to-face. The black dots in the figure denote the median values.

Team Creativity

Most research has focused on antecedents of individual employee creativity. To date, little empirical work has been conducted on studying

Figure 1. Media use across all teams

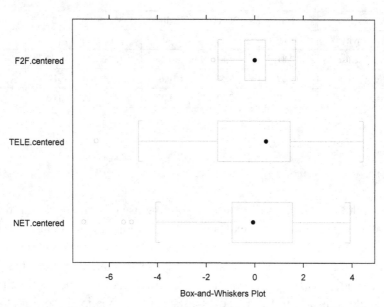

Note: For easy comparison, all variables have been centered around zero.

team level creativity of teams, although there is a large body of work on group brainstorming, team innovation, and performance on tasks requiring creative solutions that can provide some insights (Diehl et al., 1987; Diehl & Stroebe, 1987; West, 1990; Sosik, Sutton, & Hargadon, 1996; Avolio, & Kahai, 1998; Paulus, 2000; Ziegler, Diehl, & Zijlstra, 2000; Polzer, Milton, & Swann, 2002; Shalley, Zhou, & Oldham, 2004). Few studies have focused on team creativity (e.g., Nemiro, 2000; Nemiro, 2002; Taggar, 2002; Leenders et al., 2003; Gilson & Shalley, 2004; Leenders et al., 2004; Pirola-Merlo & Mann, 2004; Kratzer, Leenders, & Van Engelen, 2005). Despite the fair number of scales that exist for the measurement of individual level creativity, no commonly used scales for team level creativity exist. Much academic work in the area of creativity has been conducted and documented by Amabile (1996). As is the case with most studies on creativity, Amabile's work is largely based on experimental settings, with ad hoc teams or ad hoc tasks. Work on the creativity of actual working teams

performing their real tasks is rare (e.g., Kazanjian, Drazin, & Glynn, 2000).

In experimental research it is customary for outside evaluators to assess the creativity of a team. Raters can attach some score to the team's output per se, can count the number of ideas generated, or determine the percentage of the team's ideas that are different from that of other teams given the same task (e.g., see the first and fourth study in Ocker's chapter in this volume). In this research, however, such approaches are not possible. First of all, the variation in technology upon which the different teams base their work is too high for any evaluator to fully understand or appreciate. It is impossible to find anyone who can understand the technology each team is developing and reliably assess their creativity. Moreover, teams vary heavily in the type of product they are developing (software, a tangible measurement instrument, etc.), making it even harder for an evaluator to assess and compare team creativity. In addition, the creativity of the teams relates to highly complex and multifaceted issues, making the application of experimental-based procedures—that typically assume unidimensional, easily ratable output—problematic. The notion that evaluators need to be true outsiders, however, is not solidly based on literature. Often, researchers accept Amabile's suggestion (1983, 1996) that an output is creative to the extent that appropriate observers independently agree it is creative. In addition, judges are often not provided with scoring lists containing the items that distinguish creative solutions from noncreative ones, but it is argued that creativity is recognized by anyone knowledgeable with respect to the task at hand. Although raters in creativity research are usually outside evaluators, Amabile's arguments do not necessarily promote that. In real life settings, where teams have different tasks, tasks are complex and multifaceted, and the expertise to rate the solutions only reside within the team, Amabile's suggestions imply that creativity can be rated by employing the only true experts available in these settings: the members of the teams themselves.

We therefore relied on the few published procedures of measuring NPD team creativity (Cohen & Cohen, 1991; Kratzer, 2001; Leenders et al., 2003) and asked the team members to rate the team's creative performance. At first sight one is tempted to argue that this procedure may not be statistically reliable since it appears to rely on a form of self-report. However, since team members were asked to report on their *team's* creativity rather than on that of *themselves*, the procedure induces a form of *quasi*-self report. As Leenders et al. (2003) show, the results of such a procedure are highly reliable and stable. Using a dataset with similarities to the one in this chapter, they showed that team member assessment of the creativity of NPD teams correlated highly with the assessments by outside evaluators (for those teams for which outside evaluation was possible in their study). We therefore followed the same procedure and asked the team members to rate the team on a seven-point scale on:

- The newness and originality of the solutions your team finds to problems
- The number of possible solutions your team develops to solve problems
- The number of possible solutions your team takes into consideration in order to solve problems
- How innovative—in the sense of generating new ideas, methods, approaches, inventions, or applications in the field of work—is the project team

These items capture exactly what creativity is about in these teams. As discussed above, the NPD teams are strongly output-focused and create solutions according to clearly and deeply specified requirements. For these NPD professionals high team creativity thus derives from the solutions found rather than from social or process factors.

The descriptive of these items are shown at the bottom of Table 1. Since these four items turned out to scale reliably (details not shown here), we created an additive scale of team creativity. However, our interest is in the communication ensembles that distinguish above-average creative teams from teams with below-average creativity. Since 24 teams turned out to be above the average and 22 below—an almost equal split—we analyze team creativity as a binary: above or below the average. As a result the mean in Table 2 is .52, which is simply the fraction of the teams above the average (24/46).

EXPLORATORY ANALYSIS: CLASSIFICATION TREES

Our main hypothesis is that the difference between teams with above-average creativity and below-average creative teams resides in the way in which teams employ multiple communication media as a system. If this is correct we should find different combinations of media for each subsample of teams. An approach ideally suited for such an analysis is that of *recursive partitioning* or *tree-based models*. This essentially model-free approach was originally developed by Breiman and associates (Breiman, Friedman, Olshen, & Stone, 1984). It allows a researcher to find which (combinations of) values of a set of explanatory variables tend to be associated with particular values of the response variable. In our case we are interested in which (combinations of) values of frequency of use of three communication media tend to go with above or below-average creativity.

Tree-based models have a long history, mainly as a decision tool. The automatic construction of decision trees dates back to the work in the social sciences by Morgan and Sonquist (1963) and Sonquist, Baker and Morgan (1973). The study and use of classification trees are widely used in applied fields as diverse as medicine (diagnosis), computer science (data structures), machine learning, botany (classification), and psychology (decision theory). The idea behind classification trees is most easily understood through an example. Suppose having collected data on people in a city park in the vicinity of a hotdog and ice cream stand, the owner of the concession stand wants to know what predisposes people to buy ice cream then. The first split may be according to the weather. When it is warm and sunny 40% of all passers-by get ice cream, otherwise only 5% buy ice cream. The warm-and-sunny branch may be split further to find that 60% of those walking by with kids buy ice cream. This distinguishes them from those without kids, as only 35% of them get ice cream on a warm and sunny day. And so forth. More complex tree structures include medical classification trees (usually in the form of an expert system) or biological classification trees in which a species of animal is determined through a series of steps (e.g., number of legs → existence of wings → shape of the beak, etc.). A useful property of classification trees is that they can easily be represented graphically; a tree describes a tree structure wherein leaves (a.k.a. "terminal nodes") represent classifications and branches represent conjunctions of features that lead to those classifications (see Figure 2). Since classification trees lend themselves very well for decision-making—for examlple, a classification tree describing cloud structures could assist one in assessing the probability of rain and thus providing the decision whether or not to bring an umbrella—they are often called "decision trees." Another useful application of classification trees is the study of the origin of missing data in a data set. The dependent variable then is dichotomous (missing/present) and explanations for which data are missing are based on values of other variables and attributes of the respondents (Harrell, 2001).

The procedure of arriving at a tree is straightforward:

1. For a given variable, find the point at which the responses are divided into the two most homogeneous groups—homogeneity is measured by entropy (or Shannon-Wiener Information).

2. Choose the variable which does this best and divide the sample into two groups at this point.

3. Apply the same procedure recursively to each side.

4. Stop when either the node is completely homogeneous or contains too few observations to continue.

Often, the tree that results from such an analysis has a large number of leaves as the result of a great many splits. Such trees are needlessly elaborate and not easy to interpret. This means that an analyst has to cut the tree back to size based on cost-complexity pruning (Breiman et al., 1984). Pruning algorithms searches for subtrees that maintain acceptable levels of classification accuracy. It is beyond the scope of this chapter to discuss these algorithms, the interested reader is referred to the documentation of the many software packages that implement tree-based modeling. For the analysis in this chapter, we used two algorithms that each implement the procedure: *rpart* (Therneau & Atkinson, 2005) and *tree* (Ripley, 2005), both available in the R statistical environment. Of the two, the *rpart* algorithm is the closest to the original work by Breiman (1984). The two algorithms yielded identical trees, attesting to the reliability of the results. We also performed a complexity parameter analysis and ran computer intensive permutation tests for additional investigation of the reliability of the findings. These tests supported the tree generated by these two algorithms.

EMPIRICAL RESULTS

Figure 2 shows the final result of the classification tree analysis. It reads as follows. The first split is made according to the level of face-to-face communication maintained within the team: above or below 12.5. Of all teams with a score higher than 12.5 on face-to-face communication (leaf A), 86% have above-average creativity—the "*p*" in the figure denotes the fraction of the teams in that leaf that attain above-average creativity. This is a very intense use of face-to-face communication, since the average use of face-to-face communication is only 10.8 (Table 2). In fact, only 15% of all teams in the dataset score that high on face-to-face communication.

The teams with less intense face-to-face communication are further split according to their use of electronic communication. As can be seen from the tree, of the teams that score below 12.5 on face-to-face communication *and* score below 16.1 on their use of electronic media (leaf C) only 30% (*p* = 0.30) score above-average in creativity. In other words, such teams overwhelmingly (70%) reach below-average creative performance.

In Table 3 we have summarized the results of the classification tree in a different format, organized according to the probability of above-average team level creativity. The first column shows these probabilities; the second column shows the percentage of teams in that leaf. The

Figure 2. Classification tree explaining above or below average team creativity

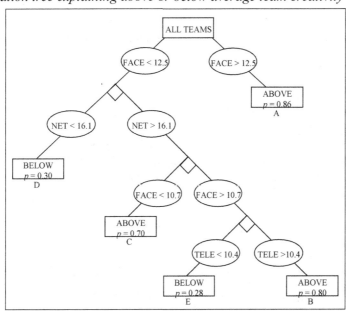

third and fourth columns of Table 3 describe the media ensemble denoted by the five terminal nodes (leaves).

Several conclusions can be drawn from the results of the classification tree. First, the first media ensemble (A) is characterized by intense use of face-to-face communication media. These teams tend to attain above-average creativity regardless of their use of other media. The media ensemble they use can therefore be described on the basis of one dimension only. This finding is in agreement with media richness theory, which states that the creativity required for new product development in complex product industries, such as that of space research, would require communication through very rich media. The use of other media does not matter in ensemble A, since the richness of face-to-face communication—formal and informal meetings—provide all the bandwidth necessary. In terms of virtuality, this suggests that colocated traditional teams that rely heavily on face-to-face interaction, have a definite advantage over dispersed teams that never meet face-to-face.

On the other hand, teams that do not score high on their use of face-to-face media can still reach a high likelihood ($p = .70$) of reaching above-average creativity by strong use of electronically mediated communication. Since there is only very little variation in the use of e-mail across the teams, this is primarily related to intranet use and, to a lesser extent, the use of Internet. This media ensemble (C) shows that it is entirely possible for a team high in virtuality to reach above-average creative performance; although the likelihood of such performance is somewhat lower than compared to that of a fully traditional team ($p = .70$ versus $p = .86$). Note, however, that none of the teams in our dataset make any use of some form of face-to-face media at all. In fact, only 37% of all teams in the dataset score below 10.7 on face-to-face. This means that we can not draw conclusions as to how the results would be for teams without any face-to-face communication. It is certainly possible that the inclusion of such teams in the dataset would lead to additional branches in the classification tree, perhaps splitting up leaf C further, showing some minimal required level of face-to-face for teams to be creative.

Ensembles B and C show the strength of ecology theories that argue that multiple media exist next to one another and that this is a requirement for performance. Ensemble B, in particular, makes this case. Teams that utilize this media ensemble have an above-average frequency of use of face-to-face communication and also score around or above the average in their use of electronically mediated communication and telephone-based communication. The value of analyzing these

Table 3. Results of the classification tree analysis

Probability above-average	Fraction of teams	Media ensemble	Media description	Ensemble
0.86	0.15	Face > 12.5	Very high on face-to-face	A
0.80	0.11	10.7 < Face < 12.5 Net > 16.1 Tele > 10.4	Fairly high on face-to-face High on net use High on tele use	B
0.70	0.22	Face < 10.7 Net > 16.1	Low on face-to-face High on net use	C
0.30	0.22	Face < 12.5 Net < 16.1	Not very high on face-to-face Low on net use	D
0.28	0.30	10.7 < Face < 12.5 Net > 16.1 Tele < 10.4	Fairly high on face-to-face High on net use Low on tele use	E

media as an ensemble is particularly clear if we compare this with ensemble E. Here, the only difference is in the use of telephone-based media—considered by media richness theory as one of the richest forms of communication. Despite the proficient use of the other two media, teams that make use of ensemble E are by-and-large not very creative.

Figure 3 provides a visual summary of the empirical findings by showing for each ensemble what level of intensity is associated with each media type. For a team to employ a particular media ensemble it needs to score within the black area of the figure and can score anywhere within the grey areas. For instance, since media ensemble A is only characterized by a high score on face-to-face contact (black) the team can occupy any level of communication within the other two media types. To the left of each drawing is the probability of above-average creativity for the particular media ensemble.

A black area denotes which part of the continuum of a particular medium is included in a particular ensemble. By extension, a team fol-

Figure 3. The five media ensembles

Ensemble A: very high on face-to-face

Ensemble B: all modes high and used in conjunction

Ensemble C: Low on face-to-face, high on net use

Ensemble D: Not high on face-to-face, not high on electronic media either

Ensemble E: Very low on tele use, face-to-face and net use can not make up for this

lowing that ensemble does not occupy a white area. The grey area can be freely used and is not of importance to the particular ensemble.

DISCUSSION: FUTURE TRENDS, FUTURE RESEARCH, AND CONCLUSIONS

In this chapter we have studied the media ensembles that distinguish NPD teams with above-average creativity from those with below-average creativity. Our main interest is in whether or not one particular communication medium can explain which teams are more creative than others. In addition, if communication media have to be studied in tandem, the question becomes which media ensembles result in high or low team level creativity. Although ample research exists on the effect of communication media on individual level creativity, theory on the association with team level creativity is scarce. This scarcity prevented us from formulating testable hypotheses and we decided to perform an exploratory study instead.

The answers to our main questions are twofold. First, it appears that face-to-face communication by itself has a strong effect on above-average team creativity. As echoed in media richness theory, the richness that face-to-face media provide is a strong foundation for creativity. However, we found that this is only the case for teams that use face-to-face interaction with great intensity. Whereas an overwhelming majority of teams with intense face-to-face communication (media ensemble A) achieved above-average creativity, lower values of face-to-face turned out to provide no guarantee whatsoever for creativity. For "example", teams with lower-than-intense values of face-to-face media use (which is true for 85% of the teams) *and* with below-average use of net-related media, largely scored below the average in creativity (media ensemble D).

Media richness theory, media choice theory, symbolic interaction theory, and other related theories tend to focus on the optimal medium for a given task. Ecology and activity-based theories tend to focus more on the repertoire of media used by individuals. The work of Nardi (Nardi et al., 1999; Nardi et al., 2000; Nardi, Whittaker, & Schwarz, 2002b; Nardi et al., 2002a) on information ecology and activity theory is influential in its argument that people tend to use several media in conjunction and that the choice for any given media is not necessarily (only) based upon their affordances in relation to the task at hand.

These theories suggest that NPD team members base their media use on at least three factors. One factor is compatible with media richness theory and refers to the bandwidth required of the medium. This suggests that teams involved in highly complex product development tasks would opt for the richest media available; in our case, face-to-face communication. A second factor is that of availability. Dispersed teams simply have less opportunity of communicating face-to-face than do colocated teams. Electronic media increasingly make some sort of face-to-face interaction possible by sending video feeds over the internet. If this becomes an important and feasible mode of communication for NPD teams, it may well affect the results of future research on the topic. In addition to technological advancements in the field positively affecting electronic interaction availability, it has been argued that managers can affect the creative performance of teams by making various modes of communication available when appropriate (Leenders et al., 2004; Kratzer et al., 2005; Kratzer et al., 2006). For example, face-to-face contact can be stimulated through increasing the size of travel budgets. Although this may appear an expensive option, the gain of increased team creativity may more than offset the financial investment. A third factor is of an entirely different nature and refers to personal preferences, team member history, and team culture. These theories suggest that team members with favorable experiences in using particular media are likely to continue to opt for their use in the future. Especially when team members have been together for a sufficient period of time, past media use becomes engrained into the team's working process and may grow resilient to changes in the tasks that are assigned to the team. If certain media ensembles worked well for the team to be creative in the past, these ensembles may become part of the team's unofficial standard operating procedure.

However, regardless of the specific reasons for the media ensemble adopted by a team, the most important finding of this study is that ensembles exist that distinguish teams with above-average creativity from teams with creativity below the average. Moreover, these ensembles tend to consist of specific combinations of all available media. We do not have enough information to perform an in-depth analysis of the reasons why the various teams adopted the five media ensembles. All three of Nardi's factors appear to play a role. NPD team members certainly attempt to use a communication medium that provides at least the bandwidth that is necessary for the goal of the particular communication. However, required media are not always available. Discussing details about possible solutions to technical problems typically requires either face-to-face meetings (with people being in the same room) or, if electronic media are used, video, audio, and additional modes of interaction. Such rich media were only available to some of the teams, or to only some of the members—this depended on their home institution. Moreover, many members of teams had worked with each other in the past, on other NPD tasks, and were prone to mainly use the media ensembles that they had used previously. As a result, some teams would use media that did not afford the richness that theory would suggest was required. Alternatively, some interaction was conducted through media providing much higher richness than necessary for a given interaction task. Face-to-face meetings were often planned long in advance

since members would have to travel across the globe to meet. As a result, these meetings were not always timely and face-to-face was therefore not necessarily used when required. In sum, the reasons for the eventual media ensembles used by the NPD teams were only partly due to active rational choice by the team members.

This study has several implications for future research. First, we did not have any teams in our sample that did not have any face-to-face communication at all. It would be interesting to study how these teams rank in terms of their creativity and whether this would give rise to new media ensembles. Most likely this would involve the study of different kinds of teams, since NPD teams almost always employ some level of face-to-face communication.

The second implication derives directly from the first: in order to assess how able to generalize the results are, future research needs to study other types of teams and/or NPD teams in other industries. All teams in our sample were involved in developing products for space research. Although the actual products varied, they all dealt with related levels of complexity and technology. In order to study whether our findings are idiosyncratic to this particular sample, it would be fruitful to study teams in entirely different industries, in particular industries that are more service-related or in which technology plays a less pervasive role. An example of an alterative research is Ocker (in this volume). In Ocker's chapter she describes four studies of the creativity of teams consisting of graduate students using communication tools with different levels of synchronicity. Several of the teams using asynchronous communication means outperform teams that are higher in face-to-face. Such studies are useful as they draw attention to other types of teams and other types of team tasks.

Thirdly, it has been commonly found that teams tend to become less creative over time (e.g., Katz, 1982; Lovelace, 1986; Katz, 1997). The main argument is that with increasing team age, problem solving and cognitive processes become more established, reinforced, and habitual through uncertainty reduction by team members. The result is a decrease in creative performance, all else being equal. This tendency can be broken in several ways, for instance by changing team composition. When new members enter the team and other leave the team this effectively revives the team, to a certain extent, with the new members not yet locked into the team's habitual and uninspired approach to problem solving. Alternatively, our findings in this chapter suggest that team managers may intervene in the media ensemble available to a team. The standardization of the team's problem solving process is likely to partly depend on the team's media ensemble becoming rigid. Once a team has adopted a media ensemble for use in its problem solving processes, our findings suggest that this should affect whether or not a team achieves above-average creativity. Breaking the status quo should therefore have an effect on the team's creative ability. For example, it is to be expected that changes in the availability and size of travel funds will affect the level of face-to-face interaction. Also, actively stimulating various modes of communication may alter the ensemble the team has locked itself into. Future research is needed about exactly how employed media ensembles in NPD teams can be altered and about the exact response in creative NPD team performance as a consequence of such changes.

Finally, this chapter has shown that tree-based modeling can be a powerful tool for exploratory analysis in the social sciences. Although it is rarely used in this field, the statistics behind it are well-developed and more than a dozen dedicated software packages exist that assist an analyst to develop trees. In addition to classification trees, where the response variable is categorical, similar analyses can be done with a continuous response variable. This produces a so-called "regression tree," comparable to forward regression methods. This does require a sufficient sample size and distributional assumptions—for example, an

obvious probability model is to assume a normal distribution within each leaf (Clark & Pregibon, 1992). Although it is often difficult to establish large datasets at the team level, such an endeavor may well serve future research potential.

The future appears to have increased development in electronic communication media in store. This will even further increase the number of teams with members that are dispersed across locations and time zones. This would suggest that team virtuality will continue to increase. However, electronic media increasingly make some sort of face-to-face interaction possible. For example, popular electronic communication media such as Skype™ or NetMeeting now include video feeds—these tools increasingly become used in the workplace. In fact, the trend in electronically mediated communication is towards mimicking as much as possible face-to-face interaction. In addition, video feeds work best when communication is synchronous. All of this makes this type of media increasingly rich and personal. It is entirely possible that electronically mediated communication will be able to substitute face-to-face interaction to a large extent in the future. However, it will be necessary for researchers to make a distinction between types of electronic media. When video feeds and synchronous rich interaction have become well-developed and data bandwidth has become abundant—a prospect that is likely to occur in the near future—it is no longer appropriate to pool all electronic communication into one category. It may very well be that teams can be highly creative by communicating face-to-face and through electronic media that mimic face-to-face contact, but that teams relying on e-mail interaction will rarely be able to achieve high levels of creativity. As technological developments advance, this study will have to be repeated to include different types of electronic communication. In addition, it may become important to distinguish different types of face-to-face interaction: face-to-face while being in the same room, or face-to-face-like interaction through computer-mediated video and speech. The different tools that allow for face-to-face-like interaction may have differential effects on creativity.

In addition to the implications for academic research, several practical conclusions can be drawn from our findings. One implication is that the media used for interaction matters. The use of different media should not be a haphazard process. The media ensemble employed by teams is a clear discriminating factor between above-average and below-average performing creative teams. Only when the combination of the intensity with which the various media are utilized follows a specific pattern, the odds of creative above-average team creativity are in the team's favor. It is therefore not enough to provide a team with one or few "random" media; the used mix has a direct effect on the creativity of teams. Moreover, providing teams with various communication media does not mean that they will use them most effectively. Project managers could monitor the use of the various communication media. If the used ensemble is far from ideal, many tools exist for NPD project managers to spur the team to use other media or change the extent to which they use a particular selection. Such tools include changing team composition, relocating team members, providing or decreasing travel budgets, changing tasks and dependencies, and several project management tools.

Since the current results are those of only one study in one industry, the "best" media ensembles may be different in other cases. However, the predominance of intense face-to-face interaction suggests that it is a manager's best bet to stimulate such interaction as much as possible—even in fully dispersed teams. This means providing media that allow for synchronous visual and auditory interaction, allow team members to interactively share drawings, test software, and databases, that allow members to discuss detailed problems using detailed material, and that allow for both planned and spontaneous interaction. But still, the findings suggest that this can not fully replace same-room face-to-face interaction. Moreover, it appears that managers would be wise to stimulate the use of noncomputer mediated interaction facilities. As follows from comparing ensembles B and E, the use or neglect of telephone-based interaction in favor of computer-based communication can have a strong effect on the ability of a team to perform creatively. Although many project workers find it comfortable to send an e-mail message rather than make a phone call, this appears to come at the expense of decreased creativity.

Finally, teams do not always need to be creative. Especially teams that are required to produce rather than develop (e.g., manufacturing vs. R&D) often have much lower creativity demands. In fact, if these teams are high in creativity this may come at the expense of efficiency. When efficiency is most important, high levels of creativity may be uncalled for. If this is the case, managers may opt to reduce the use of face-to-face media and aim for ensembles D and E. Regardless of the specific ensembles one would find in similar research in other settings, managers need to be aware that the manner in which team members communicate has an important effect on the creativity of their teams. Intervening in the used mixes of media has an effect on creativity, whether or not the intervention is deliberate. The mere realization of this fact will hopefully make managers more aware and more able to manage team creativity.

REFERENCES

Agrell, A. & Gustafson, R. (1996). Innovation and creativity in work groups. In M. A. West (Ed.), *Handbook of work group psychology* (pp. 317-343). New York: Wiley.

Allen, T. J. (1977). *Managing the flow of technology*. Boston: MIT Press.

Amabile, T. M. (1983). *The social psychology of creativity*. New York: Springer Verlag.

Amabile, T. M. (1996). *Creativity in context*. New York: Westview Press.

Andres, H. P. (2002). A comparison of face-to-face and virtual software development teams. *Team Performance Management*, 8(1/2), 39-48.

Bell, B. S., & Kozlowski, S. W. J. (2002). A typology of virtual teams. *Group & Organization Management*, 27(1), 14-49.

Bouas, K. S., & Arrow, H. (1996). The development of group identity in computer and face-to-face groups with membership change. *Computer Supported Cooperative Work*, 4, 153-178.

Boutellier, R., Gassman, O., Macho, H., & Roux, M. (1998). Management of dispersed product development teams: The role of information technologies. *R&D Management*, 28, 13-25.

Breiman, L., Friedman, J. H., Olshen, R. A., & Stone, C. J. (1984). *Classification and regression trees*. Boca Raton, FL: Chapman & Hall.

Clark, L. A., & Pregibon, D. (1992). Tree-based models. In J. M. Chambers & T. J. Hastie (Eds.), *Statistical models* (pp. 377-420). Boca Raton, FL: CRC Press.

Cohen, B. P. & Cohen, E. G. (1991). From groupwork among children to innovation teams. *Advances in Group Processes*, 8, 235-251.

Cross, R., Parker, A., Prusak, L., & Borgatti, S. P. (2001). Knowing what we know: supporting knowledge creation and sharing in social networks. *Organizational Dynamics*, 30(2), 100-120.

Csikszentmihalyi, P., & Sawyer, K. (1995). Shifting the focus from individual to organizational creativity. In C. M. Ford & D. A. Goia (Eds.), *Creative Action in Organizations* (pp. 167-173). Thousand Oaks, CA: Sage.

Daft, R., & Lengel, R. (1986). Organizational information requirements, media richness, and structural design. *Management Science*, 32(5), 554-571.

DeMeyer, A. C. L. (1985). The flow of technological innovation in an R&D department. *Research Policy*, 14, 315-328.

Diehl, M., & Stroebe, W. (1987). Productivity loss in brainstorming groups: Toward the solution of a riddle. *Journal of Personality and Social Psychology*, 53(3), 497-509.

Drucker, P. F. (1988, January-February). The coming of the new organization. *Harvard Business Review*, 66(1), 45-53.

Gilson, L. L., & Shalley, C. E. (2004). A little creativity goes a long way: An examination of teams' engagement in creative processes. *Journal of Management*, 30(5), 453-470.

Griffin, A. (1997). PDMA Research on new product development practices: Updating trends and benchmarking best practices. *Journal of Product Innovation Management*, 14(6), 429-458.

Griffith, T. L., & Neale, M. (2001). Information processing in traditional, hybrid, and virtual teams: From nascent theory to transactive memory. In R. I. Sutton & B. M. Staw (Eds.), *Research in organizational behavior*. Stamford, CT: JAI Press.

Griffith, T. L., Sawyer, J. E., & Neale, M. A. (2003). Virtualness and knowledge in teams: Managing the love triangle of organizations, individuals, and information technology. *MIS Quarterly*, 27(2), 265-287.

Gupta, A. K., Ray, S. P., & Wilemon, D. (1985). The R&D marketing interface in high-technology firms. *Journal of Product Innovation Management*, 2(1), 12-24.

Harrell, F. E. Jr. (2001). *Regression modeling strategies*. New York: Springer-Verlag.

Jarvenpaa, S., & Leidner, D. (1999). Communication and trust in global virtual teams. *Organization Science, 10*(6), 791-815.

Katz, R. (1982). The effects of group longevity on project communication and performance. *Administrative Science Quarterly, 27*, 81-104.

Katz, R. (1997). Managing creative performance in R&D teams. In R. Katz (Ed.), *The human side of managing technological innovation* (pp. 177-186). New York: Oxford University Press.

Kazanjian, R. K., Drazin, R., & Glynn, M. A. (2000). Creativity and technological learning: the roles of organization architecture and crisis in large-scale projects. *Journal of Engineering and Technology Management, 17*(3/4), 273-298.

Kirkman, B. L., Rosen, B., Tesluk, P. E., & Gibson, C. B. (2004). The impact of team empowerment on virtual team performance: The moderating role of face-to-face interaction. *Academy of Management Journal, 47*, 175-192.

Kratzer, J. (2001). *Communication and performance: An empirical study in innovation teams.* Amsterdam: Tesla Thesis Publishers.

Kratzer, J., Leenders, R. Th. A. J., & Van Engelen, Jo M. L. (2005). Keeping virtual R&D teams creative. *Research Technology Management, 48*(2), 13-16.

Kratzer, J., Leenders, R. Th. A. J., & Van Engelen, Jo M. L. (2006). Managing creative team performance in virtual environments: An empirical study in 44 R&D teams. *Technovation, 26*, 42-49.

Leenders, R. Th. A. J., Kratzer, J., & Van Engelen, J. M. L. (2003). Virtuality, communication, and new product team creativity: A social network perspective. *Journal of Engineering and Technology Management, 20*, 69-92.

Leenders, R. Th. A. J., Kratzer, J., & Van Engelen, J. M. L. (2004). Building creative virtual new product development teams. In P. Belliveau, A. Griffin, & S. Somermeyer (Eds.), *PDMA toolbook for new product development II* (pp. 117-147). New York: John Wiley & Sons.

Leenders, R. Th. A. J., Van Engelen, J. M. L., & Kratzer, J. (2007). Systematic design methods and the creative performance of new product teams: Do they contradict or complement each other? *Journal of Product Innovation Management, 24*, 166-179.

Lovelace, R. F. (1986). Stimulating creativity through managerial interventions. *R&D Management, 16*, 161-174.

Lurey, J. S., & Raisinghani, M. S. (2001). An empirical study of best practices in virtual teams. *International Economic Review, 38*(8), 523-544.

Martins, L. L., Gilson, L. L., & Maynard, M. T. (2004). Virtual teams: What do we know and where do we go from here? *Journal of Management, 30*(6), 805-835.

Maznevski, M. L., & Chudoba, K. M. (2000). Bridging space over time: Global virtual team dynamics and effectiveness. *Organization Science, 11*(5), 473-492.

McLuhan, M. (1964). *Understanding media: The extensions of man.* New York: New American Library.

McLuhan, M., & Fiore, Q. (2005). *The medium is the massage.* Corte Madera: Gingko Press.

Moenaert, Rudy K., Caeldries, F., Lievens, A., & Wauters, E. (2000). Communication flows in international product innovation teams. *Journal of Product Innovation Management, 17*, 360-377.

Montoya-Weiss, M., Massey, A., & Song, M (2001). Getting it together: Temporal coordination and conflict management in global virtual teams. *Academy of Management Journal, 44*(6), 1251-1262.

Morgan, J. N., & Sonquist, J. A. (1963, June). Problems in the analysis of survey data, and a proposal. *Journal of the American Statistical Association, 58*, 415-435.

Mumford, M. D., & Gustafson, S. B. (1988). Creativity syndrome: integration, application and innovation. *Psychological Bulletin, 103*(1), 27-43.

Nardi, B. A., & O'Day, V. L. (1999). *Information ecologies: Using technology with heart.* Cambridge: MIT Press.

Nardi, B. A., & Whittaker, S. (2002). The place of face to face communication in distributed work. In P. Hinds & S. Kiesler (Eds.), *Distributed work* (pp. 83-110). Cambridge, MA: MIT Press.

Nardi, B. A., Whittaker, S., & Bradner, E. (2000, December). Interaction and outeraction: Instant messaging in action. In *Proceedings of the ACM Conference on Computer Supported Cooperative Work (CSCW '00)* (pp. 79-88). Philadelphia; New York: ACM Press.

Nardi, B. A., Whittaker, S., & Schwarz, H. (2002). NetWORKers and their activity in intensional networks. *Computer Supported Cooperative Work, 11*(1/2), 205-242.

Nemiro, J. E. (2000). The glue that binds creative virtual teams. In Y. Malhotra (Ed.), *Knowledge management and virtual organizations* (pp. 101-123). Hershey, NJ: Idea Group Publishing.

Nemiro, J. E. (2002). The creative process in virtual teams. *Creativity Research Journal, 14*(1), 69-83.

Pasmore, W. A. (1997). Managing organizational deliberations in nonroutine work. In R. Katz (Ed.), *The human side of managing technological innovation* (pp. 413-423). New York: Oxford University Press.

Paulus, P. B. (2000). Groups, teams, and creativity: The creative potential of idea-generating groups. *Applied Psychology, 49*, 237-262.

Pirola-Merlo, A., & Mann, L. (2004). The relationship between individual creativity and team creativity: Aggregating across people and time. *Journal of Organizational Behavior, 25*, 235-257.

Polzer, J. T., Milton, L. P., & Swann, W. B. (2002). Capitalizing on diversity: Interpersonal congruence in small work groups. *Administrative Science Quarterly, 47*, 296-325.

Rice, R. E. (1994). Relating electronic mail use and network structure to R&D work networks and performance. *Journal of Management Information Systems, 11*(1), 9-29.

Riopelle, K., Gluesing, J. C., Alcordo, T. C., Baba, M., Britt, D., McKether, W. et al. (2003). Context, task, and the evolution of technology use in global virtual teams. In C. B. Gibson & S. G. Cohen (Eds.), *Virtual teams that work: Creating conditions for virtual team effectiveness* (pp. 239-264). San Francisco: Jossey-Bass.

Ripley, B. D. (2005). *Tree: Classification and regression trees.* Retrieved September 9, from http://cran.us.r-project.org/doc/packages/tree.pdf

Schenkel, A. (2004). Investigating the influence that media richness has on learning in a community of practice. In P. Hildreth & C. Kimble (Eds.), *Knowledge networks* (pp. 47-57). Hershey, PA: Idea Group.

Sethia, N. K. (1995). The role of collaboration in creativity. In C. M. Ford & D. A. Goia (Eds.), *Creative action in organization* (pp. 100-105). Thousand Oaks, CA: Sage.

Shalley, C. E., Zhou, J., & Oldham, G. R. (2004). The effects of personal and contextual characteristics on creativity: Where should we go from here? *Journal of Management, 30*(6), 933-958.

Short, J., Williams, E., & Chudoba, K. M. (1976). *The social psychology of telecommunications.* New York: John Wiley & Sons.

Sonquist, J. A., Laud Baker, E.L., & Morgan, J. N. (1973). *Searching for structure.* Ann Arbor: Institute for Social Research.

Sosik, J. J., Avolio, B. J., & Kahai, S. S. (1998). Inspiring group creativity: Comparing anonymous and identified electronic brainstorming. *Small Group Research, 29*(1), 3-31.

Sutton, R. I., & Hargadon, A. (1996). Brainstorming groups in context: Effectiveness in a product design firm. *Administrative Science Quarterly, 41*(4), 685-718.

Taggar, S. (2002). Individual creativity and group ability to utilize individual creative resources: A multilevel model. *Academy of Management Journal, 45*, 315-330.

Therneau, T. M., & Atkinson, B. (2005). *The Rpart package.* Retrieved November 15, 2006, from http://cran.us.r-project.org/doc/packages/rpart.pdf

Trevino, L., Lengel, R., and Daft, R. (1987). Media symbolism, media richness, and media choice in organizations. *Communication Research, 14*(5), 553-574.

Van Engelen, Jo M. L., Kiewiet, D. Jan, & Terlouw, P. (2001). Improving performance of product development teams through managing polarity. *International Studies of Management and Organization, 31*, 46-63.

Walther, J. (1992). Interpersonal effects in computer-mediated communication. *Communication Research, 19*(1), 52-90.

Walther, J., & Parks, M. (2002). Cues filtered out, cues filtered in: Computer-mediated communication and relationships. In M. Knapp, J. Daly, & G. Miller (Eds.), *The handbook of interpersonal communication* (3rd ed.). Thousand Oaks, CA: Sage.

West, M. A. (1990). The social psychology of innovation in groups. In M. A. West & J. L. Farr (Eds.), *Innovation and creativity at work* (pp. 309-333). Chichester, UK: John Wiley & Sons.

Whittaker, S. (2003). Theories and methods in mediated communication. In A. Graeser (Ed.), *The handbook of discourse processes.* Cambridge: Lawrence Erlbaum.

Ziegler, R., Diehl, M., & Zijlstra, G. (2000). Idea production in nominal and virtual groups: Does computer-mediated communication improve group brainstorming? *Group Processes & Intergroup Relations, 3*(2), 141-158.

Zigurs, I., Poole, M. S., & DeSanctis, G. L. (1988). A study of influence in computer-mediated group decision making. *MIS Quarterly, 12*(4), 625-644.

Zmud, R., Lind, M., and Young, F. (1990). An attribute space for organizational communication channels. *Information Systems Research, 1*(4), 440-457.

Chapter V
The Building Blocks for Creativity in Virtual Teams

Jill Nemiro
California State Polytechnic University, Pomona, USA

ABSTRACT

As the popularity of virtual teams continues to rise, those who manage and are part of virtual teams must be aware of how to enhance the effectiveness of and foster creativity in virtual teams. To provide assistance, this chapter presents a model that outlines five building blocks for enhancing and supporting creative work in virtual teams. The five building blocks are—design, climate, resources, norms and protocols, and continual assessment. By building and maintaining each of the five building blocks discussed in this chapter, virtual teams may move to higher levels of creativity and ultimately success. The chapter begins with a review of the relevant literature, including prominent models of virtual team performance, and factors necessary for creativity in teams in general. The second section in the chapter describes the methodology that guided the current research from which the five building blocks model emerged. The third section of the chapter offers a detailed description of each of the five building blocks for creativity in virtual teams. Lastly, an integrative model is proposed which links the five building blocks back to the earlier discussed models of virtual team performance. The chapter closes with a discussion of the current research's limitations and ideas for future researchers of virtual team creativity.

INTRODUCTION

Organizations across the globe, and the leaders that guide them now recognize that they do not have a monopoly on all knowledge and wisdom. These same leaders also realize that business innovation, which is increasingly becoming more complex, is and will continue to be critical for company survival. To address these challenges, and strive for continual creativity and innovation in a competitive market, managers, leaders, and employees are becoming aware of the need for new forms of collaborative work structures that require working with others who cross time, geographic, and cultural boundaries.

The myriad of group collaborative structures available today include formal collaborative structures, such as teams and work groups, and informal structures, such as communities of practice, learning networks, and professional societies (Beyerlein & Harris, 2004). Advances in information technology have made feasible and more widespread the use of *virtual* group collaborative structures. In these types of collaborative structures, team members may reside across the globe and can join together and work through information technology, achieving high levels of collaboration, creativity, and productivity, without being colocated.

In addition to the challenges of global competition, the nature of work in contemporary organizations has and will continue to change. Contemporary work has been classified on a continuum from routine to nonroutine activities (Mohrman, Cohen, & Mohrman, 1995). Routine work is conceptualized as work that is programmed, involves repeated patterns, is static and can be easily understood. Nonroutine work, on the other hand, is emergent in nature, varied and unique, interdependent, dynamic, complex, and uncertain. Today, routine work is becoming automated, and much of the work that remains is knowledge-based and nonroutine.

As the popularity of virtual teams continues to rise, those who manage and are part of virtual teams must be aware of how to enhance the effectiveness of and foster creativity in virtual teams. To provide assistance, a new area of study has emerged, in which team researchers and practitioners are developing theories and tools for creating effective virtual teams. This chapter presents one such theory—a model that outlines five building blocks for enhancing and supporting creative work in virtual teams.

In the first section of this chapter, relevant background literature is reviewed, including prominent models of virtual team performance, and factors necessary for creativity in teams in general. The second section describes the methodology that guided the current research from which the five building blocks model emerged. The five building blocks are described in detail in the third section. Finally, an integrative model is proposed which links the five building blocks back to the earlier discussed models of virtual team performance. The chapter closes with a discussion of the current research's limitations and ideas for future researchers of virtual team creativity.

BACKGROUND LITERATURE

Although theoretical models of virtual team effectiveness are in their infancy stages and more are forthcoming, current researchers have identified several important factors that influence virtual team performance. One of the first models of virtual team effectiveness was outlined by Lipnack and Stamps (1997, 2000). In their model, four elements form the foundation for virtual team effectiveness—purpose, people, links, and time. All effective virtual teams, they suggest, begin with the first element—*purpose*.

Purpose is the element that sustains and initiates the work process. For Lipnack and Stamps (2000), purpose is the "source of life and inner fire" for effective virtual teams. They use the term purpose to encompass a broad range of terms—from the abstract vision to the more increasingly concrete mission, goals, tasks, and results.

The second crucial element for effective virtual teams is the very *people* that make them up. People includes team members, team leaders, the level of number of people in a particular team (rings of involvement), and the roles people play in their teams.

People in virtual teams must be connected together with the third element—*links*. Each type of link (media or communication tool) can be evaluated for features that influence its effectiveness, cost, and accessibility. Links can be classified by the criteria of interaction, speed, and memory.

The fourth element for virtual team effectiveness is time. Time is typically defined as physical, calendar or clock time. However, for Lipnack and Stamps (2000), the element of time has additional meanings as well. Time is also characterized as process time. This type of time examines the typical rhythmic pattern in which virtual teams move through periods of working together, working apart, and back together again. Time also refers to the phases of a team's development or its life cycle, which usually includes a beginning (start-up, launch), middle (perform, test), and end (deliver).

The four elements of the model are then plugged into a systems theory perspective (inputs, processes, outputs) to form a model for successful virtual teams. Lipnack and Stamps (2000) refer to this model as the "Periodic Table of Organizational Elements" (p. 240), shown below.

The periodic table is a solid beginning for looking at what elements are needed for successful virtual teaming. The model emphasizes clear and cooperative goals, shared leadership and trusting relationships, and a process that encourages interdependency and accountability, and project life cycles. However, the model does not have a strong emphasis on the type of culture, climate, or conditions that are necessary for virtual team effectiveness. This shortcoming is rectified in another model (Gibson & Cohen, 2003), where the key assumption is that virtual teams are more likely to be effective when certain *enabling conditions* exist.

In their theory, Gibson and Cohen (2003) identify three enabling conditions necessary to promote virtual team effectiveness. They are:

- **Shared understanding:** The degree of cognitive overlap and commonality in beliefs, expectations, and perceptions about a common goal
- **Integration:** The process of establishing ways in which the parts of an organization can work together to create value, develop products, or deliver services
- **Mutual trust or collective trust:** A shared psychological state characterized by an acceptance of vulnerability based on expectations or intentions or behaviors of others within the team (pp. 8-9)

Gibson and Cohen (2003) outline a series of design factors that contribute to the establishment of the three enabling conditions. These design factors include (1) the systems and structures that make up the organizational context for virtual team success (selection, education and training, and performance evaluation and reward systems); (2) the team's structure (goals, leadership, task design, and social structure); (3) the use of technology (specific types of tools used, when and how they are used, and overall accessibility to technology); (4) people (the members that make up virtual teams, their degree of lateral skills, their tolerance for ambiguity, and their unique skills, knowledge and abilities); and (5) process

Table 1. Periodic table of organizational elements (Source: Lipnack & Stamps, 2000, p. 240)

	Inputs	**Processes**	**Outputs**
Purpose	Cooperative Goals	Interdependent Tasks	Concrete Results
People	Independent Members	Shared Leadership	Integrated Levels
Links	Multiple Media	Boundary-crossing Interactions	Trusting Relationships
Time	Coordinate Calendars	Track Projects	Follow Life Cycles

(those processes the guide the team's communication behavior, decision making, and resolution of conflict).

Two important moderators are also included in the model—the degree of virtuality (electronic dependency, geographic dispersion) and the degree of differences (culture, language, organization, function) that exist within the virtual team. These moderators are thought to amplify the effects of the design factors on the enabling conditions. In other words, the greater the degree of virtuality and differences, the more difficult it is to establish the necessary enabling conditions.

In addition, the three enabling conditions influence the outcomes of virtual teams. The model includes both business outcomes (goal achievement, productivity, timeliness, customer satisfaction, organizational learning, innovation, and cycle time) and human outcomes (member attitudes like commitment and satisfaction, and team longevity).

Gibson and Cohen's (2003) model is quite comprehensive and rightly so they refer to it as a research framework that summarizes where they began, not where they expect to conclude, their work on understanding virtual team effectiveness. Perhaps a more simplified and practical, and yet still comprehensive, model is offered by Duarte and Snyder (1999) in their book, *Mastering Virtual Teams*. Duarte and Snyder offer a model that contains seven factors proposed to affect the probability of a virtual team's success. The factors include:

- **Human resource policies:** Career-development systems are needed to provide virtual team members with career opportunities and assignments comparable to those in traditional team settings. Reward systems need to reinforce and reward cross-boundary work and results. Human resources policies should also guarantee all team members have equal, adequate and immediate access to electronic communication and technical support.

- **Training and on-the-job education and development:** Both formal training curriculum and continual on-line training should be available for virtual team members to learn how to use technology and how to interact electronically as well. In addition, systems to share knowledge across functions, projects and organizations need to be developed and maintained.

- **Standard organizational and team processes:** Virtual teams benefit from developing standardized processes to reduce both the team's initial start up and to eliminate unnecessary reinvention of such operating practices as cost estimation, procurement, team chartering, project planning, maintaining documentation, and reporting and controlling.

- **Use of electronic collaboration and communication technology:** Organizations that want to reap in the benefits from virtual teams must be able to provide these teams with the necessary technology for them to perform their work, and the needed information systems staff or technical support to assist them in using this technology.

- **Organizational culture:** Virtual teams function best in organizations that are grounded in a culture that values collaboration, respecting and working with people from all cultures, keeping criticism constructive, and sharing information. An adaptive, technologically advanced, and nonhierarchical organization is more likely to succeed with virtual teams than one that is highly structured and control-oriented.

- **Leadership support of virtual teams:** Virtual teams work best in organizations with leaders who value teamwork, communication, learning, and capitalizing on diversity. Duarte and Snyder (1999) list four categories of leadership behaviors that encourage virtual team performance—communicating, establishing expectations, allocating resources, and modeling desired behaviors.

- **Team-leader competencies:** Leaders of virtual teams need to develop an additional set of competencies on top of those required for leading traditional, colocated teams. These extra competencies include coaching and managing performance without traditional forms of feedback; selecting and appropriately using electronic communication and collaboration technologies; leading in a cross-cultural environment; helping to develop and transition team members; building and maintaining trust; networking across hierarchical and organizational boundaries; and developing and adapting organizational processes to meet the demands of the team.

- **Team-member competencies:** Virtual team members also need to develop their own set of extra competencies, which include project-management techniques; networking across functional, hierarchical, and organizational

boundaries; using electronic communication and collaboration technologies effectively; setting personal boundaries and managing time; working across cultural and functional boundaries; and using interpersonal awareness.

The theories, and the predictors of virtual team effectiveness included in each, can be taken together so as to offer an integrative look at what is needed for an effective virtual team. In Table 2, all the key predictors of virtual team effectiveness included in the three models reviewed (Duarte & Snyder, 1999; Lipnack & Stamps, 1997, 2000; Gibson & Cohen, 2003) are collapsed to yield an integrative model revealing five factors for virtual team effectiveness. The first factor is *design*, which includes purpose (Lipnack & Stamps, 1997), team structure (Gibson & Cohen, 2003), and the alignment of HR policies to support virtual and cross-boundary work (Duarte & Snyder, 1999). The second category is referred to as *conditions*. Under the umbrella of conditions falls context, shared understanding, and mutual trust (Gibson & Cohen, 2003), and organizational culture (Duarte & Snyder, 1999). A third major

Table 2. Integrative model of virtual team effectiveness predictors

	Lipnack & Stamps (1997)	**Gibson & Cohen (2003)**	**Duarte & Snyder (1999)**
Design	Purpose	Team Structure	Human Resource Policies
Conditions		- Context (design factor) - Shared Understanding (enabling condition) - Mutual Trust (enabling condition)	Organizational Culture
Technology	Links	Technology (design factor)	Electronic Collaboration and Communication Technology
Work processes	Time	- Processes (design factor) - Integration (enabling condition)	Standard Organizational and Team Processes
People	People	People (design factor)	- Training, Education and Development - Leadership Support - Team Leader Competencies - Team Member Competencies

category is *technology* or the links through which virtual teams communicate. All three models have a predictor that addresses technology. The *work processes* that virtual teams move through in completing their work make up the fourth category of predictors. Lipnack and Stamps (1997) refer to this as time; Gibson and Cohen (2003) include processes and integration; and Duarte and Snyder (1999) acknowledge the importance of using standard organizational and team processes. The final category of predictors inferred from these three models is *people*. This category includes necessary "extra" competencies that virtual team leaders and members need, the importance of leadership and technical support for virtual teams, and the training and education requirements for those who work virtually.

The theories reviewed in this section, and the integrative model, offer a promising start to understanding what elements predict virtual team effectiveness. But none of the theories discussed specifically deal with what is necessary for *creativity* in virtual teams. There has, however, been much research looking at what is needed to foster creativity in traditional (colocated) teams. In reviewing this line of research, several factors emerge that are necessary for teams to be creative. These factors, and relevant references, are provided in Table 3. As will become evident, many of the factors found important in the current research on virtual team creativity echo the findings of the earlier researchers who investigated creativity in colocated teams.

METHODOLOGY

The five building blocks model described in this chapter is based on an in-depth investigation of what is necessary for virtual teams to be creative (Nemiro, 1998, 2004). This section describes the sampling techniques and research sample, and the data collection and analysis procedures that guided the investigation.

Sampling Techniques

Maximum variation sampling was the method that guided sampling in this study. Thirty-six individuals from nine different teams participated in the research. Teams were chosen if they varied on several key characteristics. First, teams varied with respect to the core business of the originating organization in which they resided, and the nature of the team's work. Virtual teams came from both organizational and educational settings.

Table 3. Necessary factors for creativity in traditional (colocated) teams

Factor	References
Goal Clarity	Amabile, 1988; West, 1990
Trust	Rogers, 1954; West, 1990
Constructive Tension	Ekvall, 1983; Runco, 1994
Challenge	Pelz & Andrews, 1966; Ekvall et al., 1983; Amabile & Gryskiewicz, 1987; Amabile & Gryskiewicz, 1989; Runco, 1995; Amabile et al., 1996.
Collaboration	Steiner, 1965; Pelz & Andrews, 1966; Ekvall, 1983; Kanter, 1983; Amabile & Gryskiewicz, 1987.
Freedom	Andrews, 1975; Ekvall et al., 1983; Amabile & Gryskiewicz, 1987.
Management Encouragement and Support for Creativity	Steiner, 1965; Andrews, 1975; Daft & Becker, 1978; Ekvall, Arvonen, & Waldenstrom-Lindblad, 1983; Baran, Zandon, & Vanston, 1986; VanGundy, 1987; Amabile & Gryskiewicz, 1987, 1989.

Second, teams varied on the extent of "virtualness", defined by both the degree of electronic interaction versus face-to-face communication used, and the ratio of members within the team that were geographically dispersed. For example, some teams interacted entirely through electronic means, while others combined electronic interaction with periodic face-to-face encounters. For all teams, however, the majority of their communication was to be through electronic means, rather than face-to-face. Further, some teams were composed of members that were all located in different geographic locations, while others had only one physically separated team member. However, a team must have had at least one team member geographically separated to be included in the study. Third, teams were chosen to vary in size, and years of existence. Lastly, individual participants varied with respect to age, gender, educational level, geographic location, and work location (home or office).

Additional criteria were also considered before including a team in the study. Much of the literature on virtual team and organizational designs relies on investigations of project or ad hoc teams, teams that come together for a particular project and then once the project is completed, disband (Davidow & Malone, 1992; Kristof et al., 1995). For this investigation, however, only virtual teams whose existence was ongoing were selected.

In qualitative research, the actual number of participants to be included in a study depends on when the criterion of *theoretical saturation* of categories has been reached. Sampling for this project occurred over a period of nearly a year, continuing until no new or relevant data emerged regarding a category, and relationships between categories were well established (Glaser & Strauss, 1967; Strauss & Corbin, 1990). It has been suggested that effective interview studies include at least 25-30 participants (Seidman, 1991). To meet these criteria, 36 participants were interviewed. However, the emphasis was not on reaching a particular number of participants, but rather on reaching theoretical saturation.

Table 4. The nature of work for each virtual team

Team	Nature of work
Organizational Consultants	
Team 1	Consulting firm that assists clients with organizational change.
Team 2	Consulting firm that assists clients with technological diffusion and implementation.
Team 3	Consulting firm that specializes in personal productivity, time management training, and helping clients streamline workflow.
Education Teams	
Team 4	Team of designers responsible for developing and maintaining an educational virtual community for primary, secondary, and college students.
Team 5	Team of MBA career development professionals that put on an annual job recruiting event for students.
On-line Service Providers	
Team 6	Team that develops and sustains a company virtual community to promote internal knowledge sharing.
Team 7	Team that produces an on-line publication.
Team 8	Team that manages an on-line forum.
Design Engineers	
Team 9	Team of product design engineers who design circuit boards for electronics in cars.

Description of the Virtual Teams

The nine teams varied with respect to the nature of their work. Table 4 briefly profiles the nature of each team's work.

Three teams were organizational consulting firms. One team specialized in organizational change; another specialized in personal productivity and time management training, and helping clients streamline their workflow; and the another team of consultants assisted clients in technological diffusion.

Two teams were in the field of education. One team was composed of 12 career development professionals from universities with small, but high quality MBA programs that had come together to put on an annual recruiting event for their students. Another team was composed of four developers responsible for developing and maintaining a text-based, educational virtual community for primary, secondary, and university students.

Three teams were on-line service providers. Two of these teams resided in the same organization, a large software development company. One of those teams was responsible for producing an online publication that featured a calendar of events and directory of content of what was happening on the on-line service network. The other team managed an online chat on religion. Another online service provider team resided in a large, multinational organization that manufactures business machines and computers. The major work of this team was to develop and sustain a company virtual community to foster knowledge sharing among globally dispersed workers in the corporation.

The final team was made up of product design engineers, all of whom worked for a large auto manufacturing company. The engineers were responsible for designing the electronic side of the car (e.g., circuit boards for radios, clusters, odometers, anti-lock brakes, and electric windows).

Members of the nine teams were mostly located within the United States (although there were some internationally dispersed team members), but were widely dispersed across the country. The size of the teams varied from 3 to 12 individuals. Team tenure (defined as the time from when the team was initially formed to the time of the interviews) also varied, ranging from one team who had been in existence for only six months to one team who had been in existence for 15 years.

Data Collection

Selected members from the nine different virtual teams (a total of 36 individuals) were interviewed individually over the telephone about their virtual teams' creative process, functioning, communication behavior, and high and low creativity experiences within their teams. All interviews were audio-taped (with permission). In the interviews, team members were specifically asked to (a) provide background on the organization in which their team resides; (b) discuss their specific role in the team and describe a typical work day; (c) describe the characteristics, behaviors, and norms of their virtual team; (d) describe what they liked and did not like about working in a virtual team; (e) address the strengths and limitations of virtual teams; (f) describe how the creative process evolves in their virtual team; (g) share two stories of projects completed by their team—one story that they felt exemplified high creativity, and one story which exemplified low creativity (Amabile & S. Gryskiewicz, 1987; Amabile, 1990); and (h) comment on how crucial several specific dimensions of the work environment were to the effectiveness of their virtual team (dimensions previously shown as important for the realization of creativity, Ekvall, 1983; and Ekvall et al., 1983; Amabile & S. Gryskiewicz, 1987; Amabile & N. Gryskiewicz, 1989; Amabile, 1990).

Data Analysis

The general approach to data analysis followed Glaser and Strauss' (1967; Strauss & Corbin, 1990) suggestion of using grounded theory techniques to generate an in-depth understanding of the phenomena under investigation. Value was placed on finding what emerged from the data, from what the participants discussed in the interviews, rather than on forcing the data into preconceived, a priori categories. Data analysis involved two major phases—data description and data explanation:

- **Data description:** The data description process involved coding the interview transcripts. Two levels of coding were involved—first level coding and pattern coding (Miles & Huberman, 1994). In first-level coding, descriptive codes were suggested and data summarized. In pattern coding, codes or concepts were grouped together or subsumed into categories, creating a smaller number of sets, themes, or constructs. HyperResearch, a computer-assisted data analysis program, was used to assist in the coding process. One of the most useful techniques during this portion of the analysis process was *memoing, "the theoretical write-up of ideas about codes and their relationships as they strike the analyst while coding"* (Glaser & Strauss, 1967, p. 83). This technique was used extensively for creating and defining new codes, combining codes, and constructing categories.

After all transcripts had been initially coded, the process of pattern coding, reviewing codes to see how they could be grouped into categories, followed. Again, the use of memoing was helpful in looking at the data from a broader level. In addition, several meetings were held with two peer colleagues to discuss the utility of the categories and codes generated, and to further brainstorm conceptual connections. HyperResearch was also useful during this part of the analysis, as the program allowed for deleting, renaming, or copying codes any number of times.

To measure the reliability of coding within categories, two independent raters check-coded (Miles & Huberman, 1994) selected portions of the interview transcripts that were originally coded by the author. Overall, inter-rater reliability was good, with perfect agreement on 70% of the quotes check-coded. Specific areas of disagreement were discussed among the original coder and the two independent raters until agreement was reached. In some instances, a code was revised and renamed.

- **Data explanation:** Explanation refers to *"making complicated things understandable by showing how their component parts fit together according to some rules—that is, theory"* (Miles & Huberman, 1994, p. 90). The analytic progression, then, moved from describing to explaining. Two techniques were useful in examining the relationships between categories—writing theoretical memos, and constructing diagrams, displays or visual representations of relationships between concepts (Strauss & Corbin, 1990; Miles & Huberman, 1994). Writing theoretical memos helped to further develop categories, and the relationships between categories. Diagrams helped to visualize and conceptualize the models of the creative process used in these virtual teams. Data displays, in particular, cross-case matrices (Miles & Huberman, 1994) were useful to visually represent similarities and differences across teams, on a variety of factors.

THE FIVE BUILDING BLOCKS

The five building blocks outlined in this section—design, climate, resources, norms and protocols, and continual assessment and learning—emerged from extensive qualitative data analysis of the interview data.

The model proposes that creativity is highest when all five building blocks are solidly in place—when the design is appropriate, the climate is supportive of creativity, the resources are sufficient, the proper norms and protocols are agreed on and adhered to, and the team takes the time for continual assessment, and learning as a result of that assessment. Each of the proposed building blocks for creativity in virtual teams is described in more detail as follows.

Building Block #1: Design

Creative Process

Four stages emerged as the path these virtual teams followed in their quest toward the production of creative results—idea generation, development, finalization/closure, and evaluation. The idea generation stage is ignited by someone on the team recognizing an unmet need, asking a question, or simply feeling that exploration of a specific endeavor would be intriguing. An individual team member or a group of individuals within the team then become(s) the kicker (the team member who initially suggests the idea to the entire team). If the rest of the team agrees that the idea is worth pursuing and committing some initial time and resources to, the kicker then champions and begins to further define and mold the idea. After the results of the kicker's efforts are drafted, presented, and disseminated to the rest of the team, an iterative stage of development follows. The team (or subset of the team) then works to develop a product, project, or service that meets the initially proposed need, answers the initially proposed question, or brings into action the specific endeavor that was found to be intriguing. Team members exchange drafts, designs, or prototypes back and forth, offer feedback to one another, and as a result, continue to make revisions. One organizational consulting team member describes the stages guiding his virtual team's creative process as a cycling of individual work and then back out to the group, led by the kicker(s),

Our stages usually are individual initiation, a couple of people kick it around, come back to a starting nucleus of possibilities. Divvy that up to people. They respond to it. Bring it back in and there's one person who usually takes the responsibility for kind of guiding it through all that iteration.

Once ideas are developed into workable outcomes, the creative products are finalized and implemented, where the team makes one last review and pulls together any last minute loose ends. Closure occurs just before implementation of the product, project, or service. After implementation, an evaluation period follows, in which team members get together and assess the strengths and weaknesses of the completed project.

The first step in mapping out an appropriate creative process is to understand what is currently in place. Virtual team members and leaders need to examine the creative process as it unfolds in their teams. After developing a thorough understanding of the current creative process, virtual teams should honestly reflect on and assess the current forums and procedures to ensure they (1) encourage initial nonjudgmental and open sharing of ideas, (2) develop specific criteria to evaluate alternative solutions once generated, (3) effectively organize development work, (4) can gain member agreement on proposed actions, (5) can reach closure of a project within the appropriate timeframe, and (6) use multiple criteria and feedback when evaluating actions taken.

Work Design Approaches

As the virtual teams moved from initial idea generation, through development, to finalization and closure of a creative effort, they utilized two work design approaches. The most common work design approach used is termed the modular approach. One educational team member succinctly described the modular approach, *"Oh, when everybody had a job and they were able to do it, and everyone did these tiny little pieces, then the final project is something impressive."* In this approach, team members meet initially to decide on the need, task, or project to be pursued. Then, as a group, the work is parceled out or distributed among team members, usually based on individual team member's expertise or interest. Team members, then, go off to work on their "pieces of the pie," sometimes by themselves, sometimes with one or two other members of the team. After the work is completed, the efforts are presented to the group for feedback before finalization and implementation. Revisions are done as needed. The entire team, then, assesses the creative outcome, which in reality was a compilation of all the individual pieces put together.

The iterative approach was often used in conjunction with the modular approach. In the iterative approach, team members engage in back-and-forth development cycles. Members work a little, present results to the team, get feedback, work a little more, present results, get more feedback, and so on until the project is finalized. E-mail technology allows team members to throw out their ideas in a more or less random fashion. Ideas can be bounced back and forth, and built on with ease. A member of an online service provider team characterized his team's creative process as a series of iterative steps, alternating between thought and action.

Ours is more an iterative close contact. We talk about it either via e-mail or via voice as we go along, and brainstorm ideas. I think that one of

the keys to our success is, as far as creativity is concerned, frequent voice contact. We're trying to do what, in software terms, is sometimes rapid prototyping, where you think a little, you do a little, you think a little, you do a little, you think a little, you do a little, rather than thinking a whole lot and then trying to come out with something that everybody agrees with the first time.

Although the most common work design approach utilized for virtual work is the modular approach, not every creative effort (or for that matter, less creative effort too) may be easily divided into sections. In those situations, a modular approach may be a poor choice for accomplishing those tasks. Another important factor, then, in mapping out an appropriate design is seriously considering whether the creative task at hand can be effectively accomplished within the specific work design approach the team is using. Some teams may find it better to adapt a more flexible design, using one work design approach for one situation, and switching to another when the circumstances call for it.

Leadership Structures

Leading a virtual team is not the same as leading a more traditional, colocated team. Even the best designed virtual team may fail if it has not adopted an appropriate leadership structure to support its work. The different categories of leadership structures that guided the nine virtual teams included:

- Permanent team leaders (the same individual or partners)
- Rotating team leaders (every member of the team is at one time the team leader)
- Managing partners who govern the overall business and rotating project leaders that supervise individual projects and tasks (a structure in which the overall business leadership stays the same, but the leadership

of a particular project varies depending on who has the appropriate expertise needed for a particular assignment)
- Specialized facilitators or coordinators (rather than full fledged leaders)
- Leaderless teams (or led by all the team members)

There seemed to be no one best way to lead virtual teams. All of the team members indicated in their interviews that they felt their teams were highly creative and productive, yet there were a variety of leadership structures followed. Nevertheless, from their stories, some recommendations for when different leadership structures might be useful can be made. Permanent leadership structures are useful in situations characterized by centralized decision making, and where the work can be parceled out to team members who possess distinct roles and different areas of expertise. Rotating leadership structures are appropriate in situations where team members' roles are less differentiated (all team members could potentially do the same tasks); where all team members have the necessary ability to effectively lead the team; where operating practices are standardized and support staff do not rotate (to assist in maintaining stability); and where there is a high level of trust among team members. Finally, leaderless structures (or what is commonly referred to as self-managed teams) work well in situations where team members come from various functions and are of equal status or rank within their various functions; where team members are equally invested in and will benefit from the team's outcome; where team members are accountable for their work; and where there is a high level of trust among team members.

Building Block #2: Climate

A climate for creativity for virtual teams includes a solid connection among team members, both at the task and interpersonal level, and appropriate team member and management conditions and competencies supportive of creativity that are developed and practiced by all. Each of these elements is described in more detail.

Connection

Connection emerged as one of the key elements of a climate necessary for creativity in virtual teams. Connection involves both *task* connection and *interpersonal* connection. Task connection was made up dedication and commitment and goal clarity. In the high creativity stories shared by the virtual team members, the teams described situations in which the members had a sense of dedication, intense involvement, and commitment to the work. The members worked hard on difficult tasks and problems and persevered. The stories also included descriptions of goal clarity, where goals were clearly defined and developed through constant clarification and feedback, and were shared by all members. For example, one member of the product design engineering team shared the following in his high creativity story:

In the design portion, we had certain goals in mind. Manufacturing had certain goals in mind, and we had certain goals in mind. And you know, obviously you're going to try to do what you think is the best alternative within the realm of your team. But in this case, it was coming up with a joint decision that would allow all of us to win. We all had the overall goal of making a product that could be manufactured, that would pass all testing, and that was inexpensive. That basic underlying goal was always there.

In highly creative experiences, virtual team members also shared that they felt strongly interpersonally connected. Interpersonal connection was made up of information sharing (regular communication, sharing the results of one's efforts, providing needed information, timely updating of information), personal bonding (a family-like feeling where team members were committed to and cared for one another), and mutual trust. In a virtual environment, team members felt trust was essential for creative work. As one member of an educational team shared,

Trust between team members? Boy, how could you do creative work without it. In our team, I'd have to say, trust is pretty high. It has to be there. And the reason is, you can B.S. out of anything if it's just typed. If you're dealing face-to-face, it's harder to not be straight. You have eye contact, you have voice, you have the integrity of the whole body language that has to be dealt with. So, the trust has to be there.

Trust was described on several levels, including (1) a sense of trust that team members will do their designated tasks within the designated time frame; (2) trust in the accurateness of the information provided by other team members; (3) trust that team members will give honest and constructive feedback on ideas, thoughts, and creative efforts shared electronically; (4) trust in one another's expertise and ability to do the work effectively; and (5) trust that team members will hold ideas shared in confidence if requested.

The importance the virtual team members placed on connection suggests that interpersonal skills are simply just as important, if not more so, for successful and creative virtual team experiences as is knowledge of collaborative technology. Training virtual team members in active listening, nonverbal communication, responding with empathy, resolving conflict, establishing interpersonal trust, and cross-cultural communication, while it may need to be crafted differently in a virtual work environment, still needs to be emphasized. To ensure the needed deep sense of connection among virtual team members for high levels of creative behavior, these interpersonal skills are critical. Some of the needed interpersonal skills are listed in the next section, referred to as competencies.

Team Member and Management Conditions and Competencies

This section describes the set of team member and management conditions, and related competencies and interpersonal skills needed for high levels of creativity to occur while working virtually. In the creativity stories shared by the virtual team members, six team member and management conditions emerged to form the situational requirements necessary for a climate for creativity within virtual teams. Those conditions include—acceptance of ideas and constructive tension, challenge, collaboration, freedom, management encouragement, and sufficient resources and time.

Acceptance of ideas refers to a situation in which ideas and input are encouraged, valued, and accepted by all members of the team without unnecessary criticism. A high degree of honesty exists among team members, leading individuals to feel comfortable not only in sharing their own ideas, but in giving open and honest feedback to one another as well. One office staff member of an organizational consulting firm commented on the high level of acceptance of ideas within her team.

What we have to say has value, even though we're not stockholders. It used to be when I first started with this team that the office staff went to tri-annual meetings just to take minutes and did not participate. And now we participate on a very high level at these meetings. And they want to make sure that we know they value our input. When this first started happening, we were a little reluctant to speak our opinions. But then we found out that they really did want to know what we thought, and we tell them.

Constructive tension also emanated from a mix of differing views and opinions within the team. Indeed, constructive tension was so valued by some of the teams that they actively sought to create it in order to achieve high levels of creativity. An organizational consulting team member shared,

We believe that creativity arises from having differences amongst the team members that sets up a creative tension, so that we're not subject to groupthink, if you will. So we will go out and attract people who agree on this basic set of beliefs, but have a different perspective, from a different technical specialty, or from a different culture, or something. That creative difference in the team helps us be creative.

Highly creative experiences were also characterized by a sense of challenge arising from the intriguing and enjoyable nature of a problem or task presented to the team, the urgent needs of a particular situation, or the desire to push for something new and move away from the status quo. In these challenging situations, team members collaborated and demonstrated the ability to pull together and work closely and comfortably together to complete the challenging task. For example, an international member of the product design engineering team described a situation in which his team was highly creative when faced with an urgent, challenging task.

The time that our team was highly creative, and obviously we get a lot of these but the one that I can recollect off the top of my head recently, would be the cluster project. I refer to this project because I've been involved right from the start in every aspect of it. Just before my vacation, we went through the whole design review, and we had to try and get everyone else's requirements in. Then suddenly the U.S. hits us with some serious major changes which were very late in the program. We had about two weeks to meet everyone's requirements, and get the board out before my holiday. Actually achieving it was really big because not only did it please me because I've got something

out the door and I could go away on holiday and not worry about it. Everyone else was pleased because the timing of the project was still on target. We all had a little celebration. It really was against the odds.

The conditions supportive of creativity in virtual teams also included a high level of freedom. Team members were given the freedom to decide how to do their work and to work at their own pace. Schedules were flexible and adaptable to individual team member's "creative biorhythms" and lifestyles, as one organizational consulting team member put it, "not being forced into a 9 to 5 creative box." Team members also reported being free from unnecessary evaluation, surveillance, or other constraints. In addition, the leaders and managers in these situations were encouraging, enthusiastic, and supportive of new ideas and new ways of doing things.

To achieve high levels of creativity, team members also shared that they needed sufficient information, human, and technological resources; and sufficient time to creatively think about a project and to experiment and try things in new and different ways. Interestingly enough, in the low creativity stories, the lack of time was a key deterrent to achieving novel approaches. (See chapter by Ocker, *Creativity in asynchronous virtual teams: putting the pieces together*, for further discussion on insufficient time as an inhibitor of virtual team success.) One organizational consulting team member described a low creativity story for her team, one in which not only did creativity suffer, but team members were merely scrambling to get the project completed on time.

It was just such a time crunch. There was no, I mean, as far as I'm concerned, there was no creativity. It was like, I'm going to spell check this, and if it looks like the sentences read okay, then it's going in. We were handing [the team leader] the binders on his way out the door, and he had

20 minutes to catch a flight. It was just about as stressed as I've ever been without there being a death involved. [laughs].

To achieve the conditions just reviewed, virtual team members, leaders, and managers need to develop and practice a special set of interpersonal competencies including: supportive communication, cross-cultural communication, conflict resolution, decision making, stress management, time management, coaching and motivating others from a distance, and knowledgeable management and information access skills. Table 5 relates these competencies to the conditions previously reviewed; in other words, what competencies virtual workers need to develop and maintain to establish each of the appropriate team member and management conditions for creativity in virtual teams.

Now it may seem that all one has to do to establish a climate for creativity within a virtual team is to eliminate aspects that hinder creativity and put in place those aspects that foster creativity. This approach, however, may be simple-minded and somewhat impractical. A more realistic approach would be to strive for establishing a balance of the necessary conditions. For example, *acceptance of ideas* is important for a creative climate, but all ideas cannot be totally accepted. In the practical business world, new ideas need to be assessed, evaluated, and some even dismissed. The most realistic and appropriate ideas are pursued. In addition, an accurate assessment of the needed competencies should allow for the fact that not all competencies may be of equal importance to every virtual team. Each virtual team will need to realistically assess both how the members of the team *currently* stand with respect to each of the competencies previously listed and how *important* they feel each of those competencies is to their team. From these individualized team assessments, action plans can be developed that

Table 5. Conditions and related competencies (Source: Nemiro, 2004; reprinted with permission of John Wiley & Sons, Inc., © 2004)

Condition	Related Competencies
Acceptance of ideas	• Supportive communication
Constructive Tension	• Conflict resolution • Cross-cultural communication • Decision making • Supportive communication
Challenge	• Developing and motivating others • Stress management • Time management
Collaboration	• Conflict resolution • Cross-cultural communication • Decision making • Knowledge management and information access skills • Supportive communication
Freedom	• Stress management • Time management
Management Encouragement	• Cross-cultural communication • Developing and motivating others • Supportive communication
Sufficient Resources and Time	• Conflict resolution • Knowledge management and information access skills • Time management

primarily focus on the most pronounced *gaps* (competencies that may be lacking in the team but are valued as important to the team), and *areas of strength* (competencies possessed by individuals on the team and are valued as important to the team).

Building Block #3: Resources

As was suggested in the early models of virtual team effectiveness (see Table 2), the selection of and access to appropriate technology and communication tools are essential for virtual teams. The building block of Resources includes the appropriate communication tools available for virtual teams. However for teams doing creative work, these communication tools need to be selected based on which tools might work best for each stage of the creative process. In Table 6, a model is presented to offer suggestions for which communication tools are most appropriate for use during each of the stages of the creative process.

Table 6. Appropriate communication tools for stages in the creative process (Source: Nemiro, 2004; reprinted with permission of John Wiley & Sons, © 2004)

Purpose	Appropriate Communication Tools
Talking - these tools provide a shared meeting place for virtual team members to interact anytime during the creative process.	• Face-to-face meetings • Synchronous computer meetings • Videoconferencing • Teleconferencing • Telephone • E-mail and instant messaging systems • Bulletin boards
Brainstorming and Generating Ideas - these tools allow team members to jointly share and build on ideas.	• Face-to-face meetings • Synchronous computer meetings • Interactive and electronic whiteboards • Teleconferencing • Chat rooms • Bulletin boards
Doing - these tools support development and design work and offer a shared workspace for development work to occur synchronously or asynchronously.	• Synchronous computer meetings • Interactive and electronic whiteboards • Videoconferencing • Asynchronous computer meetings (shared databases, shared files)
Saving - these tools are used to archive and store creative efforts and to allow these efforts to be reviewed over and over. These tools offer the capability of, as one team member put it, "holding on to the creativity." They assist in building a content repository in which past ways of approaching and resolving client needs or problems are stored. These past approaches then may become frameworks, templates, or outlines later applied to similar client situations.	• Asynchronous computer meetings (shared databases, shared files) • Chat room records • Audio-link transcripts • Interactive or electronic whiteboards (where information is stored to the computer) • Bulletin boards • Company Intranet web pages
Finalizing and Closing - these tools allow team members to pull all the elements of a project together and to make final adjustments as needed. They also assist in the process of reaching consensus and closure.	• Face-to-face meetings • Synchronous computer meetings • Shared databases • E-mail • Teleconferencing
Evaluating - these tools assist team members in reviewing and assessing creative efforts and outcomes, and capturing these assessments for future learning.	• Face-to-face meetings • Synchronous computer meetings • Videoconferencing • Shared databases (to store team's experiences and lessons for future use)

Suggestions are made for tools for talking (in a shared meeting place); for generating ideas; for doing (developing and designing in a shared workspace); for saving (storing and building a content repository); for finalizing and bringing closure to creative work; and for evaluating (reviewing, assessing, and learning). Additional resource-type information is detailed in part C of the book.

Virtual teams pursuing creative work need to utilize a variety of communication tools to bolster and sustain their creative process. However, for creative work, it is key to incorporate into the process periodic face-to-face encounters or information technologies that simulate real-time face-to-face contact, or both. (See chapter by Leenders et al. (previous chapter) for additional discussion on the importance of face-to-face communication.) Asynchronous (communication at different times) modes of interaction are beneficial, but creative efforts cannot be accomplished without the opportunity for rich, synchronous (at the same time) interactions. To illustrate, an online service provider team member shared,

I think it is necessary to speak with the people, whether it's on chat or on the telephone, at some point in the process. I don't think creativity can all be done on e-mail. You have to be together at the same moment at some point.

Building Block #4: Norms and Protocols

Norms are critical for specifying what the acceptable standards of behavior are within a team. Norms tell individual team members what is expected of them, and what they can expect of their colleagues as well. Working virtually through collaborative technology does free up individual team members from the bounds and boundaries of a traditional team, giving individual members new levels of autonomy and freedom. However, this does not mean virtual team members can use this newfound freedom to escape the pull of their

team. Armstrong and Cole (1996) suggest that a shared agreement across distance concerning how to use technology is just as important as the technology itself. Virtual teams can develop a shared agreement by taking the time to seriously address, define, and agree on what is acceptable (and unacceptable) behavior.

Two key categories of norms described by the virtual teams interviewed for this study were communication behavior and project and task management norms. *Communication behavior* norms guided the team's communication patterns and exchange of information to accomplish and perform their creative work. *Project and task management* norms assisted the teams in organizing and managing their work. Each set of norms is further described below.

Communication Behavior Norms

The myriad of communication behavior norms that virtual teams need to develop, agree-upon, and establish include:

- **Availability and acknowledgment norms:** These types of norms are needed to establish acceptable time frames and frequency for when individuals will check in various communication tools and when team members can expect others will check in and respond as well. They ensure that team members respect one another's personal time. For example, a team member of one of the organizational consulting teams described an availability norm established for the team's telephone communication, "*Senior members of the team have agreed on daily contact times. We talk to each other every day, including weekends. I know every night at 5:30 Pacific time, my partner is going to call me from wherever he is at, or I will call him. The person out of town calls home base is another rule. And so I can save up all of the things during the day, and I don't* *even have to think about that 'cause I know when that communication is going to take place.*"

- **Appropriateness of specific communication tools:** Members of virtual teams need to have discussions about what types of communication tools they will use. Further, team members need to examine and agree on when they will use each of the communication tools they have selected—for what specific purposes or in what circumstances.

- **Protocols for usage of specific communication tools:** These norms establish the specific forms of etiquette or guidelines team members will follow when using each particular type of communication tool in their communication repertoire.

- **Rules governing subgroup and information exchange:** When virtual teams are small in size, norms for governing subgroup communication may not be necessary. However, as teams increase in size, so too may the need to establish norms guiding the exchange of information between subsets within the team. For example, the largest virtual team interviewed (12 members) created a guiding norm for all communication through e-mail (the most common way this team communicated) to go out to all members. A distribution list including all the team members' e-mail addresses was created. Individual team members then agreed to send all e-mail correspondence using this distribution list. Whenever an individual team member sent or replied to an e-mail, it was sent to the entire team. Even when the team was broken down into subsets to work on particular projects, the e-mail exchanges between those subsets of members were "cc'd" to the rest of the team as well. Other teams were more comfortable with and allowed for communication to occur only between team members working on a similar project. Teams can avoid a lot of

potential misunderstandings, conflict, and wasted duplication of efforts by establishing subgroup communication norms.

- **Balance of structured and unstructured communication:** Common sense may suggest that when individuals are geographically dispersed, it takes a lot of structure to create communication exchanges between these individuals. However, the unstructured, spontaneous "water cooler" type discussions are not easily accomplished in virtual teams. Yet, both of these forms of communication—structured and unstructured—are necessary. For the virtual teams interviewed, there was no magical mixture or balance. Of the nine teams, there were varying levels of structure incorporated into each team's communication behavior. Some teams had a high level of structure, while for others communication was merely a random exchange of information. Each team will need to discuss, specify, and agree on the degree of structure or lack of structure that will be incorporated into their communication behavior patterns. These norms specify what types of communication exchanges are formally scheduled and how often, the level of acceptability for random (as needed) communication exchanges, and for what purposes it is best to use structured and planned forms of communication and use unstructured and random forms of communication.

Project and Task Management Norms

The types of norms that the virtual teams used to accomplish their shared creative work included the following:

- **Developing a creative process project life-cycle map:** Some of the teams began projects by creating a shared process for working on their joint projects (e.g., documents or products). In order to do this, the teams defined what the lifecycle of their projects would look like (or has been in the past), and recorded that process. This allowed the teams to develop a shared working picture of the creative process and to determine the boundaries and scope of the work so that it has a clear beginning, transition points, and ending.

- **Distinguishing between routine and creative tasks:** Norms need to be established so that it is evident to the team what will be done routinely and what tasks will require creativity. These norms are necessary so that efficiency is an outcome as well as creativity. Without them, there is the likely possibility that those tasks that can be effectively accomplished using routine ways of working may use up the resources needed for tasks where creativity is required. For an example of this type of norm, a member of an organizational consulting team shared that throughout the year her team follows a set system (which they do not consider that creative), but that when the team comes together periodically face-to-face for planning sessions, a creative environment is established.

Throughout the year we have our system and it functions very well. It's evolved to the point where every person who performs a specific duty knows it, does it, and communicates it. So we don't really have to talk about it too much. When we do get together, we have reports about the different areas. What's new, and that usually lasts half an hour, where every person provides information about the area of their responsibility. And then we move on to the creative part, what are we going to do now? We have all these different ideas that we're pursuing as to how we can work more collaboratively to provide services to employers and attract

them to our Consortium. So when we do get together, it's usually a planning meeting or a marketing meeting, and it's really a very creative environment.

- **Assigning roles and responsibilities:** A key element of what makes up a creative and high performing team is clearly assigning roles and responsibilities to each individual team member. Responsibility for obtaining the overall creative goal is shared by the entire team, but responsibility for individual tasks on the path to accomplishment of that goal is given to individual members within the team. If individual roles and responsibilities are not clearly specified and understood by all the members of the team, confusion and redundancy may result.

- **Timeframes and accountability measures:** Timeframes clarify when certain actions need to be completed by. Accountability norms spell out what actions will be taken to ensure on-time delivery of task-related output and what will occur if members do not meet up to their responsibilities. Agreement on timeframes and accountability norms is essential to avoid the "out of sight, out of mind" mentality that may occur with dispersed virtual team members. Further, if team members know they can rely on others to deliver what they said by when they said, trust is built. If not, trust either does not get built or disintegrates rapidly.

- **Protocols for shared workspaces and files:** A common pitfall for virtual teams is when each team member is not working from the same updated information, document, or product design prototype. As a result, misunderstandings, confusion, wasted time, and even the total or partial loss of creative efforts (e.g., one team member saving over the most current version with a previous version) can result. As the number of individuals working with a particular shared file increases, so does the risk of loss of creative output. When virtual team members work in a shared workspace and exchange files back and forth, established norms ensure that all team members have current project-related information.

- **Project review, revision, and final approval norms:** In addition to norms ensuring that team members are accountable for their parts of the shared work, norms need to be established for how the work, once initially completed, will be reviewed, revised, and approved. These norms help the team to determine when and how review of projects and work tasks should take place, and how the team will ensure review is completed as planned. These norms also establish which individuals can offer input for revision; can add, change, or delete portions of shared work; give final approval of the shared work; or need to be informed of revisions and final approval.

Building Block #5: Continual Assessment and Learning

The fifth and final building block to creativity in virtual teams is *continual assessment and learning*. As a virtual team nears the end of its creative process on a particular project, finalizes it, and brings closure to that specific creative effort, there is a tendency for the momentum to slow down. Team members may withdraw their energy and concentration as they begin to focus on other future projects. But recall the final stage in the creative process is not finalization/closure but rather evaluation. At the close of each creative outcome, virtual teams (and any team for that matter) need to take the time to evaluate and assess their efforts. Most of the virtual teams interviewed set aside time, sometimes formally, sometimes informally, to review what worked, and what could be improved on. Out of evaluation and assessment come seeds for growth and improvement leading to potentially even more

Table 7. Integrative model revisited

	Lipnack & Stamps (1997)	Gibson & Cohen (2003)	Duarte & Snyder (1999)	Nemiro
Design	**Purpose**	**Team Structure**	**Human Resource Policies**	**Design**
Conditions		- Context (design factor) - Shared Understanding (enabling condition) - Mutual Trust (enabling condition)	Organizational Culture	Climate - Connection - Conditions
Technology	Links	Technology (Design factor)	Electronic Collaboration and Communication Technology	Resources
Work processes	Time	- Processes (design factor) - Integration (enabling condition)	Standard Organizational and Team Processes	- Norms and Protocols - Continual Assessment
People	People	People (design factor)	- Training, Education and Development - Leadership Support - Team Leader Competencies - Team Member Competencies	Climate - Competencies

creative and successful future projects and ways of working collaboratively together.

The Integrative Model Revisited

In this section, the five building blocks for creativity in virtual teams are compared to the predictors for overall virtual team effectiveness. Table 7 relates the five building blocks presented in this chapter to the earlier integrative model of virtual team effectiveness predictors (refer back to Table 2).

What the table above reveals is that the five building blocks for creativity in virtual teams can be linked to indicators of virtual team effectiveness. Perhaps this is no surprise as how well a team performs is typically assessed by how a team manages the tasks it has to perform and how the relationships are managed. For example, Hackman's (1990) well-regarded model of group effectiveness included three dimensions of group effectiveness—acceptability of the team's task output to the customer, team member satisfaction, and capability of members to work together in the future. All three of these dimensions, which blend functional and interpersonal factors, must be present and positive in direction for effective team performance. The five building blocks for creativity in virtual teams led the virtual teams interviewed in this investigation not only to high levels of creativity, but also to better task performance and interpersonal relations among the team members as well.

Ultimately, the purpose of creativity in organizations (and the teams that make them up) is to create value for the company through growth and efficiency. For organizations, creativity is not viewed as some mysterious process possessed by only a few, eminent individuals, but rather an essential part of making products, services, and related processes new. Corporate creativity, as some have referred to, is viewed as vital to organizational survival and success (Robinson & Stern, 1998). It makes sense, then, that the dimensions needed for virtual team effectiveness and those needed for virtual team creativity might be more similar than initially anticipated.

LIMITATIONS

In evaluating the five building blocks model proposed in this chapter, it is necessary to consider the limitations of the investigation. In doing so, future researchers may consider adapting their research designs to avoid these limitations. A first limitation is that the data in this study are interview data. Individuals were asked to recall their creative experiences in virtual teams. Memory biases could have affected the accuracy of reporting, as recollections may have been clouded or incomplete. Particularly in studying the creative process of virtual teams, actual observations of the process while it is occurring would have added insight beyond the interview data. As virtual teams have the ability to document and archive their creative process, a review of these documents and electronic communications will be beneficial to future investigations into the creative process of virtual teams.

A second limitation concerns the assessment of high and low creative experiences. Stories of high and low creativity were shared by the team members themselves. There was, however, no validation of these high and low creativity stories with independent experts or outsiders to the team. In other words, would outsiders to the team agree that these experiences were indicative of high and low creativity? Only one team member mentioned, in his high creativity story that the client had also rated the project as highly innovative. External validation of the high and low creativity stories by outsiders to the team would be beneficial in future investigations.

CONCLUSION

The last decade has seen a tremendous increase in the interest level and use of virtual teams. Yet can all types of creative work be accomplished in virtual work structures? Although virtual teams are and will continue to be an important and necessary type of work arrangement, they are not best for all circumstances. There are situations in which virtual teams may be appropriate (for example, when work can be easily broken down and parceled out to team members) and situations in which they may not be appropriate (physical construction, geographically specific tasks, customer service). It will be the task of future researchers to determine the situations in which virtual teams are most appropriate, and when they are not.

Not only might the type of situation or work task need to be considered when deciding whether to start a virtual team or not, but also the types of individuals that will make up the team. Not all individuals "fit" with virtual work, desire to work virtually, or can be creative in this kind of working arrangement. From the interviews with virtual team members, emerged a portrayal of individuals that appear to be most appropriate for virtual work—individuals who need freedom, have a strong sense of autonomy, are self-disciplined and self-motivated, and have a strong drive to complete challenging tasks. Organizations, managers, and human resource professionals will need to incorporate into their selection procedures ways to ascertain what individuals are best suited for virtual work. Finding those individuals who are most appropriate for this new type of work design will be beneficial to employee job satisfaction and productivity and lead to higher levels of creativity as well. It is important to remember that for creative virtual work, the human side of teams does not go away, and can take on an even more important role than in face to face work.

The model outlined in this chapter is meant to assist virtual team leaders, managers, and team members in designing and sustaining a work environment that fosters creativity in the human side of virtual teams. By building and maintaining each of the five building blocks discussed in this chapter, virtual teams may move to higher levels of creativity and ultimately success.

REFERENCES

Amabile, T. M. (1988). A model of creativity and innovation in organizations. In B. M. Staw & L. L. Cummings (Eds.), *Research in organizational behavior* (Vol. 10, pp. 123-167). Greenwich, CT: JAI Press.

Amabile, T. M. (1990). Within you, without you: The social psychology of creativity and beyond. In M. A. Runco & R. S. Albert (Eds.), *Theories of creativity* (pp. 61-91). Newbury Park, CA: Sage Publications.

Amabile, T. M., & Gryskiewicz, S. S. (1987). *Creativity in the R&D laboratory* (Tech. Rep. No. 30). Greensboro, NC: Center for Creative Leadership.

Amabile, T. M., & Gryskiewicz, N. D. (1989). The creative environment scales: Work Environment Inventory. *Creativity Research Journal, 2,* 231-253.

Amabile, T. M., Conti, R., Coon, H., Lazenby, J., & Herron, M. (1996). Assessing the work environment for creativity. *Academy of Management Journal, 39*(5), 1154-1184.

Andrews, F. (1975). Social and psychological factors which influence the creative process. In I. Taylor & J. W. Getzels (Eds.), *Perspectives in creativity* (pp. 117-145). Chicago: Aldine Publishing Co.

Armstrong, D., & Cole, P. (1996). Managing distances and differences in geographically distributed work groups. In S. Jackson & M. Ruderman (Eds.), *Diversity in work teams*. Washington, DC: APA.

Baran, S., Zandan, P., & Vanston, J. H. (1986, January-February). How effectively are we managing innovation? *Research Management*, 23-25.

Beyerlein, M., & Harris, C. (2004). *Guiding the journey to collaborative work systems: A strategic design workbook*. San Francisco: Pfeiffer.

Daft, R. L., & Becker, S. W. (1978). *Innovation in organizations*. New York: Elsevier North-Holland, Inc.

Davidow, W., & Malone, M. (1992). *The virtual corporation*. New York: HarperCollins.

Duarte, D. L., & Snyder, N. T. (1999). *Mastering virtual teams: Strategies, tools, and techniques that succeed*. San Francisco: Jossey-Bass Publishers.

Ekvall, G. (1983). *Climate, structure, and innovativeness of organizations* (Report 1). Stockholm: Swedish Council for Management and Organizational Behavior.

Ekvall, G., Arvonen, J., & Waldenstrom-Lindblad, I. (1983). *Creative organizational climate: Construction and validation of a measuring instrument* (Report 2). Stockholm: Swedish Council for Management and Organizational Behavior.

Glaser, B., & Strauss, A. (1967). *The discovery of grounded theory*. Chicago: Aldine Publishing Company.

Gibson, C., & Cohen, S. (2003). *Virtual teams that work: Creating conditions for virtual team effectiveness*. San Francisco: Jossey-Bass.

Hackman, J. R. (1990). *Groups that work and those that don't: Creating conditions for effective teamwork*. San Francisco: Jossey-Bass.

Kanter, R. M. (1983). *The change masters*. New York: Simon & Schuster.

Kristof, A., Brown, K., Sims, H., & Smith, K. (1995). The virtual team: A case study and inductive model. In M. Beyerlein & D. Johnson (Eds.), *Advances in interdisciplinary studies of work teams: Knowledge teams the creative edge* (Vol. 2, pp. 229-253). Greenwich, CT: JAI Press.

Lipnack, J., & Stamps, J. (1997). *Virtual teams: Reaching across space, time and organizations with technology*. New York: John Wiley & Sons.

Lipnack, J., & Stamps, J. (2000). *Virtual teams: People working across boundaries with technology* (2nd ed.). New York: John Wiley & Sons.

Miles, M. B., & Huberman, A. M. (1994). *Qualitative data analysis* (2nd ed.). Thousand Oaks, CA: Sage Publications.

Mohrman, S. A., Cohen, S. G., & Mohrman, A. M. (1995). *Designing team-based organizations: New forms for knowledge work*. San Francisco: Jossey-Bass Publishers.

Nemiro, J. (1998). *Creativity in virtual teams*. Unpublished dissertation. Claremont Graduate University.

Nemiro, J. (2004). *Creativity in virtual teams: Key components for success*. San Francisco: Pfeiffer.

Pelz, D. C., & Andrews, F. M. (1966). *Scientists in organizations*. New York: John Wiley & Sons.

Robinson, A., & Stern, S. (1998). *Corporate creativity: How innovation and improvement actually happen*. San Francisco: Berrett-Koehler.

Rogers, C. (1954). Towards a theory of creativity. *ETC: A Review of General Semantics, 11*, 249-260.

Runco, M. A. (1994). Creativity and its discontents. In M. P. Shaw & M. A. Runco (Eds.), *Creativity and affect*. Norwood, NJ: Ablex.

Runco, M. A. (1995). The creativity and job satisfaction of artists in organizations. *Empirical Studies of the Arts, 13*, 39-45.

Seidman, I. E. (1991). *Interviewing as qualitative research.* Columbia University, NY: Teachers College Press.

Steiner, G. (1965). *The creative organization.* Chicago: University of Chicago Press.

Strauss, A., & Corbin, J. (1990). *Basics of qualitative research.* Newbury Park, CA: Sage Publications.

VanGundy, A. (1987). Organizational creativity and innovation. In S. G. Isaksen (Ed.), *Frontiers of creativity research: Beyond the basics* (pp. 358-379). Buffalo, NY: Bearly Limited.

West, M. A. (1990). The social psychology of innovation in groups. In M. A. West & L. Farr (Eds.), *Innovation and creativity at work* (pp. 309-322). New York: John Wiley & Sons.

Section II
Tales: From the Battlefield of Virtual Team Practice

Chapter VI
Fostering Creativity in Global Virtual Teams:
Conversations with Team Leaders

Margaret Oertig
University of Applied Sciences of Northwest Switzerland, Switzerland

Thomas Buergi
University of Applied Sciences of Northwest Switzerland, Switzerland

ABSTRACT

This chapter presents insights from conversations with global team leaders on how to foster creativity in global virtual project teams in the field of product development. It shows how the leaders pay attention to team formation and managing the group dynamics in order to create a climate in which creativity will flourish. They then harness creativity by balancing the roles of motivating their team members in order to encourage fresh thinking and "putting on the brakes" where necessary in order to create something both new and viable. In particular, risk-averse team members are encouraged to be matter-of-fact about risk, making risk evaluation an intrinsic part of idea generation.

INTRODUCTION

In this chapter we consider the conditions and practices which impact on the creative performance of virtual teams in the field of product development. We present the perspectives of seven experienced team leaders at ABC, a multinational blue chip company with headquarters in Switzerland. These insights emerged from a series of interviews conducted during a qualitative study investigating the challenges arising from managing virtual project teams. ABC is a pseudonym, referring to a knowledge based technology intensive industry with a long development cycle and a high level of risk and costs during the research process. The stated goal of the project management division of ABC is "to develop innovative products with strongly perceived differentiation and optimal value, according to global plans, in the shortest time possible, and at adequate cost." Basadur's (2004) description of effective organizations would apply to this organization, where adaptability entails *"deliberate discontent—discovering new problems to solve, finding new things to do and adapting new technologies and methods before anyone else"* (p. 104).

Working in geographically distributed project teams within a matrix organisation is the norm at ABC. At any given time there are 50-80 product development projects underway, each with a project leader, a project manager and a core of five to eight project team representatives from various functional areas, for example, research, technical, development, and marketing functions—the key functions are subdivided into more detailed roles which are not specifically named here, in order to protect the anonymity of the company. A project typically lasts three to five years, although some continue after a product is on the market. In addition to the core team, up to 20 others can join the team permanently or temporarily at various stages over this period to advise on specific issues. Project teams experience significant time pressure during product development. Line functions provide the staff and budget and have authority on the aspects of the project related to their functional expertise. Many of the core project team representatives also lead a subteam in their own field or function, and these are also geographically distributed.

The project leader and project manager are located in Switzerland or the USA, and tend not to be based in the same location. The secretary of the company's Innovation Board (which makes the strategic decisions as to which projects to prioritise in the company's portfolio) described the differentiation of their roles as follows:

The difference is that the project leader leads the team, representing the team and the project to top management and is responsible for the value of the project and the project strategy. The project

manager is his or her assistant and responsible for all logistics, operational issues, doing the agendas, writing the minutes, feeding the project planning system, checking the budget, resources, and so on. So the project manager is like the chief operating officer (COO) of a project, while the project leader is the CEO of the project, the strategic lead.

As CEOs of their project, the project leaders have to be highly qualified and have extensive experience leading virtual project teams in a global matrix organization. The project leader job description, made available to us, indicates that they are required to have a PhD or an MBA and 5 years of cross-functional leadership experience. It also explicitly states the expectation that they will be creative. They are described as thought leaders who are expected to push themselves and others to see new ways of achieving results. They are required to create systems and processes to exploit the organization's competitive advantages. They should have the expertise to facilitate and optimize the contribution of team members as individuals and as members of a cohesive team. Finally, they are expected to create new approaches by considering input, concepts, and experiences from across the organization. This chapter will illustrate how they go about fulfilling some of these expectations.

Our research originally had two aims. The first was to discover what the project leadership of ABC perceived as the main challenges arising from managing international teams working in geographically distributed locations, and secondly, how they managed these challenges. The research was qualitative and exploratory, taking the form of inductive thematic analysis. One-hour interviews were conducted face-to-face in the interviewees' offices in Switzerland and the USA, with six project leaders, six project managers and two ex-project leaders (who have now been promoted to be product area heads). Background interviews were also conducted with three members of senior management responsible for strategic planning, innovation management and executive information systems. 10 interviewees were based in Switzerland and seven in the USA. The nationalities of the interviewees were as follows: three U.S. Americans, four British, four Swiss, three German, one French, one French-Canadian, and one Japanese. Nine interviewees were male and eight were female.

Three major themes emerged as most significant, affecting all aspects of the project management task: the leadership challenge, virtual aspects of communication and developing trust. A further four subthemes were identified, of specific challenges to be managed: managing the task, people, language, and cultural issues as well as managing the matrix as a whole. These themes were relevant to all aspects of the teams' work, including routine tasks. A more detailed account of these general themes can be read elsewhere (Oertig & Buergi, 2006). This chapter homes in on insights which emerged from our data regarding how the project leadership fosters the team's creativity through finding new ways of working in their field. We draw on interviews with four of the project leaders, one project manager and one product area head (an ex-project leader) whose comments illustrate this best. Table 1 details each of the people in conversation.

BACKGROUND

Transnational teams today encourage cohesiveness within a company operating worldwide (Schneider & Barsoux, 2003), contributing to the organization's "glue technology" (Evans, 1992). As team members cannot be in many places at the same time, they are increasingly working virtually. The degree of virtuality of a team can be defined in various ways. Zigurs (2003, p. 340) suggests that the key factors are related to dispersion on various levels—geographical organizational temporal and cultural. The teams investigated at ABC fulfill all the categories except organizational dispersion. Martins, Gilson and Maynard (2004, p. 808) reviewed 93 empirical articles in peer-reviewed journals and subsequently defined virtual teams as teams where members use technology to varying degrees in working across location, temporal and relational boundaries to accomplish an interdependent task. They suggest that while early definitions of virtual teams sought to contrast virtual and face-to-face teams, recent definitions have instead focused on a team's extent of virtualness, on a continuum between purely face-to-face and purely virtual teams (Gilson & Maynard, 2004, p. 807; see also Rogers Leenders, Jan Kratzer & Jo van Engelen, "Media Ensembles and New Product Development Team Creativity: A Tree-Based Exploration Model," Chapter IV in this book). We consider a key impact of degrees

Table 1. Profiles of people in conversation

Name	Role	Country of origin	Current workplace
Jim	Product Area Head (Ex-Project Leader)	USA	USA
Christoph	Project Leader	Switzerland	Switzerland
Ronnie	Project Manager	USA	USA
Peter	Project Leader	UK	Switzerland
Martine	Project Leader	France	Switzerland
Chantal	Project Leader	Canada	Switzerland

of virtualness to be the degree of media richness which results from it (Martins et al., 2004). E-mail is a relatively impoverished medium of communication compared with telephoning, where voice features are added, such as tone of voice, hesitation, and degree of emphasis. Video conferencing is higher still in media richness, with both voice and body language cues. Our interviewees communicate intensively by e-mail, but also have a monthly video conference and regular telephone conferences as needed. Face-to-face meetings occur on average once a year, but more frequently in the case of heavy-weight teams on high priority projects. It is significant that the interviewees do not emphasize the fact that most of their communication is mediated by technology, seeing this as the norm. Most of them have had no experience of project management in a colocated team. Many of the interactions described next took place during their collective monthly video conference or telephone conference.

A significant goal for these teams is to be creative by finding new ways of doing things in order to develop products with a competitive edge. Kahn (1990) defines engagement in creative processes as team members behaviorally, cognitively, and emotionally attempting new things or new ways of going about their work. This might include finding better or unique approaches to a problem or seeking out novel ways of performing a task. Team members have a choice as to whether or not to engage in creative processes (Kahn, 1990, Drazin, Glynn, & Kazanjian, 1999). Gilson & Shalley (2004, p. 455) reported that the more team members who believed their job required creativity, the more frequently the team would engage in creative processes. This may have an influence on the way our interviewees exercise creativity, given their job descriptions mentioned above.

Basadur (2004, p. 118) comments that problem solving requires the creativity of all the organization's members across multiple disciplines. In his exploration of creative idea generation and creative outcomes, Egan (2005, p. 208) points out

that creative ideas cannot be generated without the benefit of contextual influences, including team member interactions and team diversity. Bell and Kozlowski (2002, p. 25) suggest that the spatial distance and use of technology impede the two primary leadership functions of performance and team development and that it is difficult for leaders to perform typical mentoring, coaching and developmental functions. They argue that the team members are expected to have the technical knowledge, skills and abilities to be able to contribute to team effectiveness, with the result that leaders can delegate aspects of these functions to the team itself and make it more of a self-managing team (Bell & Kozlowski, 2002, p. 26). Our observation from our interview data is that most team leaders do not consider knowledge and skills among team members as a guarantee that communication processes will automatically ensue that are helpful for problem solving and creative thinking. With one exception (which is described below), the team leaders describe how they take a very central and directive role, creating conditions and facilitating communication so that the latent knowledge and skills within the team can be communicated and fed into the process of exploring new ways of doing things.

Our focus in this chapter is on the specific practices of the team leaders which help creativity to flourish, including how team leaders manage the contextual influences of such a complex setting, that is, a matrix setting involving participants working at various site locations around the world, using English as a lingua franca. We therefore start by describing how the team leaders form their team and deal with group dynamics, which is impacted by personality, job function, language, and culture. We then go on to show how leaders strive to harness creativity, balancing vision with realism as the team looks for unique solutions to problems. Each topic presented is illustrated with interview quotes, giving insights into the personal experiences and perspectives of the leaders themselves. It is to be hoped that the experience shared here can be of use to others working in a similar setting.

FORMING THE TEAM

We first draw attention to the way the team is formed, as this builds a foundation for its creative processes, which can then enhance the potential for creative and innovative outcomes (Gilson & Shalley, 2004). As mentioned, each project team has representatives from a range of key functions at various stages of the development process. The role of the project team as described by Jim, an American product area head based in the USA, is to be the "collector and distiller of information." It is responsible for developing strategies and recommendations to present to the Innovation Board from across the organisation world-wide. Jim pointed out the dilemma that working virtually in the matrix setting, project team leaders in the company have no direct authority over team members, because they report to their line manager rather than the project leader. He described the challenge as follows:

Project leaders have to influence people that do not report to them in such a way that they will perform and deliver, but they have no real authority over them.

Most of the contact is collective contact by telephone, video conference, or e-mail communication. That just makes it more difficult to establish that role, a cloak of authority without actual authority.

He pointed out that, in virtual communication the possibility of misunderstanding and disagreement was great, and emphasized the importance of meeting at the outset to define "the rules of engagement, the team operating guidelines," which were formalized in a face-to-face meeting and would become the basis for how the team interacted in teleconferences, video conferences,

and e-mail. It was crucial to take the limitations of working virtually into account.

It becomes very difficult to actually fulfill those team operating guidelines because you are not communicating face to face frequently enough. You are limited by the teleconference or the video conference, so it becomes difficult to be successful in getting people to trust you and teams to work in a cohesive way. Difficult doesn't mean impossible. When I think of the people who are the best project leaders, they are the ones who acknowledge and recognize these limitations and the teams have discussions about them. So you set up rules within these limitations and this is how you operate.

He summarized the pay-off of increased awareness as follows:

I think that paying attention to how you are performing with each other is critical to success in a matrix environment. And it's also trust-building.

Jim's comments reflect to some extent the findings of Jarvenpaa and Leidner (1998) who found that the high performing teams they studied exhibited a high level of trusting behavior which may have taken the form of swift, depersonalized, action-based trust (see also Meyerson, Weick, & Kramer, 1996) combined with explicit verbal statements about commitment, support and excitement.

In addition to defining the rules of engagement and discussing limitations with the whole team, Jim stressed the importance of keeping in touch with important individuals:

Even though most of your encounters collectively are video conferences, it is important for project leaders to have one on one contact with key players, even if the basis of the discussion is contrived or informal. It's relationship building and relationship maintenance. It's important to do that because you're so dependent on people who you, again, have no authority over. So you have to bring them in and make them stay.

We see this combination of defining team operating guidelines and building relationships as an important factor in helping the team to gel and become effective in its subsequent creative tasks.

GROUP DYNAMICS

The practice of group creativity does not take place in a vacuum. The atmosphere in the group plays a part as do the roles taken by the individual group members. For many, feeling comfortable is crucial to forming and expressing new ideas. The team composition and individual qualities of team members are factors influencing how well the team functions. Christoph, a Swiss project leader based in Switzerland saw being "team players" as more important than technical brilliance:

I had a very good team for 5 years, and if you would look individually, probably none of the people were individually absolutely outstanding, the best people we had in the organization technically for doing that job. They were very good people but they were all willing to work together and that made it one of the best teams. If I have three or four individualists who may be technically superior but they are not willing to work together, I probably have a weaker team at the end, and I have a poorer outcome.

Ronnie, an American project manager based in the USA described what he considered to be an unusual team, which was together for two years and worked very creatively:

People would argue and discuss with each other like a brother and sister fighting or kids arguing

with the parents, something like that. So there was this very unique dynamic, you could see it, you could feel it. You could really feel you were part of the team.

He put the unusual richness of perspectives down to the team's diversity, not least as having people with decades of experience in the team:

In terms of the demographics we had a spread of team members of different ages, different views, of different levels of experience. I think that is missing today. It's really rare that you see people around here in their 50s or early 60s still walking around.

In view of the fact that the composition of the team had a significant impact on the dynamics, project leaders were asked whether they could choose their team members. Their answers reflected a high degree of realism and willingness to compromise, showing that it is not easy to obtain ideal team members. Jim commented that if he lost an important team member he might be able to request a "crack person" as a replacement. However, as other interviewees also pointed out, he said that there were too many project teams who naturally all wanted "the best people", and it was difficult to even keep an overview of who the best people were in such a large organization. Another approach was to understand the constraints of the line functions that provided the team member, take the person offered and only have them replaced if they proved to be unsuitable. Jim explained this as follows:

What you can do at any point in time is try to work with that person to make sure they understand what their responsibilities are and that they have to deliver. If that doesn't work over a period of time, then certainly, you get in touch with their manager or the line function head, and you say, "This is not working, and I would really like someone else." So you can select your team member by getting rid of them, if you see what I'm saying. But again, this depends on the project. The line function has a limited number of people, some of whom are new, and they have a great load that they have to accommodate. You have to be pragmatic about what you can expect to get and what you can deliver. There's ideal visions and then there's working necessity.

Christoph also expressed the importance of making the best of the situation with less than perfect team members:

And of course you also try to rather find a way to integrate the person in the team than just say "Okay, I want to have him replaced", because most of the time you get someone else, and most of us are not perfect and you get some positive and negative sides anyhow. The next one will just be different, so you will have probably different strengths and weaknesses.

How Long Members Have Known Each Other

Another important factor in relation to group dynamics is how long the team members have been working together. In the literature a moderate amount of organizational tenure has been suggested as ideal for employees to engage in creative processes (Gilson & Shalley, 2004). Project leaders were also asked how important they thought it was that the team is together for a long time. Their answers varied. Ronnie stressed the importance of achieving a balance when bringing in new people and thought newcomers to the company needed time to learn about the project processes in order to apply learning to the next stage of the project:

The more you practice, the better you get. If people have no internal network and no project history, they are really behind. You've really got

to work on something like that much more vigorously with a new person than with someone who's been with the company for 5 years or so. When you bring a group of people together, they've got to learn about each other, on the personal level, then they've got to learn the processes, and implement them, and the more you practice the better you get. The oral history of the project is invaluable. If I've been on a team with someone for two or three years, I can come to you and say, 'remember two years ago when we did this and that?' and, boom, you're there. Whereas if you're just rotated in, you may or may not have read up on that, you may have no idea what I'm talking about. So a group of people who've gone through the project, they've resolved the problems, they know the obstacles, it's all in your memory, so if you want to apply learning from that to the next stage it's kind of there.

Peter, a British project leader based in Switzerland, did not find how long team members had known each other particularly significant:

If someone's competent and has a personality that's not getting in the way, then it shouldn't really matter in a pure professional sense. People recently joined my team. They'd come from another company, but their being new didn't impact. A couple of them were very knowledgeable, which was great. They just jumped straight in—smart people—picked up the issues, no problem.

It was Peter's opinion that if people needed a long time to get to know others, they should not be in project work:

Well, in project teams, as far as I'm concerned, you can't sit quiet. The person sitting at the table is the functional representative for their function in that project. 'You are the specialist on this issue'. And so everybody has to have an audible voice at the table. Otherwise they shouldn't be there.

However, having said this, Peter later reported that in practice, he took action to encourage quiet team members with new ideas to speak up, as will be shown.

Christoph found that professional team building exercises helped a lot to build a team culture:

It helps people to open up and express a little bit, how they feel in the team, what is difficult for them, what they enjoy in a team, what they don't enjoy. The problem here is that when you build a new team, you should start with that. We usually wait until the team is in such deep trouble (laughs) that someone says, "Now, listen, we have to DO something."

Impact of Personality and Functional Roles

Team leaders also reported that it was important to consider the impact of personality and functional roles on group dynamics. Once the team had formed, attention had to be paid to how the members interacted. Those leaders who thought it was important for team members to stay together for a while usually related this to the need to get to know the other members, work with their personality styles and encourage their contributions. Christoph talked of how introverted team members might have a lot to contribute, but needed to get to know the team at a face to face meeting before they could express the communication challenge they faced:

Typically, in a face to face meeting where you start understanding that person, they are able to express themselves and say, "It costs me. I just can't jump in and speak, if I always have these people who talk all the time. I just wanted to say something, but I need more than two seconds of silence to start my sentence." And if the others start realizing that, they're willing to give way. But it needs the whole team who helps, and someone who says,

"Listen, this person has not been speaking, and what do you think about it? Now everyone else shut up, and you listen to him."

Christoph estimated that a team had to have been together for at least a year for this kind of open communication to be possible. We note in this respect that team building with an outside facilitator at a later stage (in addition to the classic initial team building to help the team form) could be fruitful to help members air issues which had arisen over the year.

As shown above, Christoph valued having the team together for as long as possible and saw the time factor as important to help the team itself take responsibility for its group dynamics issues. Peter took the approach that new members were a fact of life and always welcome, if they could "jump right in". For him it was the leader's task (rather than the task of the whole team) to use his or her interpersonal skills to facilitate the sharing of ideas, in particular if someone in the team always thought they had the right answer and sounded very confident and knowledgeable:

If that person's on a roll, you have to interject, "Okay, thanks. Got your point. Thanks very much. So, Sam, what do you reckon about this?" You just have to be very directive.

He described how he would have to make sure that the right people were coming forward with their ideas:

I would say to the under-talkative person: "I know you may not feel too comfortable sometimes but you've got a lot to contribute, I'd really like you to do that, because I'd like the team to hear what you've got to say." Often they're not permanent members of the team, but when they come along, I say, "I'd like you to talk." I want them to, actually, for their own development.

Peter also described the role he played as a mediator between specialists in different functional areas who did not understand each other's language:

The essence of a team, of a project team whether it's national or international, is clear communication across all of the functions. If that's not there, then you don't have an effective team, and effective has to be measured upon getting a product to market. And you have to have clear communication between the technical group and the marketing group and often those two don't understand each other's language at all. There are certain traits, Technical will ask: "How many widgets do you need?" Marketing will answer: "I don't know, just a couple of lorry loads, enough to fill the shop shelf." So they are talking different languages. This is where I come in, and try and find something they will both understand … I try and explain why someone needs something and then break it down into smaller chunks, because often they'll throw out a demand which is misunderstood—it's all in acronyms, or it's just the style.

Impact of Language and Culture

Language and cultural differences were a further key factor. Bell and Kozlowski (2002, p. 37) report that the difference in values across cultures may require leaders to tailor their actions to coincide with a particular team member's orientation. Several interviewees referred to the need to pay attention to different ways of communicating and working in different cultures and at different site locations. Peter sometimes had to remind team members that they should not be country-bound:

You may occasionally get someone saying "I do it like this in the U.S." But that's not so much necessarily a cultural thing. It's just that they've forgotten that they're working in a global set up. And they say: "Over here we do it this way," and I say, "I don't mind where you're sitting, whether

it's Timbuktu, irrespective, we're working as a global team." And communicating that takes a while. I am just reminding them that I don't want any geographic arguments.

Graen and Wakabayashi (1994) suggest that leaders need to implement a leadership structure that builds a unique or "third" culture. Ronnie describes global team members as "bridge people", possibly functioning in the mode of a "third culture" (this concept is also discussed in this book, Chapter VII, "Rethinking Virtual Teams for Streamlined Development" by Larsson et al.).

Most international team members are steeped in a global mentality, and tend not to be locked into a "This is the way we do it, so tough!" way of thinking. If someone is going to be promoted to be a global team representative, they look for people who can bridge the language and culture gap.

Martine, a French project leader based in Switzerland, described how she had bridged the gap by taking a different approach in communication with her Japanese team members:

We started to have additional teleconferences where they tried to explain things to me. I asked questions. I said, "We don't understand. Why do you need to do it this way?" And they tried to explain the cultural subtleties of why they had to do it that way. And what would be the consequences if they were not doing it this way. So they took the time to brief me and then I explained that to our other colleagues.

Jim described it as a challenge to get accurate information when communicating by video conference with the Japanese side. He used the following strategy to clarify what was agreed in the meeting:

I've found the best way to move towards understanding and agreement is to have someone from the Japanese side summarize in English what was agreed to. And send that to us as a draft. So, rather than my summarizing something as a draft, I have someone from their side summaries it as a draft. Generally it's been my experience, if they write something they're agreeing to, then that is closer at least to an agreement and understanding. Although it is often amazing that what is written bears little relationship to what was actually discussed and agreed to. So it's an eliminative process.

The interviewer asked Jim whether his Japanese colleagues omitted details when summarizing, or added new points. His reply was as follows:

No. Actually they're pretty comprehensive. I've been amazed and pleased, often, where there will be a summary which will be reasonably accurate as to a complex issue, what was discussed ... There will be a clarification of their position which was not communicated well verbally but is communicated much better in writing, particularly after a meeting, where there is the protocol of who speaks and when they speak and then there's the caution which many Japanese have, of speaking the language because they don't feel they speak English well.

HOW CREATIVITY IS HARNESSED

The interview extracts above show how the project leaders find it important to actively foster a creative team climate by paying attention to the team's conversation dynamics over time, with particular regard to the personalities, functional, and national cultures of team members. This may involve encouraging people to speak up or be quiet, as described above by Christoph and Peter, or getting clarity across cultures as described by

Martine and Jim. We see these aspects of leadership as prerequisites for the sharing of creative ideas. In this section, we show more specifically how the leaders balance the role of "motivator" to encourage fresh thinking leading to a competitive edge with "putting on the brakes" if team members get carried away with their vision. We refer to their style of facilitation as "harnessing" in the sense of a means of directing which involves both exploiting the power of a group and keeping it in check (see www.wordreference.com/definition/harness). Creative thinking needs to be harnessed in order to create something both new and viable. The following comments from Chantal, Jim and Peter illustrate this point.

Chantal is a French Canadian project leader responsible for two projects, one of which is in the early research stage, involving mainly technical team members, and the other for a product on the market, with mainly marketing team members. She described the impact of personality on brainstorming, and how she plays the extrovert with the more introverted research team:

So if the personalities of the people are more introverted, I say:

"What are we doing next?"

Silence.

"Come on guys, what are the challenges?"

Silence.

I have to be the one that pushes; I have to be the one that says, "Yes maybe it's possible, you know, we have to see outside the boundary." And with the extrovert team I have to moderate that. So it just depends. You have to adapt to the members of your team.

She described her role with the more research-focused team as "the motivator" and compared it to her approach with the extroverted marketing-focused team. There she had to play the introvert and "plead rationality":

My role in the product that is marketed is more "Whoa, whoa ..." I'm more like the peace-keeper.

Jim took this idea of the different dynamics further, and described a variety of approaches within teams regarding how people from different functional areas provide their understanding of the viability of the project:

Some people, like the marketing side for instance, will be more into championship, while the technical development side will be more into the absolute facts about the material.

He saw it as important that the project team leader helped the team to define reality, rather than just aim for success:

The role of a project team in the project management function is not to be the champion of the success of the project. Many times, people think that their role is to make the project successful. And while ultimately we all want that to occur, in fact the role is to define what is reality, in our best understanding, and then what are our best options based on that reality. And then we move ahead to provide the best opportunity. If that reality tells us that the best answer is a negative answer, then we must inform our management that this is the reality, our options are limited and the option for success is no longer viable and this option, the reduced option or failure option is the only way to go.

He saw the project leader as playing a crucial role in helping push the team towards developing objectivity:

You have this group of people based around the world that are trying to fulfill this objective of defining reality and defining options. And either you enter into providing information factually, or you color it in terms of where you want to go, which is the championship approach. And I think one of the hard things to do is to ensure that there is a very objective view and that objective view is maintained, and I think it is an important role of project management to ensure that objectivity, to know when to ask the next question: 'Is this your extrapolation of what you know or is this just the limits of what you know?' Just to make sure that it's focused to push people away from championship but to push them towards being objective viewers of what could be, as opposed to wide-eyed visionaries of what could be. Doing that in virtual settings is very, very hard.

Jim went on to refer to cross-functional aspects of team conversations, describing how he would like technical people to contribute more in general discussions to find new ways of solving problems:

In a good functioning team with its virtual dynamic everyone takes part. Technical people are as smart as the others. They're just responsible for different things. They can apply those thinking skills to a complex question, whether it's associated with a marketing dynamic, or it's associated with a technical dynamic. Some people maybe have some specialized knowledge, but whether you have the specialized knowledge or not, the rational thinking that you apply to a problem in terms of putting pieces together and then leaping into the next decision, we all have that ability.

Peter saw the challenge of fighting against the temptation of continuing to do things as they were done before:

The norm people go for is, "If it ain't broke, don't fix it, don't change it," They will do it the way they did it before. But we're always seeking a competitive edge. And sometimes you have to think, "Well I know we've done it that way," and then you do it a different way, to show a differentiation, a uniqueness.

He found it important to help technical people to express their concerns about the risks involved in a course of action, in particular when looking at something that has never been looked at before:

They're generally more limited in their scope of thinking because they're working to strict guidelines. "It says this, you need to do this, you're not allowed to do that and you can't promote this." They're very structured and strict, and when you get into "Well I know it says that but we're looking beyond that, because in fact what we're looking at is a scope that has never been looked at before, because we're first in the class, because we're new." Technical people, it's the technical mind. They're not risk takers at all. It's lovely if a technical person says, "You know I've thought about x ... if we did this beforehand ... " which happened this week. Someone saved us a significant amount of time. So I said to this gentleman, "Thanks very much for that suggestion, you've just saved us. Yes there's a risk to it, there's a risk to everything." So I asked him to communicate that. Put down what the risks are, so we know what the trade-off is. So that was lovely to see.

In referring to the trade-off, Peter encouraged people to be matter-of-fact about risk, instead of allowing it to block them in their thinking. He described risk evaluation as a central part of the job of the project team:

If I did this and went down this avenue, what's the risk and what's the benefit? If I went down another one, what's the risk what's the benefit? Weigh it up, come to a decision. That's what our job is to do. And those risks are not just from the techni-

cal perspective, it's the marketing opportunities. What else is happening in the market place? What competitors might be out in the meantime? So it's weighing all of those up.

Another point raised by Peter was how to move forward when the team was in new territory and the project leader knew less about the subject than some of its members:

Part of my rationale weighing something up is "How does this decision impact the other activities that we've got?" And so if you've got two specialists arguing about, "I think we need to do this, that and the other," and you don't know what they're talking about, try and say, "What's the meaning of that? For a statistical analysis, do we take means, mediums, modes or whatever? What's the impact? If we did it this way, what does it mean? What are our competitors doing? How do they analyze the data?" Because ultimately we are going to be asked to compare, "How are you stacked up? What did they do? What method did they use?"

In this way he turned the team's attention to the focus on the consequences of the action in the market place rather than how knowledgeable or authoritative the speakers were perceived to be.

CONCLUSION

The objective of this chapter was to provide perspectives from experienced global project team leaders on the conditions and practices which impacted on the creative performance of their virtual teams. Their reflections lead us to the following conclusions:

Firstly, we note that team leaders working in complex settings such as a global, virtual matrix organization are performing a balancing act requiring great skill and a high degree of realism as they build their team. Although they expressed their views about ideal team members and conditions, for example, having diverse team members with a richness of perspectives and experiences who are excellent team players and good communicators, working together for a long time in the same team, they assume that the reality will be different. They are very proactive in developing strategies to manage the less-than-perfect situation in a virtual context in which they have ever-changing teams with inexperienced or challenging team members. Team-building, communicating ground rules, maintaining face to face contact with key players, working with weaker members, sometimes "giving them back" to the line function, are all steps taken to facilitate the forming of an effective team.

Secondly, we conclude that the group dynamic process is addressed by these leaders on an ongoing basis, whenever communication is taking place. Considerations of communication styles related to personality, job function, language, and culture are not just a one-off team building topic, but have to be given constant attention. In order to develop new ideas, people have to be thoroughly informed about the project status from the point of view of different line functions and site locations. Leaders act as facilitators, mediators and bridge people, making technical and marketing people more understandable to each other (Peter). They take responsibility for the gap in their understanding of their Japanese colleagues and apply techniques such as asking open questions to get clarity regarding the rationale for Japanese processes (Martine) and to encourage Japanese colleagues to reveal their true thinking after a meeting (Jim).

With regard to managing group dynamics, we note an interesting variation in attitude between Christoph and Peter. Christoph hopes to have a team together for a long time and sees it as the job of the whole team over time to manage its personalities and dynamic processes over time.

Peter does not think it should be necessary to have the team together for a long time, and takes a more hands-on role himself in managing the team dynamics. This topic related to leadership styles may be of increasing significance given the greater mobility and ever-changing team composition in multinational companies in Europe in the 21st century.

Thirdly, and most central to fostering creativity, team leaders have to harness the creative thinking of the team. Encouraging some team members to "think beyond the boundary" (Chantal) while "restraining the wide-eyed visionaries" (Jim) involves a balancing act. Success is not the only option. As Jim points out, a "reduced option" or "failure option" may on occasions be the only objective view. Peter's technique is to use well-constructed questions to open up the discussion and encourage risk-averse specialists to verbalize the risks and assess them in relation to the benefits. In this way they make explicit what might otherwise be unspoken barriers to taking their thinking further in a new direction. At the same time, he asks those strongly advocating new ideas some questions to help them examine the implications of implementation in the marketplace. Basadur (2004, p. 106) describes how leaders can help others to execute the basic creative thinking skills of deferring judgment, keeping an open mind and thinking divergently. When confronted with new ideas, people are often prematurely critical, shutting down the flow of productive thinking. He advises that leaders can model open-minded thinking and reinforce training in behaviors to separate idea generation from evaluation through deferral of judgment (Basadur, 2004, p. 108). It would appear that, in contrast, Peter's team members learn to expect that while final judgment will be deferred, risk evaluation will be part of idea generation, and that this provides the safety net they need to verbalize their creative ideas.

We see future research possibilities in an in-depth exploration of the conversational dynamics which help foster creative thinking in successful virtual teams. We see a particular need to address the communication challenges which have to be managed due to the range of personality types and functional roles represented, with the result that some specialists feel less knowledgeable or even intimidated by the communicative ability of others. This chapter has highlighted the importance of asking well-constructed, open questions to encourage idea generation, and at the same time encouraging concern about the risks involved to be verbalized. We believe it would be useful to make a more detailed study of the range of approaches and facilitation techniques used by successful teams and their leaders. This will help to elicit crucial information and explore new ways of doing things, in turn leading to higher creativity and new products with a competitive edge.

ACKNOWLEDGMENT

Our grateful thanks go to the senior management of ABC for their kind permission to conduct this research, as well as to the interviewees in Project Management who generously shared their expertise with us.

REFERENCES

Basadur, M. (2004). Leading others to think innovatively together: Creative leadership. *The Leadership Quarterly, 15*, 103-121.

Bell, B. S. (2002). A typology of virtual teams. Implications for effective leadership. *Group & Organization Management, 27*(1), 14-19.

Drazin, R., Glynn, M. A., & Kazanjian, R. K. (1999). Multilevel theorizing about creativity in organizations: A sensemaking perspective. *Academy of Management Review, 24*(2), 286-307.

Egan, T. E. (2005). Creativity in the context of team diversity: Team Leader Perspectives. *Advances in Developing Human Resources, 7*(2), 207-225.

Evans, P. (1992). Management development as glue technology. *Human Resource Planning, 15*(1), 85-106.

Gilson, L.L., & Shalley, C. E. (2004). A little creativity goes a long way: an examination of teams' engagement in creative processes. *Journal of Management, 30*(4), 453-470.

Graen, G. B., & Wakabayashi, M. (1994). Cross-cultural leadership-making: Bridging American and Japanese diversity for team advantage. In H. C. Triandis, M. D. Dunnette, & L. M. Hough (Eds.), *Handbook of industrial and organizational psychology* (Vol. 4, pp. 415-446). New York: Consulting Psychologist Press.

Jarvenpaa, S. L., Knoll, K., & Leidner, D. E. (1998). Is anybody out there? Antecedents of trust in global virtual teams. *Journal of Management Information Systems, 14*, 29-64.

Kahn, W. A. (1990). Psychological conditions of personal engagement and disengagement at work. *Academy of Management Journal, 33*, 692-724.

Martins, L. L., Gilson, L. L. & Travis Maynard, M. (2004). Virtual teams: What do we know and where do we go from here? *Journal of Management, 30*(6), 805-835.

Meyerson, D., Weick, K. E., & Kramer, R. M. (1996). Swift trust and temporary groups. In R. M. Kramer & T. R. Tyler (Eds.), *Trust in organizations: Frontiers of theory and research* (pp. 166-195). Thousand Oaks, CA: Sage Publications.

Oertig, M., & Buergi, T. (2006). The challenges of managing cross-cultural virtual project teams. *Team Performance Management, 12*(1-2), 23-30.

Schneider, S. C., & Barsoux, J. (2003). *Managing across cultures*. Harlow, Essex: Pearson.

Zigurs, I. (2003). Leadership in virtual teams: oxymoron or opportunity. *Organizational Dynamics, 31*(4), 339-351.

Chapter VII
Rethinking Virtual Teams for Streamlined Development

Andreas Larsson
Luleå University of Technology, Sweden

Tobias Larsson
Luleå University of Technology, Sweden

Nicklas Bylund
Volvo Car Corporation, Sweden

Ola Isaksson
Volvo Aero Corporation, Sweden

ABSTRACT

Much of the research on creative teams tends to focus mainly on relatively small teams working in the fuzzy front-end of product development. In this chapter, we bring a complementary perspective from an industry context where creativity is often perceived as risky business—yet a precondition for success. Here, we focus closely on people and teams that might not usually describe their own work to be of a primarily 'creative' nature, and that currently work under circumstances where traditional approaches for enhancing creativity might no longer be applicable. Drawing from experiences in automotive and aerospace development, we argue that it is time to radically progress our current understanding of how creativity could be introduced in organizations where factors like legal demands and contractual agreements severely restrict 'outside-the-box' thinking, and where well-known creativity enablers such as trust, shared goals, and shared culture are becoming increasingly difficult to accomplish.

INTRODUCTION

The motivation for this chapter is to question, or at least provide a reality check on some of the 'quick fix recipes' for virtual team creativity that often seem to take a rather idealized perspective on how creativity might be infused in geographically dispersed development teams. Our stance towards creativity techniques is generally positive. Not surprisingly, we too believe that creativity is a crucial building block of successful product development in just about any industry context. However, much of the research on creative teams tends to focus mainly on relatively small teams working in the very front-end of product development, such as in the initial idea generation phase of a consumer electronics project. If anything, such development projects explicitly target the creative aspects of collaboration to showcase innovative concepts for a future market. We bring a complementary perspective from an industry context where creativity is often perceived as risky business—yet a precondition for success.

Consequently, we direct our focus to what we have chosen to call 'streamlined development'—here defined as development activities which are considered as relatively mature with respect to achieving accelerated development and significant cost reduction, while maintaining or increasing product performance. We do not imply through this term that the 'fuzzy front-end' of innovation (so called due to the high level of uncertainty encountered during the initial states—this concept is discussed further in Chapter X of this book, "Virtual Teams in Practice: Tales from the Battlefront of the Fuzzy Front End of the Innovation Process," by John Feland) is entirely free from harsh deadlines, demanding industry regulations, downstream production planning, or supply chain integration issues. We merely want to focus more closely on the concerns of virtual teams that might not usually describe their own work to be of a primarily 'creative' nature. First and foremost, we are interested in the individuals and teams that enter the field after the contracts have been written; the people whose job it is to 'deliver what has been promised.' Not only do we realize that these teams are in serious need of appropriate creativity enablers, we also realize that these teams currently work under circumstances where traditional approaches for enhancing creativity might no longer be satisfactory.

Drawing from experiences in highly streamlined product development work in the automotive and aerospace industries, we aim to provide insights into the complex relationships between geographically dispersed team members and the day-to-day activities through which they collectively create the cars and aero engines of tomorrow. The overall business context in these industries is rapidly and continuously changing, which has serious implications on how global partnerships are formed and sustained. For the virtual teams engaged in such partnerships, creativity is undoubtedly a key to success. However, as this chapter will highlight, we argue that it is time to radically progress our current understanding of how creativity could be introduced in organizations where factors like legal demands and contractual agreements severely restrict 'outside-the-box' thinking, and where well-known creativity enablers such as trust, shared goals, and shared culture are becoming increasingly difficult to accomplish.

Some overall characteristics of automotive and aerospace development in a global perspective are elaborated upon using examples from two Swedish companies that have already taken significant steps towards realizing the Virtual Enterprise vision. This chapter's 'tales from the battlefield' are also taken from these companies and are based on observations and experiences from two car platform development projects at Volvo Car Corporation, and from two aero engine development projects at Volvo Aero Corporation. These tales are thematically organized around four different dilemmas, which fundamentally implies that while establishing trust, shared goals, and so forth, seems to be highly important for successful collaboration in virtual teams, the special conditions under which these virtual teams work are often not conducive to building those creativity enabling properties. Furthermore, these dilemmas also imply that, for example, trust as a creativity enabler is not about an unconditional either/or question. Briefly stated, it is about knowing *when to*, and subsequently *when not to*, trust someone or a piece of information.

CORPORATE CONTEXTS

Today, globalization is a reality and not simply a matter of choosing whether or not to make use of worldwide production facilities and geographically dispersed product development teams. Considering this increasing 'virtualization' of companies, an overview of the corporate contexts in which our forthcoming 'tales from the battlefield' are embedded is provided below. We initially describe some characteristics of automotive development, a business-to-consumer industry, where brands join forces to develop common platforms to reach scale advantages. Descriptions follow of some characteristics of aero engine development, a business-to-business industry, where component manufacturers create solutions in very close partnerships with several engine manufacturers (who are essentially fierce competitors).

Automotive Platform Development

The product life cycle in the automotive industry has been reduced to produce more and more models in a shorter time span. A typical life span of a car model is five to seven years. However, manufacturing techniques still rely heavily on a billion Euro investment for tooling and assembly equipment, and the development cost is hundreds of millions of Euros. To amortize the investments and development costs, companies are seeking scale advantages. If several automotive brands use the same platform, the volume of shared parts increases, meaning less customized manufacturing equipment, and so forth.

In the last 10 years, more and more automotive groups have been created. Very few independent manufacturers of size, such as BMW and Porsche, now exist. However, the idea of

forming automotive groups is not new. For example, Chrysler Corporation joined the brands Chrysler, Dodge, Plymouth, and DeSoto already in 1928, and then merged with Daimler-Benz to form DaimlerChrysler in 1998. General Motors' (Chevrolet, Pontiac, GMC, Saturn, Hummer, SAAB, and Cadillac) history of mergers dates back to 1899, when Olds Motor Vehicle and Olds Gasoline Engine Works merged to form Olds Motor Works.

Note that an automotive platform does not just mean that some kind of go-cart like structure is made and different 'top hats' are put on. Although it is true that the lower part of the car body and the suspension are important parts in a platform, there are also important synergy and scale effects regarding commodities, such as tires, batteries, fasteners, paint, sealers, electronics, electrics, as well as more complex systems such as steering servos, antilock brake systems (ABS), air bags, and climate systems. Using engine and gearbox units in different cars on the same platform is also attractive because of the high development cost. There are even automotive groups, such as PSA, that develop engines to be used by other automotive groups.

To amortize investments and development costs over a longer period, the life of a platform for a car can be extended to cover several car models. This is especially valuable if the base program platform has shown its strength in successfully being used in a variety of cars for several car brands in an automotive group, for example, station wagons, sedans, SUVs, convertibles, and minivans. New legal demands and higher customer expectations on the next generation of cars, together with increased competition lead to a situation where higher performance is needed at a lower or maintained price. The upgrade must start in time so that new models are ready to replace the old ones at the end of their designated life cycle. Based on data from all platform models, which come from different brands on the platform, a discussion is held about the possibilities and hindrances for upgrading the platform. Every brand has its profile, identity, and customer segment meaning different priorities. Since the budget is limited and fixed and will most likely be reduced later on, it is necessary to know how the upgrades, that is, the changed requirements, impact the cost. It is about balancing the content of the upgrade package. The whole procedure of agreeing on the requirement levels and basic solutions are made within both colocated and virtual teams, and enabling these teams to collaborate more effectively is undoubtedly a key priority for all participating brands.

Aero Engine Development

The aerospace industry provides another example of an area where there is pressure to perform the product development on a global arena with many partners representing different companies—yet with a common business interest. Since development in commercial engine programs follows contractual agreements and the customers are professional organizations (i.e., airliners) rather than the actual users of transport services (i.e., passengers)—the lead time pressure will always be there. Once the airliners have placed their orders for a new aircraft and selected the engines, the development race starts.

It is important to recognize the huge program coordination required to certify new aircraft and their engines. In practical terms—there are some rather hard targets for all involved development teams to meet. From a technical perspective an aero engine is a thermodynamic machine, most often a gas turbine. The trade off is to balance technical system performance (weight, thrust, noise, and emissions etc.), durability and safety with the cost. While the system performance is designed and 'owned' primarily by the original equipment manufacturer (OEM), the development of the engine components involves several different companies sharing both technical and financial risk (and also revenue, of course). Set-

ting up a complete set of technical requirements sufficient for component design from day one is difficult, thus close collaboration with those partner companies is a must.

Another trend of the aerospace industry is that because the cost of development is increasing, and lead-time pressure is continuous, the 'window' for design and engineering work shortens. As a reference, the lead-time from signed contract when the actual development is launched to first engine to test (FETT) decreases about 6 to 7% annually. Currently, development lead time is less than one and a half years. The time available for product development consequently decreases while, essentially, the same amount of decisions has to be taken. This is an immense challenge for any design team and is exacerbated by the challenges of collaborating effectively between different sites and different organizations. The design teams must reach peak performance each time, and failure to do so cause costly solutions that affect the entire life cycle of the engine in operation (about 40 years). The opportunity to modify already certified designs is limited due to the extensive certification process required for air worthiness.

Consequently, there are many incentives and drivers to more effectively enable the development teams to perform at their absolute best. We will discuss later situations that illustrate some of the challenges experienced in two recent engine development programs.

TALES FROM THE BATTLEFIELD

In this section, we have chosen to emphasize the so called 'live experience' of engineers who work under the conditions described above; the engineers who are called to the 'battlefield' on a day-to-day basis and have to submit to the rules, regulations, procedures, and routines that govern their work in the global product development projects in which they partake. These tales are based on experiences and observations from global product development projects carried out in the automotive and aeronautical industries, and we note that even though Volvo Car Corporation and Volvo Aero Corporation provide the primary source of information here, we have also collected insights from complementary sources within these global partnerships. It is not our intention to promote any kind of 'us vs. them' analytical lens and the examples we provide are thus not intended as examples of good or bad practice, rather our objective is to tell it as perceived by members of these global teams, that is, we discuss 'real' problems that engineers encounter while trying to get the job done. We neither give both sides of the coin, nor do we judge which corporate culture is 'best.' We merely offer you the opportunity to get some insight into the kinds of barriers to collaboration one could expect if embarking on global, boundary-crossing product development projects in streamlined industry domains.

First, we reconnect to the earlier description of the two main industry contexts, or 'battlefields' if you will, that we are dealing with: automotive platform development and aero engine development. Then, we have organized the tales from the battlefield according to four dilemmas. The reason for doing so is mainly that that we need to seriously reconsider some of the 'creativity enablers' that have, more or less, come to be taken for granted when discussing successful and creative virtual teams. Having said that, we do not imply that these well-known enablers are entirely useless—on the contrary, we applaud just about any initiative to enable creativity in virtual teams. All we are saying is that there are particular circumstances of so called streamlined development that increase the complexity of global business partnerships, and which create barriers to creativity that are not easily forced. We would like to point out that the chosen dilemmas should not be considered as the only interesting aspects in this field, but as a selected set of issues that have been particularly prominent in the settings that we have participated in and studied. Also, we are using the term 'dilemma' rather loosely, to signify perplex situations that require making choices between equally unfavorable options, such as choosing between risking a joint partnership to secure individual rewards, or risking the individual rewards to reap potential future benefits of a joint partnership.

To illustrate our point, we make reference to Sutton's (2001) basic principles for differentiating between 'innovative work' and 'routine work' (see Table 1). As Sutton (2001) notes, both principles are necessary for moving forward, and the real challenge is thus not to choose between the two columns, once and for all, but rather to know when it is beneficial to exploit old ways and when it is time to explore new ways.

With the below observations from the battlefield, we want to highlight that we are looking at global business partnerships where several fundamental pillars of a creative environment, at least according to conventional wisdom, seem to be missing (or at least seem extremely difficult to achieve), and yet these partnerships would cease

Table 1. Basic organizing principles: Exploitation vs. exploration (Source: Sutton, 2001, p. 7)

Exploiting Old Ways: Organizing for Routine Work	Exploring New Ways: Organizing for Innovative Work
Drive out variance	Enhance variance
See old things in old ways	See old things in new ways
Replicate the past	Break from the past
Goal: Make money now	Goal: Make money later

to exist without creativity. Also, we are looking at situations where there are specific constraints that essentially force companies towards the left column of Table 1—requiring that they efficiently manage to both replicate past successes and to know when to break completely new ground, thus moving to the right-hand column of Table 1.

Battlefield A: Automotive Platform Development

Project A1: Compact Car Platform

Several years ago, a medium-sized platform was developed at Ford Motor Company (FMC), including brands in Europe and Asia. The platform has proved successful and all three brands have made profit on vehicles based on the platform. Recently, a decision was made to update this platform to meet new legal requirements and new customer expectations. This process is essentially about defining improvement actions at minimum cost with respect to sourcing (i.e., finding the right supplier at maximum advantage), engineering and factory changes at the different brands. This is a fierce fight about getting the most from the platform and it is complicated by the different strategies of the constituent brands—a low cost brand will naturally have very different priorities from a premium brand. When this update started, some resident engineers were installed, as leaders, in order to 'fight for the brand' requirements. Since the brand that has the earliest production date locks the updated platform capability, it is important to be active already at the beginning even if the start of production is far in the future.

Project A2: Full-size Car Platform

This project is shared among three European brands within FMC and aimed to develop next generation full-size cars of different types. Here, one of the smaller companies within FMC has the lead of the platform—meaning that it is re-

sponsible for the 'orchestration.' In order to do this, the smaller company has needed to adapt to FMC's systems and routines, which has not been an easy feat. Early mistakes in the documentation and lack of understanding of the importance of formal agreements within FMC have lead to a lot of frustration and extra work. In FMC, a platform is 'remote controlled' by the documents, while in other brands, the development is often made more directly.

Battlefield B: Aero Engine Development

Project B1: Large Commercial Jet Engine for an Airbus Aircraft

A few years ago, when the engine for the new Airbus 'super jumbo' (A380) was in the development stages, Volvo Aero was responsible for the development of an integral, mechanical structure in the engine, and several other companies had similar responsibilities for interfacing components in the engine. Once the contract was signed, the team was set up to start the development work. Until then, the OEM had been responsible for predevelopment but now the time had come to define the component in detail. The technical challenge was obvious, since the engine included many geometrical interfaces, and a complex geometry requires advanced castings in advanced materials (which consequently results in long lead time). The interaction with neighboring development teams and their design models, and with the engine system level needed particular attention. These factors impacted on the decision to colocate the Volvo Aero design team with their colleagues at the OEM site, and to support that remote team with back-office resources.

All involved were experienced in collaborating, highly dedicated, and aware of the importance of colocation to succeed. Ideally, the selection of such a team should be carefully planned, powered by training, team building, and IT tools for

143

engineering and communication before 'take off.' Here is where reality strikes back. The first technical decision review gate was only a couple of weeks ahead. The conceptual design had been made by another team at the other company and needed to be understood quickly. A coordinator was sent to the 'hot zone.' The hunt for team members able to commit to staying abroad for a long period (starting immediately) was intense and the team on site was soon under intense pressure. The effort to support the team from back-office was also in start-up mode, which took time. As a consequence, the team on site needed to deal with more issues than originally planned.

Project B2: Large Commercial Jet Engine for a Boeing Aircraft

This project is more recent, and deals with the development of structural components for an engine that will be used on, for instance, the 787 Dreamliner from Boeing. The technical pre-conditions were quite similar to Project B1, with several partners codeveloping the engine together with the integrator (the OEM). When the design team was set up, the plan was to quickly colocate the core team at the Volvo Aero office in Sweden, mainly in order to better use routines and the more sparsely used resources outside the core team. Coordination and collaboration with the engine system level of design, as well as other design teams (from other companies) working on other

components and subsystems in the engine, had to be facilitated by other means than colocation.

The collaboration between the design teams, coordinated by the integrator, relied to a much higher degree on e-tools for collaboration, such as sharing meeting documents in virtual meetings. Also, several applications allowed Volvo Aero to remotely access tools and resources at the OEM. After a few initial weeks, Volvo Aero only needed to keep a representative on site, whose main task was to facilitate and coordinate communication between the design team in Sweden and the integrator. Figure 1 illustrates the difference in collaborative set-up between Project B1 and Project B2.

Dilemma I: Trust

The dilemma of trust is, in basic terms, that you need trust to develop trust, and to be trusted you must also trust others. The most important thing is that the concept applies only to situations where there exists some degree of uncertainty or risk. To a certain extent, virtual enterprises are about sharing risks and managing uncertainties in highly competitive markets.

Davidow and Malone (1992) note: "To achieve true partnership, customers and suppliers must share information—on new products, designs, internal business plans, and long-term strategy—that once was closely guarded" (p. 145). Although we are in general agreement with this statement,

Figure 1. Comparison between Project B1 (left) and Project B2 (right)

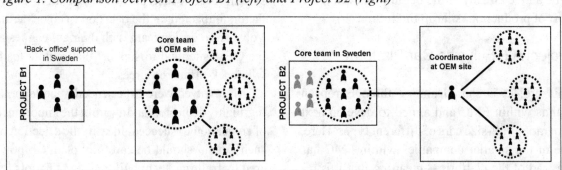

we would like to take the notion of true partnership a bit further. In our opinion, trust is not created once and for all; it is a highly context-dependent concept and thus changes over time. As we will highlight with examples below, it is crucial to know when to share and, subsequently, when not to share information or knowledge. In streamlined business areas, it is absolutely critical to continuously assess advantages and drawbacks on the individual, team, company, and virtual enterprise levels. In the case of automotive development, what is best for one brand has to be considered in relation to what is best for the common platform. In the case of aero engine development, what is best for one component must be related to what is best for the overall system.

It seems like we sometimes take incentives for collaboration too seriously and automatically assume that just because you may have a joint business offer you are eager to collaborate and will do everything in your power to make the relationship work as effectively and smoothly as possible. We think this is a too simplified view on the situation that many global companies face. Relating to the concept of 'coopetition' (Brandenburger & Nalebuff, 1997), you have to collaborate to survive, but you also have to protect your own brand and expertise in order to stay competitive and to be perceived as a preferred partner in the future. Companies are struggling to know when, where, and how to draw the line. As one project leader at Volvo Aero commented on the close relationship with three major engine companies (General Electric, Pratt, & Whitney, and Rolls-Royce):

We never share anything which could harm these three companies. If we fall into disfavor with them it is a catastrophe for us. We never present evidence from [a company's] engine program to a competitor in order to come to a solution ... we'd rather back off and find another way of proving our case.

If we consider trust to be a cornerstone of creativity, we must seriously think about the boundaries of such trust. In the above situation, the ability to establish mutual trust and respect is absolutely critical to set the stage for creative collaboration. Surely, these teams and companies need to trust each other to some extent in order to achieve the contract they have jointly agreed to, but in fulfilling their contract obligations, they should not be allowed to be 'too creative' or 'too trusting', thus risking to spoil future contracts, possibly with another partner. So, from a Virtual Enterprise perspective, with whom are you allowed to be really creative with, and with whom is it merely 'business-as-usual'? In a discussion about how creativity plays out in global aero engine alliances, one team member commented:

Creativity mostly happens in local teams, but sometimes also in distributed teams ... but then you have to think about how you expose yourself.

In automotive development, similar problems are faced in terms of staying loyal to the brand or staying loyal to the automotive group. Here, trust has a lot to do with the expectations of what each partner has to contribute to the common platform. Partly, this is a financial issue where the automotive group is calculating the sales volumes for each brand and the total project cost, which is then shared (in relation to expected sales) between platform partners. This means that there is a lot of documentation describing what each brand should deliver for a certain amount of money. It is thus absolutely crucial to keep tabs on what development is 'brand unique' (used only by one brand) and what is 'platform-wide' (used by all platform brands). For instance, there could be reinforcements to the platform floor, which are only needed by one brand. There are even parts that should be developed by the platform project, but which will only be used by one brand. Naturally, documents and contracts are highly important in such work to avoid bias.

The nice form of creativity...figuring something out together ... this is more a paper war. It is about knowing that on page six-hundred-and-twenty-two in the thousand-page document it says "this is what the platform is doing, this is what the brand is doing.

Another aspect that complicates the whole trust and bias discussion is that each brand has the responsibility for one platform size. This means that the brand that has 'lead' on a certain platform takes on a dual role: as platform leader and as brand representative in the platform project. This also impacts individual team members who have to move as seamlessly as they can between 'platform thinking' and 'brand thinking.' A similar situation arises in aero engine development, when Volvo Aero team members need to move between 'component thinking' (i.e., loyalty to own brand) and 'system thinking' (i.e., loyalty to engine manufacturers, aircraft manufacturers, and even airliners). The issue of allegiance was commented on by a member of a global automotive platform team:

There are those in the platform project who take responsibility for all brands, but there are also those who want to transfer [responsibilities] to the other brands. It is easy to favor the own brand ... you are affected by your environment. You should be 'genderless' when working for the platform. Most of the people working with the platform check things with their own brand first, perhaps because of the contacts that they have at their own brand and because of the lack of contacts at other platform brands.

When it comes to creativity in these kind of virtual teams, the conditions are more than a little constraining because team members always have to think long and hard about the downstream effects of 'creative propositions.' It can, for example, be extremely difficult to get acceptance for a creative idea that contributes

to a cheaper platform, but which at the same time requires serious investments at another of the participating brands. An obvious reason for mistrust, and the essence of the trust dilemma, is that it is very difficult to make judgments about where collaborators' loyalty lies under various circumstances. For example, one person might be completely trusted when it comes to making platform decisions with minimum financial impact on her/his own brand, but when the stakes are higher, the same person might not be trusted since there is a risk that she/he will prioritize the brand before the platform. In one of the global automotive platform development projects, a team member noted:

[They] want us to release our material five weeks earlier than we do now, and they will get results and details from tools 15 weeks later than we would have got ... it's a difference of 20 weeks. It's not logical. We should have the same amount of time ... [They] have just looked out for their own interests, that we have a joint platform seems to be a minor detail here.

Since trust in virtual teams is very much based on the knowledge that persons have of each other, the work they do, and the work they have done in the past, it seems absolutely crucial to achieve a greater sense of social connectedness in virtual teams. "Gaining a better understanding other people's priorities and problems, is highly important since it fundamentally sets the context for your own work." Observations have shown that engineers very often turn to a person for information rather than to a database or a file cabinet, and people seem to rely heavily on colleagues they know and trust. This raises questions of how to provide enough 'social lubrication' in virtual teams. Although permanent virtual teams are becoming increasingly common, many virtual enterprises face a reality where teams are formed and dissolved rapidly, and there is not a lot of time to make these teams 'gel.' Furthermore, there is a steady influx of temporary team members, consultants, experts, and so forth, and they must also be natural partners in the strive for 'team-level creative synergy' (Kurtzberg & Amabile, 2001). To recap, trust is contextual. It varies from situation to situation, and you trust people for different reasons. In the industry context we describe, it is dangerous to assume that trust has automatically been created just because the contracts have been signed, or that trust exists just because the appropriate security strategies have been put in place when it comes to data and information sharing over networks. For virtual teams that aim to be truly creative, trust can not be assumed, it has to be collectively created.

Dilemma II: Shared Corporate Culture

The dilemma of shared corporate culture is that when combining different corporate cultures, which is essentially what Virtual Enterprises are about, you are in effect creating a new culture. There are a lot of practical problems in this respect, some of which relate to the kinds of cultural traits that are transferred from the individual companies to the common Virtual Enterprise culture. Here, we are talking mainly about culture-as-practice, meaning 'the ways we do things around here'; ways of working that have evolved through the years and which are so deeply rooted in each company that they are more or less taken for granted.

Since an automotive platform development project is about joint commitments, which is also true with respect to joint life cycle commitments in the aerospace industry, we cannot assume that a shared culture already exists just because the paperwork has been signed. It is appealing to think about virtual teams creating 'virtual cultures', without necessarily having to change the internal corporate cultures that have been successful in the past. For example, we can speculate that the 'Toyota Way' (Liker, 2004) is based on a set of

beliefs, values, and principles that are not easily transferred into a Swedish business context, just in the same way as the 'Volvo Way' relies on approaches that might create havoc in other circumstances (even if applied to other Swedish companies). One Swedish automotive engineer with experience from global development had the following to say about differences in corporate culture:

The Swedish style is open dialogue, no prestige ... as a person you can say "I think like this." The Japanese style seems to be that you say something in the name of [the brand]. In the U.S., everything seems to be more individually oriented, but much more hierarchical than in Sweden.

Another Swedish automotive engineer further commented on pros and cons of various cultures:

When we were at [a company] in the U.S., two researchers from a university participated. Their first question after the meeting was "who of you is the boss?" From the discussion, they couldn't understand who was the boss. We had five or seven people there and everyone was talking. ... but sometimes it seems like we are not as well aligned as [they] are. It is not good that we sometimes take a discussion with our boss during a meeting. [They] seem to have gone through such things beforehand, they are better prepared.

On a practical level, corporate culture impacts which things you prioritize. As in the section on trust, particular ways of working are sometimes viewed with suspicion from the perspective of other organizations, maybe because these approaches differ from what people in other organizations usually expect. For example, an automotive engineer working in global platform projects experienced differences in the way that stage gates were understood:

We have not cleared cost and weight for the next gate. For [them] it is crucial that we're clear until then. We see it more as a way of highlighting problems at the gate ... we tell it like it is and that is not always popular ... there are often a lot of risks.

Similar observations were made by an aerospace engineer working in global partnerships:

My feeling is that we are very honest. We flag when we have a problem, while others hide them. But that's just our point of view, it's an appraisal. Other people make other judgments. We wave our flag ... now we have trouble ... very early. Not the smartest way when the project is running since it puts us in the spotlight ... but after the project we probably have a good result, while others might come up with late problems.

The engineers that we talked to seem to be very aware of differences in culture, and they are often quick to point out that their remote colleagues in partner companies probably do have similar concerns. Again, this is not about defining best-practice and worst-practice; rather to highlight some of the barriers to a shared, 'creative' culture. It is also a highly political game, where participants can use other organizations' cultural traits (e.g., work methods and principles) to their own advantage. When doing risk analysis, for example, 'waving the flag' or 'reporting red' can also be a conscious choice rather than simply a forced decision that attracts unwanted attention:

As a project leader, you can be sly and put in a red marker ... then you will come up high in the organization and say "we need more resources to reach our goals." So, you can use that tool the other way around. Sometimes you flag red and end up in an undesired situation, sometimes you can get the things you want. That you've flagged red once in a while is forgotten in the end if you deliver what is expected.

In the case of automotive platform development, one of the project leaders commented on the importance of doing things in ways that are 'recognizable' to the partner's corporate culture, to increase the acceptance rate of their work outside of the internal organization:

[They] have a certain way of doing things. If they recognize things, it is easier for them to accept something. It is not only about documentation, but also about the way it is documented and presented. [They] often see problems in our presentations; they do not see it as feasible solutions. They are hung up on things that haven't been done. We should have followed [their] way of working from the start ... I guess we wanted to keep [our] way, and I think that's one of the biggest problems.

Another interesting aspect that relates to shared culture, and how it impacts virtual teams and their creative boundaries, has to do with industry culture. Taking the aerospace industry as an example, there are very special demands that seriously affect a virtual development team's degree-of-freedom. There are regulations and contracts that govern what a system or a component must accomplish. To a certain extent, there are also regulations for what the processes (e.g., test routines) that lead to a finished product should look like. There is a striking difference between this reality and that of industries where you can repair faulty products after they have been released to customers, or those consumer-based industries where the customer might simply decide not to buy the product because it does not meet their demands.

What does this mean for virtual team creativity? On one hand, product failures could result in massive and hugely expensive recalls (such as in the automotive industry). On the other hand, product failures could also put lives at danger, summarized here by Volvo Aero Corporation's former president and CEO, Fred Bodin:

As far as quality is concerned Volvo Aero must be in a class of its own. In the aviation industry quality and safety go hand-in-hand. A car can be recalled, but in aviation everything has to be right the first time. (Volvo Aero Corporation, 2005, p. 14)

Kurtzberg and Amabile (2001) note that diversity among team members can be both positive (i.e., presenting a heterogeneous set of perspectives for consideration) and negative (limiting shared understanding by creating such divergence that damaging conflict occurs). In this light, we think that Hirshberg's (1999, p. 33) concept of 'creative abrasion' is very appealing. It deals with the need to handle colliding cultures and conflicting viewpoints *"without discarding or allowing either to dominate."* Creative abrasion recognizes that friction has positive properties that are crucial in making things work (e.g., friction as a source of electricity), and that we need to better understand when these abrasions have creative potential, and when they have not. As we see it, it could be useful to think in terms of creating 'third cultures' (Graen & Wakabayashi, 1994)—a way of working in global teams that is not necessarily based on colocated models of collaboration, or based on a single dominating worldview. Instead of saying that streamlined development is not favorable to creative activity, we might try to identify the positive abrasions between corporate cultures that can help spur creativity, and try to better understand the ways in which the nature of streamlined industries actually empowers, rather than limits, our creative potential.

Dilemma III: Shared Goals

The dilemma of shared goals is that in order to fulfill them you often have to take on individual, team, or organizational commitments and responsibilities that could involve conflicting subgoals. From a Virtual Enterprise perspective this relates

closely to our previous discussions about both trust and culture: of course these concepts are enmeshed in each other in that they are all about accomplishing a sense of shared understanding of the project, the roles of the participants, and the expectations on what every partner should bring to the table to fulfill the joint contractual agreement. It is important to discuss them separately as they affect creativity in different ways.

In our discussions with automotive engineers, they often talk about 'finding the best compromise.' Everything you do to optimize a particular component might have serious negative effects on other components or on the system as a whole. So, even if you are able to find a 'creative solution', you are soon under pressure to explain how your solution influences the commonality (which in turn has to do with economies of scale), and how your idea relates to the manufacturing tools that are currently available at the plants, and so forth. Also, as we touched on earlier, you could come up with a brilliant solution that is of great benefit to all platform partners (e.g., increased commonality with improved performance), but which could at the same time result in major and expensive upgrades to your own part of the platform. Here, it is easy to understand that low-level actions (such as making a minor design change) could bring about consequences of unforeseen proportions—an incentive as good as any for staying 'inside-the-box.' One of the automotive engineers we have talked to says the following about shared goals in platform development:

Each brand wants to have products that are profitable. If Volvo makes a profit, it goes into Ford, but a certain amount goes back to Volvo for the next model. [Another brand] is completely dependent on [their automotive group], so they can't do any development on their own. Shared goals could mean making a profit in order to keep your freedom.

From an aero engine development perspective, a project leader commented on the difficulty of knowing whether or not the distributed team really have shared goals and priorities:

I have probably not really understood what the others think is important. Priority one is to deliver, but after that ... You would think that you could read it in the contract ... [Engine manufacturer] and [airline] might not agree with each other, but we haven't talked to [the airline] that many times. It's difficult to get the whole picture ... some of the things are kept secret. Their problems might be based in earlier engine programs and business relations.

It is rather obvious that engineers working in such global, cross-boundary alliances constantly have to deal with conflicting demands. It is not simply the case of sitting down at a table and definitively deciding on shared goals and objectives. Rather, they have to move between different levels of abstraction in that some goals are of superior importance in particular circumstances, but of inferior importance in others. High-level objectives, such as meeting new flight regulations concerning noise, must be assessed in relation to lower-level objectives, such as making strength simulations of a modified engine casing to allow for noise reduction. Also, the engine manufacturer (e.g., Rolls-Royce) have separate contractual agreements with the aircraft manufacturer (e.g., Airbus), and this information is mostly not available to the component manufacturer (e.g., Volvo Aero). A Volvo Aero project leader comments on the difficulties of relating their own goals, based on written contracts, to the higher level goals that might be part of undisclosed business agreements between the other partners:

We must hope that they've written clear enough contracts with us ...requirements specifications, penalties etcetera. We have demands to deliver on time, at a certain weight, but we don't know

what the penalty structure between [engine manufacturer] and [aircraft manufacturer] looks like. [The engine manufacturer] might choose between a weight penalty and a delay penalty, and decide that it's better to deliver late. If they don't feed this down to us, we have a hard time seeing the type of trade-offs we do at our level. And even if we meet our demands, [the engine manufacturer] might have other problems that result in penalties. We only get a small piece of the puzzle.

Apart from contractual obligations, there are flight safety regulations that impact how companies work and how they document their work to ensure traceability. Further, an individual aero engine component has clear interfaces to other components that make up the engine, so the geometrical 'envelope' together with the very high performance requirements means that the creative boundaries have, at least to a great extent, already been set. Of course, this is also true in automotive development, where engine envelopes, foot envelopes, wheel envelopes, and so forth, govern the geometrical boundaries (i.e., 'vehicle packaging'). Just as all components need to fit into the car and contribute to the overall performance, the aero engine is also a system that must work together with the airplane. All parts must contribute to the overall system performance and we must therefore consider that a modification requiring 1000 hours of work on the system level might render 3000 hours for every component in that system. Whose goals are really targeted, who gets the benefits of reaching those targets, and who is paying for the work to reach them? A Volvo Aero project leader highlighted this problematic situation:

[The engine manufacturer] owns the engine certificate, so their perspective is what's best for the engine. If we and [our competitor] stand there, [the chief engineer] will choose what is best for the engine, that's what makes the engine sell. But if you are at a crossroads ... we are partners and carry the costs ... [the chief engineer] doesn't

consider our economical aspects, but will take what is best for the engine. My gut feeling tells me that they look more carefully when they're paying for things themselves. We are also thinking 'Volvo Aero'... we can have our own purchasing strategies ... We are working for Volvo Aero; we must have our own interests.

When discussing shared goals we are really discussing 'collective commitment.' What are the goals that we all are committed to achieving, and what are the goals that only apply to some of us? This relates to how we define our virtual teams: are we considered a team just because we are all engineers, are we considered a team because we are tied together in the organizational chart, or are we considered a team because we have joint commitments that we achieve together rather than individually? Sometimes it is obvious that team members have the same perception of the goal, but radically different views on how to reach that goal.

We believe that the notion of a virtual team, at least in streamlined development, involves often conflicting worldviews, approaches and priorities. Again, the challenge is not necessarily to completely merge these different perspectives, but to raise awareness of their complementary nature, and to help virtual teams know when they have to collaborate, and when they might be better off on their own. Being able to effectively identify critical collaborative activities, or 'interfaces' between individuals and teams, might be more interesting than always striving for close collaboration.

Dilemma IV: Creative Priority

The dilemma of the creative priority is that *not* investing in creativity could in fact increase the creative output. What we are saying here is *not* that companies should refrain from dedicating extra time, money and resources into creativity-enhancing approaches. Rather streamlined development means that those extra resources are

often not available, and furthermore, the immense pressures of such industries could actually prove to be a driver of creativity and innovation. In the words of an aero engine project leader: *"He who suffers conquers."*

This comment should be seen as a general comment on the current incentives for creativity and collaboration that are available to engineers working in global product development of the Virtual Enterprise kind. Relating to the introduction of this chapter, where we talked about 'creative work' versus 'routine work', we could ask ourselves if more time and money automatically results in more creative work, or if *"work expands so as to fill the time available for its completion,"* as Parkinson's law (Parkinson, 1958) states. What does it mean to put a priority on creativity? Will people be more creative just because they have more time, or could it be that creativity is needed the most, and is also most applicable, when enmeshed in daily, supposedly 'routine' work, such as designing aero engine components or automotive platform components as part of highly streamlined and regulated processes? As one of the automotive engineers put it:

When should you be creative? You can be creative and cut costs. When can you afford to be creative, and when can you not afford to be creative?... creativity can be to do the same thing cheaper. Creativity can be to cut costs with sustained or increased performance. Cars get cheaper every year ... we have to try to lower the price without making the product worse."

Another automotive engineer had similar thoughts:

We have to be creative to put together a product where several brands take part and we have different production plants. The biggest challenge is the complexity... very many boundaries are set with respect to five production plants.

When we have talked to engineers working with streamlined development, we have seldom heard them talking about creativity, at least not in those terms, until we have explicitly asked how they relate to creativity. Part of this could imply that they do not really consider 'streamlining' to involve creative activities. It could also be that they are not that concerned if other people consider their work to be creative or not. They are working towards meeting deadlines, satisfying requirements specifications, fulfilling contract agreements—they are doing what they have to, solving problems as they arise. One aero engine project leader summarized the demands on his team in the following way: "*The biggest problem of all is to deliver on time.*"

Investing in creativity is truly a hard sell considering the lead times that development teams face. From one project to the next, Volvo Aero cut their lead time (design to delivery) from 19 months to 12 months, which caused one of the engineers to comment: "*Innovation disappears when the contract is written. After that, it's only about bringing the stuff out.*"

One of his colleagues, a project leader, added to this comment:

We have very little time for innovation ... we have to go for safe solutions. We have to know that what we're doing works to ninety-five percent. You glance a lot at how earlier generations look ... we go for the things that give us a competitive advantage ... and with low risk. No customer wants us to take big risks.

In a way, our observations and experiences tell us that creativity flourishes under pressure. Creativity inside-the-box is entirely possible; otherwise these companies would not be able to deliver innovations to the market. Considering the creative boundaries that are inherent in streamlined industries, it is amazing that creative activities do not cease to exist. One of the reasons for this might be that the 'not invented here' syndrome is not given enough time (or funds) to develop. New work methods and design solutions seem to gain acceptance more easily when teams are under pressure, perhaps because stakeholders are forced to find the 'best argument' or 'best compromise,' regardless of the origin of the idea. Interestingly, this implies that although the high industry demands and complex business relationships provide a rather narrow window of opportunity for creative freedom, it is these very same constraints that encourage participants to really collaborate, find shared understanding, and reach acceptable compromises that 'do the job.'

When seeing the pressures of streamlined development not as something entirely negative, but as a sometimes crucial component of creative work, we can make the analogy with athletes that get into 'game mode' by, more or less consciously, using their pre-game stress to stimulate the flow of adrenaline into the bloodstream. One of the problems here is that virtual teams often seem to play on different battlefields. When the adrenaline is pumping in Detroit due to near-deadline design changes, the people in Gothenburg might be out playing golf, and vice versa. In discussions with aero engineers, for example, they mentioned the problems of 'distributing heat,' meaning the possibility to make off-site team members aware of the severity of a particular situation.

FUTURE TRENDS

One of the key messages that we take from the battlefield tales above is that the applicability of information and knowledge is a continuously moving target. The problem you start out working on is often not the same problem a few weeks down the line, and the solutions you discarded in previous projects might very well prove to be useful in future projects, due to rapid and radical advances in both supporting methods and technologies. Furthermore, the agility required of future enterprises forces them to quickly decide when collaboration is beneficial, when it is too risky, and on what level of interaction that collaboration should best be carried out. In many previous cases, the focus has been directed on the technical challenges that virtual teams face, while it has been repeatedly discovered that communicative aspects have a decisive impact on the success of the team performance (i.e., how well virtual teams actually come to understand and jointly deal with those technical challenges).

The status, applicability and validity of dispersed knowledge resources needs to be continuously assessed, updated and effectively spread to all stakeholders in a project to ensure that no time, money, or intellectual resources are lost on activities that are based on inaccurate (or irrelevant) information. Here, we are basically talking about knowledge efficiency, where the competitive edge lies in a company's ability to pick out the useful knowledge, while leaving out the irrelevant, and to take advantage of that useful knowledge quicker than their competitors. Using an organic analogy, we need to aim for a high 'knowledge metabolism.' Being in possession of information and knowledge is obviously crucial, but putting it to use, in the right context, at the right time is essentially what decides if it is the 'right' information and knowledge or not. Information and knowledge thus needs to be shared on all levels of maturity—from sketchy ideas to minutely detailed contracts—so that useful ideas and concepts are shared when needed rather than when defined in the stage gate process. Today, such informal knowledge sharing is extremely difficult to achieve across geographical, functional, and organizational boundaries. This has to change. Here, it is of great interest to explore the concept of knowledge readiness level (KRL), brought forward by NASA along the same lines as their technology readiness level (TRL) concept (Chiaramonte & Joshi, 2004). Future KRL systems could help virtual teams assess both the current status of their knowledge capability and devise strategies to reach a satisfactory level.

Future enterprise environments will be characterized by multicontext collaboration, where people will need to move seamlessly between different teams, projects and priorities. They will need to switch effortlessly between total task-focus and multitasking, between high-level goals and low-level goals, and between individual work and exceptionally close teamwork. Further, people will have to move fluently between both virtual and physical team spaces, all the time with uninterrupted access to colleagues, information systems and other knowledge resources that are spread all over the world. Taken together, this is pointing towards an anyplace/anytime vision of collaborative engineering, where virtual teams are so commonly used that it will be very difficult to draw the borders between the colocated and the virtual workplace. Most likely, even physically colocated team members will communicate to a greater extent in a virtual mode, enabling all virtual team members to more easily stay aware of what is going on at partner sites. The transparency and seamlessness of collaboration implies that engineers will be allowed to focus more closely on the job of work (i.e., delivering the goods) and that they, in doing that job, will be less bound to physical spaces and less dependent on the immediate availability of their colocated colleagues.

This multicontext perspective on collaboration further implies a need for automated capabilities to link virtual team members to relevant information and knowledge, reducing the necessity to clearly know what you are looking for. Further, it is unlikely that future enterprises will be able to maintain their agility if they are constantly forced to homogenize the IS/IT environment to include all partner's needs and requirements. Instead, there is a clear trend towards supporting heterogeneous enterprises with service-oriented architectures, allowing companies to share data, information and knowledge regardless of which vendors and systems have been selected at each partner site. The 'Virtual Enterprise Collaboration Hub,' currently under development in the EU FP6 aeronautics project VIVACE (2005), provides one example of how such a neutral collaboration platform could be realized. So, even though we can see a convergence in terms of the capabilities that virtual teams would need to succeed in global collaboration, such as having one-click access to audio, video, and web conferencing, it does not imply that these capabilities should be delivered by one and the same vendor. Rather, there is going to be an increasingly open 'knowledge market-place' where service providers of all sizes will be able to contribute with, for example, simulation capabilities that can easily be incorporated into a partner's workflow without exposing any con-fidential information ('black box' approach with internal system properties hidden from view).

Best practice until quite recently for teamwork in engineering has been to rely on physical coloca-tion for intense collaboration. As a consequence of escalating globalization, development is now conducted worldwide in highly heterogeneous teams, which makes physical colocation extremely difficult. In relation to the industry contexts we have discussed earlier, we can see the following general trend in virtual team collaboration as seen in Table 2 (although there are many dimensions that we do not consider in Table 2).

CONCLUSION

This chapter uses observations and experiences from real industry practice to point out that we might be in need of a more balanced view on creativity's role in virtual team collaboration—particularly when applied to so called streamlined development. Although we are generally positive to the quest for 'creativity techniques', we are also painfully aware of the severe constraints that currently impair creativity. Furthermore, we firmly believe that many of these constraints are here to stay and that they are going to be even more impeding in the future. This means that we should not assume that companies will 'get the point' and start investing heavily in creativity

Table 2. Towards future enterprise collaboration

As-Was	As-Is	To-Be
Most team members located at partner site, with back-office support.	Virtual teams with some on-site ('coor-dinator') representation.	Completely virtual teams. No on-site representation. Even colocated teams are 'virtual.'
Global person-to-person collaboration (with back-office) occurs predominantly in formal meetings.	Global person-to-person collabora-tion occurs predominantly in formal meetings.	Global person-to-person collaboration oc-curs 24/7 in varying degree of formality.
Several employees are detached from their mother company.	Few employees are detached from their mother company.	No employees are detached from their mother company.
Several employees are dedicated to single projects.	Few employees are dedicated to single projects.	No employees are dedicated to single projects.
On-site team members are disproportion-ately affected by pressure from the partner company.	Coordinators are disproportionately affected by pressure from the partner company.	Pressure is evenly distributed.
High social connectedness with colocated team members (at partner site). Low social connectedness with back-office members (at mother company).	High social connectedness with colo-cated team members. Low social con-nectedness with virtual team members.	Social connectedness is less dependent on physical proximity.
Culture assimilation: 'guests' are expected to follow the work approach governed on-site.	Culture dominance: work approach is dominated by 'lead' partner.	Third culture: work approach is sensitive to the interests of all partners.

and in 'creativity enabling' activities. The fact is, many companies have already done so—with poor resulting ROI. What has been gained in one dimension (e.g., social connectedness) has often been lost in another (e.g., effectiveness), and this is partly because these 'investments' seem to require substantial downpayments in terms of each team member's time and devotion. This is a major flaw.

We need to build social connectedness as a natural part of day-to-day work, we need to create trust through everyday interactions between virtual team members, we need to encourage creative work in just about everything we do in the workplace—but we simply have to understand that when we focus explicitly on 'creativity' or 'trust', or any other concept, we naturally lose some of our main focus, to 'deliver what has been promised.' Virtual teams that will be able to build the foundation for creativity in natural, seamless, and effortless ways will be way ahead of their competition.

On a positive note, there are already trends that point towards a business environment where the open source and standards movement will play an increasingly important role. In terms of virtual teams and creativity, this movement is acknowledging that highly heterogeneous enterprises must be given a 'common playground' where true, hugely creative collaboration can take place in spite of the rich diversity of backgrounds, cultures, organizational, and technical setups and so forth, that the various partners embrace. If we can create this common playground, we might more truthfully say that we have reached success 'because of' diversity, rather than 'in spite of' diversity. Furthermore, in the spirit of true collaboration and joint creativity, future books on the subject might be drawing on 'tales from the playground' rather than 'tales from the battlefield.'

REFERENCES

Brandenburger, A. M., & Nalebuff, B. J. (1997). Co-Opetition: *A revolution mindset that combines competition and cooperation: The game theory strategy that's changing the game of business.* New York: Doubleday/Currency.

Byrne, J. (1993, February 8). The virtual corporation. *Business Week*, 98-102.

Chiaramonte, F. P., & Joshi, J. A. (2004). W*orkshop on Critical Issues in Microgravity, Fluids, Transport, and Reaction Processes in Advanced Human Support Technology* (NASA/TM—2004-212940). Retrieved October 30, 2006, from http://peer1.nasaprs.com/peer_review/prog/ahst_2003.pdf

Davidow, W. & Malone, M. (1992). *The virtual corporation.* New York: HarperCollins.

Graen, G. B., & Wakabayashi, M. (1994). Cross-cultural leadership-making: Bridging American & Japanese diversity for team advantage. In H. C. Triandis, M. D. Dunnette, & L. M. Hough (Eds.), *Handbook of industrial and organizational psychology* (Vol. 4, pp. 415-446). New York: Consulting Psychologist Press.

Hirshberg, J. (1999). *The creative priority.* New York: HarperCollins.

Kurtzberg, T. R., & Amabile, T. M. (2001). From Guilford to creative synergy: Opening the black box of team-level creativity. *Creativity Research Journal, 13*(3&4), 285-294.

Liker, J. (2004). *The Toyota way.* New York: McGraw-Hill.

Parkinson, C. N. (1958). *Parkinson's Law: The Pursuit of Progress.* London: John Murray.

Sutton, R. I. (2001). *Weird ideas that work: 11½ practices for promoting, managing, and sustaining innovation*. New York: The Free Press.

VIVACE Project. (2005). *Virtual Enterprise Collaboration Hub—Services description*. Retrieved October 30, 2006, from http://www.vivaceproject.com/content/advanced/vechsd_full.pdf

Volvo Aero Corporation. (2005). *AERO: News, Views & Interviews*. Number 3.

WebEx Communications, Inc. (2006). *Web conferencing, online meetings, and video conferencing*. Retrieved April 30, 2006, from www.webex.com

Chapter VIII
Enabling Creative
Virtual Teams in SMEs

Avril Thomson
University of Strathclyde, Scotland

Angela Stone
University of Strathclyde, Scotland

William Ion
University of Strathclyde, Scotland

ABSTRACT

Many SMEs struggle to support virtual teams effectively within distributed design projects, hindering their creative potential. It is not uncommon for SMEs to have tools and working practice imposed on them by collaborating multinationals to meet the requirements of the multinational. SMEs however, need to develop their own working practices to support effective, virtual team design within their own organisation or extended design team. This chapter describes, through a series of four case studies, how a typical SME achieved successful virtual team working within their organisation. A "strategy for enabling creative virtual teams" encompassing the processes, methods, and tools developed and implemented within the company to achieve this success is presented. Generic and transferable findings drawn from this two year study aimed at helping other SMEs, form the conclusion of this chapter.

INTRODUCTION

This chapter is concerned with supporting creative virtual teams within small and medium sized enterprises (SME). Specifically, it focuses on virtual teams formed to carry out the creative process of design in a distributed manner. Many issues affect creative virtual teams. It is essential that virtual teams within the SME environment overcome these issues and operate efficiently and effectively thus providing the company with a successful, competitive edge. Initially, this chapter investigates and identifies specific issues facing creative virtual teams within the SME environment. A strategy aimed at overcoming these issues is then described and evaluated.

Readily available and affordable groupware, conferencing tools, and internet technologies such as IP-phones and Skype™ mean that sharing information and data within virtual design teams is simple and affordable. However, many SMEs struggle to support virtual teams effectively within distributed design projects, hindering their creative potential. Furthermore, as part of the extended design team of large multinational companies it is not uncommon for SMEs to have tools and working practice imposed on them to meet the requirements of the multinational. SMEs however, need to develop their own working practices to support effective, virtual team design within their own organisation or extended design team. The success of SME is vital to the European economy as they account for 93% of enterprises in Europe (Observatory of European SMEs, 2002).

This chapter describes, through a series of case studies, how a typical SME achieved successful virtual team working within their organisation. A "strategy for enabling creative virtual teams" encompassing the processes, methods and tools developed and implemented within the company to achieve this success is presented. In total, four live case studies, spanning a 2 year period, are described, two initial studies focus on current virtual design team practice clearly highlighting issues and areas for improvement, leading to the development of processes, methods, and tools which form the support strategy. Its evaluation through two further live industrial case studies is then described.

The case studies themselves together with the processes, methods, and tools developed by this company could be adopted by other SMEs directly, to achieve the same success. Generic and transferable findings drawn from this study

aimed at helping other SMEs form the conclusion of this chapter.

BACKGROUND

As companies grow and expand, they may shift from a single office to a multioffice environment, often spread over a wide geographical area. If this happens, it is vital that unity is maintained in the products or services offered. In order for the company to grow in the same direction, knowledge and resources need to be shared throughout the company, rather than being limited to individual offices allowing each office to take on bigger, more complex projects than they might be capable of if limited to local resources. This can be achieved through the formation of virtual teams, allowing key skills and specialisms to be exploited. Benefits often documented by companies adopting virtual working within the design process include (Top Gear, 1996):

- Improvements in the flow of work allowing companies to move and react faster
- Product development lead time, time to market and costs reduced while maintaining or improving quality
- Quality failure costs reduced
- Sharing of information and expertise between organisations/departments improved
- Relationships between manufacturers and suppliers strengthened
- Efficiency of day to day dealing with customers improved

However, the practice of virtual design does not always meet its full potential (MacGregor, Thomson, & Juster, 2002) and more often than not, in virtual design projects, designers do not feel entirely satisfied with the product or service provided. Designers are often discouraged from participating in virtual teams due to negative experiences, or worse still by reports of negative experiences from others. In addition to this, working practices are often so far out of synch that any work produced remotely needs to be re-worked when the distributed phase of the project is complete. Human nature dictates that people take time to develop trust and good working relationships (Williams, 1977; Rocco, 1998; Zheng, Veinott, Olson, & Olson, 2002), however, members of virtual teams regularly feel distant and disconnected from their remote colleagues.

Existing studies have shown that an increase in distance between team members results in more problems in the design team. Bradner and Mark (2002) monitored the behaviour of subjects who were unknowingly sat in adjacent rooms and told they were various distances apart. They demonstrated that increasing the distance that partners believed themselves to be separated by, made them less likely to cooperate, less susceptible to persuasion and more likely to deceive. Trust, which is harder to build and sustain in virtual environments, has been shown to be a critical factor in the success of teams (Jarvenpaa & Leidner, 1998; Lipnack & Stamps, 2000). Trust is shown to be greater amongst individuals who have met face to face, or exchanged a photograph prior to working in a distributed manner (Zheng et al., 2002). Increased dispersion inevitably results in a loss of rich subtle interactions meaning work takes longer to do (Herbsleb, Mockus, Finhohlt, & Grinter, 2000). In order to increase the effectiveness of remote collaboration, Herbsleb et al. recommend making greater use of electronic tools. The practice of using electronic tools to facilitate distributed collaborative working is known generically as computer-supported cooperative work (CSCW).

Introducing CSCW systems can be potentially hazardous and although an organisation may have the best intentions when introducing systems to share information and knowledge, users often end up confused as to its function

and purpose (Orlikowski, 1993, 1996; Hayes & Walsham, 2000).

Greenberg (2003) tells us that that CSCW must support two essential elements, telepresence and teledata. Telepresence means a system will allow transmission of subtle and explicit dynamics such as body language, hand gestures, eye gaze, presence awareness, and so forth, to help orchestrate interaction, whereas teledata requires the system provide a mechanism for bringing work and materials into the meeting. Even the best research systems can only support partial telepresence and although some developments, such as Clearboard by Ishii and Kobayashi (1992), satisfy many of the telepresence requirements, there are as yet no commercially available products that provide an acceptable solution.

Teasley, Covi, Krishnan, and Olson (2000) showed that teams work better when they are physically close to each other by grouping software development teams in "war rooms" and comparing their productivity to those in a regular software development environment. They demonstrated that productivity (in terms of functions per staff month) doubled and cycle time was cut by almost one third. The dramatic increase in productivity was attributed to the fact that the team was physically close, could overhear conversations, were constantly aware of each others' presence, and to an extent what they were doing, and were able to seamlessly share artefacts. Although this research did highlight some disadvantages, mainly that the war rooms removed all privacy and sometimes ruined concentration, it confirmed that for teams to succeed they must be made to feel "close."

To summarise, there are many and varied areas of research under way to develop CSCW systems that will allow remote colleagues to feel "closer." Most important is an understanding of the cultural and social issues that are central to virtual teams. Before any successful collaboration can take place, participants need to get to know and trust each other, and that the only satisfactory way to build trust is to meet face to face. Although there are many IT tools available to facilitate virtual teams, the correct systems, procedures, and philosophy must be in place to allow this to happen.

The motivation for this particular study was therefore, to bridge the gap between distributed design sites in an SME (within the context of an engineering design consultancy) in order to:

- Encourage trust and good working relationships between virtual team members
- Rationalise and streamline systems and procedures such that work produced in any site is relevant in any other site to support effective virtual team working
- Increase the satisfaction felt by members of virtual teams

Building a firm foundation in each of these areas will facilitate the efficiency and effectiveness of virtual teams. Improving each will allow virtual design teams to focus on the actual creative process of design and the quality of its output.

CASE STUDY METHODOLOGY AND CURRENT VIRTUAL DESIGN TEAM PRACTICE

Methodology

A case study-based approach was adopted to investigate current virtual design team practice. Yin (1994) defines the case study as "an empirical inquiry that investigates a contemporary phenomenon within its real life context."

The approach adopted was similar to that of Jagodzinski, Reid and Culverhouse (2000) summarised as:

- Immersion of the researcher in normal day-to-day activities of the people under

study, occasionally as a participant, but most frequently as an observer or interviewer
- Gathering data from a wide range on sources, including observation, interviews, conversations, and documents so as to build up a rich and detailed picture of participants, their purposes, and activities
- An open-ended approach to gathering data, so that key issues can emerge gradually through analysis

Several methods of data collection were used including:

- **Daily "e-mail diaries":** These were submitted by the participants detailing their level of collaboration within the virtual team each day. Participating designers responded to an e-mail sent to them each day containing five short questions designed to take only a few minutes to complete.
- **Questionnaires:** Various questionnaires were used throughout the study to survey opinion and determine working practice. The questionnaires took various formats depending on the type of response required, for example, short answer, multiple choice, or quantifying opinions or attitudes.
- **Semi-structured interviews:** These were frequently used to acquire rich data to supplement the information gathered through the diaries and clarify or develop any issues that arose through the questionnaires
- **Observation:** A great deal of rich data and understanding was gained through observation of activities and conversations/discussions.

Two initial case studies were undertaken to identify current practice and develop a 'strategy for enabling creative virtual teams.' Evaluation and development of the strategy was facilitated through two further case studies.

Company Background

All of the case studies took place within a UK-based mechanical and electrical engineering design consultant referred to within this chapter as "The company." The company has approximately 130 staff, with 60 based in the head office in Glasgow, Scotland which was established in 1953 and the rest distributed throughout eight regional UK offices specifically, Edinburgh (est. 1989), Aberdeen, Inverness, Epsom (est. 1992), London, Birmingham (est. 1990), Manchester (est. 1998), and Bristol (est. 2000). The company has been adopting virtual teams to support distributed design projects since the establishment of the regional offices. It is essential for the company to form virtual teams consisting of designers from their various offices for several reasons:

- Skills and resources can be leveraged
- Lower cost resources in Scottish-based offices can be exploited including highly skilled, experienced staff
- Agility allows the company to respond to the markets throughout the UK independent of location
- Stability is achieved by spreading business across the UK leaving the company less vulnerability to regional fluctuations within the UK market

The regional offices have grown, both organically and through merger and acquisition, over a period of 15 years and, despite best efforts, drifted in terms of the systems and procedures adopted throughout the design process. As a result, virtual design teams inevitably have difficulty sharing data, thus hampering the effectiveness of the distributed design process, inconveniencing the designers, and projecting an unprofessional image to clients due to an inconsistent interface. Not surprisingly, initial interview data in the company highlights low levels of satisfaction with the work produced during distributed projects with designers often being reluctant to work as part of a virtual team.

Company practice for distributed design projects is shown in Figure 1. The project is managed from a "lead office" located closest geographically to the actual "project site." The lead office correspond with the external design team members and relay information back to designers in a "support office" with the appropriate resources including skills, knowledge and time to complete elements of the design work.

Case Studies of Current Distributed Design Practice

Two case studies were undertaken to ascertain the current status of virtual team working within

Figure 1. Company practice: Distributed projects

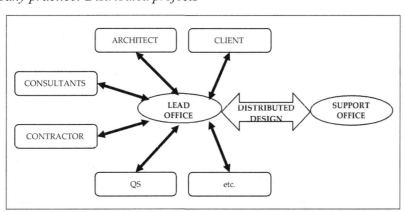

the company. The main findings from each case are presented in terms of the project stages, as follows:

- **Project initiation**
- **Distributed design phase:** Where the main design work is carried out by the virtual design team
- **Project handover:** When the project is completed by the virtual team and handed back to the Lead Office

Case Study Project One

Due to a shortage of resources in the lead office, assistance was requested from the support office to perform the mechanical and electrical design for two new build schools. A virtual design team was formed consisting of designers from two company offices—a project team based in the lead office with the support office providing virtual team members in the form of one mechanical and one electrical engineer. All correspondence with the external design team members was channelled through the lead office. Project one lasted five months.

Project Initiation

There was no formal briefing meeting where the virtual team could meet face to face to discuss the project. The only way to build trust and good working relationships is to meet face to face (Rocco, 1998). The team had never met before, and in fact did not meet during the entire project, leading to several problems at the outset of the project, most notably:

- The project brief and background information was e-mailed from the lead office to an absent virtual team member for distribution amongst the virtual team. It remained unread for over a week in his personal inbox, drastically affecting initial design progress.

- The virtual team did not have an opportunity to discuss the project brief resulting in incorrect assumptions being made and elements being designed that were not required.
- Some of the designers in the virtual team were unaware of the contract details for example, a preferred manufacturer list.

Delays were incurred when queries requiring clarification were e-mailed back and forth between the virtual team members when they could have been clarified at a single face to face briefing meeting.

Distributed Design Phase

During this phase of the project, problems arose through a lack of proactive communication. These were compounded by the problems encountered during the project initiation stage:

- Some members of the virtual team were unaware of project deadlines and missed them. This can be attributed to the fact that no programme was agreed at the outset and there were no regular discussions to check progress.
- There were no midproject face to face meetings to review progress and re-evaluate objectives, therefore team members assumed the design was progressing.
- Drawings were produced using the wrong template.
- There were substantial differences in the design methods employed within the virtual team for example mechanical design tools ranging from spreadsheets through to commercial mechanical design software packages.
- Team members were unaware of their virtual team colleagues' activities. This is confirmed by analysing the shared project correspondence database "project desk" activity between the lead and support of-

fices during the distributed design phase of project one shown in Figure 2:

- ° There were an average of less than 0.3 outgoing e-mails and less than 0.3 incoming e-mails logged in the database per week. It is expected that a project of this size and nature would generate significantly more e-mail. It is clear that the shared project correspondence database was not being used for sending and storing project e-mails.
- ° Faxes were managed more effectively, there were on average three to four incoming and outgoing faxes logged in the system each week.
- ° The support office appeared to be logging more internal correspondence than the lead office, further investigation uncovered that the support office were logging on receipt from the lead office.

Project Handover

There was no review of the design produced between virtual design team members for project one. As a result:

- There was no opportunity to query and comment on the design.
- The virtual team did not receive feedback on the work completed.

Furthermore, poor briefing procedures during the project initiation phase led to a lack of understanding of drawing requirements within the virtual team. This resulted in substantial rework of drawings prior to issue.

Design Team Satisfaction Survey

The virtual team members in this project were not at all satisfied with the systems and procedures in place to facilitate virtual working. Completed

Figure 2. Shared project correspondence database activity during distributed design phase of Project 1

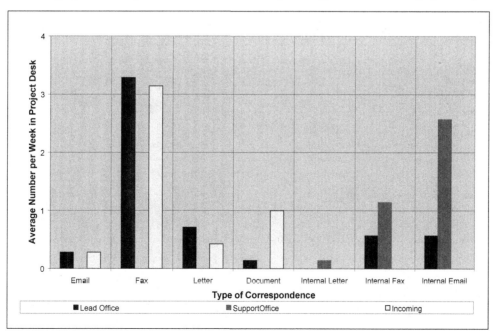

survey results are shown in Figure 3. In general, team members were less than 40% satisfied with the current systems and procedures. Correspondence management within designers' own office was rated below 60%, suggesting a major lack of awareness of team colleague's activities.

Conclusions of Case Study One

Problems arising throughout each of the phases of this project hindered the creative potential of the virtual team. In particular, the virtual team member lacked face to face interaction with no initial meeting and no project handover. Furthermore, the shared project correspondence database illustrates a lack of awareness between virtual team members.

The key lessons learned from this case study were:

- There must be a briefing meeting to explain the project background, agree roles and responsibilities and set an internal programme.

- The drawing and design philosophy must be agreed at the outset and any changes must be discussed between team members.
- There must be more proactive communication and regular checks of progress against an agreed programme.
- The correspondence management system was not being used appropriately and required development and a training plan to make it work in the modern business environment.

Case Study Project Two

The scope of project two was to design the mechanical and electrical services for an online bank's customer service centre. The lead office requested assistance, due to an excessive local workload and restricted resources. The design was split into two packages with the mechanical elements being designed in the lead office and the electrical elements being designed in the support office. The lead office was responsible for all correspondence with the external design team members.

Figure 3. Project 1: Participants satisfaction with systems and procedures

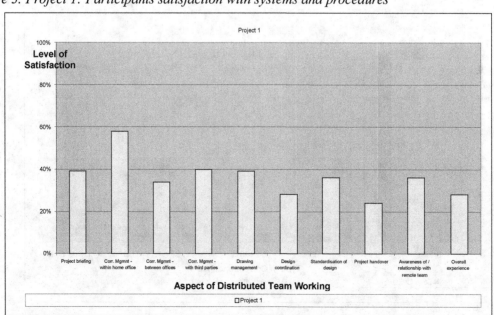

Project Initiation

A face to face briefing meeting took place at the start of the project. The virtual team had never previously collaborated and appreciated the opportunity to meet, discuss the project and start to form a relationship.

Distributed Design Phase

A face to face meeting took place half way through the project to discuss progress and to re-evaluate the programme. This meeting went well with progress decisions being made. However, this project was of a particularly dynamic nature with high levels of correspondence coming from the external design team in a short period of time after the initial meeting. This meant that most of the agreements made during the meeting were irrelevant shortly afterwards and the project fell into a period of poor correspondence management and control.

Data from the shared correspondence database, Figure 4 shows:

- There were less than 0.5 outgoing e-mails being logged each week, which is below what would normally be expected.
- The support office was logging more internal project correspondence than the lead office, suggesting that they were more comfortable with the system.

Project Handover

Similar to project one, there was no handover meeting. The project tailed off and transferred back to the lead office in a similar manner to project one. As a result similar to project one, drawings were not suitable for issue and had to be reworked following handover.

Figure 4. Shared correspondence database activity during distributed design phase of project two

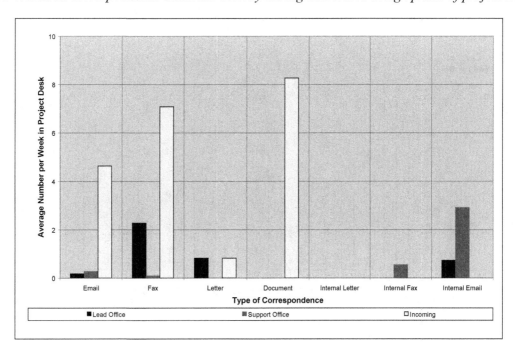

Design Team Satisfaction Survey

The results of the design satisfaction survey shown in Figure 5 again show poor levels of satisfaction with existing systems and procedures. The project briefing [1] scored slightly higher than project one (53% compared to 39%) because a face to face meeting actually took place and, although the information issued was limited and subject to change later, it provided individuals with a chance to meet each other. The overall experience [2] was rated more highly than the first project highlighting the fact that the team involved appreciated the opportunity to have someone else vet proposals and offer constructive criticism.

Discussion and Conclusion of Case Study Two

This was a particularly difficult project to support virtually due to the high rate at which information was being exchanged between the lead office and the external design team. In this situation, to allow the team to release its full creative potential it may have been beneficial to either:

- Arrange for all team members to reside permanently in one location for the duration of the project.
- Use virtual team working to resource another less demanding project allowing resources to be reassigned and this particular project to be handled by a team working within a single office.

Although communication in this project was slightly better than the first, and the participants did begin to build better relationships following an initial and midproject face to face meeting, there were still problems through lack of awareness of remote colleagues. Some team members were not being informed of all correspondence emanating from the external design team. As such they were often working with inaccurate or out of date information. In order for virtual

Figure 5. Projects One and Two: Participants satisfaction with systems and procedures

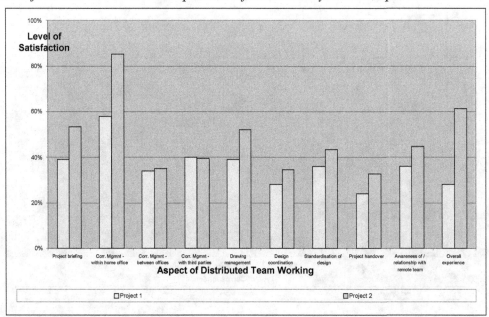

team working to be effective, all correspondence needs to be shared between team members in an efficient transparent manner.

The key lessons learned from this project are:

- Greater thought and discussion should take place prior to undertaking virtual team working to ensure it is the correct solution for the problem.
- Existing systems, such as the project database need to be developed and used to share and store all project correspondence.
- All notes and minutes from meetings or discussions with external design team members should be stored in the shared correspondence database for future reference.

A STRATEGY FOR ENABLING CREATIVE VIRTUAL TEAMS

Following analysis of the key lessons learnt from projects one and two, four key areas were highlighted for development. A strategy for enabling creative virtual teams was developed addressing each lesson highlighted from the first two cases, specifically:

1. Developing a distributed design process map
2. Upgrading the shared correspondence management system
3. Standardising design tools and methods
4. Designing and implementing a corporate intranet

Distributed Design Process Map

The distributed design process map is a procedure aimed at improving the effectiveness of the virtual team and the distributed design process. Improving the efficiency and effectiveness with which the virtual team communicate and work

allows them to focus on the creative process. The virtual design team process map is shown in Figure 6.

Each stage in the distributed design process map is explained in more detail:

- **Decision to seek assistance:** If an office does not have enough resources locally the project director may make the decision to seek support from another office.
- **Check suitability for distributed collaborative design:** Each potential distributed project should be checked to ensure using a virtual team it is the best solution. The following should be considered:
  ° The project should be easily and logically split into packages.
  ° The project should have well defined start and end dates.
  ° The project should not require excessive visits to site, that is, new builds are preferable to refurbishments.

A cost/benefit analysis should be performed to ensure that resources saved by using virtual design teams outweigh potential costs.

- **Select support office:** A resource request manager should be nominated to take responsibility for overseeing resource requests and coordinating distributed resources.
- **Confirm project details:** At this stage the following should be discussed and confirmed before any design work commences:
  ° Virtual design team personnel
  ° Time scales and deadlines

Careful planning and discussion at this stage and selection of appropriate staff will ensure a successful virtual design team. If possible, select designers who have worked together successfully in the past, one of the biggest obstacles to distributed working is building trust and relationships in a short period of time, therefore shortcuts, should be exploited.

Figure 6. The distributed design process map

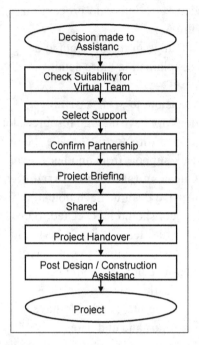

Project Briefing Meeting

A project briefing is critical, providing an opportunity to discuss technical, commercial, and political issues relating to the project. It also gives the virtual team members a chance to meet each other and start to build relationships and trust. The meeting should be minuted to record that the key issues have been discussed and made accessible to everyone working on the project. It is important at this stage that ownership of the relevant design elements is acknowledged between team members.

The following key points that should be addressed at the briefing meeting:

- Review the project history and discuss the design brief
- Define support office and lead office objectives, responsibilities, and deadlines
- Draft an internal project programme and agree who is responsible for monitoring progress
- Agree design tools, methods, and appropriate standards including responsibility for design coordination
- Arrange for regular progress reviews and meetings
- Agree appropriate level of quality control

Distributed Design Phase

During the distributed design stage, the virtual design team should work to meet their objectives as defined in the project briefing meeting. The following tasks should be evident:

Figure 7. Recommended communication structure

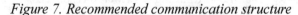

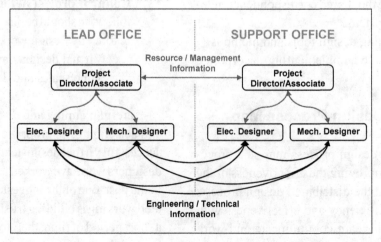

- All correspondence with the external design team should be shared throughout the virtual design team using the shared project correspondence database. Phone calls should be used to communicate project issues between the virtual design team.
- There should be as many face to face meetings as the project budget and programme allows, otherwise telephone is the best medium for discussion. E-mail and fax should be used primarily for the transfer of documents and technical information.
- Design tools and methods used should be consistent with those detailed in the standard design guides detailed on the corporate intranet unless specifically agreed otherwise at the project briefing meeting.
- Weekly progress discussions must occur between the lead engineers in each distributed location with any amendments to the internal project programme being made available to all virtual team members.
- Any assumptions made by a virtual design team member must be checked and approved with the rest of the virtual design team. Proactive communication relating to technical matters is strongly encouraged between members of the virtual design team. Resource or management information should be discussed between the project directors. If workload or priorities change and resources need to be diverted, then this must be agreed at director level and communicated to the designer.

Project Handover Meeting

A face to face handover meeting should take place following completion of design work to allow the team to review the design. This allows smooth transfer of ownership back from the Support Office to the Lead Office. The handover meeting should be scheduled to allow enough time for final checks and modifications prior to design issue.

Post Design / Construction Phase Assistance

Depending on the type of contract, the design team may or may not have responsibilities for overseeing procurement, installation, and design revisions during the construction phase

Project Review

In the interests of continual improvement, every member of the virtual design team should participate in a project review highlighting strengths and weaknesses of the project.

Shared Correspondence Management System

The first two cases highlighted several key problems:

- Poor management of e-mails
- Lack of training and support
- Inconsistent and user-unfriendly interface
- Poor contact management

A great deal of care has to be taken when developing groupware systems within an organisation. Orlikowski and Hofman (1997) highlight the need for improvisation and reacting to events as they occur during development. The project correspondence management system development

Figure 8. The plan-do-check-act (PDCA) cycle

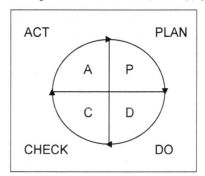

Figure 9. Electrical design tools utilised

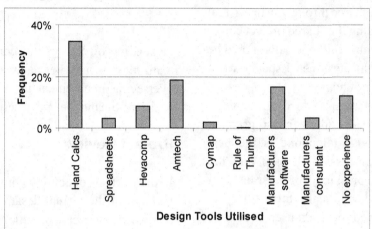

Figure 10. Mechanical design tools utilised

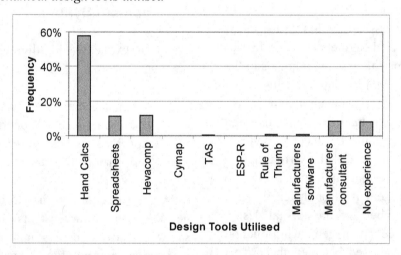

followed a plan-do-check-act (PDCA) cycle. This is one of the key concepts of the Kaizen[1] management theory, which as Imai (1997) explains, focuses on continuous improvement of working practices and personal efficiency.

The development process used within the company is explained briefly below:

PLAN

• **User forum:** A user forum was held with a cross-section of engineers, administration personnel, IT personnel, and a meeting facilitator. During this forum, the current correspondence management system was reviewed in its entirety and users given a chance to express their opinions on the current system and make suggestions for improvement.

• **Create brief:** From the minutes of the user forum, a detailed brief was developed that outlined the proposed development of the system. The brief was revised and reissued for approval following review amongst key personnel.

DO

- **Development of solution:** The project correspondence management system (PCMS) was developed in accordance with the brief to fit alongside existing systems and with minimum disruption and retraining for designers.

- **Training:** Prior to rolling out the revised system, all users were briefed and trained in the functionality and philosophy of the PCMS. This ensured everyone throughout the company knew how to use it, why the development was required and where to go for support or advice. A user manual was compiled and made available to all staff.

- **Rollout:** The revised project data management system was rolled out to all offices over a single weekend so that when staff arrived for work on Monday morning the new system was up and running and all historic correspondence databases had been migrated to the new system. This caused minimum disruption and ensured that all distributed and collocated staff was using the same system from day one.

CHECK

- **Feedback:** A review questionnaire was issued to all designers in order to gauge their reaction to the new system in comparison to the old system. Feedback was very positive throughout almost all aspects the general consensus being that the system was much better and easier to use. Selected results show that:
  - 91% of staff surveyed thought that sending project related correspondence to external design team members was easier or much easier.
  - 82% thought that their awareness of correspondence received by other virtual design team members had improved.
  - 86% thought that joining a project is (or would be) easier or much easier.

ACT

- **Continual improvement:** Feedback from users was handled in-house through a formal feedback database, with serious bugs being fixed immediately and minor bugs and suggestions for additional features being logged and batch processed as appropriate.

Figure 11. Project correspondence management system database usage during project 3

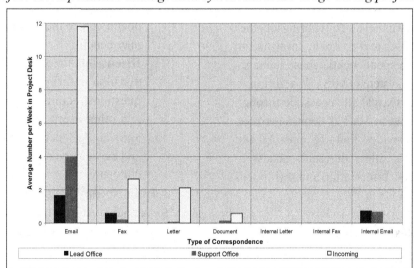

Design Tools and Methods

Case studies one and two highlighted a variation of packages being adopted within the company. Standardising and controlling the tools throughout the company would improve the efficiency of information and data sharing between offices. A design standards review forum was set up consisting of four senior engineers. The forum met initially to discuss the findings of a company wide survey of design tools utilised, shown in Figures 9 and 10—and reconvened regularly to develop and refine proposals for standardising the design tools and methods. Members of the forum analysed the various options available before recommending software packages as "the company standard." To ensure maintenance and continued adoption of the standard design guides and tools a company wide design standards group was set up.

Corporate Intranet

It became apparent from projects one and two that unless an individual had collaborated with another office in the past, they knew very little, if anything, about their distributed colleagues. This lack of awareness of colleagues and associated skills and knowledge could be addressed by creating an online community for the staff to get to know more about the people in the company. A corporate intranet was developed to bring together all existing databases and company information such as project correspondence database, management information systems (MIS), in addition to a new suite of databases, all accessible through a common portal set by staff as their homepage. The homepage provides links to existing and new databases that allow designers access to company standards, information and staff pages as described below:

- **Design notes:** This section contains the following databases:

  ° **Design guides:** This gives best practice advice, company standard design methods including approved software and spreadsheet solutions, relevant standards, and guides.

  ° **Drawing guide:** This is an online CAD manual to be adhered to by all designers and CAD staff ensuring that when drawings are produced during distributed design projects, they are of the same quality and standard throughout the company.

  ° **Distributed design process map:** This is to be followed when embarking on a distributed design project. This is explained in more detail in the section "Distributed Design Process Map."

  ° **QA :** This provides details of the company quality assurance procedures.

  ° **Staff notes:** This raises awareness of remote colleagues and broadens the pool of skills, knowledge, and experience that staff can draw from; this includes databases including news, people, offices, and company handbook.

  ° **Library:** This includes company standard documents such as design spreadsheets and checklists in addition to copies of electronic documents. Designers are encouraged to submit these documents to the library so that others may benefit.

  ° **Discussion forum:** This is a typical discussion forum where users post questions, comments or observations and other users respond accordingly, allowing designers to tap the knowledge and experience of staff throughout the company.

- **Admin Notes:** This section provides links to management information systems (MIS) such as timesheets, expenses, and fee invoice databases.

- **Marketing notes:** This section provides links to other databases such as project registration database (PRDB), ACT (marketing contacts database), and submissions databases.

EVALUATION OF THE STRATEGY FOR ENABLING CREATIVE VIRTUAL TEAMS

The strategy as described previously was evaluated through two further case studies. These projects made use of all aspects of the strategy.

Case Study Project Three

Case Study Three was of three months duration. The project brief was to design mechanical and electrical services for the extension to an existing shopping centre. A virtual team was created led from a regional office and supported by two electrical engineers from the head office, both of whom had historical knowledge of the project.

Project Initiation

As the distributed design process map recommends, a structured face to face briefing meeting took place to allow the Lead and Support teams to discuss the project. Notes from the meeting were stored in the shared project correspondence management system. Some of the members of the virtual team had worked together previously.

Distributed Design Phase

This period worked well largely due to the fact that some members of the virtual design team had collaborated on previous jobs and had already developed good working relationships. Other members of the virtual team who had not met prior to the briefing meeting quickly bonded and there were frequent pro-active telephone calls to discuss matters arising and to check progress. The PCMS was used extensively. Analysis during the distributed design period of this project shows (Figure 11) there were significantly more incoming e-mails being logged—11.8 per week

Figure 12. Project 3: Participants satisfaction with systems and procedures

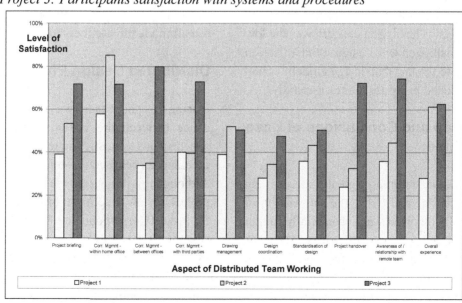

compared with projects one and two. This is a direct result of the improvements made to the system, which allowed designers to easily share and store e-mails within the system. It is also a result of a greater amount of training and support being offered in the use of the system.

Project Handover

A handover meeting did take place. However, not all members of the team could attend. Minutes were taken during the meeting and shared amongst the team using the project correspondence database.

Design Team Satisfaction Survey

The results of the design team satisfaction survey (Figure 12) show increased levels of satisfaction in key areas such as correspondence management [1], [2], project briefing [3], project handover [4], and general awareness and relationship with the remote partner [5]. It must be noted however, that although the participants in this project were more satisfied with most aspects of virtual team working, there were still concerns over drawing management and design standardisation [6], [7], and [8]. It is appropriate to note that drawing management was not addressed within the scope of this project. The biggest concern was the low levels of satisfaction with design standardisation [8] relating to the fact that design guidelines had been introduced just prior to the case study.

Discussion and Conclusions of Case Study Three

Project three was definitely a greater success than both projects one and two. The satisfaction of the designers involved was substantially higher in most areas. Furthermore, there was no re-work required following the project handover. Virtual team members involved in project three indicated the development of the shared correspondence

system helped to improve awareness of virtual design team colleagues. The distributed design process map, also added value to the process—team members agreed that it was extremely useful to have a structured briefing meeting to discuss the project and to have the opportunity to form a good relationship from the outset. Improving each of these areas allowed the virtual team to focus on the creative process of design.

Case Study Project Four

Case Study Four lasted for 1 month and was undertaken by a virtual team consisting of designers from two offices. The head office provided two virtual team members in the form of one engineer and one company associate. The project brief was to provide mechanical and electrical support for an office redevelopment.

Project Initiation

A structured project briefing meeting took place as recommended, the technical and commercial aspects of the project were discussed along with the objectives, responsibilities, and timescales. Similar to project three some key members of the design team already had a strong working relationship through previous collaboration whilst, the remaining team members had never met.

Distributed Design Phase

During this phase there was frequent correspondence between the virtual design team, both synchronous—mostly via telephone and face to face, and asynchronous—mainly through e-mail. Although this project only lasted 1 month, a mid-project review meeting took place. Analysis of the Project Correspondence Management System (Figure 13) shows both offices corresponding with external design team members, with internal correspondence being logged extensively [1]—4.75 per week, compared to 3.14, 3.64 and 1.29 for

Figure 13. Project correspondence management system activity during distributed design phase of project 4

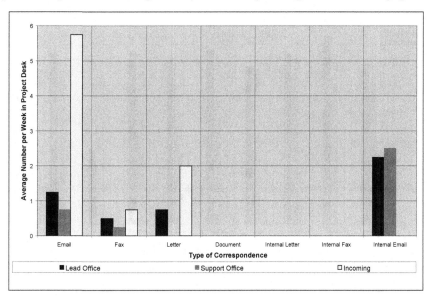

projects one, two, and three respectively. The fact that there was so much internal correspondence being logged shows that the improved system provided a convenient method for sending and crucially recording internal correspondence. We also notice that the usage is more evenly split between both sites of the virtual team showing confidence in using the system throughout the company.

Project Handover

Time constraints within both offices meant there was no handover meeting to transfer ownership back to the lead office.

Design Team Satisfaction Survey

If we look at the results of the design team satisfaction survey Figure 14, it is obvious that the participants of this project were more satisfied with the systems and procedures than in any of the previous projects. The greatest difference can be seen in the areas of design standardization and

drawing management [1], [2], and [3]. This may be attributed to various factors:

- Key members of the virtual team had worked together previously.
- Design tools and methods to be used were discussed and agreed in detail at the briefing meeting.
- A midproject review picked up minor deviations in design before they had gone too far down the wrong road.

The lack of a structured handover meeting meant that this was rated low in the satisfaction survey [4].

Discussion and Conclusions of Case Study Four

Overall this was a successful distributed design project. Deliverables were issued in the timescale required and were of appropriate quality. Similar to case three, this project was made easier because of the tools and procedures specified by the strat-

Figure 14. Project 4: Participants satisfaction with systems and procedures

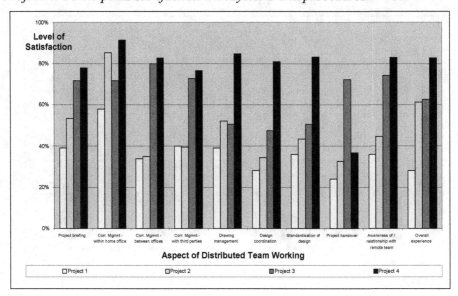

egy for enabling creative virtual teams. The virtual team's satisfaction with the improvement in each key project areas is highlighted in Figure 14. The creative design process was facilitated further by the fact that key team members already had a good working relationship. Through the distributed design process however, other designers within each office were able to form relationships that may be exploited in future. The importance of face to face communication was highlighted through a midproject progress meeting which picked up several misinterpreted design features.

CONCLUSION

This chapter describes a study of creative virtual teams within an SME environment. The study spans a period of 2 years with four separate case studies being presented each based on live projects. Two initial case studies, described in the third section, highlight issues and areas for improvement within virtual team working practice, which are addressed through the development of a strategy for enabling creative virtual teams. This strategy addresses four key areas: distributed design pro-

cess map; project correspondence management system (PCMS); design tools and methods; and corporate intranet. Each of these is described in detail in the fourth section.

The strategy is evaluated through two further case studies again based on live projects; these case studies prove that successful virtual design teaming is achievable with appropriate systems and procedures in place, thus releasing creative potential. The PCMS ensured that designers' were aware of latest developments regardless of where they were located. Analysis of system data shows a dramatic increase in its usage from case studies 1-4. Demonstrating a clear improvement in the effectiveness with which the virtual teams are communicating and managing their communication. The corporate intranet helped by giving designers in remote locations information about people, skills, knowledge and news about people from all around the company, helping to instil a sense of association with the company as a whole rather than each office being an island. Following the distributed design map has improved the efficiency and effectiveness of the process. Misinterpretations are identified before they have a major impact with the need for rework diminishing to zero in projects three and four. Furthermore, from cases one to four the team are more satisfied with the various aspects of the distributed design process in particular the greatest improvements occurring in:

- Correspondence management between distributed team offices – 147%
- Design coordination – 115%
- Standardisation of design – 133%
- Awareness of relationship with remote team – 133%
- Overall experience – 121%

Making improvements in each of these areas is critical to releasing creative potential within virtual teams. This is emphasised through quoting a company director on the results of this project. "Overall the entire virtual design team experience is much happier. The new correspondence management system and design standardisation has vastly improved design coordination. Teams are working more closely through the adoption of the distributed design process map—instead of struggling to produce one design that meets the requirements virtual teams are more efficient allowing them to produce, explore and select the best from multiple design options."

In addition to offering an evaluated strategy, this study highlights and reinforces several issues well founded in the literature such as higher trust between individuals who have met before, and the essential nature of face to face meetings. Furthermore, this study recognises that strangers working in virtual teams with other team members who know and trust each other bond faster and more effectively and that it is important to identify critical points within the distributed design process for face to face meetings. Value is added by the fact that these results are based on real "live projects" rather than laboratory tests which have been the focus of many studies to date.

This study focuses on distributed design practice within a medium sized company who like many other SMEs had the technology to support virtual team working in place, but needed to improve existing company processes and systems, adopt appropriate tools and methods, and address management issues to achieve greater effectiveness from virtual design teamwork. Many companies, especially SMEs face the problems and issues highlighted in case studies one and two and could therefore, make use of the developed strategy. In particular, other SMEs could benefit from:

Distributed design process map—this step by step approach to setting up and undertaking a distributed design project using a virtual team is presented in a straight forward manner. Critical stages are highlighted and proven methods for achieving success are presented. This map could easily be modified to suit specific companies and their business requirements.

Development of the shared project correspondence management system—in this study the company adopted a plan-do-check-act (PDCA) approach to develop their PCMS. This chapter provides a description of how the company used this method to their benefit. Others SMEs may find this approach useful for developing their own company specific systems and will find the description of how the case study company used this approach both informative and encouraging.

Standardisation of design tools and methods—many SMEs struggle to achieve and maintain standardisation of tools and methods. This chapter presents a successful method adopted by one particular company. Others SMEs could adopt a similar approach or select particular elements of the approach described within their company.

Others SMEs will find value in the 'tales' described in this chapter, and should be able to modify the developed support to suit their own circumstances. Whilst this work focuses on virtual design teams within one company, the strategy could be applied to achieving and maintaining effective virtual team design between organisations. The success of the cases was determined by measuring the satisfaction of designers since they were the people using the systems and procedures, and were best positioned to comment on their effectiveness.

REFERENCES

Bradner, E., & Mark, G. (2002, November). Why distance matters: Effects on cooperation, persuasion and deception. In *Proceedings of the ACM Conference on Computer-Supported Cooperative Work (CSCW 2002)*, New Orleans (pp. 226-235). New York: ACM Press.

Greenberg, M. H. (1993), S real time distributed collaboration. In P. Dasgupta & J. E. Urban (Eds.), *Encyclopedia of distributed computing* (pp. 241-254). Amsterdam: Kluwer Academic Publishers.

Hayes, N., & Walsham, G. (2000). Competing interpretations of computer supported cooperative work in organizational contexts. *Organization*, 7(1), 49-67.

Herbsleb, J., Mockus, A, Finholt, T. A., & Grinter, R.E., (2000, December). *Distance, dependencies and delay in a global collaboration*. In *Proceedings of the ACM Conference on Computer-Supported Cooperative Work (CSCW 2000)*, Philadelphia (pp. 319-328). New York: ACM Press.

Imai, M. (1997). *Gemba Kaizen: A common sense, low cost approach to management*. New York: McGraw-Hill.

Ishii, H., & Kobayashi, M. (1992, May). Clearboard: A seamless medium for shared drawing and conversation with eye contact. In *Proceedings of the ACM CHI'92 Conference on Human Factors in Computing Systems*, Monterrey, CA (pp. 525-532).

Jagodzinski, P., Reid, F., & Culverhouse, P. (2000). A study of electronics engineering design teams. *Design Studies*, 21(4), 375-402.

Jarvenpaa, S. L., & Leidner D. E. (1998). Communication and trust in global virtual teams. *Journal of Computer Mediated Communication*, 3(4). Retrieved November 1, from http://jcmc.indiana.edu/vol3/issue4/

Lipnack.A., & Stamps, T. (2000) *Virtual teams: People working across boundaries with technology*. New York: John Wiley & Sons.

MacGregor, S. P.; Thomson, A. I., & Juster, N. P. (2002, July). A multi-level process based investigation of distributed design. In *Proceedings of the Engineering Design Conference 2002 (EDC 2002)*, Kings College London, London.

Observatory of European SMEs. (2002). *Enterprise and industry business statistics*. European Union Publications. Retrieved October 20, 2006, from http://ec.europa.eu/enterprise/enterprise_policy/analysis/observatory_en.htm

Orlikowski, W. (1993, November). Learning from notes: Organisational issues in groupware implementation. In *Proceedings of the 1992 ACM Conference on Computer-Supported Cooperative Work*, Toronto, Ontario, Canada (pp. 362-369).

Orlikowski, W. J. (1996). Evolving with notes: Organizational change around groupware technology. In C. U. Ciborra (Ed.), *Groupware and teamwork—Invisible aid or technical hindrance?* (pp. 23-59). Chichester, UK: John Wiley & Sons.

Orlikowski, W. J., & Hofman, J. D. (1997, Winter). An improvisational model of change management: The case of groupware technologies. *Sloan Management Review*, 32(2), 11-21.

Rocco, E. (1998, April). Trust breaks down in electronic contexts but can be repaired by some initial face to face contact. In *Proceedings of CHI'98*, Los Angeles, CA (pp. 496-502). New York: ACM Press.

Teasley, S., Covi, L, Krishnan, M. S., & Olson, J. S. (2000, December). How does radical colocation help a team succeed? In *Proceedings of the ACM Conference on Computer-Supported Cooperative Work (CSCW 2000)*, Philadelphia (pp. 339-346). New York: ACM Press.

Top Gear. (1996, March 7). Ford Motor Company case study. *Computer Weekly.*

Williams, E. (1977). Experimental comparisons of face to face and mediated communication: A Review. *Psychological Bulletin, 84*(5), 963-976.

Yin, R. K. (1994). *Case study research: Design methods* (2nd ed.). London: Sage Publications.

Zheng, J., Veinott, E., Bos, N., Olson, J. S., & Olson, G. M. (2002, April). Trust without touch: jumpstarting long distance trust with initial social activities. In *Proceedings of the Conference on Human Factors in Computing Systems (CHI 2002)*, Minneapolis, MN (pp. 131-146). New York: ACM Press.

ENDNOTE

[1]   "Kaizen" is Japanese for "continuous improvement."

Chapter IX
Virtual Teams and Creativity in the Mondragón Cooperative Corporation

Javier Fínez

Mondragón Innovation & Knowledge & Mondragón Cooperative Corporation, Spain

ABSTRACT

For companies in this age of globalization and innovation, creativity is a core activity in a growing section of the economy. Since virtual teams are a relatively new organizational form, very little research has been carried out on their structure, performance, routines, and of course, on their creative ability. In this chapter, a detailed insight will be provided of three experiences of virtual teams built into Mondragón Cooperative Corporation (MCC) cooperatives, providing an overview of the company's activity, going into greater depth regarding the needs and opportunities behind the decision to set up a virtual team, detailing the organizational structure adopted in each case, the dynamics incorporated to achieve higher creativity, and suggesting some practices that can put the reader on the path towards common drivers for virtual creativity.

INTRODUCTION TO THE MCC BATTLEFIELD AND CHAPTER OBJECTIVES

Surfing papers, folders and electronic devices, traveling miles with nothing more than the click of a mouse and a tiny Web-cam presiding over his desk, and chatting with Ian: *"How do you fancy this idea ... I like it a lot ... could you develop this part further while I check with Karl how things are going with the offshore team ... and later we'll all meet on the Chat platform at 14:00 GPM and discuss the next steps."*

This *'modus operandi,'* which we may think is far ahead of everyday practice and reserved solely for top executives spread out across the four corners of the globe, in charge of technological mega platforms, is nevertheless becoming an increasingly regular picture in all companies. Due to such factors as the internationalization of business, the externalization of noncore activities, and the inclusion of suppliers and customers in projects, companies need to get together and redesign their creative processes so as to actively take part in the age of globalization.

This is the case of the Mondragón Cooperative Corporation (MCC), the largest cooperative conglomerate in the world, founded in the village (Mondragón, in the Basque Country in the North of Spain) from which it takes its name, in 1956. Nowadays, MCC is a business group made up of 264 companies and entities organized into three clusters: The Financial Group, which includes activities such as banking, social welfare, and insurance; the Industrial Group, which comprises eight divisions dedicated to the production of goods and services, and the Distribution Group, which is made up of various commercial, distribution, and agricultural-food companies. There are also a number of research, vocational training and teaching centers, including a university which has over 4,000 students. See MacGregor, Arana, Parra, and Lorenzo (2006) for an example on how co-creation proceeds within this unique environment.

At this point we dare to make a small plea in favor of cooperativism, because we think the choice of MCC as one of the battlefields to benchmark virtual teams and creativity is no accident. Some of the essential values of cooperativism, such as collaboration, transparency, equity, democratic management, and so on seem to be equally relevant to teamwork, members' camaraderie, personal involvement, and the like. Among the principles of cooperativism, revised by the International Cooperative Alliance (ICA) in Manchester in 1995, it is stated:

Cooperatives are voluntary organizations, open to all persons able to use their services and willing to accept the responsibilities of membership. (p. 45) (Closely related to subjects such as involvement and collaboration within teams)

Cooperatives are democratic organizations controlled by their members, who participate in setting their policies and making decisions. Men and women have equal rights and are organized in a democratic manner. (p. 45) (Closely linked to the fact that equity, democracy and transparency are generally recognized as key factors for successful team management)

Cooperatives serve their members most effectively and strengthen the group movement by working together as autonomous, self-help organizations controlled by their members. (p. 45) (Here we see the concept of democratic team management which is discussed later as an important principle of team management)

At MCC, individual cooperatives constitute the basic organizational structure, with the General Assembly acting as the supreme body to express the will of the members and the sovereignty of the cooperative, and the Governing Council acting as the ultimate body for management and representation, bearing responsibility for the appointment of the managing director.

This structure and the constant effort in favor of internationalization and integration has allowed MCC today to have 57 production plants in 16 different countries, which accounted for 18% of total industrial production in 2005 and for 12,858 jobs. If we add the numbers of personnel working in corporate and sales offices abroad and the jobs that Eroski provides in its shopping centres in the south of France, the foreign workforce total reaches 14,121 people (at the end of 2005) which is 18% of the total corporate workforce of MCC, calculated at nearly 70,000 people throughout the five continents.

Having presented MCC and, by extension, the cooperativism battlefield where virtual teams flourish, we will provide in this chapter an insight into various experiences of virtual teams built into MCC cooperatives, and discuss how different issues such as structure, management type, and technological means are reflected in virtual creativity. For each of the experiences, an overview of the company's main activity will be presented together with the needs and opportunities behind the decision to set up the virtual team; the organizational structure adopted in each case; the dynamics to support virtual creativity and the best and worst practices as related by people closely involved in these virtual teams.

With these objectives in mind the next section provides a brief preamble to the relevant themes (virtual teams and creativity), and is followed by tales from the MCC battlefield, featuring three of the leading companies in the implementation of virtual teams, who were asked to share their amazing experiences specifically for this book. Finally, in the "Towards Common Drivers for Virtual Creativity" section, we discuss the three cases in unison to help the reader in making cross-comparisons and to summaries the main findings uncovered in this research exercise.

THE ROOTS OF VIRTUAL TEAMS AND CREATIVITY

One of the more accepted definitions for the word 'team' comes from Katzenbach and Smith (1993):

A team is a small number of people (from two to twenty five) with complementary skills who are committed to a common purpose, performance goals, and approach for which they hold themselves mutually accountable. (p. 45)

Although there is no clear, single definition for 'virtual' team, the common factor in most of them is that members of virtual teams are physically scattered (in time and/or space) and that their interaction is predominantly electronic (The Networking Institute, 2000).

In this way, companies that are geographically isolated or eager for participation and interaction have turned to virtual teams as a response to the increasing need for coordination and collaboration brought about by an era of globalization of clients, suppliers, markets, and production plants. This response depends on the sophistication of Information and Communications Technologies (ICTs) and arises, in the words of Ruben Igual, Project Manager at household appliances multinational Fagor Electrodomésticos:

... due to sheer need. Because you want to have the best people with you, but they may be so far away that you cannot meet everyday, or even once a week ... and yet their initiative, knowledge and creativity are an absolute 'must' if we are to go on being the best.

With respect to the other aspect in which we are most interested in this chapter, the phenomena of 'creativity', there exists more than fifty different definitions just from the psychological point of view (Albert & Runce 1999). To adopt a commonly accepted definition, 'creativity' is a mental process involving the generation of new ideas or concepts, or new associations between existing ideas or concepts. Evidence shows that the capacity to think creatively is common to everyone (Kirton, 1989); the differences appear in the way people express it.

Different authors (Ekvall, 1997; Fairbank, Spangler, & Williams, 2003; Proctor, Tan, & Fuse 2004; Shalley, Zhou, & Oldham, 2004) as well as people interviewed for this publication who are involved in the everyday routine of these teams, have agreed on two basic archetypes of creativity, namely, incremental creativity and radical creativity. This duality, incremental vs. radical, has also been widely studied and analyzed with reference to the concept of innovation (Balachandra & Friar, 1997; Veryzer, 1998; Koberg, Detienne, & Heppard, 2003), the principles and drivers behind creativity being quite similar in essence to those behind innovation.

Incremental creativity, also known as adaptive or sustained creativity, refers to small changes and improvements aimed at modifying the dynamics, functionality, processes, and features of the product or service that the creativity process is concerned with. Normally this incremental creativity is produced in a cumulative way, with a continuing evolution-improvement cycle based on an already existing line of work, re-framing the ways in which a product category or service is perceived.

Radical creativity, on the other hand, also known as revolutionary, disruptive or boundary crossing creativity, involves a substantial breakthrough in thinking about the existing established line of work. This could be based, for example, on a totally different point of view or way of conceiving a process, or technology, which generates substantially new products, processes or services that cannot be understood as a natural evolution of the already existing core 'knowledge base.' For more information on definitions and distinctions between both types of creativity, see Ekvall (1997).

Figure 1. Incremental and radical creativity

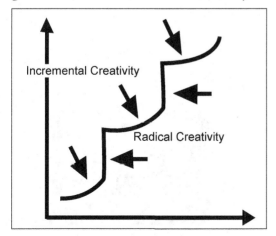

The differences between both types of creativity can also be observed graphically, as in Figure 1, where radical and incremental creativity strokes alternate. As seen in the chart, incremental creativity is marked as a horizontal line with a very gradual slope, which represents small changes or improvements upon an already existing line. Intermittently, prominent vertical lines interrupt the quiet flow of the chart, marking a disruptive breakthrough in the way the idea, process or product is conceived. This is so-called 'radical' creativity.

A final element of course regarding virtual teams and creativity is technology—yet sophisticated ICTs are not enough to enable truly creative virtual teams. Emphasized on several occasions by managers interviewed for this chapter is the importance of an adequate operational structure—of which technology in only a part. In the next section, we move on to the core of the chapter, describing in detail three cases of companies that have shaped different organizational structures for their virtual teams. In this way we will illustrate how factors such as operational structure, management, objectives, and type of work can help towards, or result in, higher levels of creativity.

CASE ONE: VIRTUAL TEAMS AND CREATIVITY IN FAGOR ELECTRODOMESTICOS (HOUSEHOLD APPLIANCES)

Fagor Electrodomésticos is a prime example of the internationalization process undergone by companies at MCC. Conceived under the name of ULGOR in Mondragon towards the end of 1956, it started off manufacturing paraffin stoves for the national market. Fifty years on, Fagor Electrodomésticos has consolidated its position as one of the major companies in the global home appliances market, operating in eight different business areas, including: refrigerators, dishwashers, driers, ovens and hoods. The company has 16 production plants in six countries across Europe, America and Africa, a presence in more than 100 countries and a staff of nearly 12,000 employees.

In order to analyze the organizational revolution brought about by this complexity in the evolution of virtual teams at Fagor Electrodomésticos, we met Xabier Elizetxea, Research and Development Manager for the baking area and Rubén Igual, Project Manager. Rubén is one of the people involved in the everyday functioning of virtual teams and he remembers his first experience dating back to 2001, which came about in response to the need to integrate the main suppliers with whom they were working:

We want to work with the best, and they are not usually by your side. We need to integrate them at earlier and earlier stages of engineering, design, marketing, and of course, accomplish all this efficiently and cost-effectively.

Since 2001, Rubén has taken part in multiple virtual teams that have contributed to forging a virtual culture in the company and a new organizational model. These teams, called operational virtual teams (OVT), aim to gather the best human team, regardless of their geographical location, and to develop a given task in an innovative way within a fixed deadline.

It is something similar to the way the movie industry works: the director, the actors, the technicians and the producers get together to carry out a common project, work together sharing their creativity for a while, and then part to start up new projects.

Virtual Team Structure

From a conceptual point of view, the structure of an OVT is similar to that of a sphere, see Figure 2. In an OVT there is only one boss, called the

leader, and a base team that is usually formed by between ten and twelve people working in concentric spheres of three to four people each. These concentric spheres are determined by the fields of knowledge which are necessary to develop the assigned task. As a general rule, in Fagor Electrodomésticos these spheres of knowledge usually correspond to the Engineering, Design, Production, and Marketing Departments of the different plants they have throughout the world. The first important feature of OVTs is that they are multidisciplinary:

This prevents them from being formed solely of experts in just one area who may set out looking at the problem from just their own point of view. As they work with experts belonging to other fields, they can look further to more daring solutions.

Moreover, experience has shown that renewing the membership in each virtual project is not only good practice but also advisable as a means to encourage innovation.

These aspects, together with a multicultural approach constitute good starting conditions that encourage creativity in our teams.

The triggering factor of an OVT coincides with a meeting, ideally face to face ... :

... with all the members of the team, not just with those responsible for each sphere. Having some

Figure 2. Structure of an operative virtual team: Creativity sphere

prior physical contact is a determining factor when it comes to working virtually. It allows people to get involved in the task, creates empathy among the different members, and makes them proactive and creative in problem solving.

Furthermore, this meeting gives the leader an opportunity to specify the goals of the OVT in a univocal way, thus ushering in the collaboration process so as to achieve the expected results.

These leaders are not chosen because they are particularly communicative or skilled in new technologies, but because they know a lot about the specific field they will develop, they have organizational and consensual skills, and because they are able to unify expectations and get the best out of the different team members. In this way the OVT is launched, and in its conceptual structure—Figure 3—the leader is seen as the nucleus of the sphere and the concentric spheres are the different departments involved in the team.

Each of the concentric spheres is formed of people belonging to the same field of knowledge but geographically spread out in different plants. In a typical example, the first sphere, closer to the leader, is made up of those members of the team belonging to the engineering department of the different plants, the following concentric circle is formed by those belonging to the design department and the third sphere comprises people from the marketing area that are involved in the virtual team.

Reflection on Creativity

This organizational structure has a special influence on the OVT's creativity, as it allows the exchange and creation of knowledge among the members of the team to take place on two different levels:

- On the one hand, those who are experts in the same field work very hard on an intra-sphere basis—concentric collaboration—together with the rest of the experts from the geographically distributed team. It is this collaboration that is the main source of so-called incremental creativity.
- On the other hand, they also collaborate on a more sporadic basis with members from other fields (or spheres), thus exchanging knowledge in radial collaboration. It is in these concentric multidisciplinary leaps that radical creativity is more commonplace.

As can be seen, the spherical structure that appears in the virtual teams of Fagor Electrodomésticos enables a first moment of 'intra-spherical creativity':

Figure 3. INTRA/INTER-spherical structure of creativity in the OVT

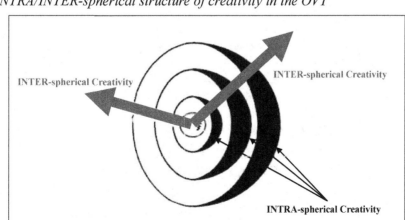

... and this is the result of each member of the subteam studying the problem from its own corner, sharing it calmly with other team mates from the sphere under no pressure, and with enough time that the final result of this creativity is to some extent studied and structured so that it does not make the rest of the team waste their time. This is unlike what can happen in local teams where the leader sets the line of thought for the whole group.

Ideas, innovations and suggestions that arise during this stage of intra-spherical exchange, when taken as a whole, *comprises* the so-called intra-spherical creativity which is usually incremental in nature, as the collaborating members belong to the same field of knowledge resulting in very few radical innovations. Communication and incremental creativity usually materializes through phone calls, Web conferencing or chats with other members of the sphere to exchange impressions, possibilities, and so on. Later, the result of this creativity is communicated to the leader of the OVT by phone or e-mail.

Once the leader has been informed, he or she activates his or her radial communication channels with the rest of the concentric spheres to let them know about the solutions proposed and weigh up how these may affect both the project and the rest of the OVT. This leader-spheres communication is two-sided, since stimuli arise in the core to be radially communicated to all the concentric spheres, and these in turn react with creativity, new suggestions and ideas, looking for synergies and adapting to the new suggestions posed from the core.

The activity produced in the radial axis is the so-called radical creativity. It provokes larger qualitative leaps in creativity since it is motivated by people from other disciplines with more ability to consider the situation from different points of view. It usually materializes in the form of a video-conference or e-mail communication sent either to the leader or to all the members of the OVT.

In this way we go back to the starting point of the creative cycle, see Figure 4, because as a result of the radical creativity produced inter-

Figure 4. Creative cycle of OVTs

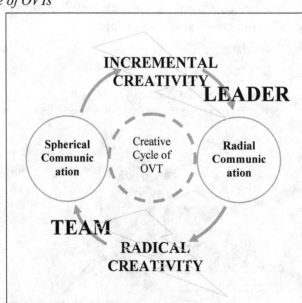

spherically, further intra-spherical analyses of the contributed new solutions are produced, stimulating creativity in each of the spheres in response to the new situation.

Apart from the permanent members of the OVT, in this spherical structure we also find the figure of the "satellite." The satellite, a political position within each organization, is the member that orbits outside the spheres. He or she does not take part in the OVT itself but plays two main roles:

First, in monitoring meetings he or she supervises the development of the project and might play an important role in the radical creativity as he or she has nontechnical training which might help pose interesting and different points of view. He or she will benefit from having, at the same time, a global view of the organization and the skill to look for synergies.

Also, he or she is the person you turn to when the OVT doesn't work properly and the leader is at a loss and needs a different kind of help—so to speak—"from the highest authorities."

The 'political aspect' enables him or her to strike up conversation with other 'satellites' responsible for the rest of the organizations taking part in the OVT and to take decisions at the highest level:

Resorting to political means is very rare; you are not supposed to do so unless it is a real emergency and only the leader is entitled to take this course.

Along with the virtual team members there are also temporary recruits who carry out occasional tasks. Nevertheless, these tend to be kept local, that is, unless the need exists, the rest of the members do not actually know of their existence, as they might contribute to causing unrest in the OVT. Their function is channeled through the member

of the OVT that belongs to the intra-sphere in which they take part.

Further Insights

Apart from considerations of structure and creativity, there emerged some other findings that are worth presenting to contribute to later discussion and cross comparison. A so-called "Theory of the Volume of the Virtual Team" has been observed which arises from the working model described; the higher the concentration in the sphere, the smaller the diameter so the greater the cumulative creativity and, in turn, the more scattered the sphere, the greater the radical creativity. In other words more volume involves more viewpoints, more multidisciplinarily teams, more chaos and thus more possibilities of radical creativity. Less volume means more uniformity in the points of view, less disciplinary richness and more incremental creativity.

Digging deeper into the concept of creativity, Rubén remarks that he has also noticed that the type of creativity and the space—time communication channels used to interact are somehow related:

At any given time, the members of the team know which communication channel to use, depending on the urgency of the communication and on whom they want to contact—the leader, inter-spherical or intra-spherical team mates.

This space-time communication vs. creativity type can be summarized in the following chart, Figure 5 (see Chapter IV of this book by Leenders, Kratzer and van Engenlen, "Media Ensembles and New Product Team Creativity: A Tree-Based Exploration," for an investigation of media use and creativity):

- E-mail is used both intra-spherically and with the whole OVT to circulate nonurgent documentation—that is, that which can wait until the following day. It is also a means to put across ideas or concepts in a clear way, avoiding any misunderstandings:

However, such a cold means as e-mail can be interpreted in very different ways depending on the moment it is received, the mood of the recipient, the usage of capital letters, opening and closing remarks, and so on.

- The telephone (Web-cam usage is not so widespread yet) is mostly used for urgent communication and to share emotions in a spontaneous way. Most of all it is for intra-spherical communication or for personal contact with the leader.
- Chats are used as an all-with-all intra-spherical means of communication and are not normally used to contact the leader.
- The video-conferencing room is used as an all-with-all inter-spherical tool to generate and coordinate new ideas and also for team operational and organizational routine sessions. These operational sessions are scheduled and subject to an agenda:

We carry out monitoring videoconference sessions once a week. In these sessions each subteam shares what they've achieved in their intrasphere with the rest of the subteams. This moment is prone to radical creativity, as this inter-spherical exchange leads to people considering the work from a multidisciplinary point of view, looking for synergies, unification, and so on. Although this exchange of knowledge does not always produce great ideas or stimulate creativity in the OVT, it is vital to maintain it, at least, as a way to check that everything is moving forward, meeting deadlines and, as expected.

There is also a close link between relationship/communication intensity and creativity. Firstly, the relationship/communication intensity phenomenon is different in each of the spheres that take part in the project. Communication is deeper and more frequent among the members of the intra-sphere and between these people and the

Figure 5. Communication mode vs. creativity type

	Incremental Creativity				Radical Creativity		Ordinary Coordination		
	Urgent spontaneous communication	Ad-hoc Communication	Leader-Member Communication	Intensive Intra-sphere Communication	Inter-sphere Communication	Predetermined Communication	Communication on organizational and operative aspects	Non-Urgent Documents	Routine Communication
Email					■		■	■	■
Telephone	■	■	■						
Web-conferencing	■	■	■						
Chat				■	■				
Video-conference					■	■	■		
Document Management Platform					■	■	■		

leader in spheres which are closer to the nucleus. Thus, the farther we are from the center, the less decisive becomes the inter-sphere relationship and the members' communication with the leader. Finally, Xabier and Rubén admit that:

The moment the team begins to go through operational tensions like not meeting deadlines, or when there's a reluctance or lack of trust among people, that's the moment when the leader should call an all-in meeting and use face-to-face contact, body language, tone of voice and everything else to redirect the situation. In general, we only resort to physical meetings when we have used up all our other options without success.

CASE TWO: VIRTUAL TEAMS AND CREATIVITY IN MAIER

Maier is part of the Automotive Division of MCC, a sector characterized by the existence of gigantic clients (car makers) with extremely high negotiating power over smaller suppliers like Maier. Set up in Gernika (Spain) in 1973, it manufactures plastic injection parts and groups of parts mainly for the automotive industry, but also for household appliances and consumer electronics. Nowadays, within Europe, Maier is at the forefront in the development and manufacture of body-color painted

front grilles, chrome wheel-trims, hub-caps and petrol-cap covers, and so forth, see Figure 6, with five production plants, sales of € 220 million and a workforce of nearly 2,200 people.

Given this complex, highly-competitive sector, Maier set up the Maier Technology Centre (MTC) at their headquarters in Gernika. MTC is designed to be the centre for virtual teams structuring and to coordinate the great quantity of research and development activities carried out among the five manufacturing plants distributed across three European countries. See Figure 7.

In order to get to know the organizational structure of virtual teams in Maier, we met Álvaro Páramo and Eneko Santiso, a studies manager and systems engineer respectively, who are involved in the everyday functioning of virtual teams:

The first virtual teams were born spontaneously to connect the diverse national and international plants and arose from the need to coordinate people. Things were usually coordinated over the phone or by e-mail, but one had to travel whenever the issue was something important.

Formally, virtual teams are framed within the structure of project planning management at Maier, which specifies the people, positions and responsibilities in those groups:

Figure 6. Some products marketed by Maier

Figure 7. Production plants throughout Europe

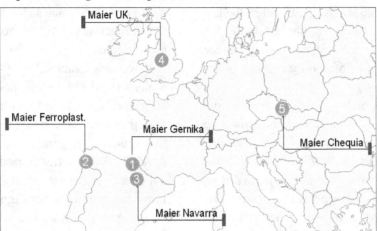

... *which are characterized by being made up of members who cyclically go in, do their job, and leave, in order to successfully carry out projects that take an average of two years from the elaboration of the initial viability studies and the offer on the contract, to the testing of the necessary equipment prior to the mass production of the piece.*

Virtual Team Structure

Conceptually, the organizational structure of the standard virtual team at Maier looks like a spiral, see Figure 8, which has a beginning (the initial bid for a contract) and end (the manufacturing of the contracted parts in the plants). The person in charge throughout the whole of the project is the project leader (who is also the team leader) and the members of the team are determined by the different stages (or 'spiral phases') that the project goes through:

As a general rule, all the departments in the different plants and in MTC collaborate in some way at some stage of a given project, which is a practice we have found especially satisfactory as it favors the transmission of knowledge and encourages creativity within the company.

As a result of this 'in and out' rotation in the virtual team, coordination work has to be more structured and organized than in ordinary groups. With this aim in mind, they use the usual communications technology as well as two management platforms: ARTEMIS and an in-house developed project management platform. Moreover, it is difficult to gather the whole team due to dissimilar timetables in the different regions and the members' availability, among other things, which is why ...

... *one has to make the most of those video-conferences in which all the members of the virtual team take part, respect rules on punctuality, get to the point, don't beat about the bush, and so on.*

It can be compared to a "long-distance romance" in that you have to pamper and look after it much more carefully than normal if you want to "keep it alive."

As a rule, the virtual team, whose first mission is to make a bid for the contract according to the customer's requirements, is made up of people from MTC and from the Commercial, Costs, Purchasing, and Production Departments as well as the customers themselves. People who are going to form part of the initial team are appointed by those in charge of each department

Figure 8. Structure of a virtual team at Maier: Creativity spiral

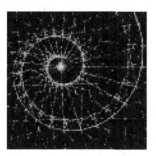

part and shares his or her progress with the rest of the team members. It is a process we could call constructivist, moving forward along the spiral (see Figure 9).

As the project moves forward in time and completes this stage, it goes towards a follow-on phase in which some of the members of the virtual team stop or reduce their involvement while other departments from the plants join in to contribute their knowledge to the next stages of the project.

bearing in mind such issues as their knowledge of the family of components to be offered, any prior work with the same client, and so on. The launch of the process usually coincides with an initial meeting between the members of the team—either physically or through video-conferencing—to consider the offer from the different points of view represented, and to design the best possible strategy to land the contract.

Collaboration among the members of the team could be called 'cyclical'; that is to say, each member works locally on his or her own

If we land the contract, the contribution to the virtual team of people from Costs, Commercial etc. decreases, and new functions join in, such as the product developer, the production processes developer, quality control, simulations and so on, that take over the previous work and lead to further progress along the spiral.

Reflection on Creativity

This organizational structure, based on multi-disciplinary teams that rotate according to the

Figure 9. Alternation between radical and incremental creativity in the project spiral

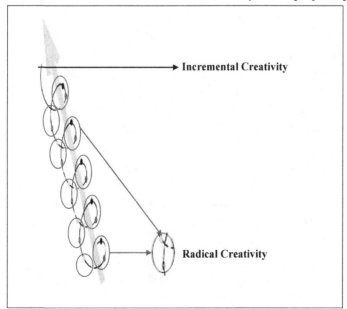

skills needed to move along the project planning management process, affects virtual team creativity in fundamental ways that becomes apparent with greater or lesser intensity. First, when the distributed virtual team of experts is formed, they take over the corresponding previous part of the work:

They work it out locally without the passivity often generated by the lack of oral fluency in a foreign language or by the omnipresent face-to-face brainstorming sessions which are supposed to encourage creativity but are, in most cases, a waste of time.

They talk things over and new work ideas arise. They go over them again locally and then share their work once more. This interchange of "local work—sharing of ideas" brings about proposals, attempts to find synergies, reconsiderations of the problem, the search for an alternative method. These elements, taken as a whole, lead to incremental creativity.

The second moment takes place as a result of the incorporation of new members into the team as the different stages of project initiation come to an end. These new incorporations receive a project that they have to get to know, and contribute their points of view by posing questions like: 'Why don't we try doing things this way?' 'Let's introduce this new parameter to see if works out,' and so on. In this way they produce successive moments of collective catharsis, of great creativity that can change the running of the project for the better and bring about radical or deeper creativity:

This creativity is boosted by the fact that it is virtual. As the new members get in touch with others they probably do not personally know, whose opinions on common issues they are not aware of, it is easier to leave personal issues aside and go straight to the point. These forms of creative behavior are not so easily accomplished in ordi-

nary, nonvirtual teams, which are usually biased because members already know each other. They know how they think, what they are allowed to put forward, what cannot be done. In other words, there are in fact some assumed roles discouraging creativity that a virtual team does not have.

A third moment, which is usually the most critical one for the virtual team, takes place when the customer changes the initial requirements, thus obliging the team to force their creativity so as to adapt to the new terms. These changes are the most critical ones, particularly in a virtual team since at the beginning, confusion prevails and the isolation factor becomes more evident. (Late customer changes may require the need for greater process *flexibility*, a concept detailed by Preston Smith's chapter, "Enhancing Flexibility in Dispersed Product Development Teams," Chapter XII of this book).

These dramatic swings produce a moment of great effervescence, of catharsis in the team, of re-situation which, at the very least, leads to urgent video-conferences and loads of all-to-all communications to exchange impressions. There will be brainstorming to offer solutions to the new situation and, if the worst comes to the worst, one follows the spiral back to a point where it is possible to resume the problem.

Although this third 'creativity booster' is the most critical one, these are the situations in which one can really measure the team's creativity, their maturity and their capacity to collaborate.

In Figure 10, each of the shaded areas represents people participating in the virtual team who belong to the different departments of the plants taking part in the project. In this way, by means of the cyclical combination of the stages of radical creativity (new incorporations and, to a lesser extent, changes in the customer's requirements) and incremental creativity (once the team has settled and every one is working on his or her own piece of the puzzle) the virtual team carries out its development function (co-creation) until it reaches the final stage. This, in the case of Maier, is the one prior to mass production.

Further Insights

Leaders of virtual teams at Maier have long been working with this structure and agree that it works for the profile of the company and type of activity entrusted to the teams. However, they have noticed that performance and creativity fluctuate according to activity, stage, experience of the team and so on. In collaboration with the interviewees

we have identified several variables that greatly influence performance and creativity.

At least two different types of variables were present at team level. 'Intellectual variables,' values intrinsic to the person, but which affect the group, cannot be transferred from one to another, and are very difficult to measure. Also important are 'team set-up variables,' which are extrinsic to the group, can be altered easily for better performance and are very easy to quantify.

Further, intangible variables may be defined as: motivation (intrinsic motivation), creative skills, and expertise or knowledge. Towards the end of this chapter, in the section entitled "Towards

Figure 10. Rotation in the virtual teams vs. creative phases through the project's different stages

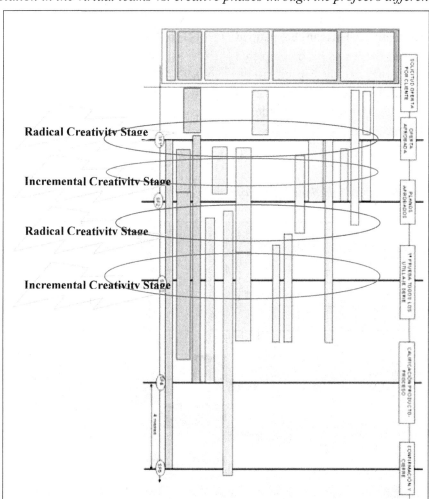

Common Drivers for Virtual Creativity," these will be discussed in greater depth.

Among the team setup variables found were: the number of people in the team, member rotation, the number of departments represented, and the stage of the project. To illustrate how these setup variables interact, Figure 11 analyses variables in pairs, which either results in radical, incremental, or little/no creativity (note that in Figure 11, the central diagonal section is not applicable since this area corresponds to the same sets of variables).

Several comments and general criteria concerning creativity in this case can be highlighted:

- The final stages of the project are apparently more likely to produce incremental rather than radical creativity. This can be explained by the fact that the teams have completed most of the journey and the capacity to introduce radical changes in the project, even for the better, has to be limited in order to get the job done and meet the deadline.

- Radical creativity appears to be scattered over the chart, but seems more frequent when there is a high occurrence of 'in and out' rotation within the team and when more departments are represented. This chart serves to corroborate the above mentioned theory, that the more multidisciplinary viewpoints there are, the more chance the team has to produce vertical breakthroughs.

- From the unshaded areas, it seems that there are also situations where, apparently, creativity type cannot be defined in advance or is less prone to arise, and where it does, it will be of very low intensity.

CASE THREE: VIRTUAL TEAMS AND CREATIVITY IN MCC GRAPHICS

MCC Graphics is a completely different case from companies one and two: the company was conceived to be virtual and, due to its small size, it is possible to observe more clearly than in the

Figure 11. Project variables and their connection with creativity in the virtual team

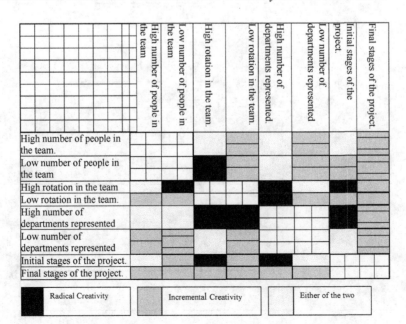

previous examples 'the feeling of its cooperative spirit.'

MCC Graphics, the graphic services division of MCC, was set up in the late 1990s as the commercial and marketing image of two already established cooperatives: Elkar S. Coop. and Danona S. Coop. Later on, and under this virtual 'umbrella,' they were joined by Rotok in 2001 and by Evagraph S. Coop. in 2005, thus establishing their dominance in the commercial printing and publishing market in both the North of Spain and the Southwest of France. With 40% of production exported to France, the United Kingdom and Germany and total sales expected by the end of 2006 to reach €30 million, the group employs nearly 150 people. All of the four cooperatives are spread out across diverse parts of the Basque Country.

MCC Graphics is not a typical case, as detailed by company representatives:

It did not appear as a reactive response to reality, but as a conscious gamble on creativity brought out by virtuality as opposed to the homogeneity generated by hierarchy and presence; in favor of collaboration between teams rather than competition among parallel productive structures. It is a unique new form of organization needed to face up to the complex scenarios that dominate the sector more efficiently than would four autonomous and distributed realities.

To talk about this virtual cooperative we met Javier de la Fuente, export manager and Ignacio Varona, head of technologies at MCC Graphics, who are involved in the organization of virtual work and technological support for the teams:

Virtuality determines the whole structure and day-to-day working of the company and allows us to manage the four productive realities MCC Graphics encompasses as just one unit.

Virtual Team Structure

The four companies that constitute MCC Graphics keep independent accounting and sales figures, but have provided themselves with a unique, 'distributed' virtual structure that unifies managerial issues (Joint Management, the Board of Directors and the Advisory Council), the Commercial Department, Financial Management and Production Management. This is achieved in the form of multidisciplinary teams assisted by a powerful management tool called AURKINET which allows access to the information systems of each company and consolidates scattered information (unification of orders, invoicing, offers, etc.).

Conceptually (Figure 12), the structure of MCC Graphics can be compared to that of an atom, with the nucleus (protons), the joint productive structure of the different companies, remaining mainly static. Around it, the virtual teams (neutrons) orbit and provide services to this productive structure. These virtual teams can be of two different types:

- **Stable virtual teams (SVTs)** are formed by people who share the same function in each of the four different plants, along with the international branches in France, Germany, and Great Britain. These people share knowledge, a common language and insight, and utilize a restricted area on the technological platform, work according to predetermined team events, and so forth. In MCC Graphics these stable teams are commercial, offers, coordinators, plant managers, and production managers.
- **Project virtual teams (PVTs)** are born of the 'virtual resources' of MCC Graphics and combine groups of seven to eight people, each of whom belongs to a stable virtual team with their own particular field of knowledge, goals, tasks to develop, and so on. These PVTs, together with occasional contributions from other experts, "... are

able to provide, in a creative way and in a very short time, solutions to problems of logistics, supplies, resource availability, etc. so as to meet orders in due time and live up to the high standards demanded by our customer."

The first essential feature that differentiates both types of team, and which provides the PVTs with a fundamental part of their creative muscle, is that they are both emergent and ad-hoc. No meetings are held either to launch the virtual team or to get members together. On the contrary, when faced with the need to produce, let's say, an estimate, they burst onto scene and under self-management, evolve towards their goal:

... not in a chaotic way or by defending the particular interests of their respective plants, but with all the generosity, professionalism and commitment infused by the cooperative spirit, as well as all the richness and creativity this entails.

Another characteristic that should be pointed out is that teams neither follow an obvious leader nor select their members beforehand, as is the case at both Fagor Electrodomesticos and Maier. On the contrary, they are teamed up through natural selection:

Figure 12. Conceptual structure of MCC Graphics

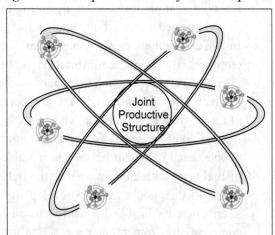

Following a customer's phone call, the commercial unit that holds the data and deadlines concerning the offer contacts the department in charge of estimates, which in turn gets in touch with coordination, which in turn... And so on. It is in this process that each position—the people in charge of the commercial part, the estimates, pre-printing, production, etc.—is self-selected to take part in a multimarket, multiplant, multiproduct and multicreative virtual team.

Reflection on Creativity

It is precisely here, in this natural selection, through emergence and cooperative spirit, that the creative seed of these virtual teams can be found. The process encompasses two phases. The first can be seen as an 'internal assessment and launch-pad towards the next phase,' Figure 13. It is iterative, and is carried out in all the necessary SVTs to meet the requirements of a project, producing mostly incremental creativity:

In practice, the commercial agent asks the SVT in charge of offers for an estimate, and they get together to analyze it, check availability, requirements and resources, and so on. They then provide a partial assessment of the project and contact the SVT of Coordinators who again get organized to analyze the proposal.

This process manifests itself in creative cycles of 'assessment-launching' which are encouraged by the fact that, with the way the teams are distributed, they work on things locally, exchange suggestions, contribute and recombine different solutions. In this way, they generate more creative solutions than they would if they were working on the basis of face-to-face meetings, where there is always the risk of people choosing the easiest approximation to consensus due to constraints of time, language, and pressure, or indeed blindly accepting the course promoted by the leader of

Figure 13. Radical and incremental creativity hotspots

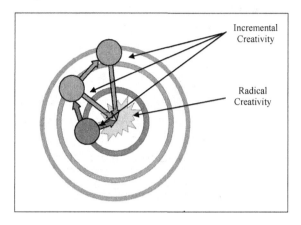

the meeting, or one that has not been explored in sufficient depth by everyone.

However, it is important to bear in mind that the individual solution outlined at this stage by the particular SVT is intuitive, 'partial,' so to speak, as they have yet to get coordinated with the remaining SVTs that are expected to contribute different resources and solutions. Therefore in order to advance towards the unified solution, the SVT selects a member to monitor the process and to take part in the project's virtual team. This

person will also be the one in charge of launching the partial solution towards the next SVT in the structure.

Thus the same scheme is reproduced again and again: the corresponding SVT gets coordinated, goes over the requirements and comes up with 'their' solution at the same time as they appoint a member for the project virtual team, who is responsible for launching the proposal onto the next SVT ... And this happens successively in exactly the same way throughout all the SVTs involved in the solution, right up to the SVT just before the beginning of mass production at the plants. See Figure 14.

It is upon reaching this last step that we get into the second phase, where the PVT, made up of representatives of all the SVTs of MCC Graphics relevant to the reaching of a solution, is ready to act. It is precisely this multidisciplinary, multi-viewpoint, and virtual type of team that creates the appropriate breeding ground for radical creativity to arise. This is because the team has to alternate between working locally and in coordination with distributed colleagues to adapt the different partial solutions that have been proposed and then draw up a solution. This solution must be one that simul-

Figure 14. SVT iterative process followed to join the PVT

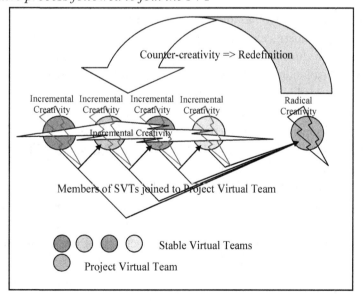

taneously considers the expectations, resources, requirements, and points of view of all the different parts represented and also be competitive as far as the customer is concerned.

It is therefore the opposite order to that followed when incorporating into the PVT, that is, starting with those closer to manufacturing, the team starts to coordinate and contribute the necessary interphase creativity so as to fine tune a global solution to the project. Compared to ordinary teams, this one will have the advantage of allowing every member to study the options slowly and locally, to be able to check and contrast the requirements with other members or superiors before committing themselves, thus avoiding stress, the lack of decisiveness and the time pressure one can come across in face-to-face meetings, "with the certainty that this way, we will reach the best possible solutions, even though this may happen at a slower but more creative pace." It is specifically in this pressure-free contrast with superiors and with local reality that one can most easily find the clue to radical creativity and great ideas.

Further Insights

If the above explanation of creativity sounds idealistic, it also has its pitfalls, its darker side. Virtuality sometimes makes it easier for people to feel frustrated or confused, as well as making it impossible to unify the concerns expressed by different members. This produces a phenomenon of countercreativity and isolation, of getting lost in thought. It is characterized by the absence of a dialogue among members that could lead to the redefinition of requirements established in previous stages, changes in the composition of the PVT, actions taken in order to explore new and more creative means that, this time, must bring together the solutions proposed by the SVTs and the customer.

Curiously, the fact is that the day-to-day reality of these teams shows us that the higher the number of SVTs taking part in the project, the

more incremental creativity is produced. This, however, leads us to the following paradox: the possibilities for creativity within the PVT to be more brilliant increase as more points of view, requirements, resources, means, and so forth are considered, but, at the same time, for this very reason there are also more chances that there will be no agreement or solution on the basis of the expected specifications. When this happens, the phases and members of the team have to be restructured, resulting in the nonrecommendable stage of 'redefinition.'

Finally, according to Javier:

MCC Graphics is characterized by two key factors; firstly, by the fact that it is a cooperative and secondly, by its virtual condition. We have had to deal with distance using work routines and communication tools which are different from the traditional chats around the coffee-machine or at a desk. In this way you encourage values like generosity both at an individual level and on a team basis when it comes to the point of taking decisions that may minimize benefits to your plant in favor of another plant; values like the creativity to develop virtual tools and means of coordination with your colleagues. It also promotes a higher level of personal professional expectation to assume tasks that, due to virtuality and the lack of a rigid hierarchy, are not defined by the duties of different posts but are none the less essential to allow the project to reach a satisfactory conclusion and the virtual structure to go on.

TOWARDS COMMON DRIVERS FOR VIRTUAL CREATIVITY

Through the case experiences presented in this chapter, it can be observed that creativity is achieved through the different organizational structures of the virtual teams. Although it is difficult to measure the success of this virtual creativity, we can confirm that it does exist, and on a solid basis, and that several strings pulled together correctly can lead to creative virtual environments. As a summary, Figure 15 presents a cross-case comparison of important virtual team creativity features in each company.

Regarding the pursuit of virtual team creativity, while a company can plan and invest to kit the team out with state of the art technology for interaction, decide the number of participants, schedule rotation within the team, and so on, there still exists other ingredients that are highly dependent on the individual people making up the team. This is where the aforementioned "intellectual variables" which were touched upon in the second case come up again. Factors such as intrinsic motivation "for its own sake," creative thinking skills (how flexibly and how imaginatively the team faces the activity) or expertise ("technical and intellectual experience") are always going to play a critical, yet unpredictable role in the creativity of virtual teams.

Another issue important to highlight is that the individual's working environment and by extension that of the whole team may affect creativity. With this in mind, the most often repeated working conditions that have arisen throughout the conversations held with the experts are presented below in Figure 16. The inferred relationship between members' working conditions are depicted, the type of creativity most likely to arise from these conditions, and the effect that virtuality has on them.

While the above chart has been drawn up entirely by interpreting interviewees' comments, and the surface of these subjects have only just been scratched, we dare to draw the following hypotheses (which are far from being rigorous) and leave them completely open to discussion:

- Those working conditions that seem to provide a more suitable environment for creativity to arise are generally encouraged

Figure 15. Summary of experiences for cross-case comparison

	FAGOR ELECTR. S. COOP.	MAIER S. COOP.	MCC GRAPHICS S. COOP.
STRUCTURE			
CREATIVITY			
DEFINING DRIVERS	- The figure of the Satellite. - Space / Time Communication versus Creativity Type. - Interaction Intensity versus Creativity.	- Virtual Teams Setup Variables. - Intellectual variables. - Creativity forced.	- Cooperative values. - Counter-Creativity. - Working Conditions / Environment.

Figure 16. Working conditions, creativity and virtuality relationships

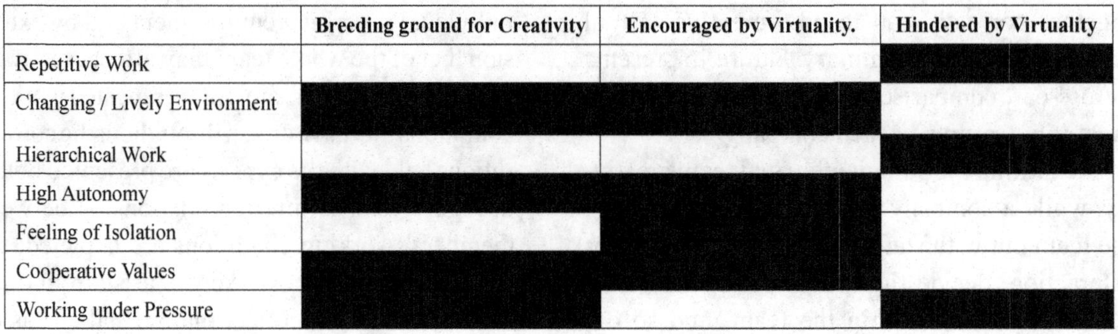

	Breeding ground for Creativity	Encouraged by Virtuality.	Hindered by Virtuality
Repetitive Work			■
Changing / Lively Environment	■	■	
Hierarchical Work			■
High Autonomy	■	■	
Feeling of Isolation	■	■	
Cooperative Values	■	■	
Working under Pressure	■		■

and augmented when they take place in virtual conditions. For instance, working in a changing and lively environment seems to be a favorable condition for radical creativity to appear, and the fact of working virtually increases this feeling of liveliness and change. We can infer, therefore, that virtuality emphasizes this kind of creativity.

- In repetitive or highly hierarchical work environments, the fact that activity takes place under virtual conditions lessens the effects of these repetitive and/or hierarchical circumstances. It seems, therefore, that virtuality encourages dynamism and autonomy, which are working conditions that favor creativity.

- Apparently, there exist two exceptions to the above mentioned rules; one is the sense of isolation and the second is working under pressure. The former is an unfavorable negative condition that goes against creativity, and yet it is increased by virtuality. Consequently, constant communication and interchange are good practices in virtual teams in order to avoid the negative effects of this feeling of isolation. Working under pressure, however, is a different phenomenon. Statements like 'I concentrate and work better and faster when under pressure' corroborate the fact that creativity seems

to be encouraged by these circumstances. Nevertheless, virtuality alleviates the pressure in these situations, allowing people to exchange ideas locally, calmly, off-line, and so forth. These are conditions which involve greater relaxation than being in ordinary groups where pressure and responsibility can more easily be exerted. As a result, in this particular case virtuality would lessen creativity, which is negative from the creative point of view but positive if one considers peoples' stress levels.

REFERENCES

Albert, R. S., & Runce, M. A. (1999). *A history of research on creativity.* Cambridge: Cambridge University Press.

Balachandra, R., & Friar, J. H. (1997). Factors for success in R&D projects and new product innovation: A contextual framework. *IEEE Transactions on Engineering Management, 44*(3), 276-287.

Ekvall, G. (1997). *Organizational conditions and levels of creativity. Creativity and innovation management, 6*(4), 195-205.

Fairbank, F., Spangler, W., & Williams, S. (2003). Motivating creativity through a computer-mediated employee suggestion management system.

Behaviour and Information Technology, 22(5), 305-314.

International Co-operative Alliance (ICA). (1995). *Statement of co-operative principles.* Retrieved November 15, from http://www.ica.coop/coop/principles.html

Katzenbach, J. R., & Smith, D. K. (1993). *The wisdom of teams.* Boston: Harvard Business School Press.

Kirton, M. (1989). *Adaptors and innovators.* New York: Routledge.

Koberg C. S., Detienne D. R., & Heppard K. A. (2003). An empirical test of environmental, organization, and process factors affecting incremental and radical innovation. *Journal of High Technology Management Research, 14*(1), 3, 21-45.

MacGregor, S. P., Arana, J., Parra, I., Lorenzo, M. P. (2006). Supporting new product creation in the Mondragon valley. *European Journal of Innovation Management, 9*(4), 418-443.

Proctor, T., Tan K. H., & Fuse K. (2004). Cracking the incremental paradigm of Japanese creativity. *Creativity and Innovation Management, 3*(4), 207-215.

Shalley C. E., Zhou, J, & Oldham G. R. (2004). The effects of personal and contextual charasteristics on creativity: Where should we go from here? *Journal of Management,* 30(6), 933-958.

The Networking Institute. (2000). *Virtual teams booklet.* Retrieved September 12, 2006, from http://www.netage.com/learning/mini_book/Mini_book.html

Veryzer, R. W. (1998). Discontinuous innovation and the new product development process. *Journal of Product Innovation Management, 15*(4), 304-321.

Chapter X
Virtual Teams in Practice:
Tales from the Battlefront of the Fuzzy Front End of the Innovation Process

John M. Feland
Human Interface Architect at Synaptics Inc., USA

ABSTRACT

A growing number of enterprises are building virtual teams to assist in crafting new opportunities in the fuzzy front end of the innovation process. Using the tools of design thinking, these creative virtual teams have different management requirements than virtual teams used in the more routine efforts of product development. This chapter uses examples from industry to examine the challenges of managing customer expectations, explore the membership dynamics of virtual teams, and suggest a new framework for assessing the progress of creative virtual teams, concept maturity. An example from the creative virtual team at Synaptics, the Red Dot Award winning Onyx mobile phone concept, is used to delve deeper into these concepts. Finally, trends for the diffusion of creative virtual teams as well as potential challenges in bringing such teams into your organization are investigated.

INTRODUCTION

The first decade of the 2000 millennium could easily be called the decade of design. Design is on the lips of all the business pundits and has been the target investment of many funding agencies for academic research. The classic path to bringing design thinking into your organization is the hiring of a design firm, such as IDEO

or SparkFactor. These engagements range from complete turnkey interactions to the inclusion of these firms as members of your virtual innovation team. Utilizing these firms can be expensive both in time and money. The benefits can be significant, especially to firms that are new to design thinking and are committed to acting on the paths such firms recommend. One of the hidden costs of working with these firms is the time and personnel resources consumed in educating the firm on the client's core competency. The design firm must take the time (on the client's purchase order) to understand enough of what ever technology, market, and business issues face the client for the design thinking strategies to be effective. Unfortunately the economics of consulting engagements do not support using these firms to deploy these methods throughout the firm. As a result, a growing number of businesses are building internal design services to support creative engagements with customers, end users, and other critical stakeholders of the innovation process. In March of 2005 Hitachi announced the establishment of five design centers worldwide. The formal goal of these centers is to assist customers "integrate hard drives into consumer electronic devices." (http://www.physorg.com/news3210.html) Synaptics, maker of human interface devices, has had some form of design services group since 2001. Recently they consolidated the human factors, usability, and product design functions into one team focused on creating and validating new user experiences that leverage Synaptics interface technology. These new in-house design services groups are themselves virtual teams, bringing together resources from internal and external resources to support rapid concept creation and validation.

These virtual innovation teams bring with them a mixed bag of challenges and opportunities. They can be used to create new 'sandboxes' for the enterprise to experiment with advanced concepts. Utilizing these teams can also generate an overwhelming management overhead as their leaders work around the organizational policies and procedures that typically prevent, albeit by accident, virtual innovation teams from existing in the first place. To complicate the matter further, traditional project management metrics fail to represent the value of these teams. Couple the nuanced style required for managing creative teams and the resulting situation seems untenable at first; yet many companies have been success-

ful at utilizing these teams to drive innovation, both internally and externally. This chapter will explore in more detail the challenges faced by these teams and their management, along with a few suggested paths of inquiry that promise to reduce the overhead requirements for such teams. A detailed case from Synaptics will also be used—the Red Dot design award-winning Onyx Concept Phone.

BACKGROUND

Virtual teams are a growing part of how businesses operate today. They offer benefits of reduced fixed personnel costs in a single location, potential for work across time zones, or outsourcing of functions that can be fulfilled more effectively outside the firm such as some human resource functions. In the past, virtual teams have been used in places were the process and procedures are mature and well understood. The concept prototyping team at Synaptics focuses its efforts in the 'fuzzy front end' of the innovation process—the early stages where the majority of challenges are met due to high levels of uncertainty; see for example, Khurana and Rosenthal (1997), Reinertsen (1999), Koen et al. (2001), Trygg and Nobelius (2002). It is also the most important given the influence decisions at this stage have on downstream performance. Poskela et al. (2004) propose the use of road-maps to aid in structuring the fuzziness of this early phase yet more tools are needed, especially in a virtual context. Increasingly, enterprises are using virtual teams to address the challenges of this fuzzy front end and Synaptics is no different.

Synaptics is a supplier of human interface solutions to the consumer electronics industry. It was founded in the late 1980s to leverage the parallel developments in CMOS semiconductors and the maturing artificial intelligence domain of neural networks. The company sought to develop neural network analog chips in an effort to possess competencies in fast hardware based neural nets. The natural evolution of Moore's law eliminated the bottleneck of simulating these neural networks in software. As a result Synaptics applied their expertise in pattern recognition and mixed signal semiconductor design to create a novel pointing device for notebook computers, the touchpad. As manufacturers began to push for thinner, lighter notebooks, the touchpad began to displace the then dominant notebook pointing device, the trackball, and Synaptics grew to be the leading player in the market.

Synaptics began to branch out from notebook pointing devices when one of their major customers came to them with a strange request. The customer wanted Synaptics to utilize their capacitive touch sensitive technology to create a new interface device for their new music player. The success of the Apple iPod® pulled Synaptics into the public limelight, increasing demand for their interface solutions but also increasing the number of competitors in their market. One of the main methods Synaptics used to compete was through regular customer road shows to show innovative concept prototypes. The team that conceives and constructs these demonstrations is the concept prototyping team. These prototypes are the main form of demand generation for Synaptics' many product lines.

Creative work forms a larger percentage of the concept prototyping team's efforts than in more traditional virtual teams. As such, the team has a different set of challenges and opportunities in how they build and rebuild their virtual team in order to be successful at innovation. In this chapter, experiences at Synaptics will be generalized to address what are considered to be common issues faced by distributed virtual innovation teams, and which are becoming increasingly commonplace in the modern enterprise.

EFFECTIVELY MANAGING VIRTUAL INNOVATION TEAMS

Managing virtual teams chartered with delivering creative results is a challenging and rewarding experience. Creative work offers opportunities for improvement along much different vectors than routine work. The personnel required for creative work have very different management needs than those of more routine tasks. The measures of creative work are also different. Additionally the context in which creative work takes place has a significant impact on the results. Distributing teams across political, cultural, field of expertise, and corporate boundaries complicates the technical, business, and human challenges that face managers today as they seek to increase creativity.

The new product release cycle for most consumer electronics markets is decreasing at a rapid pace. As such, most development teams have little time to perform the risk reduction activities required to integrate a new technology or radical new feature into their product offering. Firms in their value chain realize this and are assembling virtual teams to support customers in rapidly beating out the risk of bringing new ideas into the marketplace. Many firms are using virtual innovation teams to assemble innovation "tiger teams,"[1] aimed at rapidly bringing together critical stakeholders in the innovation process to generate a diverse range of effective alternatives. Synaptics assists customers in rapidly assessing and reducing the risk of the integration of creative ideas. This speeds the integration of new technology into innovative products for customers, shortening the new product development cycle.

A Useful Model of the Innovation Process

There are several models of the innovation process, each offering different perspectives on issues to be addressed, obstacles to overcome, and opportunities to be exploited. Marquis' model (1988, p. 81) of innovation will be used to aid this discussion. He uses six stages of innovation starting with the recognition of a compelling solution or need, all the way through to the utilization and diffusion of the innovation. We will use these stages to explore how the needs of creative teams change through the innovation process with special attention on team structure, concept maturity, and management needs over time. Our attention is focused on the first four stages. Stages 1 and 2 form the fuzzy front end of the innovation process. Stages 3 and 4 raise concept maturity to a stage that the opportunity can be passed to the development organization within the enterprise and eventually be launched into the market.

As chapter focus is on the exertions of virtual innovation teams, the last two phases of this view of the innovation process will not be considered. This is because Stage 5: development and Stage 6: utilization and diffusion, consist of more routine work as compared to Stages 1-4. This is not meant to belie the importance of these later stages of the innovation process. Many great ideas never become great products. This discussion is focused on forming and managing the virtual team that

ensures the enterprise has enough good ideas to utilize.

Building and Supporting Virtual Innovation Teams

Throughout the phases of the innovation process, the members of the virtual innovation team change. For the team at Synaptics, the stakeholder diagram in Figure 2 represents a typical concept development engagement—the connections represent normal communication channels throughout the creative process. Virtual innovation teams in other enterprises encounter similar changing team structures throughout projects.

Several firms use this type of virtual team structure for design thinking projects. The connections between actors in Figure 2 highlight the communication channels used during projects. Notice that the Core Design team has primary responsibility for coordination among all the actors, a significant overhead cost. Intel's concept prototyping group creates and produces several "concept cars" every year for the Intel Developer Forum. In 2005, the Intel concept team produced a prototype experience based on a medical tablet PC, thinking through scenarios of patient records,

Figure 1. Marquis' innovation process is a useful model to support this discussion of virtual innovation teams

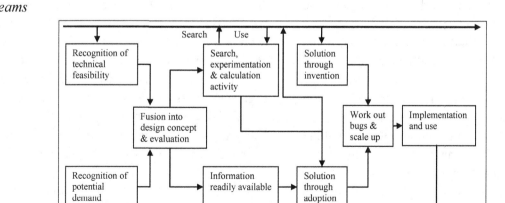

Figure 2. Simplified value chain to illustrate a typical set of actors involved in a virtual innovation team

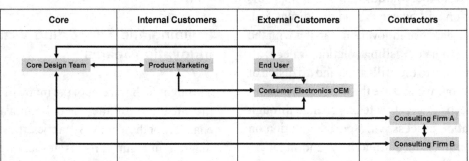

doctor annotation of notes, issues of pharmaceutical safety, and even a Bluetooth stethoscope configuration to allow amplification and recording of heartbeats. Intel did not possess all the knowledge to create this novel experience and notebook inside the corporate walls. The goal was to construct a fully functional prototype that enabled doctors and others to test drive these novel medical interactions. To achieve this goal, Intel solicited support from design firms, doctors, nurses, patients, original design manufacturers (ODM) of notebook computers, and component companies like Synaptics.

Intel was working with Whipsaw, an award winning design firm in San Jose, to design first the experience and then the actual tablet PC. Whipsaw engaged the concept prototyping team (CPT) at Synaptics to work on codesigning the capacitive button interface that allowed the user to control some of the advanced functions of the notebook while also providing an indication of status including battery and WIFI connectivity. Synaptics was asked to help because we could produce interfaces that allowed the notebook to be easily cleaned with an antiseptic, something that is critical for hospital use. This required our team at Synaptics to join the virtual team that Intel had constructed to build the device. We joined later in the Solution phase of Marquis' innovation process. The Synaptics CPT was brought into the virtual team by Whipsaw and immediately en-

gaged with Intel, the ODM for the medical tablet, and Whipsaw on this project. Thought it was an Intel project, Whipsaw provided all the project 'on-boarding' support to Synaptics, including the communication of the design intent, introductions to the stakeholders involved, and the brokering of communication between the various actors. The virtual team for Intel's medical tablet project grew and shrank throughout the project—Synaptics being one of the last component suppliers engaged in the project. Different on-boarding and off-boarding windows as seen in the Intel medical table virtual team is typical within the process of creative collaboration (see Figure 3).

The diagram illustrates when the various stakeholders enter into the creative efforts of the virtual team. This time phase diagram demonstrates how the various actors introduced in Figure 2 engage with the virtual team over time. The core design team is active throughout these first four phases of the innovation process, while the internal customer, end user, and external customer are engaged as part of the virtual team at different phases of the creative process. Consulting firms that provide additional support phase in when their additional expertise is appropriate. Notice that the internal customer, end user, and external customer have several entry and exit points. These are critical points of collaboration within the team where the project risk increases dramatically due to the gap in knowledge, and lack of shared context between the new or returning team members and the incumbents.

Every time a new stakeholder joins the virtual team, there is a need to make the current state of development explicit so that the new team member may contribute to project success as soon as possible. This is complicated by the fact that during creative work, especially in the fuzzy front end, the innovation exists almost exclusively at a tacit level. There is significant implicit knowledge stored in the team. The team develops its own language around the particular project, creating code words and other shorthand to speed sharing of context. Hargadon and Sutton (1997) identify knowledge brokers within the team structure as being critical to this process. Without explicit and tangible artifacts to point to and scaffold the integration of new team members, managing constant on-boarding and off-boarding of team members is difficult indeed.

Additionally, each stakeholder has different motivations and reward structures. An external customer is focused on how the project will help their efforts in creating a market for their new offering. The end user is selfishly motivated to address their own needs, rightfully so. The core design team enjoys the challenge of the project and celebrates their contributions. The consulting firms that augment the resources of the core design team seek both intellectual and financial rewards. The internal customer is focused on managing the relationship between the enterprise and the external customer. Each stakeholder has

a different set of needs to be addressed in this process. As such, what works for motivating the end user to participate fully with a given virtual team does not hold the same weight with the internal customer.

There are further complications such as how to manage intellectual property or the added layer of complexity generated by having all the stakeholders engaged in multiple creative endeavors at once, at times splitting their attention so fine that little creative work is actually accomplished.

The virtual innovation team at Synaptics is routinely engaged in more than one project per person. This is only possible by integrating extracorporate members into the team in the form of contractors, end users, or the development teams of partner corporations. While interactions with these virtual members are not as efficient as the internal team members, this structure allows for increased capacity to scale the resources as compared to hiring more permanent employees. SparkFactor Design is a small Silicon Valley firm that has created a core business around providing virtual team members. Different from the talent houses that match firms with independent contractors for short term contracts, SparkFactor is a full service design firm, which carefully screens talent for integration into their clients' virtual teams. In supporting design firms and internal development teams at large OEM clients, Sparkfactor is able to onboard their employees rapidly, enabling their clients to create a more agile and efficient virtual innovation team.

Figure 3. Illustrative on-boarding and off-boarding diagram for a virtual team engaged in creative collaboration during the first four phases of the innovation process described earlier

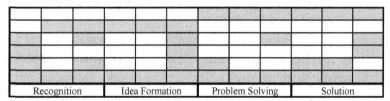

Context of Creative Work

There are certain conditions that assist virtual innovation teams in delivering on the goals of the innovation project assigned to the team. MacGregor (2002) proposes a specific framework for distributed (virtual) design that segments the conditions required to support distributed design teams into four steps: build distributed infrastructure, define project context, create a distributed design space, and map the distributed design journey. These conditions can also be segmented into three categories: *People*, *Place*, and *Process*.[2]

Within the category of *People*, there is need for individuals that are very comfortable with ambiguity. Trust is an essential element of these teams as well. Wrestling with the intangibles of early stage creative work, these teams work almost like improvisational theater groups in that though a team member may be headed down an unexpected path, there is sufficient trust within the team to follow through. Building and sustaining this trust is complicated by the temporal and geographic separation of team members. Common wisdom says that regardless of the duration of the project, virtual teams require a face-to-face kickoff meeting to set strong foundations of trust for the duration of the project. Additionally, feedback seems to play an important role in maintaining the motivation and performance of these teams. Both positive and negative aspects are welcome as members—especially of the core design team—routinely seek to improve their skills. Unfortunately the pace of these types of projects coupled with common failings of corporate cultures today results in an environment where positive feedback is rare and negative feedback is rarely constructive.

The notion of *Place* is complicated with virtual teams. Many consider *Place* an open office environment covered with whiteboards, old coffee cups and foam rockets. These benefits are lost over distance and time. *Place* is used in this context

to represent a quartered off set of resources to support creative work and the support required. This includes freedom to fail early in the process, as long as the team utilizes the failure to improve upon their efforts. *Place* also includes space to play, in an intellectual sense. Collocated teams uses project rooms to accomplish this need extensively. These rooms allow a persistence to team workflows, offering opportunities for both synchronous and asynchronous communication and knowledge creation. In the virtual environment the asynchronous communication tends to be more verbal and written, and less visual in comparison.

The *Process* viewpoint suggests that a documented and repeatable process, even a simple one, is crucial to successful innovation. While this chapter does not reveal any perfect process that can be applied by readers, it is the author's hope to share some process characteristics that are important to consider. One critical feature is the notion of clear goals but fuzzy means. At the extremes, a good creative team will require freedom to determine their own path towards the clear goals set out by key stakeholders; a poor virtual team's best hope of delivering anything of value is to cling to the goals when all else seems to fail in their creative efforts. Additionally it is difficult to force a creative outcome within a constrained timeline. Few and far between are teams that can deliver a creative outcome at the same time as meeting aggressive milestones. Ensuring that the team is not put in a situation where there is insufficient schedule flexibility to allow for a successful, innovative outcome, is paramount.

Management of Virtual Teams

The management of virtual teams is a challenging role, which is amplified in the context of creative work. Two issues that continue to be themes for many virtual innovation teams are the metrics to assess team performance and stakeholder communications, more specifically expectation management.

Performance and Process Measures

One significant challenge faced by the managers of virtual innovation teams is measuring progress toward the project goal. This is important for the manager for two reasons. An accurate assessment of the team's progress is critical information for a manager trying to change course, address concerns, and celebrate successes. Additionally the manager requires sufficient status information to report on the team's progress to key decision makers within the enterprise. This is difficult for the same reasons the constant shift in team structure creates challenges. Much of the efforts of virtual innovation teams deal with implicitly held beliefs, attitudes, and concepts that are difficult to represent effectively to those not immersed in the context of the creative effort. This is especially complex for the team at Synaptics where our primary customers are not so familiar with the technical or end user aspects of the projects. As a result there is more than ample opportunity for the beliefs and expectations of the project to diverge significantly throughout. Short of having our internal customer sit with the team everyday, we have no effective means of representing the

gradual maturing of the intangible aspects of the concepts being developed. Even then, from the outside the team's efforts may appear a random walk where our customers may expect a linear path.

The diagram in Figure 4 helps to understand why the community refers to this phase of the innovation process as the Fuzzy Front End. In much the same way that humans take between 15 and 21 years to mature into adults (though some might argue it takes longer) ideas and concepts created and nurtured by creative virtual teams take time to mature. As such, there are two areas of performance assessment that need to be considered in deploying and managing a virtual team. The first is managing the expectations of critical stakeholders as to what type of project the team is about to embark on. The second is the development of a shared framework to assess the maturity of the project as time passes. As can be surmised in Figure 4, significant effort occurs prior to the project maturing to the milestone of prototype development, at least in the idea case.

Managing Critical Stakeholder Expectations in the Start of a Project

Expectation management is a continual challenge for the managers of any team, virtual or not. This

Figure 4. Representation of the random walk of design thinking from the outsiders' point of view as represented by the design practice, Central Office of Design (www.c-od.net) in San Francisco

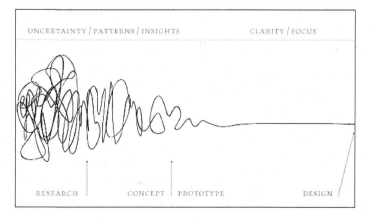

is especially critical during the formation of a new team while the challenge is exacerbated in virtual teams as the stakeholders are typically separated by space, time, and/or language. It is critical for the team and its customers to understand and agree on the scope of the creative work being taken on. One model that has proved useful to design firms and technology firms alike is Eddie Obeng's framework for project types. Obeng's model (1994) divides project types along two axes, if the knowledge exists of how to meet the goals of the project and if the solution required to meet the goals exists. This creates four categories of projects: "Paint by numbers, Making a movie, Lost in the fog, Going on a quest." These are illustrated in Figure 5.

Paint by Numbers projects assume that both the process and the solution of choice are well understood and can be executed with minimal risk. Most projects taken on by virtual innovation teams fall into the remaining three categories, often contrary to the perceptions of the client. *Making a movie* supposes that although the outcome is not known, the process is well understood. Regardless of the final outcome, you still need actors, sets, and a producer. In *going on a quest* the ends are well known yet the means lack clarity. Your team may be clear on creating a music experience

that competes with the iPod® but uncertain as to how they are going to develop the means of doing so. The riskiest project type is being *Lost in the fog.* There are no indications as to which process would be effective. The goal is nowhere in sight, leaving the team with the responsibility to define both the objective and the process by which the objective is achieved. Many of our projects for the virtual innovation team at Synaptics fall into the *Lost in the fog* category: "We don't care how you do it but we need new concepts for X and they better displace our competition." I am sure many others have had similar missions proffered to them with that same shiver of fear crawling down your spine when you realize that, although your customer thinks that you are doing a *Paint by numbers* version of the Mona Lisa, your team has just been placed in the middle of a body of water surrounded by fog with limited resources for survival. This creates tremendous tension throughout the project as schedules slip, requirements change, and costs exceed even the most liberal budget explanations—in truth, few will be *Paint by numbers.* The challenge comes in deciding and coming to consensus as to which of the other three types of projects the assignment is. This challenge is made more acute by the distributed nature of virtual teams. Converging on the shared viewpoint required to successfully initiate and complete the project requires significant communication of implicit information. This is especially complicated when different pieces of expertise are scattered throughout the team and the customer's knowledge is limited regarding the requirements to achieve their goal. The delicate dance of managing the customers expectations, while at the same time managing the activities of the team as activities and expectations converge on a shared project vision, is not well supported by existing tools and methods.

What is needed is a framework that provides a shared language for discussing progress towards conclusion. The passage of time and expenditure of financial resources are poor surrogates for

Figure 5. Obeng's (1994) framework of project types represented in a matrix

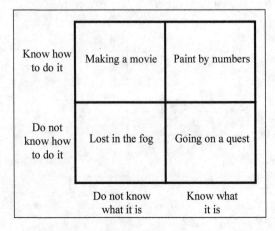

measuring progress towards a compelling innovation during a design thinking project. The notion of concept maturity that follows seeks to be a useful framework to support both intra team discussions of progress as well as discussions with the ultimate customers of the project.

Concept Maturity as a Performance Assessment Framework

Concept maturity is a process measure—the assessment of the uncertainty remaining regarding the future success of the path being taken by the team. If the manager and the team have a firm grasp of what risk items remain to be addressed through all phases of the creative process, then managing the expectations of critical stakeholders is simplified tremendously. One perspective that can be used in applying this notion of concept maturity to virtual teams is the comprehensive design framework that considers technical, human, and business aspects (Feland, Leifer, & Cockayne, 2004). IDEO product development refers to this framework as the Innovation Engine as reported by Laura Weiss (2002) in the *Design Management Journal*. Feland, Leifer, and Cockayne published a slightly modified version applied to design curriculum called *comprehensive design engineering* (2004). Others have adopted similar frameworks to structure curriculums (the Designium at the Helsinki University of Art and Design) or design practice (Design Continuum uses a similar notion to represent their expansion into design strategy to clients). This framework is being used by design firms and technology companies to ensure that all three perspectives are represented in product teams, thereby supporting business decisions. At Synaptics, we use it informally to guide discussions regarding the quality of a new concept, highlighting potential weaknesses and assessing if and how those weaknesses could be addressed. It is only recently that this framework has been applied to the notion of concept maturity.

Concept maturity should improve over time, as each stage of innovation is achieved. The task of the virtual innovation team is to manage this maturation process. In the early stages, maturing the concept too quickly can reduce the design freedom of the team, through ignoring new technology that could improve the offering. A delay in maturing the concept can place the entire project at risk, requiring the influx of additional resources to later accelerate project progress.

Figure 7 shows how concept maturity changes in a qualitative sense through the six phases of the innovation process. The oscillations maturity in each phase represents the multiple divergent and convergent design cycles that exist within each phase. The oscillations represent the multiple divergent and convergent cycles within the process. Notice that the concept never reaches 100% maturity, even after being launched into the market. This is important to note from a performance measurement point of view: should concept maturity assessment occur at an infrequent interval, then there is a danger of increasing risk perception by only noting the divergent activities, building a persistent perception of continued immaturity.

The next figure illustrates the relative changes in concept maturity as coded by the three domains

Figure 6. Comprehensive design engineering framework considers technical, business, and human aspects of design and innovation

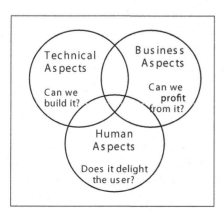

Figure 7. Qualitative graph of concept maturity over the size phases of the innovation process

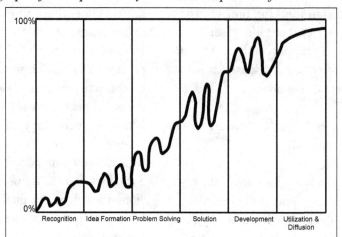

Figure 8. A qualitative illustration of how concepts mature with respect to technical, business, and human aspects of the product offering

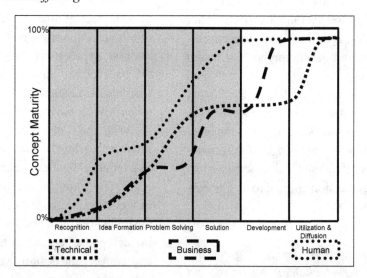

in the comprehensive design engineering framework. The shaded region highlights the stages this chapter is focused on. Note that for the phases of innovation where virtual innovation teams have the most impact, there are different rates and levels of maturation depending on whether technical, human, or business aspects are being considered. This is part of what drives the modifications in the membership of virtual innovation teams through the process.

Most virtual innovation teams in modern enterprises focus almost exclusively on the tech-nical aspects, assuming that human and business aspects are being addressed by others in the organization. There is a need therefore to expand the membership of these virtual teams to include the stakeholders responsible for maturing human and business elements of the concept maturity. Synaptics, when building virtual innovation teams charged with creating new concepts to drive future revenue, brings together a diverse group of actors to ensure the team contains the resources to address all three domains. This is a difficult task in most enterprises due to a diverse range of issues, cultural differences, organizational structure, lack of senior management support, to name a few. It is a challenge to demonstrate the value of such a complex and intense teaming for innovation.

Larger design firms have been successful in building such integrated teams, especially for design strategy projects. Their engagements tend to connect with senior business decision makers. Design firms such as IDEO and Design Continuum provide the expertise in the human and some of the technical aspects of the project, while the client enterprise provides the virtual teammates that contribute to the understanding of the business aspects as well as coverage of the client specific technical aspects.

The dominant metrics of cost, schedule, and product performance do not adequately represent the value of such teaming. Measuring concept maturity, specifically as it relates to the maturity of technical, human, and business aspects would provide additional metrics to support the creation of such virtual teams. Feland (2005) demonstrated that enterprises that show evidence of operating according to the comprehensive design engineering framework have increased revenues, stock price, and return on assets. Using a portfolio of metrics organized into domains of product financial capital, product intellectual capital, and product social capital, the performance of Palm, Handspring, the Mini Cooper, and Ford Thunderbird could be modeled better than using traditional financial metrics. Product financial capital measured the financial resources consumed and generated in the development of products, including gross margin and cost of goods. Product intellectual capital includes patents, R&D expenditures and new product introductions, all measures of the generation of intellectual capital during the innovation process. Product social capital measured the strength of the relationship between the end user and the product using online customer reviews. Design thinking has the greatest impact on product social capital, which was

a leading indicator of future revenues and stock price for all cases considered. As such, creative virtual teams can have a significant impact on downstream revenues and stock prices by designing a usage experience that fosters a strong relationship between the end user and the product or service being designed.

There is ample support for building virtual innovation teams that can actively evolve concepts across the three domains of technical, business, and human issues. Additionally, concept maturity metrics would provide the evidence essential to educate key decision makers regarding the benefits of complicated, yet effective virtual innovation teams. The outcomes based metrics of the product capital model provide a starting point for thinking of concept maturity metrics but as yet, no metrics exist to assess the evolving maturity during the overall innovation process.

CASE STUDY: ONYX PHONE CONCEPT

In order to delve deeper into the challenges in managing creative virtual teams, the development of the Onyx Concept Phone is presented. Our efforts were recognized by winning a Red Dot design award in the Design Concept Category in 2006. However, winning an award does not mean the process was not without its challenges. The process of forming and managing the virtual team responsible for the Onyx will be shared using the frameworks discussed earlier.

The Onyx mobile phone experience was launched to the press in August of 2006. This advanced mobile concept prototype reflects the joint collaboration of Synaptics (being an interface component company based in Silicon Valley, California) and PilotFish, an industrial design firm based in Munich. The Onyx began as an internal effort by Synaptics to demonstrate to potential customers the benefits and opportunities of ClearPad—a touchscreen technology that has significant advantages over the more ubiquitous resistive touch screens most consumers have used on their smart phones and supermarket checkout counters. We knew from previous experience at Synaptics that technical and user experience benefits of the core technology had been difficult to communicate to prospective customers through the more traditional marketing collateral of PowerPoint slides and nonfunctional mechanical samples. The product marketing manager for mobile phones came to the internal concept prototyping team for help. What arose out of literally months of discussion was the most ambitious project this team had taken on to date, to design a functional mobile phone experience prototype. Luckily the team was not constrained by more onerous requirements like actually making phone calls or fitting inside the shrinking phone form factor. The focus was on new user interactions and industrial design elements that were enabled by the ClearPad technology. The Synaptics concept prototyping team did not have all the skills necessary to design and manufacture the prototype, and therefore formed a virtual team to ensure that all the required skills were available.

Structure of the Onyx Project Virtual Team

As mentioned above, the Onyx Project required expertise not available in the Synaptics concept prototyping team. The team is staffed with a product designer, an electrical engineer, a systems engineer, and receives part-time assistance from software and firmware resources. The team was lacking in industrial design, graphic design, and user interface design skills. During the almost twelve months of the Onyx project, the concept prototyping team continued to produce over 40 additional prototypes. As a result the team required additional resources to augment the core resources in mechanical engineering, software, manufacturing, and electrical engineering. Figure 9 shows the number of stakeholders involved as well as the normal communication channels between the members of the virtual team.

The first member of the virtual team outside of Synaptics was PilotFish. PilotFish is an industrial design firm based in Munich, Germany, with offices in Taipei, Taiwan. In the end, PilotFish provided the industrial design and graphic design skills necessary for the project. The team at Synaptics not only provided the overall concept architecture but also did the interaction design. The graphic user interface was a joint collaboration between the PilotFish and Synaptics design teams. Other resources were brought in as contractors to support the core team with additional prowess in electrical engineering, manufacturing, software development, and Adobe Flash programming. The following table describes the roles and responsibilities of the various virtual team members.

Figure 9. Stakeholder network for the Onyx Project. The actors are grouped according to their affiliation to the concept prototyping team during the project.

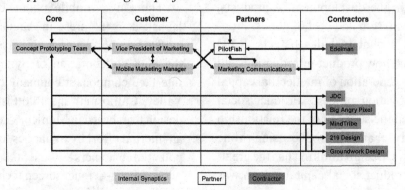

Engagement Cycles of Onyx Stakeholders

Different stakeholders came in at different times in the development of the Onyx prototype. There was even time when no one was actively involved in development. Figure 10 illustrates when the various actors in this production entered and left the stage. The top section shows when the various virtual team members on-boarded and off-boarded the project. The bottom sections illustrate the overlapping evolution of the innovation stages.

As shown by the early design phases (Figure 10) most of the recognition phase was completed inside Synaptics. PilotFish was brought on board during the Idea Formation phase. Contrary to common wisdom in forming distributed design teams, the Synaptics and PilotFish teams have never met face-to-face. As such, much of the early phone conferences were spent not only sharing project information but also building a rapport and a foundation of trust. This took longer than in virtual teams where face-to-face meetings kick things off. As such, it took many months to have the foundation of trust necessary to effectively support the creative work we were engaged in. This trust was especially important for the relationship between Synaptics and PilotFish. Most engagements with industrial design firms involve a client-contractor relationship, with the client paying for the services rendered by the industrial design firm. For the Onyx project, this was a partnership relationship, with both Synaptics and PilotFish contributing their intellectual capital to the project. The preliminary rules of engagement between the two firms were set in an initial partnership agreement. This agreement attempted to anticipate what path the project would take as well as likely contributions by both parties.

As the interaction design and industrial design began to mature, the project transitioned from idea formation to problem solving. Additional firms were recruited to join in the project. Each new firm brought into the virtual team after PilotFish was a contractor for Synaptics. As each new actor entered the stage, there were certain challenges associated in bring them into the production. The first was in the sharing of the Onyx project vision. Some contractors entering in later stages

Table 1. Members of the Onyx creative virtual team and their responsibilities

Member	Role and Responsibility
Concept Prototyping Team	Project Management, concept architecture, interaction design, integration and test, usability testing
Vice President of Marketing	Eventual internal customer for Onyx Project
Mobile Marketing Manager	Initial internal customer of Onyx project
Marketing Communications Group	Internal group that orchestrates outbound marketing
PilotFish	Industrial Design Partner
Edelman	Synaptics PR firm assists with outbound marketing of Onyx Concept
219 Design	Preliminary component sizing to support industrial design
JDC	Mechanical design support and vendor coordination
MindTribe	Electrical engineering of main boards and ClearPad driver software
Big Angry Pixel	Graphic Design for Preliminary Interaction Design Prototype
Groundwork Design	Development of Adobe Flash software

Figure 10. Engagement diagram for the Onyx Project

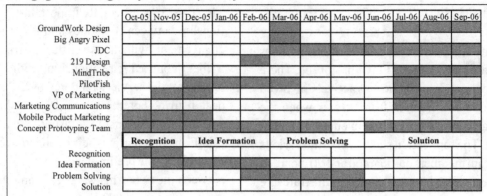

such as problem solving attempted to shift their efforts back to idea formation. Other contractors held on to assumptions that this would eventually turn into a real product, applying overly rigorous constraints to their design efforts. In the later stages of the project, the complex interdependencies between the electrical, mechanical, and software subsystems required tight collaboration and open information sharing. For a few of the contractors involved, this pushed beyond their normal mode of operation, requiring the project manager to constantly facilitate communication between the actors. Tracking project status was made more difficult by the lack of proactive communication from these novice virtual team members. The exchange of hard currency eased some of the complexities involved in the Onyx virtual team.

Though partnership mentality pervaded the entire project, in the end Synaptics had the ultimate decision responsibility for Onyx. This form of structural power was critical during periods of the project where some virtual team members were not collaborating effectively. In these times of conflict over *who did what wrong when*, having a central decision authority helped the team focus on solving the problem rather than bickering over who caused it.

The constant shift in the membership of the Onyx virtual team presented several challenges.

The first major challenge experienced had its root in the collaboration and knowledge sharing infrastructure for the project or the lack thereof. E-mail was the main collaboration tool for the Onyx team. Internally Synaptics has other collaboration tools such as an internal wiki or Microsoft Sharepoint, but these tools were not accessible by virtual team members outside the corporate firewall. The team's reliance on email also hampered the sharing and version control of large files such as computer-aided design (CAD) databases for the mechanical parts of Onyx. This was not an issue of having appropriate technology; rather that the corporate policies and information system architectures were too inflexible to fully support distributed virtual teams.

Additionally, Onyx team members worked across multiple software environments, making it difficult to review interim progress on various tasks. Not only were file viewers not readily available for software like Adobe Illustrator but for those viewers that were available, lack of team familiarity lessened the efficiency of joint review. Three-dimensional CAD geometry requires different review tools and skills than that of a human interface specification.

Finally, off-boarding was a sporadic, sputtering process as the transfer of knowledge was often incomplete. So much tacit knowledge is created in creative projects. In tightly coupled teams, this tacit knowledge is made explicit by human knowledge brokers in a "just in time" fashion. With members coming and going on this project, the tacit knowledge of crucial project details was often absent during critical decision points. At these times, former members were asked to come back in, even for just a short time, to broker the required knowledge transfer. In contrast to the rapid step like on-boarding process, off-boarding of team members on Onyx seemed to sputter along until the required tacit knowledge was shared.

Dynamics of Concept Maturity in the Onyx Project

Originally named for the technology that offered the greatest constraint, the ClearPad Phone was focused on demonstrating novel user experiences that could be uniquely enabled with transparent capacitive touch sensors. This constraint pervaded every aspect of the project, from industrial design to interaction design, LCD selection, mechanical design, and so forth. The first task in the project was to develop a shared understanding between the internal customers and the concept prototyping

team as to what type of project Onyx would be. Prior to partnering with PilotFish, the first several weeks were spent agreeing on the scope and goals for the project. In the end all involved agreed that this would be the Concept Prototyping team's first *Lost in the Fog* project. There were clear goals for the project though we were unclear how the team would achieve those goals and what would be the final deliverable. The process that played out over the next several months is represented qualitatively in Figure 11.

Notice that the technical maturity takes a significant leap in the early phase of this project. This is because of the initial constraints of the ClearPad technology, an anchor that drove many of the design decisions. As PilotFish is brought on board towards the end of the Recognition phase you see the Human aspects of the project maturing as well. The team did several prototypes of the interface along the way that provided sporadic leaps in maturity. This happened in parallel to the hardware development. The team took a great risk in pursuing parallel development of all of the critical components of the systems, hoping that when these disparate pieces were first integrated

Figure 11. Concept maturity qualitative graph for the Onyx Project

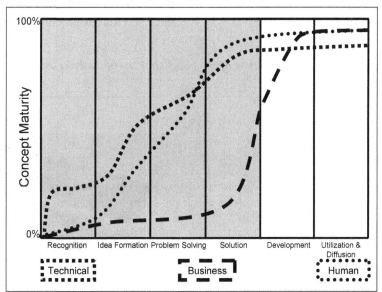

the Onyx would work fine the first time. As a manager, I used these notions of concept maturity to decide where to focus my attention and therefore resources during the project.

The first part of the Onyx architecture comprised the stages of industrial design and mechanical design. Based on some initial geometry studies done by 219 Design, PilotFish was able to craft several compelling concepts of the form for Onyx. Figure 12 shows the progression from rough form studies to the final industrial design. Based on this design language, JDC began detailed mechanical design of the components. This was difficult since many of the components inside the phone had not yet been specified or designed, such as the main PCB that held the processor, speaker, and charging circuit among other features. MindTribe started the detailed electrical design once the overall dimensions of the mechanical components were designed. While JDC and MindTribe were working through the mechanical and electrical interfaces, PilotFish and Synaptics turned their attention to the interaction design.

The interaction design was led by Synaptics with PilotFish providing the professional polish and consistent design language for the graphic elements of the interface. The Synaptics team took a scenario-based approach, conceiving artificial personas to design for. The team also generated a list of potential technologies and interactions that could be showcased during the demonstration of the concept prototype to potential customers. This list of application interactions was trimmed and focused by the mobile product marketing manager—the preferred application interactions being woven together to create a coherent narrative. Blending the use of several applications to support the activities of the fictional user, the Onyx user interface sought to flatten the navigation hierarchy of traditional mobile phone interfaces. Allowing simultaneous access to phone, music, location based services, and calendar/social networking functions, the Onyx interactions were designed to be intuitive yet powerful.

As can be seen in the concept maturity graph in Figure 11, the business issues received very little attention until late in the project. As the design team neared completion of the hardware prototype, the Synaptics Marketing Communications Group began working with the vice president of marketing to craft a publicity strategy for Onyx. The main goals of the Onyx project were to help Synaptics launch the new ClearPad technology and have a demonstration platform around which to discuss potential opportunities with customers. During this phase, photorealistic renderings of the as yet nonfunctional Onyx made their way out to the press while PilotFish prepared the entry into the Red Dot design competition.

Figure 12. Rough industrial design sketches of the candy bar motif evolved into the finished form of the Onyx concept

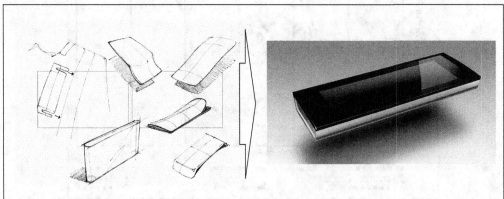

Figure 13. Interaction design and graphic design of main menu for Onyx showing the maturing from rough sketch to final implementation in Adobe Flash on the hardware platform

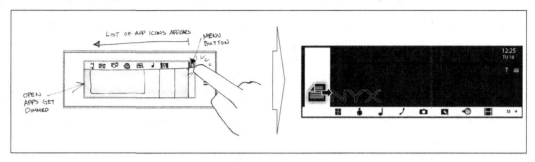

Figure 14. Functional Onyx prototype demonstrating the use of a virtual scroll wheel to control the volume of music playback

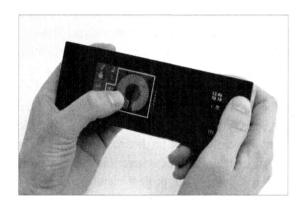

In the end, most of the disparate components came together without any major design flaws. The biggest challenge is that the final prototype appears as mature as a shipping product, creating a communications challenge for the sales and marketing teams when the prototype behaves as only prototypes can. Staying aware of the dynamics of concept maturity across the three domains of comprehensive design engineering was critical to the successful management of this project. More formal metrics and better tools for assessment of the changing concept maturity would be a tremendous help, especially in the context of managing virtual teams engaged in creative work where normal metrics of routine work, lines of code or engineering change orders, have no value.

Reflections on the Onyx Virtual Creative Team

The Onyx virtual creative team was very successful in creating a novel mobile user experience using Synaptics' proprietary ClearPad technology. In addition to winning a 2006 Red Dot design award in the Design Concept category, the Onyx project has generated significant worldwide press attention for both Synaptics and PilotFish. The project was not without its challenges. The constantly changing roster of team members, each with different points of view, methodologies, and toolsets, created significant management overhead for the project as compared to a nonvirtual team doing routine work. Working in the fuzzy front end of the innovation process brought additional overhead in aligning customer expectations with the processes the team were engaged in as the Onyx concept matured. Achieving initial agreement as to the type of journey this was likely to be, *Lost in the Fog* was critical to the continued support and eventual success of Onyx.

FUTURE TRENDS

As global enterprise matures, their ability to increase profits by cost reduction efforts, outsourcing to regions of lower labor costs, and merging with other firms to share common resources, will diminish rapidly (Hamel, 2002). This leaves only one path to continued growth, innovation. Effective creation and management of global distributed innovation teams will be critical in ensuring the best minds are focused on the greatest opportunities at the right time. This will only get more difficult. Current best practice is to have small copies of complete innovation teams embedded in the local context, one in Europe, one in Asia, and one in North America. In the future this will be cost prohibitive, especially for smaller firms seeking to compete in the global marketplace. Teams will need to be more agile and effective while maintaining their commitment to delivering creative solutions to innovative opportunities. As the pressure to shorten product development lifecycles rises, the temporal resources available to support these teams will shrink dramatically. Such pressures will push virtual innovation teams to deliver immature concepts, creating substantial risks for the enterprise seeking to innovate. There needs to be recognition that giving birth to an innovation, like giving birth to a child, cannot be accelerated beyond a certain limit.

The growing emphasis on the importance of design to business success (Nussbaum, 2004) will raise the demand to support virtual innovation teams beyond the capacity of the enterprise. Without robust metrics, improved methods of on-boarding and off-boarding team members, and proper cultural accommodations for such teams, the success of bringing design into the enterprise will be dampened significantly. Should the development of supporting methodologies keep pace with the adoption of such teams into the corporate tool chest then building and supporting virtual innovation teams will be simplified and the sponsoring enterprise will enjoy greater success.

Industry cannot rely solely on the natural growth in bandwidth and other technological means to ease the adoption and implementation of virtual innovation teams. New business models and methods of dealing with intellectual property (IP) will also be required. Current IP policies ensure that the legal wrangling surrounding a multinational, multifirm virtual team can easily consume more resources than the creative work itself, often taking months to agree upon contractual language for a two week project.

CONCLUSION

Virtual innovation teams are an increasingly powerful asset many enterprises utilize to 'turbo-charge' their innovation process. The management of these teams has a unique set of challenges that distinguish it from routine work done by virtual teams and from creative work done by collocated teams. Creating the environment to support creative work across cultural, enterprise, geographical, and domain specific differences is problematic with the tools currently available. Additionally, the overhead of managing the integration and engagement of the various actors involved with a specific project over time generates additional project risk stemming from the time required to bring new members on board, the knowledge lost when team members leave the team, and the need to offer enough project visibility to satisfy the customer's need for process and progress transparency.

Assessing the concept maturity across the technical, human, and business aspects of the project provides managers with an important tool for determining and communicating the projects state of health. It is critical that prior to the commitment of precious resources to a new project, that all stakeholders agree upon the scope of the effort required. This classification needs to be revisited throughout the innovation process to ensure that both the customers and virtual team members continue to have congruent points of view with respect to the scope of work and the desired deliverables.

Virtual innovation teams offer significant benefits to the enterprises that utilize them. In the future, firms will gain significant competitive advantage if they can learn to deploy such teams effectively. There are many challenges in building and managing these teams, some of which have been shared here while tools and methods needed to overcome some of these challenges are detailed in other parts of this book.

REFERENCES

Feland, J. M. (2005). *Product capital model: modeling the value of design to corporate performance*. Unpublished doctoral dissertation, Stanford University.

Feland, J. M., Leifer, L. J., & Cockayne, W. R. (2004). Comprehensive design engineering: Designers taking responsibility. *International Journal of Engineering Education, 20*(3), 416-423.

Hamel, G. (2002). *Leading the revolution: How to thrive in turbulent times by making innovation a way of life*. New York: Penguin Putnam.

Hargadon, A., & Sutton, R. I. (1997). Technology brokering and innovation in a product development firm. *Administrative Science Quarterly, 42*, 716-749.

Khurana, A., & Rosenthal, S. R. (1997). Integrating the Fuzzy-Front-End of new product development. *Sloan Management Review, 38*(2), 103-120.

Koen, P., Ajamian, G., Burkart, R., Clamen A. et al. (2001). Providing clarity and a common language to the "fuzzy front end." *Research and Technology Management, 44*(2), 46-55.

MacGregor, S. P. (2002). *Describing and supporting the distributed workspace: Towards a prescriptive process for design teams*. Doctoral dissertation, DMEM, University of Strathclyde, Glasgow, UK. Retrieved October 15, 2006, from http://www.design4distribution.com

Marquis, D. G. (1988). The anatomy of successful innovations. In M. L. Tushman & W. L. Moore (Eds.), *Readings in the management of innovation* (pp. 79-87). Boston: Ballinger Publishing Company.

Nussbaum, B. (2004, May 17). Power of design. *BusinessWeek*, p. 86.

Obeng, E. (1994). *All Change! The project leader's secret handbook*. London: Pitman. Retrieved January 8, 2006, from http://www.physorg.com/news3210.html

Poskela J., Berg P., Pihlajamaa J., Seppälä J., & Feland J. (2004, April). The role of roadmaps in fuzzy-front-end phase of innovation process. In *Proceedings of IAMOT 2004, 13ᵗʰ International Conference on Management of Technology*, Washington, DC.

Reinertsen, D. G. (1999). Taking the fuzziness out of the fuzzy front end. *Research and Technology Management, 42*(6), 25-31.

Trygg, L., & Nobelius, d. (2002). Stop chasing the front end process—Management of the early phases in product development projects. *International Journal of Project Management, 20*, 331-340.

Weiss, L., (2002). Developing tangible strategies. *Design Management Journal, 13*(1), 33-38.

ENDNOTES

[1] The term "tiger team" was first introduced to me during the spread of Total Quality Management in the late 1980s and early 1990s. Organizations would form multidisciplinary teams to "attack" quality issues. In the context of this chapter, these tiger teams are "attacking" innovation instead of quality.

² This triad of *People*, *Place*, and *Process* comes from discussions with Rickson Sun at IDEO. Rickson serves as IDEO's head knowledge broker, moving through teams and projects trading bits of pertinent insights. Part of his responsibility is to reflect on what makes IDEO work. The three P's represent a framework that he uses to support his efforts to improve the performance of their design teams.

Section III
Tools: Unlocking the Power of Virtual Teams for Creativity

Chapter XI
Tools and Technology to Support Creativity in Virtual Teams

Julian Malins
Gray's School of Art, The Robert Gordon University, UK

Stuart Watt
School of Computing, The Robert Gordon University, UK

Aggelos Liapis
School of Computing, The Robert Gordon University, &
Gray's School of Art, The Robert Gordon University, UK

Chris McKillop
School of Computing, The Robert Gordon University, &
Gray's School of Art, The Robert Gordon University, UK

ABSTRACT

This chapter examines the ways in which currently available software applications can support the creative process in general, and designers, in particular, working in virtual teams. It follows the main stages in the design process, examining how existing software can support the creative process. Emerging innovations for each stage of the design process are also presented. The chapter provides examples of tools, considering their strengths and limitations, and speculates on future directions for software development to support creativity and collaboration within virtual teams.

INTRODUCTION

As the Internet develops many more of us are getting used to working with colleagues as members of virtual teams. No longer is it necessary to be in the same physical space as someone you are working with or even in the same time zone. This chapter focuses on the work of designers working collaboratively in virtual teams and software tools which can support them. The 'team' in this context includes a wide range of stakeholders, clients, designers and specialists, and virtual teams are groups working collaboratively within a virtual space. This may or may not include working at a distance; in this virtual space colleagues may be working in a conventional face-to-face relationship at the same time as occupying the virtual space with others. We have chosen design as the focus because it raises a tension between the creative aspects of practice and the professional aspects of commercial reality—this tension underpins many of the issues that influence the choice of tools to support teams and is a thread that will run through the rest of this chapter.

Although there are software applications available that can support various aspects of the design process, they are fragmented: there is no commonly accepted single environment that supports the entire design process for a virtual team. There are two main different types of tool: those which support tasks specific to certain stages of the design process, and those which enable a virtual team to operate as a cohesive and creative unit throughout the process. Furthermore, as will be discussed, although there are many technologies which support parts of the design process (such as prototyping and modelling), of critical importance to the subsequent success of a project is the initial dialogue and understanding which takes place long before the formulation of the design brief. This is particularly important given the range of stakeholders involved in the process, but is not well supported by technology.

While in the future, we envision a true collaborative virtual design environment, made up of a wide range of tools accessed over a network; this is very much a long-term vision. In this chapter, we will focus principally on creativity in virtual teams and how (and even if) today's tools genuinely provide a framework that permits virtual teams to work in a creative way. We will return to this vision at the end of this chapter. First, the

nature of creativity in collaborative teams is examined, and is followed by a systematic analysis of presently available tools and their ability to support and enhance this creativity.

To illustrate the overall framework used in the rest of this chapter, consider the following scenario, which reflects the nature of the design process in an imaginary virtual team:

Scenario: *Megalith Sound Inc. has commissioned a small design consultancy, Carnelian, to design their new range of MP3 players. Sandy, senior partner in Carnelian, calls their lead designer, Alex, to set up a team to work on the design. Alex e-mails a few of their affiliated designers, with different specialities: Pat and Terry. Pat usually works from home and Terry is freelance, but Alex knows from one of her old e-mails that she has worked on a similar project. They look at the messages from Megalith, and put together a rough brief, exchanging word-processed e-mails. After getting feedback from Megalith, who provides more detailed technical information, they refine the brief, and Alex begins to plan and cost the design project. Meantime, Pat has been sketching out a few rough ideas and Terry has been building a mood board by collecting together a set of images. After exchanging e-mails, they call Alex (Pat uses Skype™ extensively) who pulls together a more focused set of alternatives. Pat uses Rhino to develop a range of 3D models, which they can run by Megalith; Terry and Alex amend the designs to refine the color and design detailing. Alex uses the in-house rapid prototyper to make a few samples, and emails the model files to Megalith.*

This simple scenario is pretty typical of how people can work together today as a virtual team in the design industry.

Figure 1 illustrates how many technologies are already integral to the design process. A wide variety of tools are used, some so ubiquitous that they are almost invisible. E-mail is important, but so is searching old e-mail, browsing and searching the Web, and word processing, as well as tools that more explicitly support parts of the process such as 3D modelling, project management, and spreadsheets.

Two other points are worth commenting on: first, that the formation of the team is fairly complex: it involves a wide range of stakeholders and constraints that become important parts of the early stage design process; and second, that a wide range of communication and sharing tools are both essential and used throughout the whole process. However, this communication and sharing needs to support two different aspects of the work within the team:

a. Creativity within the team
b. Convergence on a design solution

These are two very separate issues and there can be a significant tension between them, particularly in a team which is not well synchronized. The tools and technologies which exist today are not neutral in this respect, as we will see, some are better at (a) and others are better at (b). In the third section of this chapter, we will return to the tools, and look at how they measure up against these two aspects, but before doing so, it is important to look at individual and collective creativity in more detail.

CREATIVITY IN VIRTUAL TEAMS

The detailed nature of creativity is still very much in question (Taylor, 1988; Boden, 1994), but by and large, there are two main different types of creativity. According to Langer (1989) when looking at a new problem, we can either look for differences from other problems, or we can look for similarities with other problems. These result in two distinct creative processes, the first involves deriving new solutions from old ones, 'case-based' design, or what Guilford (1967) calls "divergent production." The second involves transforming solutions by shifting contexts, thinking by analogy. Boden's (1994) model is slightly more complex, but in outline similar: allowing different kinds of divergent production, allowing new solutions by association, analogy, exploration, and transformation.

Design problems come in different sizes. Dym (1994) describes the differences between 'creative' design, 'variant' design, and 'routine' design. For Dym (1994), creative design is the 'hard problem' of design—new design, usually where there is a lack of knowledge on the part of the designers. Variant design involves adapting existing designs. Routine design makes no demands on new knowledge.

So on the one hand, the nature of the problem influences the kind of creativity that is likely to

Figure 1. An overview of a typical collaborative design process, and common tools to support it

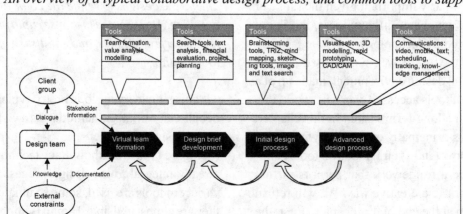

be relevant to it. This is not the only, or even the most important factor: there are at least two other important sets of factors: individual factors and external conditions as described by Rogers (1954):

Factors relating to the individual:
a. They should be open to experience
b. Evaluative judgment should be internal
c. They should be able to 'toy' with elements and concepts

Factors relating to the context of collaboration:
X. **Psychological safety:**
   X1. Contributors should be accepted for their own worth
   X2. External evaluation should be absent
   X3. Contributors should be understood empathically
Y. Contributors should be given freedom of symbolic expression

Although this model is not oriented to design specifically, the issues that it raises are general to all types of creative work. Importantly, this model reveals the tension between the creative individual and their social and collaborative context—this dynamic is central to virtual teams (as illustrated in the scenario) and it is clear that the factors that promote true creativity cannot be fully reconciled with the need for the team as a whole to deliver a unified design. For example, external evaluation can not be totally absent when there are external stakeholders.

On the other hand, some aspects of this approach to creativity can be effectively enhanced through tools and technology. Search engines, for example, provide new ways for helping designers to associate concepts, form analogies, explore alternatives, and transform problems. And 'designers' here means teams of designers whose expertise may cover a wide range of specialist knowledge, as the days of the inventor locked in a garden shed are increasingly less representative of modern design (Broadbent & Cross, 2003).

So on the one hand, true creativity can perhaps best be achieved by free creative individuals, given respect and freedom to solve complex problems in ways that they feel reveal their unique potential, yet the realities of design usually involve other stakeholders, who make their own evaluations of the work—whether it will help creativity or not! The challenge for a virtual team is to provide the kind of support that will enhance creativity, while still delivering a quality result. Tools and technology can assist, by mediating the most harmonious balance within this framework.

COMPUTER SUPPORTED CO-OPERATIVE WORK

The rapid development of new communications technologies both supported and was driven by, the geographical spread of organizations, leading to a range of new "computer-supported co-operative work" (CSCW) technologies, that changed the ways in which teams communicated and worked. According to Suchman (1987), CSCW arose in the mid to late 1980s as a response to the formalism of human-computer interaction, at that time dominated by cognitive models of human action. The research field of CSCW provided technologists and social scientists with the opportunity to consider the social-scientific factors of technology. Workplace studies in CSCW (Orlikowski, 1992) demonstrated how the wider context was critical to successful collaboration.

Today, modern CSCW technologies include e-mail, threaded discussion boards, wikis and news groups, along with more technologically advanced synchronous chat systems, remote access and screen-sharing tools, and group decision support and brainstorming systems. They vary widely from synchronous tools (e.g., voice over IP, screen sharing) where collaborators are present at the same time, to asynchronous ones (e.g., e-mail, discussion groups) where they are not. Asynchronicity makes interaction more convenient but creates new coordination problems.

As CSCW technologies transform computer networks into teams, they have built social networks on the technology and social factors become critical to their success or failure (Grudin, 1994). CSCW relationships are often narrowly focused, geared to accomplishing tasks through coordinating activities and providing information. Although emotional support and sociability often accompany these exchanges, this communication is secondary to the specific tasks in hand and relationships often remain limited in content and emotionally distant. By contrast, virtual or electronic teams involve sociability, emotional support, and a sense of belonging, even though they are often accompanied by exchanges of information.

The task-oriented focus of these technologies can reduce social presence and social cues (Rice, 1984; Sproull & Kieser, 1991). While it may be good for giving and receiving information, opinions, and suggestions, it is less suited for communicating agreement and disagreement, and is worse for social-emotional tasks involving conflict and negotiation, such as showing tension or tension release (e.g., laughing) or showing strong emotions (Hiltz, Johnson, & Turoff, 1986). Successful CSCW depends on respecting the social dynamics of team collaboration—a real challenge for technologists (Grudin, 1994). These can be avoided to some extent by letting people shape the collaboration process rather than imposing it through technology, making participants equal within an environment, and avoiding 'turn-taking,' so all participants can key in entries whenever they like.

Virtual teams are often hard to divide into off-line and on-line types. Most use of CSCW occurs in social networks that are at least partially colocated, so online contact is interspersed with face-to-face, telephone, and written contact. In such situations, the norms of the team may shape the use of the technology. In other situations, the network is formed and primarily sustained online, a scenario most likely to be adopted by organizations that are dispersed geographically, especially between time zones. In these cases, traveling for meetings is not practical, and asynchronous CSCW is often used; for example, email communities are widely used in international organizations for knowledge sharing (Moreale & Watt, 2003).

TOOLS AND TECHNOLOGY TO SUPPORT VIRTUAL TEAMS

The main aspects of the design process are now examined in more detail with an outline of existing tools and technologies to support virtual teams at each stage. We will broadly follow the process laid out in Figure 1, but, obviously, the design process is not entirely linear and some tools span several stages of the design process. For each aspect, we will draw out the main issues involved and look at the strengths and weakness of each tool and technology in supporting virtual teams. These are based on our experiences of using these tools.

We will also discuss some key innovations in this area; many are not yet proven, but are likely to have an impact on future practice in virtual teams. There is an element of future-gazing here, obviously, and there are likely to be many new innovations above and beyond the ones described. These are relatively promising, however, we feel they are all likely to have an impact, directly or indirectly, in the way that teams operate.

Perhaps more interestingly, they generally strike a different balance to the tools in terms of the tension between creativity and collaboration. These more innovative technologies appear to afford individual creativity slightly more emphasis than the established technologies, in several ways. The key themes in these innovations are:

- **Improved connectedness:** Making it easier to make connections, both with people and concepts
- **Improved usability:** Making it easier to use the tools effectively
- **Improved immediacy:** New tools helping people to work at the same time

TEAM FORMATION

Virtual teams require tools to help establish the core values and aspirations of the key stakeholders. Tools are also required to help inform the decision process prior to the formation of the design brief.

Informing the team itself, especially when the team is geographically distributed, it is important that roles complement each other. Psychometric tests can play a useful part here: they enable the members of a team to explore and reflect on their individual strengths and weaknesses, ensuring that the team as a whole is complementary. In collaborative design, a useful framework is Belbin's (2003) team role inventory, which maps out each person's natural roles, and how they affect team working.

Communication is also key to forming a team, as well as being an integral part of working within a virtual team. Regarding formation, there is relatively little in the way of support currently, as shown in the scenario, where team formation depended largely on preexisting contacts.

Key existing tools:
- **Team evaluation metrics:** For example, Belbin's team role inventory (http://www.belbin.com®). These tools help ensure that the team has complementary skills, so that highly creative contributors are counterbalanced by those who ensure communication and cooperation is effective. Belbin's model suggests that creative contributors are often

too distracted to communicate effectively with other members of the team.

The Web is taking on a social twist, with the advent of Web 2.0 (discussed later in the chapter). Essentially this is not a technology, but a trend to a more interconnected approach to Web developments, where people can easily make associations and connections with others as equal individuals. Good examples of this trend are MySpace.com® and eBay™, which provide a whole new way of finding people with particular skills and services to offer. Gone are the geographical limitations of national boundaries. Gone too are the limitations of marketing and advertising, anyone with the relevant skills can share their skills with others.

Key innovations:

- **Social networking systems:** For example, Elgg.net (http://elgg.net/), MySpace.com (http://www.myspace.com/)

MySpace.com first came to fame as a forum for musicians, but it provides a forum for other creative disciplines and services, such as photography and publishing. It breaks down the need for a large corporate presence, and individuals can find and connect to others with complementary skills. Elgg.net is similar, with a learning orientation and very good support for portfolios. Strengths: easy networking, access to skills without barriers. Weaknesses: still a fairly small base in some areas.

Figure 2 shows how one of these sites, MySpace.com, can be used to find people with skills in a particular location.

BRIEF ANALYSIS

Some parts of the brief are easier to work on than others. All design briefs should contain the following information (Press & Cooper, 2003):

- Background of the company
- Identification of the design problem
- Design specifications and product attributes
- Some consumer and market information
- Approximate costs
- Timescales

The design brief should identify the problem being addressed whilst avoiding suggesting solutions. It identifies a likely selling price, user population, product requirements, and so forth. Because there is a definite costing and project management aspect to this part of the design process, tools such as Microsoft® Project and Excel are likely to prove useful. Increasingly, these tools are becoming 'Web enabled' to allow for dissemination, if not collaboration, on the information they embody. We will come back to the project management issue later, as this cuts through the design process.

Finally, and critically, the design brief sets out the design goals' major constraints and the criteria for evaluating a successful solution. This information may appear in any order within the document (design briefs are generally text-rich documents). Support for design brief preparation, especially collaboratively, is currently weak—e-mail was used in our example scenario, and this is far from unusual.

Key existing tools:
- **Office suite:** For example, Microsoft Office (http:www.microsoft.com), OpenOffice (http://www.openoffice.org/)

Figure 2. Example of finding skills in MySpace.com

For managing the basics of a brief, a good word processor, a drawing package, and a spreadsheet are the most important tools required. A key requirement is that these documents can be shared effectively; here Microsoft document standards, despite being both complicated and proprietary, are also supported by most alternatives. Strengths: use is widespread and well supported. Weaknesses: support for collaborative authoring is limited, drawing tools may be awkward. Microsoft Office is a commercial product.

OpenOffice is an open-source project released under the GNU public license. The Office suite as well as the source code can be downloaded from: http://download.openoffice.org/index.html

The issue of working with design briefs is currently open, with no significant tool support. The design brief analysis is designed specifically to help the client and the designers identify the key points of the design brief. Developing a tool to provide an analysis of this type of document, allowing the information to be clarified, categorized and essential points highlighted, provides another opportunity for a new software solution.

We are currently developing a specialized brief analysis tool that allows the designer to manipulate the design brief and give an alternative format based on the keywords underlined manually or automatically by the application. The core of the specific tool is founded on a database based on TRIZ algorithm (Altshuller, 1994), automatically highlighting key words and phrases. The specific tool may benefit end users by helping them identify all the important parts of the design brief finding a common language between client and designers in significantly less time. The design brief analysis tool aims to assist the client or the designers to identify the key points of the design brief by helping them identify related sources based on their selections.

Key innovations:

- **Google(TM)Docs** (docs.google)

Google Docs provide a Web-based word processing tool that is designed for collaborative authoring. It is still in beta release (as of April 2007) but shows promise as the first of a range of AJAX (asynchronous JavaScript and XML) tools equivalent to a standard Office environment. Strengths: collaboration on word processing. Weaknesses: can get complicated without a clear division of responsibilities.

IDEA GENERATION

Generating ideas returns to the different kinds of creativity outlined by Boden (1994)—ideas can be generated by association, by analogy, by exploration, or by transformation. Tools exist which support all of these, although they are disconnected. In practice, the design stage does influence the usefulness of some techniques; for example, 3D modelling (which is a relatively expensive and time-consuming approach to exploration) is more effective later in a design process, less so at the stage of idea generation. Association, by contrast, is relatively cheap.

Two techniques deserve particular mention. The first is brainstorming, which is a highly successful method, but requires significant support to be successfully used in a virtual setting. There are two essential stages to any brainstorming process: the first being to generate as many ideas as possible (this is Guilford's (1967) 'divergent production'), the second being to categorize or evaluate the ideas that have been generated. Iterative cycles of convergence and divergence is a common feature of the design process as detailed by Pugh (1990). Mind maps can assist the brainstorming process by allowing the structuring of abstract concepts as well as concrete ones. The use of color or other ways of emphasizing or highlighting links can contribute to the usefulness of the mind map (Buzan, 1988, 2005; Driscoll, 2000; Frey, 2003).

The second useful technique is TRIZ (http://www.mazur.net/triz/), which in contrast to techniques such as brainstorming (which is based on 'random' idea generation), aims to create an algorithmic approach to the invention of new systems and the refinement of old systems. In practice, TRIZ provides a large body of proven design heuristics, which offer set ways of transforming problems (in Boden's terms)—and, therefore, a sound basis for creative idea generation.

Images are a powerful resource to convey meanings, particularly emotional values, and experiences. Their application can serve as an important tool to communicate values that cannot be expressed easily through words (Sharples, 1994). Images are able to convey less tangible aspects of the users' experience (feeling, mood), thus giving users a medium to express them. Likewise, designers often tend to prefer visual information due to its accessibility. The image can offer the designer and user a shared language—thus aiding the communication. For example, designers can use mood boards to immerse themselves into a particular state of emotions associated with a task or product. Mood boards are a collection of visual images (e.g. photographs, material samples) gathered together to represent an emotional response to a design brief.

During the implementation of the project a moment of creative insight emerges, when designers discover a new or previously hidden association between a certain piece of information and what they want to design (Sharples, 1994). Designers then apply the association to their design and produce a potentially creative design. They reflect on the design and decide whether they like it or not in the evaluation phase. These stages are repeated until a satisfactory result is achieved (Gardner, 1985; Gero & Maller, 1993; Dartnall, 1994; Gross & Do, 1996).

Key existing tools:

- **Image searching:** For example, desktop—Picasa (http://picasa.google.com/), closed collections—Dreamstime™ (http://www.dreamstime.com/), Web—Google (http://www.google.com/), Web—Delicious (http://del.icio.us/)

All these tools support good image searching; however, they depend on good levels of meta data—image retrieval technology is far less advanced than text retrieval. Strengths: support for individual creativity, easy access to a wide range of images. Weaknesses: lack of associations between images.

- **Encyclopedias and thesauri:** For example, Wikipedia (http://www.wikipedia.org/), Visual Thesaurus (http://www.visualthesaurus.com/)

Wikipedia has taken concept association to a new level and provides a network of more than a million concepts and entries, which can be freely and easily browsed with some additional image entries. Strengths: support for individual creativity, exhaustive association between concepts. Weaknesses: often predominantly textual, no well-defined connections between concepts and visual images. Wikipedia is an open-source online encyclopedia and its source code as well as its entire list of archives is released under the GNU public license and can be downloaded from: http://en.wikipedia.org/wiki/Wikipedia: Database_download. Visual Thesaurus® is a commercial product available as a Web-based service or a stand-alone application. It provides a visual overview of the relationship between words.

- **TRIZ:** For example, Goldfire Innovator (http://www.invention-machine.com/)

Goldfire Innovator uses TRIZ as its basis, helping to assist creative problem solving. However, it also includes a range of other methods appropriate to the earlier parts of the design process. Strengths: especially useful in larger organizations, as many of the tools are oriented to corporate knowledge management. Weaknesses: principally intended for engineering- and design-related disciplines.

- **Mind mapping:** For example, Inspiration (http://www.invention-machine.com/)

Visual tools to assist mapping out concepts can be a good approach to encouraging creativity, especially for individuals and for groups where the maps are coconstructed. The software allows the map to be converted directly to an HTML document which can be viewed as a Web site. When used in combination with Macromedia's Contribute, team members can continue to develop the mind map and modify the Web site.

Strengths: easy to use, good way of drawing out issues. Weaknesses: one person's map may be hard for another to interpret. Inspiration is a commercial product. A trial of its latest release can be downloaded from: http://www.inspiration. com/freetrial/index.cfm

- **Brainstorming:** For example, FacilitatePro (http://www.facilitate.com/)

Brainstorming is essentially a range of psychologically-derived techniques for creativity. There is a range of techniques that can be used, but the process is specifically designed to meet the rules of Rogers' approach to creativity, for example, by withholding judgment during the creative parts of the process, and respecting other people's contributions. Strengths: the process is sound for encouraging creativity. Weaknesses: tools do not generally support the whole process. ePro is a Web-based commercial product.

Figure 3. Image searching and collecting tools

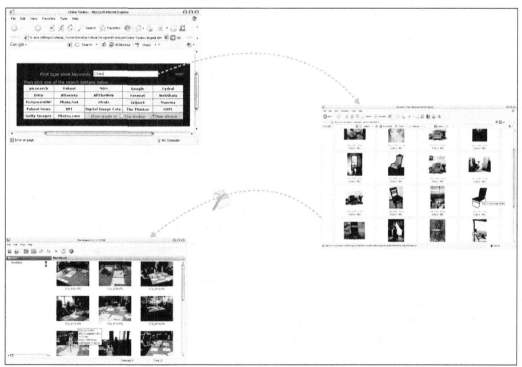

Despite the wide variety of searching tools, there is a weakness in the connection between textual and conceptual exploration, and the use of images. We are developing a tool to enhance idea generation, illustrated in Figure 3, which integrates searching by concept with image retrieval. This is not an image retrieval tool in itself, but is designed to afford the 'toying' with concepts and visual elements required by creative designers. Clicking on a concept can bring up a palette of related images, which can then be collected, for example as part of a virtual mood board.

However, there are other innovations which show significant promise as additional support to this aspect of the design process.

Key innovations:
- **AACECAD DigiMemo** (http://www. acecad.com.tw/)

This is simply a pad which records what you write or draw, and enables it to be uploaded onto a computer for further work. It is ideal for sketching, as it uses a real pen (unlike a tablet) and does not require to be connected to a computer constantly. Strengths: excellent for quick sketching and enables the sketches to be shared digitally. Weaknesses: additional software needed for handwriting recognition. ePro is a commercial product.

- **DENIM** (http://dub.washington.edu/denim/)

DENIM is a sketching tool developed at the University of Washington, mainly intended for interface and Web design. Best used with a graphics tablet or Tablet PC, its strength is speedy pen-based sketching, and its ability to animate these sketches. Tools like these are ideal for quickly bringing early stage designs to life. Strengths: speed of use, good for storyboarding. Weaknesses: particularly designed for Web and

interface design. Denim is an academic project and can be downloaded from: http://dub.washington. edu/projects/denim/download/.

VISUALISATION AND MODELLING

Exploration is an important part of the creative process, and sketching tools enable designers to quickly explore and share ideas. Sketching is frequently used during the early stages of conceptual design when ideas are still unfinished. The lack of precision implied by the strokes seems to increase the tolerance of the initial estimate of shape. Thus, sketching has been recognized as an important tool for communicating ideas and concepts.

While it is traditionally performed using pencil and paper (at least in the early stages of the design process), the ability to interactively explore and refine the original thoughts in a collaborative environment can provide a sense of shared design space, allowing the easy creation of different versions of the project and serving as a valuable brainstorming tool.

A second issue at this stage of the design process is that different kinds of design differ significantly in the tools they may use. Graphic designers will use different tools to industrial designers, textile designers, and architects, for example. This is a particular issue for virtual teams, as shown in the scenario, where despite its lack of reliability, e-mail is far and away the most common file-sharing tool today.

Key existing tools:
- **Sketching tools:** For example. Adobe® Photoshop® (with a graphics tablet)

Quick sketches are an ideal start to the design process, as they can take seconds to prepare and share. These applications usually support 'layers' which allow aspects of a drawing to be combined and recombined, which is a useful way of exploring alternatives quickly. Strengths: speed of sketching, easy to share results. Weaknesses: can be on the complicated side, hard to amend and refine sketches. Adobe Photoshop is a commercial product. A trial of its latest release can be downloaded from: http://www.adobe.com/downloads/.

- **Drawing tools:** For example, Adobe Illustrator or Macromedia Freehand

For more precise drawing, vector graphical applications have a number of advantages. They are generally easier to amend and polish than raster (bit map) applications like Photoshop. They do tend to be more complex, though, and require a little practice; and putting together an image will generally take longer, even though the result will be of a higher standard. Strengths: high quality, easy to amend in details, files can be exported to form the basis for geometries which can be used in 3D packages. Weaknesses: slower to use for quick sketching. Adobe Illustrator and Macromedia Freehand are commercial products. A trial of the Adobe Illustrator latest release can be downloaded from: http://www.adobe.com/downloads/.

- **3D modelling tools:** for example, Rhinoceros® (http://www.rhino3d.com/)

These are the 3D equivalents of the vector drawing tools like Illustrator, and essentially have the same strengths and weaknesses compared to sketching, only more so. They are designed to be used closer to the end of the design process and take longer to learn and to use. Strengths: results can be used directly in the manufacturing process, high quality visuals. Weaknesses: slow to amend, harder to use for quickly exploring alternatives. Rhinoceros is a commercial product. A trial of its latest release can be downloaded from: http://download.mcneel.com/rhino/3.0/eval/default.asp.

- **3D printers:** For example, InVision LD (http://www.3dsystems.com/)

The smaller (and significantly cheaper) siblings of rapid prototyping machines, these now cost under £10,000 and will easily fit in an office. Strengths: good for quickly and relatively cheaply making models for discussion within the team and with clients. Weaknesses: limited in materials and size of models.

This is an area where standards are always changing, as it is the part of the design process which is most closely associated with the type of design being done. Tools in this area are always emerging, but it is hard to identify any clear winning trends in the near future. However, there is a clear trend towards increased usability and access to these tools. Past CAD tools were highly complex, and required specialized hardware. Today, a cheap PC costing a few hundred pounds will do for many purposes. The software has also become much easier to use, all in all, partly through improvements in modern operating systems, and partly through the effects that these operating systems have had on encouraging better usability design in software developers.

Key innovations:
- **Google SketchUp** (http://sketchup.google.com/)

Google Earth (http://earth.google.com/) enabled free access to satellite imagery. Google SketchUp allows people to make simple models in 3D and place them in Google Earth for others to see. It is strikingly easy to use, and although the free version is limited to simple shapes, the 'pro' version allows freeform editing. Here, usability is a key innovation—Google has definitely pioneered enabling access through usability. Google SketchUp has also enabled a large community to grow, with easy sharing of models through a Web site associated with Google Earth. Strengths: very easy to use, very good support for creativity within a community. Weaknesses: not as powerful as other 3D modelling environments.

COLLABORATION

Collaborative environments allow a team to share their work, seeing how others are communicating and working. Collaborative environments can be very helpful at certain parts of the design process, particularly after a brainstorming phase, when results need to be integrated. However, they can actively inhibit creativity, as they expose work to a community, and without the 'rules' of brainstorming to promote openness to ideas and alternatives, and acceptance of other people's contributions, they can discourage people from contributing. This has been especially well observed in discussion groups, where a few extrovert individuals will often tend to dominate discussions, unless good moderation is in place.

Within the field of design, a number of more specialized collaboration environments have been developed to help teams work together more effectively.

Key existing tools:
- **Collaborative design spaces:** For example, OneSpace.net (http://www.cocreate.com/onespace.net.cfm)
- **AutoDesk® Buzzsaw®** (http://usa.autodesk.com/adsk/servlet/indexsiteID=1231 12&id=2407898)

These enable a workflow to be established and tracked, and document sharing and basic communication. Strengths: good for ensuring visibility and tracking. Weaknesses: overused, they may provide too strong an evaluation framework to encourage individual creativity. OneSpace.net and Autodesk Buzzsaw are both commercial products.

In the real world it is possible to see and manipulate objects. A standard metaphor for virtual collaborative environments is the room which can contain people, objects, information, for example, books, notes, or whiteboards. Topics and projects can be housed in different rooms providing a framework or structure that can be used to separate different activities (Harmut, 2000). Additionally, these objects are arranged in sublocations within that room (e.g., shelves, drawers, folders, etc.), enabling people to find and organize specific information. Rooms are therefore also a means to structure information. (Metaphors are used extensively in Chapter XIV in this book.)

Current collaborative technology still fails to support real life collaboration (Mulder & Swaak, 2003). This problem is a direct result of not looking at the dynamic aspects of work. In designing technology that is able to support real-life interaction processes we need to pay attention to the fact that real-life situations are dynamic and involve complex tasks. A collaborative design environment pays attention to the complexity and dynamics of the teams, but also enables the team to complete the task effectively; in our original scenario, collaboration around ideas was weak, mainly because designs were hard to share. As a result, that team divided into well-defined roles, with creative collaboration largely confined to the details.

There have been several approaches to transfer the metaphor of rooms into computer supported cooperative work systems (Roseman & Greenberg, 1996). A principal advantage with the use of this metaphor is its relationship with the real world. The virtual room metaphor supports group structures/relations by providing a spatial analogue to group relations (Agarwal, 2004). It can be adapted to support the requirements of different groups, for example, client-designers, designer-designer or designer-other professionals (Toomey, Adams, & Churchill, 1998). It allows users to engage in a range of tasks, for example, brief analysis, storyboards, presentations, problem-solving, and brainstorming (Greenhalgh,

1997), and allows the control of interaction as required through the use of access rights (Pfister & Wessner, 1998). Virtual rooms are one potential way of providing flexible structures which can contain relationships and communication, and provide an overview of content (Marcus, 1997; Barbiery, 1999; Powel, 2004).

However, there is one big caveat to all this—as discussed in the section on creativity, to be successfully and constructively creative, evaluative judgment needs to be driven by the individual and external evaluation needs to be handled very carefully. Making all work public can seriously inhibit creativity; for this reason, there needs to be private rooms where people can work individually, until they are happy for others to see their work. (This phenomenon is highlighted through the public and private spaces of the virtual platform as described by Thomas Leerberg, "A Spatial Environment for Design Dialogue," Chapter XIII in this book.)

Improving the efficiency of the collaborative design process requires a better understanding of the dynamics of how the design process is conducted. Existing collaborative environments do not take enough account of the design process and are difficult to control. Improvements could be brought about by the use of real time remote access, the development of brainstorming tools and advanced image search engines, improved Web conferencing using new voiceover Internet protocols, synchronous and asynchronous collaboration using forums or Wikis to overcome a lack of communication and to enhance reliability and usability.

Key innovations:
- **Wikis** (http://en.wikipedia.org/wiki/Wiki)

Wikis are a relatively old Web technology, dating back to 1994 when the Web was in its infancy. Essentially, they are Web pages which have an extra button: "Edit this page" allowing anyone to edit and even create pages, using a few simple text formatting rules. Newer wikis support images, tracking, and searching. Strengths: easy to use, especially in large groups, good support for individual creativity. Weaknesses: public wikis can be subject to vandalism—adding 'undo' mechanisms may help to overcome this.

COMMUNICATION

Throughout the design process, the team needs to be able to communicate effectively. This is especially the case for creative people where, as Belbin (2003) identified, there is a tendency for a lack of communication while they are actively being creative.

An additional aspect is presence—simply being aware of when the other person is available. Open plan offices provide this—it is one of their key advantages over closed offices, that it is easy to see when people are likely to be available. This concept of 'awareness' has been approached by both technological (Greenberg & Fitchett, 2001) and design management (MacGregor, 2002) perspectives.

Key existing tools:
- **E-mail**

A widespread and ubiquitous communication system, e-mail is probably still the most commonly used communication tool on the Internet, despite its many limitations for working in teams. Strengths: widely available, easy to share digital information of any type. Weaknesses: asynchronous and occasionally unreliable, can get hard to track multiple contributions.

- **Voice over the Internet:** For example, Skype (http://www.skype.com/)

An emerging technology, Skype, and similar tools make voice communication cheap and easy. Some new operating systems (e.g., Apple®'s

MacOSX Tiger) make these kinds of tools available as standard. They are particularly at home in conference calling, which can be expensive and difficult through other telephone systems. Strengths: cheap, good conference calling. Weaknesses: not ubiquitous, hard to integrate with telephone systems.

- **Desktop sharing:** For example, Webex™ (http://www.webex.com/)

It is increasingly easy to share work by using a desktop sharing program where everyone can see what others are doing, as they do it. Especially when combined with voice, either by telephone or as above, this is a great tool for discussing and sharing design ideas. Strengths: good visibility, so everyone can see the same things. Weaknesses: tend to enforce a workflow that can exclude contributors unless the team dynamic is right.

Predicting the future of new communications technologies is hard: there have been some surprises, such as the dramatic growth in mobile phones, texting, video messaging and so on; but despite this, desktop computers today are fundamentally similar to those of twenty years ago. Most of the technologies we have described were available ten years ago. The problem is one of integration and consolidation, rather than development. An important force for change is likely to be open-source software, which allows components to be freely re-used and adapted without the same dependence on closed commercial software packages. Having said that, there are a few innovations starting to happen: technology is becoming more affordable—good examples include 3D screens, rapid prototyping, virtual reality software, and hardware. All of these are orders of magnitude cheaper than ten years ago, and are now within easy reach of smaller design practices.

Another likely change is the growth in mobile telecommunications. 'Always on' mobile Internet connections mean that people can be kept informed and brought in to address particular problems, as and when they are needed. This is common with colocated teams, skills can be borrowed informally as and when required—how this will work on a worldwide scale remains to be seen.

Key innovations:
- **3G mobile communications**

3G technologies allow video to be shared far more easily than previously. Its role in the design process is still emerging, but a good example is that a short video clip, moving around a 3D model, can now be cheaply and quickly transmitted to stakeholders and fellow designers for immediate feedback. Strengths: speed of delivery, able to disseminate widely. Weaknesses: quality of video still relatively poor compared to Internet communications.

- **3D projection theatre:** For example, The Macaulay Institute's Virtual Landscape Theatre

3D wraparound projection technology is now at least affordable, if not exactly cheap. The Macaulay Institute, Aberdeen, Scotland, has used this to create a participatory design environment for wind farms, which enables local communities, in groups of about 40 people, to explore different views and their environmental impact. Strengths: able to create a strong sense of presence for stakeholders. Weaknesses: expensive to develop good models, equipment still pricey.

KNOWLEDGE MANAGEMENT

Designs rarely begin from scratch. In industrial design, typically more than 70% of design information comes from previous design work. This is a consequence of the fact that the majority of design work is variant design—neither wholly creative not wholly routine. Under these circumstances, the knowledge needed to form a successful design often already exists within the organization, even if it is not currently available to the designers. This is where knowledge management techniques become important, enabling designers to find the information they need.

Designers may begin the design process by either referring to case-based design solutions (Domeshek & Kolodner, 1992) or by applying their own design knowledge to retrieve information from their own resources (Fischer, 1997; Nakakojin, 1999). Creativity is not limited by these theories or approaches—ideas and alternatives can be generated by a wide range of intuitive and systematic creative problem solving techniques.

Even apart from previous solutions, design knowledge is often widely distributed through an organization; email is especially valuable as an experience sharing environment, and many large organizations rely on it as a collective experience. Shared documents, including past briefs and design descriptions, can also be valuable. The challenge for finding this past knowledge is a challenge of information retrieval.

Key existing tools:
- **Desktop searching:** For example, Spotlight, Google Desktop (http://desktop.google.com/)

Finding previous relevant design issues/solutions can be hard. Good searching is essential. Since AltaVista Discovery, a range of desktop searching tools have come through, best represented at the moment by Google Desktop and Apple's Spotlight. Strengths: good at finding relevant texts, especially in email and other types of document. Weaknesses: no provision for searching other people's information.

Supporting a team portfolio requires an advanced file repository system, capable of mediating and sharing the contributions of the team. The portfolio will need to allow users to create projects, to add documents or files, and to manage

the project. In the collaborative design process, sharing and privacy of design information are both required. All members of the team need to be able to view, share, and modify files, with changes tracked and logged. Detailed meta-information such as the name of the contributor, time and date, versioning as well as appropriate commentary on future changes or possible objections in a project are essential features of such tools.

There has been something of a shift in Web technologies towards systems that draw out individuals and communities, enabling individual communication rather than the 'publish to the world' model of the current World Wide Web. Good examples include MySpace.com, blogging, and now vlogging (video blogging).

Knowledge management techniques come in a variety of different forms, according to the roles they play in the design team (Masterton & Watt, 2000). For example, knowledge management tools can play a role as a 'critic' in a design team (Fischer et al., 1993), as a 'bard'—telling stories about past successes and failures (Schank & Cleary, 1995), or as a 'matchmaker'—helping find people with needed knowledge or experience (Collison & Parcell, 2001).

Key innovations:
- **Web 2.0** (http://en.wikipedia.org/wiki/Web_2)

"Web 2.0" is a term given by O'Reilly Media in 2004 to refer to the move to a more socially- and collectively-oriented set of technologies emerging across the Web. Key examples include MySpace.com and Wikipedia. The full direction and impact of this trend is still unclear, and it is intertwined with ideas from the 'open-source' movement (discussed next), but it seems to be particularly promising as a way of enabling artistic and creative expression. Strengths: good for enabling individual creativity and expression. Weaknesses: can be hard to maintain an overall unifying style.

PROJECT MANAGEMENT

Bringing a team together is one thing, keeping it on track towards successful completion is another. There are a good number of commercial tools to support project management, although these are generally disconnected from any particular field or type of project. The iterative methodologies of design sometimes struggle to fit into linear project planning tools.

Scheduling is a key concept of particular importance in a situation involving multitasking, which is the standard condition in a design project. In a collaborative design environment having a scheduler ensures that designers can meet critical deadlines (with the use of an integrated reminder) or join synchronous collaborative sessions.

Key existing tools:

- **Basic project management tools:** For example, Microsoft Project

These tools can help both with the calculation of costs and with the management of resources; they allow tracking of a project against a defined work plan, and revision of plans when needed. Strengths: good visual overview of a project, very detailed planning possible. Weaknesses: limited effectiveness for 'informal' project plans. Microsoft Project is a commercial product. A beta version of the 2007 version of its latest release can be downloaded from: http://www.microsoft.com/office/preview/beta/download/en/default.mspx

- **Collaborative project tools:** For example, AutoDesk ConstructWare & Streamline (http://www.autodesk.com)

A chat- and whiteboard-based collaborative project management tool, which allows tracking of design phase issues and comments, and a file management and sharing tool which complements

it. Strengths: good project tracking and search, synchronous communication. Weaknesses: limited to chat communication and basic file management. Both products are commercially available.

In the world of computing, "open-source" technologies are causing a quiet revolution in the management of large software projects. New Web-based technologies now provide frameworks for version tracking (e.g., Tigris.org, 2001-2006b), issue tracking (e.g., Tigris.org, 2001-2006a), and project quality monitoring (e.g., Apache, 2001-2006). Although these primarily focus on development and maintenance, and not design, they allow very large-scale distributed collaboration between thousands of people around the world, to a level where they are creating systems that often exceed commercial systems in quality.

Underneath these technologies, the enabling change is in the process of development. Open-source development teams may be very large, potentially thousands of members. The quality of their work is at least as good as commercial equivalents—often better because the larger team ensures better testing and evaluation. A range of 'agile' project management approaches (Highsmith, 2004) have arisen—these emphasize process over planning, and people over documents, and set out to build dynamic and flexible teams which aim to enhance creativity. Much of this is still aimed at software development (where these techniques first arose) but it is now starting to have an impact on product development. Tool support for these approaches is still emerging, but rapidly.

The full impact of these approaches in other fields remains to be seen, but there has been a tradition of embedding open-source technologies, and it seems likely that at least some of these will become part of frameworks to support design in a wider context in the future. And in some ways, successful teams have always used agile practices, even if not explicitly—the initial scenario presented in the introduction emphasized people over process and the need to continually engage with client feedback (Bernstein, 1988), characteristics of agile approaches. (See "Enhancing Flexibility in Dispersed Product Development Teams" by Preston G. Smith, Chapter XII in this book, for a deeper discussion of the agile approach and its relation to creativity.)

Key innovations:
- **Subversion** (http://subversion.tigris.org/)

Subversion is an open-source file versioning system released under the GNU public license. It is relatively simple to use, and the effect is to create an audited log of changes to files. All previous versions are recorded so that people can return to an early version, while 'branching' is allowed, so that individuals can make an alternative set of files to explore and experiment, before 'merging' their work with collaborators. Strengths: free, simple, and easy to use. Weaknesses: for network use, requires specially managed (although free) Web server software.

- **Tracking systems:** For example, TRAC (http://trac.edgewall.org/)

The open-source approach to project management uses issue tracking where ideas, comments, and problems, even constraints, can be tracked and assigned to individuals or groups. TRAC actually combines issue tracking with Web access to Subversion, and a Wiki for collaborative editing. Strengths: good community support for passing ideas and thoughts as well as problems. Weaknesses: can expose individuals to public critique.

TOWARDS A VISION OF THE FUTURE

These innovations are largely disconnected, both from each other, and from the design process. However, there is a potential emerging for a new concept of a design environment which can help assist virtual teams to collaborate, and to collaborate creatively. We are working to integrate some of these tools into a single environment—or what can be seen from each participant's point of view as a single environment—and which can help to draw these different aspects of the design process together. This is very much a work in progress, and there is a significant amount of evaluation to do as we explore the nature of the support it can

Figure 4. The main interface of the envisioned environment, with associated tools

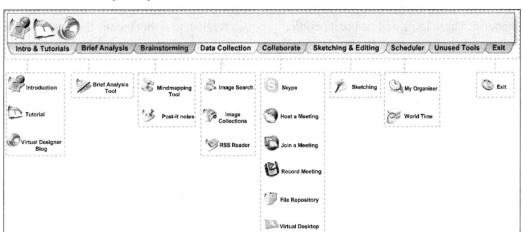

provide for the design process, but the direction seems promising.

A successful environment will depend on a close fit between the needs of the team and the task to be achieved (Grudin, 1994). For design, this needs a hands-on, constructivist, environment (Malins et al., 2003)—an environment where individuals can safely collaborate, while respecting their individual approaches to knowledge and practice. By tightly coupling tools which allow designs to be externalized with those which allow communication and collaboration, an integrated environment, like that shown in Figure 4 and currently under development, will enable virtual teams to form and work more effectively. Both shared practice and communication are essential for this: as Reddy (1979) described, without the shared practice, the basis for collaboration in a team is lost. This requires careful handling, however; to promote creativity, an environment needs to support private work as well as public, and ensure that the individual factors and external conditions which promote creativity are met (Rogers, 1954). There has been too much emphasis on generic collaboration, outside the context of the task in hand.

Returning to the story of Megalith Sound's MP3 player—in the future, Megalith (a future subsidiary of Google Galactic Inc.) will likely follow a similar process, but with each stage supported by a new range of innovative tools. Some of these will specifically support design, but many will be generic. These tools will connect people, assisting creative collaboration by encouraging an exploratory playfulness with concepts and ideas. Teams of designers will continue to seek out new tools and new processes, transforming their ways of working in the future.

CONCLUSION

In order to enhance virtual team collaboration, we should provide designers with technology that actually supports their collaboration, for example, technology that makes collaboration better, easier, and faster. Due to the fact that so far technology fails to support the collaborative design process, designers tend to prefer face-to-face collaboration, as a result delaying the entire process (Mulder & Swaak, 2003). As this chapter shows, also, today's tools are still somewhat limited in their support for individual creativity within that collaborative process.

Technology has great potential to support genuinely creative virtual teams, but is currently fragmented, existing in diverse separate applications that may have been adapted from their original use and not specifically designed to support the design process. Future directions will provide better access to existing knowledge bases and new technologies, and provide a framework that allows much easier collaboration and sharing of knowledge within the design process.

The science fiction writer Arthur C. Clarke, writing in the 1960s, predicted the growth of tele-working as a result of geocentric low orbit communication satellites. His vision described individuals working in isolation from one another, using communication tools. The virtual team model, whilst including remote working, stresses the importance of collaboration and the use of computer networks to access resources on a global scale.

To remain competitive in the global economy, it is essential that virtual teams of designers can be creative, and this means they need to balance improved communication with improved tools, in order to enable exploration of concepts and alternatives. Greater communication, by itself, may actively reduce creativity by making evaluation of alternatives too easy, too early in the process. Computer tools need to be properly designed within this understanding of the collaborative and creative processes, so that as the world becomes more complex so must the virtual teams' response become more sophisticated and informed.

REFERENCES

Agarwal, S. S. (2004). *Supporting collaborative computing and interaction* (No. LBNL-50418): Office of Advanced Computing Research, U.S. Department of Energy.

Altshuller, G. (1994). *The art of inventing (and suddenly the inventor appeared)*. Worcester, MA: Technical Innovation Center.

Apache. (2001-2006). *Maven*. The Apache Foundation. Retrieved from http://maven.apache.org/

Barbiery, T. T. (1999). *Networked virtual environments for the Web: The WebTalk-I & WebTalk-II architectures*. Department of Computer Engineering—Politecnico di Milano. Milano, Italy.

Belbin, R. M. (2003). *Management teams—Why they succeed or fail*. Oxford: Butterworth-Heinemann.

Bernstein, D. (1988). The design mind. In P. Gorb (Ed.), *Design talks!* London: London Business School/Design Council.

Boden, M. A. (1994). Precis of "the creative mind: Myths and mechanisms." *Behavioral and Brain Sciences, 17*(3), 519-570.

Broadbent, J. A., & Cross, N. (2003). Design education in the information age. *Journal of Engineering Design, 14*(4), 439-446.

Buzan, B. T. B. (1988). *Super creativity*. New York: St. Martin's Press.

Buzan, B. T. B. (2005). *The history of memory techniques leading to mind maps by Tony Buzan*.

Collison, C., & Parcell, G. (2001). *Learning to fly: Practical lessons from the world's leading knowledge companies*. Oxford: Capstone Publishing.

Dartnall, T. (1994). *Artificial intelligence and creativity: An interdisciplinary approach*. The Netherlands: Kluwer Academic Publishers.

Domeshek, E. A., & Kolodner (1992). A case-based design aid for architecture. In J. Gero (Ed.), *Artificial intelligence in design '92* (pp. 497-516). The Netherlands: Kluwer Academic Publishers.

Driscoll, M. P. (2000). *Psychology of learning for instruction*. Boston: Allyn and Bacon.

Dym, C. L. (1994). *Engineering design: a synthesis of views*. Cambridge: Cambridge University Press.

Fischer, S. G. (1997). Computational environments supporting creativity in the context of lifelong learning and design. *Knowledge-Based Systems Journal, 10*(1), 21-28.

Fischer, S. G., Nakakoji, K., Ostwald, J., Stahl, G., & Sumner, T. (1993). Embedding critics in design environments. *The Knowledge Engineering Review, 8*(4). Retrieved October 15, 2006, from http://journals.cambridge.org/action/displayJournal?jid=KER

Frey, C. (2003). The creative thinker's unique approach to mind mapping is a winner. *Innovation Tools.*

Gardner, H. (1985). *The mind's new science: A history of the cognitive revolution*. New York: Basic Books, Inc.

Gero, J., & Maher, M. L (1993). *Creativity and knowledge-based creative design*. Hillsdale, NJ: Lawrence Erlbaum Associations Inc.

Greenberg, S., & Fitchett, C. (2001, November). Phidgets: easy development of physical interfaces through physical widgets. In *Proceedings of the 14th Annual ACM Symposium on User Interface Software and Technology*, Orlando, FL.

Greenhalgh, C. (1997). *Creating large-scale collaborative virtual environments*. Department of Computer Science, University of Nottingham.

Gross, M. D., & Do, E. (1996, October). *Ambiguous intentions: A paper like interface for creative design*. Paper presented at the ACM Conference on User Interface Software Technology (UIST) '96, Seattle, WA.

Grudin, J. (1994). Groupware and social dynamics: Eight challenges for developers. *Communications of the ACM, 37*(1), 92-105.

Guilford, J. P. (1967). *The nature of human intelligence*. New York: McGraw-Hill.

Harmut, D. (2000). *SKETCHAND+: A collaborative augmented reality sketching application*. Retrieved September 20, 2005, from http://www. technotecture.com/media/papers/seichter_caadria03_web.pdf

Highsmith, J. (2004). *Agile project management: Creating innovative products*. Boston: Addison-Wesley.

Hiltz, S. R., Johnson, K.D., & Turoff, M. (1986). Experiments in group decision making: Communication process and outcome in face-to-face versus computerized conferences. *Human Communication Research, 13*(2), 225-252.

Langer, E. J. (1989). *Mindfulness*. Cambridge, MA: Da Capo Press.

MacGregor, S. P. (2002). *Describing and supporting the distributed workspace: Towards a prescriptive process for design teams*. Doctoral dissertation, DMEM, University of Strathclyde, Glasgow, UK. Retrieved October 15, 2006, from http://www.design4distribution.com

Malins, J., Gray, C., Pirie, I., Cordiner, S., & McKillop, C. (2003, April). *The virtual design studio: Developing new tools for learning, practice and research in design*. Paper presented at the 5th European Academy of Design Conference. Barcelona, Spain.

Marcus, A. (1997, April). *Metaphor design in user interfaces: how to effectively manage expectation, surprise, comprehension, and delight*. Paper presented at the Conference on Human Factors in Computing Systems (CHI '97), Atlanta, GA. Retrieved November 20, 2005, from http://portal. acm.org/citation.cfm?doid=223355.223728

Masterton, S. J., & Watt, S. N. K. (2000). Oracles, bards, and village gossips, or, social roles and meta knowledge management. *Information Systems Frontiers, 2*(3/4). Retrieved October 15, 2006, from http://springerlink.metapress.com/content/1572-9419/

Moreale, E., & Watt, S. N. K. (2003, March). *An agent-based approach to mailing list knowledge management*. Paper presented at the AAAI Spring Symposium on Agent-Mediated Knowledge Management (AMKM '03), Stanford, CA.

Mulder, I., & Swaak, J. (2003). ICT innovation: starting with the team: A collaborative design workshop on selecting technology for collaboration. *Educational Technology & Society, 6*(1). Retrieved October 15, 2006, from http://ifets.ieee.org/periodical/vol_1_2003/v_1_2003.html

Nakakojin, K. (1999, October). *A framework that supports collective creativity in design using visual images*. Paper presented at the Creativity and Cognition '99 Conference. Loughborough University, UK.

Orlikowski, W. J. (1992, October-November). *Learning from notes: Organizational issues in groupware implementation*. Paper presented at The Conference on Computer Supported Cooperative Work (CSCW '92), Toronto, Ontario, Canada.

Pfister, C. S., & Wessner, M. (1998). *The metaphor of virtual rooms in the cooperative learning environment CLear*. German National Research Center for Information Technology.

Powel, A. (2004, October). Virtual rooms, real meetings. *Ariadne, 41*, 9. Retrieved October 15, 2006, from http://www.ariadne.ac.uk/issue41/powell/

Press, M., & Cooper, R. (2003). *The design experience: The role of design and designers in the twenty-first century*. Aldershot: Ashgate.

Pugh, S. (1990). *Total design: Integrated methods for successful product engineering*. Wokingham, UK: Addison-Wesley.

Reddy, M. J. (1979). The conduit metaphor—A case of frame conflict in our language about language. In A. Ortony (Ed.), *Metaphor and thought* (pp. 284-324). Cambridge: Cambridge University Press.

Rice, R. E. (1984). *The new media*. Beverly Hills: Sage Publications.

Rogers, C. R. (1954). Towards a theory of creativity. *A Review of General Semantics*, *11*(4), 249-260.

Roseman, M. G., & Greenberg, S (1996, November). TeamRooms: Network places for collaboration. In *Proceedings of the ACM CSCW '96 Conference on Computer Supported Cooperative Work*, Boston.

Schank, R. C., & Cleary, C. (1995). *Engines for education*. Hillsdale, NJ: Lawrence Erlbaum Associates.

Sharples, M. (1994). Cognitive support and the rhythm of design. In T. Dartnall (Ed.), *Artificial intelligence, and creativity* (pp. 385-402) The Netherlands: Kluwer Academic Publishers.

Sproull, L., Kiesler, S. (1991). *Connections: New ways of working in the networked organization*. Cambridge: MIT Press.

Suchman, L. A. (1987). *Plans and situated actions: The problem of human-machine communications*. Cambridge, UK: Cambridge University Press.

Taylor, C. W. (1988). Various approaches to and definitions of creativity. In R. J. Sternberg (Ed.), *The nature of creativity: Contemporary psychological perspectives* (pp. 99-121). Cambridge: Cambridge University Press.

Tigris.org. (2001-2006a). *Scarab*. Retrieved October 15, 2006, from http://scarab.tigris.org/

Tigris.org. (2001-2006b). *Subversion*. Retrieved October 15, 2006, from http://subversion.tigris.org/

Toomey, L. A., Adams, L, & Churchill, E. (1998). Meetings in a virtual space: Creating a digital document. In *Proceedings of the Thirty-First Annual Hawaii International Conference on System Sciences (HICSS)* (Vol. 3, p. 236).

Chapter XII
Enhancing Flexibility in Dispersed Product Development Teams

Preston G. Smith
New Product Dynamics, USA

ABSTRACT

Highly creative product development teams are exploring the unknown. Initial plans are likely to change as they understand better how the customer will use the product they are developing, as competitive products appear, and as new technologies evolve. Thus, a creative team must remain open to change as its plans shift. If the team is dispersed (virtual), the complications of dealing with changes in plans magnify. This chapter provides tools and approaches for being flexible to such changes as creative teams proceed. These include ways of lowering the cost of change, anticipating change, isolating change, and maintaining options as late as possible. Such tools and approaches will help teams working on highly creative projects to take advantage of their creativity, even when they are dispersed over time and distance.

INTRODUCTION

Dispersed[1] product development teams have become increasingly popular over the past decade, especially with large multinational companies. In many cases, these teams span multiple continents and time zones. In order to maintain control over such a far-flung organization, management generally imposes procedures and plans so that all parts of the team remain focused on a common objective.

While they clearly have their strengths, such procedures and plans can undercut creativity. They encourage heavy upfront planning and reward sticking to plan. In contrast, creativity requires experimenting, trying things out, and adjusting as better solutions appear. In short, dispersed teams are easiest to manage when they can execute their original plans without change, but creativity requires change.

This chapter addresses this paradox by introducing the notion of flexibility in dispersed teams and by showing how one can enhance the flexibility of a team to deal effectively with change.

Creative product development teams need the flexibility to be able to explore options and make changes, even late in the development cycle. Unfortunately, such flexibility is difficult to achieve, especially for dispersed teams. This chapter will explore flexibility and offer flexibility-enhancing tools aimed at teams spread across various locations.

What Flexibility is and Why it is Important

Flexibility is the ability to make changes relatively late in a project without being too disruptive. The later one can make changes or the less disruptive they are, the more flexible the process is. One usually measures disruption in terms of the money, labor, or time lost in making the change. See Figure 1, in which, after the initial planning period, the restricted flexibility level locks too much down too early, but the completely flexible level leads to chaos at the end of the project. Thus, the rate of convergence must be managed consciously throughout, as shown in the moderately flexible level.

Change can appear in many forms. A common one in product development is a change in product requirements, which may occur because the developers neglected to identify a requirement earlier, because feedback from prototypes or market research has uncovered a new requirement, or because a competitor has just offered new functionality. Technical change is another source, and it can occur when a new technology appears, when the capabilities of a technology expand, or when developers discover weaknesses or limitations in a technology that they are planning to use.

Flexibility is important because the essence of product innovation is change, as discussed below. Productive innovation benefits from change, and inhibiting change stymies innovation.

Flexibility and Creativity

Product development is the creation of something that has not existed before, and as one pursues this creative act, unplanned changes will occur. Creativity involves generating, assessing, and choosing among options. Creative professionals are trained to generate many options without

Figure 1. Three levels of managing flexibility in a development project (Source: 2007 by John Wiley & Sons; used with permission)

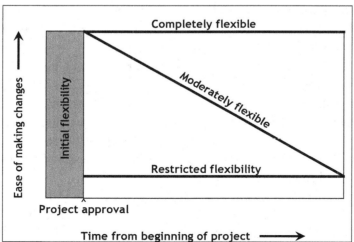

judging them, then to narrow them gradually toward a final solution.

In effective product development, the customer drives these choices and the team often implements them using some type of technology. Customers often clarify their thoughts as to what they really want only after they have tried a model or prototype, and as engineers get into a design and start testing it, they often find that a technology does not work as originally envisioned. Thus, the need for a change arises, and it can arise at any time during the project.

The more creative the project is in terms of satisfying new customer desires and the more adventuresome engineers are in applying new technology to unmet needs, the more change is likely to occur. Effective innovation encourages such change, and resisting change inhibits innovation.

James Adams, author of the classic on creativity, *Conceptual Blockbusting* (Adams, 1974), connects creativity and change thus: "Creativity and change are two sides of the same coin. They are often linked, in that creativity is needed to respond successfully to change and creativity, in turn, results in change" (Adams, 1986, p. 3).

There are alternatives for dealing with changes. One is to discourage them after a certain initial point in the project ("freezing" the design), but this will clearly diminish creativity and result in inferior products as better information arrives later in the project. Another is attempting to predict change, but this is likely to be frustrating and result in a rigid process that impedes creativity. Perhaps one could hope that change will not occur and then deal with it when it does, but such behavior will erode project performance, because developers will not be prepared to deal with change when it occurs.

Consequently, this chapter takes the position that change will occur and applies practices that will diminish the impact of changes, even when they occur relatively late in the project. In short, the goal is to put practices in place that will allow the team to accommodate and even to embrace change. For a dispersed team, these practices must work in a dispersed environment.

BACKGROUND

Change—even disruptive change—is becoming more common and more frequent in business today (Brown & Eisenhardt, 1998). This is especially true in new-product innovation (Christensen & Raynor, 2003; Christensen, Anthony, & Roth, 2004). On the other hand, business managers, hard-pressed to perform under competitive stress, are moving toward more sure-fire methodologies that focus on minimizing variation and eliminating mistakes, waste, and rework. These include phased development, such as Stage-Gate®[2] (Cooper, 2001), Six Sigma (Eckes, 2003), and lean product development (Mascitelli, 2004).

Phased development organizes the product development process so that important steps, especially in the front end, are not skipped. Six Sigma, as its name suggests, continually refines business processes to minimize variation. And lean development, which has grown out of lean manufacturing in several different directions, centers on strengthening processes to eliminate waste. This can either be waste in the design phase or downstream in the manufacturing phase. As different as these approaches are, however, they all have one characteristic in common: they all attempt to improve the business by strengthening processes.

Strengthening processes has been beneficial in general—but it carries with it a side effect. It tends to make the process rigid so that it must be followed and cannot be changed easily. Consequently, as management moves toward stronger business processes, they tend to move away from flexibility.

As discussed, flexibility is connected with change and innovation. Predictably, as firms move away from flexibility, they are having more difficulty being really innovative with their new products. This is reflected in recent data, which show that from 1990 to 2004, more innovative products (new-to-the-firm products and new-to-the-world products) have declined substantially in product portfolios while safer ones (additions, improvements, and modifications to existing products) requiring less flexibility have increased, as shown in Figure 2.

Although flexibility is a new topic in nonsoftware product development, the software development community has practiced it for several years under the name of agile development. Larman (2004) provides an overview of agile development, including descriptions of several popular agile methodologies. Boehm and Turner (2004) show how to balance the need for agility and the need for discipline on a specific project and, in the process, illustrate the factors that determine whether a given project should follow a more fluid or a more structured process.

Lessons from the agile software arena point the way for flexible development and establish the guiding principles and values. Yet it is not possible to apply the techniques of agile software development directly to nonsoftware projects. Several characteristics unique to the software medium allow the agile tools to work there, for example, object technologies and the ability to automate the build process so that the team can build an update of the product cheaply and daily. In general, these characteristics do not apply to other types of products, so for nonsoftware products the need exists for solutions other than the agile development tools in order to enhance flexibility.

USING FLEXIBILITY TOOLS AND APPROACHES

The tools and approaches described in this chapter work in various ways to improve flexibility:

- They may isolate or encapsulate change so that a change does not ripple through the whole product causing massive redesign.
- They may allow one to move ahead iteratively with lots of feedback when it is not possible to see very far ahead.
- They may expose new options through experimentation and intentional expansion of the design space.
- They may keep options open longer by delaying decisions (but still without affecting the project's overall schedule).

Figure 2. Product innovation has decreased dramatically since 1990 (Source: Cooper, 2005. Figure copyright 2007 by John Wiley & Sons; used with permission)

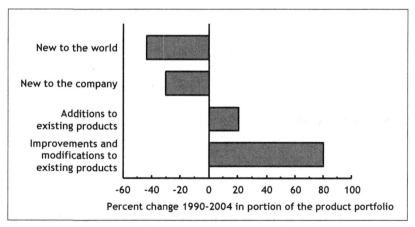

- They may reduce the cost of change by maintaining backup positions or understanding the consequences of a choice.

These tools must be used selectively. Each tool has types of projects where it fits well and others where it fits poorly. Just as with a set of mechanic's tools, it is not a matter of using all of the tools for every job but one of selecting the tools that fit each job and using an appropriate combination. In general, each project will require a different combination.

However, one lesson that carries over from agile software development is that the tools tend to fit together in a mutually supportive way (Beck, 2000, Chapter 11). There are synergistic effects of combining the tools. Consequently, do not focus on just one tool, but try to apply a group of them that will support each other.

In most cases, a tool focuses selectively on anticipated types of uncertainty. Usually, it is not possible, or economical to encompass all types of uncertainty with one application of a tool or approach, and providing flexibility in one area may limit your flexibility in another area. Thus, it is usually necessary to make choices as one proceeds as to where change is most likely to occur and focus the tools on areas where flexibility might have the greatest payoff in allowing change with little disruption.

As Boehm and Turner (2004) illustrate, these tools and approaches can have undesirable side effects. Flexibility and stability need to be balanced, and the more dispersed a team is, the more the balance is likely to shift toward stability—to the detriment of creativity.

THE TOOLS AND APPROACHES

This section covers eight types of tools and approaches that enhance flexibility:

- Customer understanding
- Product architecture
- Experimentation
- Set-based design
- Product development teams
- Decision making
- Project management
- Development process

After describing each tool, the chapter closes with further discussion on how they can be combined.

Customer Understanding

It is fundamental that the needs of customers drive the development of successful products. Good practice normally is to assess the needs of customers, capture the essence of these needs in a document often called a product specification, and design according to this specification. Seldom does this work well in actual projects:

- Writing is an inadequate medium to describe the complexities of customer use or customer desires.
- Often time pressure forces developers to start designing before they have all customer requirements.
- Customer usage patterns are complex and change over time.
- What is essential to one customer is unimportant to another.
- Customers change their minds after they see how a product works.
- Customers use products in ways never considered by the designer.

This means that the specifications will change over the course of development. Depending on how innovative the product is, they could change a little or a great deal.

The first tool for dealing with such changes is to build an early warning system, that is, a system to alert you to changes in the customer environment and allow you to check out your designs early. There are no standard prescriptions for doing this, because experience shows that the best solutions invariably are the ones created by a company to meet its specific needs. But here are some guidelines:

- To get advance notice of potential changes, get in touch with lead users, as popularized by von Hippel (1994). These are the people who are leading change and are likely to modify your product to suit their leading requirements.
- Get the designers themselves in direct contact with users of the product. They see different things than marketing or sales staff, which inadvertently filter out valuable clues.
- Get in touch early in the project, and—most importantly—keep in touch throughout the project. You never know when change will occur!
- To balance exceptional or noncharacteristic incidents that designers might see in isolated cases, have marketing people survey the customer arena regularly to provide balance and interpretation of incidents.

In most cases, a dispersed team will have additional challenges in putting its designers in ongoing contact with customers. Because economics often drives dispersion, your designers are likely to be in a low-wage region of the world, such as India or China, while your intended customers are located in a wealthier region of the world, such as North America or Europe. Thus, putting designers in contact with customers may be a challenge.

Another approach is to emphasize product descriptions at a level that is less likely to change. For instance, most developers work from a product specification that is a detailed list of features or requirements. Such details are almost bound to change as you learn more about your customers and the design space. Instead, place primary emphasis on a product vision (Clark & Fujimoto, 1990), which is a short statement (100-200 words) that describes the distinctive characteristics of this product relative to other products within the company's portfolio, or indeed the competition. The vision is far less likely to change.

Related approaches that center on aspects less likely to change are ones that attempt to capture the customer. One is personas (Cooper, 1999), which are descriptions of archetypes of predominant classes of users, each carefully created from methodical customer research. Suppose you were designing a waterproof digital camera, and your primary persona were Jeslyn, a white-water kayaker. Then if you were considering a change in camera operation that would require two hands on it, someone would immediately object, "We can't do that! Jeslyn will have the paddle in her other hand." A similar tool is use cases, which software engineers use to describe how a user would interact with a product to perform a certain task (Cockburn, 2000).

Product Architecture

Just as one may put fences around pastures to avoid chasing livestock across the countryside, one places "fences" around chunks of a product to contain design changes to relatively small parts of the product.

There is lots of talk about product architecture, but it is a rather abstract subject addressed from many different perspectives. It is therefore useful to start with an example of an architectural choice. Figure 3 shows two different architectures of a corded telephone. Both of them share the same functional schematic, but the architect chose to put the keypad function in different chunks of the physical product.

From this figure follows a useful definition of product architecture: Architecture is the way in which the functional elements of a product are

Figure 3. Two different architectures for a corded telephone (Source: Copyright ©2007 by John Wiley & Sons; used with permission)

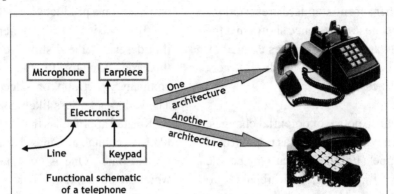

assigned to its physical chunks and the way in which those physical chunks interact to achieve the product's overall function.

One reason this is a confusing subject is that designers can use architecture to achieve many different ends, so each person discusses it in terms of what he or she wants to achieve. Some possible objectives include:

- Product development flexibility (our objective)
- Manufacturing flexibility
- Product distribution flexibility
- Time to market
- Product serviceability

Each objective will result in a different architecture. It follows that architecture is a strategic decision, and you must choose your business objective before you can create an appropriate architecture.

Even narrowing to product development flexibility, there are still architectural choices to be made. Usually, it is expensive or impossible to find one architecture that will facilitate any kind of design change. Thus, one must make some assumptions as to where change is most likely to appear and design the architecture accordingly.

An important consequence is that architectural choices should not be technical decisions but instead business decisions. This may seem obvious, but too many companies turn such decisions over to their engineers and thus forfeit the business benefits.

Product architectures span the range from modular to integral, as illustrated in Table 1. Each approach has its place, and most implementations are somewhere between these two extremes. Modular architectures are advantageous for flexibility, because they allow us to place "fences" around portions of the product most likely to change so that the change is limited to that portion of the design. The fences are actually called interfaces, and interface design and location is thus a critical part of organizing a product for flexible development. Like fences, developers must maintain interfaces consistently over time or they will decay and lose their "fencing" power.

What is special here for dispersed teams? First, recognize that architectural choices are important, and they are made quite early in the project (often even in preceding projects!). Because these are business decisions, you will somehow have to assemble your dispersed business team early in the project to plan the architecture for flexibility—or whatever other business objective you choose. Do not assign this task to the engineering team, even if it is all in the same location.

Second, you will need to designate someone to maintain the architecture. Although an engineer should not be the primary creator of the architecture, an engineer might be the ideal candidate to be responsible for maintaining it, because most of the violations are likely to arise in engineering as designers make design compromises.

Experimentation

In a project with little change—and thus little creativity—traditional methods of project planning, management, and control work well and are efficient. When change is commonplace, planning requires a shorter horizon, and management and control take on more of a cut-and-try style. Cut-and-try is just another name for experimentation, which could encompass formal or quick experiments, simulations or analysis, prototypes or mock-ups, models, tests, and tryouts.

Not only does experimentation assume a central role in the flexible approach, but recent developments in experimentation technology have made many types of experiments ten to 100 times faster, cheaper, and more effective (Thomke, 2003). Many managers shift to these new tech-

Table 1. Comparison of modular and integral architectures (Source: Copyright ©2007 by John Wiley & Sons; used with permission)

Type of Architecture	Modular	Integral
Characteristics	Chunks are decoupled, operate independently	All portions are interdependent
Example	Desktop Personal Computer	Walkman®*
Advantages	Can change design easier, test independently, reuse portions	Cheaper to make, lighter, more compact
Limitations	Planning time, performance weaknesses, integration burden	Difficult to change, late testing

*Note: * Walkman is a registered trademark of Sony Corporation.*

Table 2. Observe the great differences between traditional and front-loaded prototyping, which open up possibilities for more iterative processes that fit with changing environments (Source: Copyright ©2007 by John Wiley & Sons; used with permission)

	Traditional prototyping	Front-loaded Prototyping
Number of prototypes	Few	Many
When used in development	Late	Throughout
Prototype's objective	Verify	Learn
Prototype cost	High	Low
Prototype build time	Slow	Quick
Prototype attractiveness	Refined	Perhaps crude
Prototype's scope	Broad, vague	Narrow, specific
Departmental orientation	Primarily engineering	Any and all departments

niques and pocket the savings. Others recognize that such great improvements open new process possibilities, as Thomke and others (Smith, 2001) have shown. Specifically, they allow you to run many more experiments, run them much earlier in the development process, and use them for learning and direction rather than their traditional role of verification. Table 2 contrasts a traditional with a so-called front-loaded process. Although this table is specifically for prototyping, it applies similarly for other types of experimentation.

Projects with little change benefit from an established process and known steps to reach a predetermined goal. With lots of change, the development team has little or none of this benefit. It must operate in a more iterative, cut-and-try mode. Experimentation fits this mode perfectly, but it requires a new mode of operating, as shown in Figure 4. This loop starts with a formulated hypothesis for the outcome of the initial experiment and repeats throughout the project. In fact there are likely to be multiple loops (experiments) proceeding simultaneously.

The key part of this loop is the hypothesis, which serves to focus the experiment and enable drawing actionable conclusions. If you wish to test two hypotheses, it is usually best to run two experiments.

Failure plays a critical role in such hypothesis-based experiments. Corporate cultures usually discourage failures while paying lip service to accepting them. But there is something much more fundamental at stake. If your hypothesis is that the experiment will succeed and it does succeed, you haven't learned much (the purpose of an experiment is to learn so that you can move forward). Consequently, if you plan a sequence of experiments with success as the expectation and success as the outcome, progress will be slow (little learning). In contrast, the experiments from which you learn the most are those where a priori expectation is a 50-50 split between success and failure. This is how you should plan each loop for maximum rate of progress.

Thomke makes another important point about failure. He distinguishes between failures and mistakes. Mistakes are poorly planned experiments or ones with uncontrolled extraneous variables. With these, when you reach the end of the loop in Figure 4, you cannot reach clear conclusions, and the experiment is wasted. Failures are valuable, but avoid mistakes.

Regarding the aversion to failure, corporate cultures often discourage the early, quick-and-dirty prototypes that might expose one's ignorance. Although designers are taught in university to make lots of simple prototypes early to explore options, many corporate cultures actually reward refined prototypes made late in the process when most uncertainties are resolved. For instance, see

Figure 4. An iterative experimentation process (Source: Copyright ©2007 by John Wiley & Sons; used with permission)

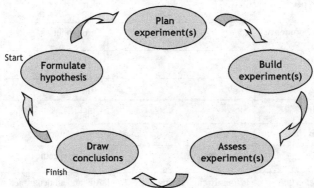

Kelley and Littman (2001), which is the story of the renowned product development firm, IDEO. Although this book touts quick, early prototypes, the books photos reveal only beautiful, late-stage prototypes.

The conclusion: although supporting failure and quick-and-dirty prototypes are well-known means of facilitating innovation and are given a great deal of lip service, fitting these styles into a corporate environment will require ongoing effort and executive support.

For dispersed teams, experiments present special challenges, because many experiments, by nature, exist in only one location. A test is run in a specific laboratory, and the broken parts that may result exist only there. A prototype is built in only one model shop. A simulation is run on one engineer's computer. Thus, with a dispersed team, there is the added challenge of dispersing experimental artifacts and results. Some experimental tools work well for this. For instance, an especially fast and inexpensive type of rapid prototyping system is called a conceptual modeler (Smith, 2001), or more colorfully, a 3D printer, because when connected to a desktop computer, it "prints" three-dimensional plastic parts. If connected to a remote computer over the Internet, it thus becomes a so-called 3D fax machine that can provide prototypes to remote members of the team in real time.

Set-Based Design

Set-based design comes from Toyota's thoroughly studied "lean" product development process. Because Toyota is generally regarded to have the best automotive development system in the world (Sobek, Ward, & Liker, 1999), this unusual and somewhat counterintuitive system has attracted much attention.

Consider a simple nondesign example to convey the concept. Suppose that Emery (leader), Susan, and Walter need to meet. Emery suggests Tuesday at 10:00, to which Walter immediately

objects (out of town). So Emery proposes Thursday at 3:30, but Susan has a conflict then. This continues for several more iterations—and it would be even more difficult if the participants were in different time zones. Such a process corresponds to a conventional so-called point-based methodology. The parallel in set-based operation would be for Emery first to ask Susan and Walter for their calendars for the week. Then he picks a clear time for all of them. Not only are they finished quickly, but Emery has some back-up meeting times in case the primary one fails. Observe that contemporary information technology, such as Microsoft® Outlook®[3], facilitates set-based scheduling, and this works equally well for a dispersed team.

Conventional point-based design technique is based on making *choices*. The designer keeps making choices at forks in the road to improve the design until it is good enough. In contrast, set-based design operates on *constraints*. The designer explores the constraints that limit the design, for instance:

- Which types of solutions won't work?
- What would be too expensive or take too much time?
- What would have reliability or safety problems?
- What would be difficult to manufacture?

The objective is to see how much of the design space is open and where it is open rather than to arrive at a design immediately.

Toyota follows the constraints approach for different reasons than those enhancing flexibility do. For Toyota, exploring the design space results in better, more robust solutions because the point-based approach may proceed into an area that is suboptimal, and they would not know this because they would have no visibility into other areas; they remain unexplored. More importantly, with point-based processes, developers may go out on a branch that does not work out and have to retreat. Thus, although progress may be slower in set-based, they are much less likely to have to back out and find a new route. That is, design convergence is far more likely.

The advantage of set-based design for flexibility is that it defers decisions. Deferred decisions are discussed shortly, but the idea is that developers will not have to reverse a decision that they have not made yet. This maintains our options and our flexibility as long as possible. The team spends its early time not on making decisions that might have to be changed but on assembling information on their constraints and options so that they can make decisions quickly and confidently when the time comes.

Figure 5 illustrates how a set-based design progresses. As the team discovers additional constraints, the design space shrinks at a controlled rate (not too fast, not too slow), by adding constraints progressively to shrink the design space. This continues to leave space to maneuver, although the maneuvering space shrinks to the best solution over time. This convergence rate is Toyota engineering management's primary lever for controlling the set-based process. They want the space to shrink continuously but not too quickly.

Toyota's application to automobile design is a mature product area. Set-based design is effective for modest uncertainty, as one would encounter in automobile design. When uncertainly is great, however, one could converge into a solution space that turned out to be inadequate. In such cases, one faces so-called unknown unknowns (unk unks), where assumptions of convergence and nearby solutions are often unfounded (Loch, deMeyer, & Pich, 2006). Experimentation is a better approach here.

Dispersed teams pose no major challenges for set-based design. Toyota uses it in their functional organization, in which the members of one development project are dispersed throughout the facility, although generally all in the same city. It is mostly document-based, as practiced at Toyota. The process is not simple, however. They apply it with lots of training and mentoring, which is the company culture.

Product Development Teams

As discussed earlier in the "Background" section, the principles and values of flexible development stem from agile software development. One value that is central to agile development and embedded in every agile methodology is that people are more important than process. This comes directly from the Agile Manifesto (Beck et al., 2001), which compares four values that set agile projects apart from traditional ones. The first of

Figure 5. The team manages set-based design to converge at a desirable rate (Source: Copyright ©2007 by John Wiley & Sons; used with permission)

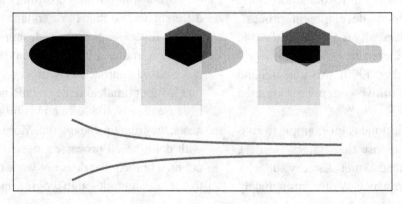

the four comparisons states that people and interactions are more important than processes and tools. Thus, this "Product Development Teams" section should be placed at the top of this discussion—but you will notice that the Process section falls last for this reason.

This said, this is an entire book about teams, and you will find countless dispersed team insights and tools throughout it. Consequently, this section will be short to cover only two tools that you might overlook otherwise.

The first tool is to establish the team's authority clearly. If you think about the environment in which teams operate, you might notice that the team needs certain types of authority to operate effectively. For example, the team may find that in order to be most creative, it needs to be able to:

- Remove a cynic from the team
- Have an on-demand account at a local model shop
- Have a 3D fax machine (see above) in its Singapore office
- Set its work hours in each facility

Thinking more broadly, you will find that someone in every company needs the authority to make dozens of types of decisions regarding a project, such as a decision to hire staff, a decision to proceed to the next phase of the project, and a decision to invest in buildings and equipment. Try creating such a list specifically for your organization. It is likely to have about 50 types of authority on it.

This list is useful for two purposes. First, you may observe that the team and management are unclear on just what kinds of authority the team has. Often, management assumes that the team has a certain type of authority, but the team is reluctant to move ahead because management has not granted this authority explicitly. Thus, the team is hamstrung by an unclear set of operating rules. The solution is for the team to discuss the aforementioned list of authorities with manage-ment and agree explicitly both on the team's areas of authority and on where the team will need to obtain management approval.

Also, you can perform a triage on your list. You will find that some kinds of authority the team clearly already has, so they are not issues. Other types the team does not need or want (they are more work than they are worth, for instance), such as obtaining a new building. But in the middle there are likely to be a few types of authority that the team does not have now but it could operate more effectively if it did have this authority. Then you can discuss this short list with management.

The second tool is partial colocation. By definition, a dispersed team is not colocated. But there are clear advantages to colocation for creative teams. Fortunately, once you appreciate what it is that makes colocation valuable, you can find ways of approximating these characteristics. For instance, if the team has one chance to come together as a team, ensure that this happens at the beginning of the project, when it is most valuable. Try to colocate clusters of team members in a location. If your members are split among three locations, for example, make sure that all team members in each location are colocated. And make sure that your communication media work for you; for example, if delays in e-mail response are slowing the team down, establish team protocols on how quickly an e-mail will receive a reply.

Decision Making

If you dissect the product development process down to its core, you will find that the core process is decision making. The literature has emphasized the few major decisions that come at the end of phases (Deck, 2002), but more important are the thousands of daily decisions made by the team and by individuals as they work their way forward in the design. These decisions cumulatively determine not only the quality and attractiveness of the resulting product but also the performance level of the development team.

How you approach these many decisions should be determined by what you wish to emphasize in your development. If speed of development is your priority, you should find a way to make such decisions quickly. If productivity (products developed per unit of resources) is your objective, accurate decisions (do it right the first time) should drive your process. And if your first priority is flexibility, you should make decisions in a way that facilitates flexibility.

The key to making flexible decisions is not to make them until you have to, because you have more flexibility before you commit to a decision. This leads to the concept of the *last responsible moment*. The last responsible moment is the earliest time when:

- An important option expires
- The decision goes onto the critical path
- The expense of carrying the decision rises dramatically

It is important to recognize that this is not procrastination. On the contrary, one actually works quite hard on the decision from the time that one sees that a decision will be needed until actually making it by collecting information that will support making a better decision when its time comes. That is, you defer the decision itself, but you do not defer the data collection and analysis needed to make the decision. This results in not only more flexibility but also in better decisions, because they are based on fresher, more complete information.

The last responsible moment should not be applied to all decisions. Sometimes the decision is clear (only one reasonable choice) or it can be reversed easily later if necessary. Then the decision can be made early so that it is not a threat to the critical path.

Many analytical and computer-aided tools are available to help make decisions. Savage

(2003) provides several, complete with supporting software. One is decision trees, which is a graphical technique that lays out a sequence of linked decisions together with the uncertainties involved so that one can see the complete picture before committing to the first decision. Another tool is Monte Carlo simulation, which allows the decision to be "played out" involving uncertainty to understand what the probability distribution of the outcome will be.

Consensus is an important part of group decision making, especially for a dispersed team. Many decisions require the consensus of several parties with interests in the decision. This is more than just being nice. If you do not take the dissenters' opinions into account when you make the decision, dissenters are likely to undermine future activity related to the decision. Thus, consensus means full agreement to move forward together.

Obtaining such agreement can be difficult for dispersed teams. One tool that is helpful here is a consensus gradient. Everyone involved votes on the proposition under discussion using a carefully arranged scale that goes from full agreement to veto, such as:

1. Completely agree and commit
2. Agree (and commit)
3. Don't disagree (but commit)
4. Some reservations (but commit)
5. Veto

You tally the results first by addressing the vetoes. Any vetoes must be resolved to have a consensus. Then see if there is a preponderance of votes in categories 3 and 4. If so, there is little energy behind the proposal and it is likely to die.

Note that the consensus gradient is easy to use in a dispersed environment, once team members understand how to use it. Beyond this, in a dispersed environment, you will need to ensure that the communication channels are wide open to facilitate good decision-making. For example, ensure that delays in responding to e-mails (mentioned earlier) are acceptable.

Project Management

The contrast between a flexible project and a traditional one is perhaps greater in the project management area than in any other. The *Agile Manifesto* (Beck et al., 2001) illustrates this for software projects, but the contrast also carries over to nonsoftware projects.

Consider project planning. The traditional way of doing this is to plan the whole project in uniform detail from beginning to end. However, agile software developers produce only an overview plan of the whole project initially and then plan the details of each iteration as they enter it. In fact, the team often does the final level of planning within iteration as it proceeds. The process they use is similar to the rolling-wave project planning approach that is applicable to nonsoftware projects (Githens, 1998).

Another contrast with traditional project management is in how the team views corrective action. Traditionally, corrective action is "Documented direction for executing the project work to bring expected future performance of the project work in line with the project management plan" (PMI, 2004). In contrast, because agile and flexible developers place less credence in the overall project plan, they are just as likely to suspect the plan as the execution when execution does not match the plan and correct whichever one they find to be wrong.

More broadly, the two approaches view the project objective—and thus what constitutes project completion—differently. In general, traditional project managers work to complete a list of deliverables that they established at the project outset. When they deliver all of these, the project is complete. Again, agile and flexible development managers place less emphasis on the original list of deliverables, because it, or whatever was influencing it, may have changed.

Thus, they must look more fundamentally at delivering value to the customer. This is clearest to see in software information technology (IT) projects, where an actual customer is likely to be on the development team, and the team delivers features in iterations. At the end of each iteration, the team and the customer jointly decide if they have delivered enough value to call the project complete. Notice that this could include more or fewer product features than originally planned, and there is often little commitment to complete the original list. In nonsoftware projects, the product is not so easily divisible into features and value may not be so easy to assess, but the emphasis is still more on delivering value than on predefined deliverables.

The development process is different. One normally views a traditional project as being sequential, with one task leading to the next in a progressive manner. But a flexible process proceeds in a more iterative manner (iteration is actually a part of a traditional innovation project too, but it is often ignored in planning). Observe that Microsoft Project is a popular tool for planning and scheduling traditional projects. However, Project will not allow iteration: if you try to make a task feed back into an earlier task, you will receive an error message in Project. Project has no way to escape from iteration, so it does not allow it.

Finally, project risk management is fundamentally different. In the traditional approach, risk management is an identifiable set of activities that, when done well, begin at project planning stage and are well integrated with other project activities (Smith & Merritt, 2002). In a fast-changing project, the risks change often and initial risk identification is of little benefit, because most risks are unknown at this point. Consequently, the entire development process *is* risk management—the iterations; prototyping, testing, and experimentation; parallel development paths, and project staffing (Loch et al., 2006).

Data management presents a special dilemma for flexible teams. In general, agile and flexible teams eschew detailed documentation and find simple ways to document things. Often, this means using wall charts and sticky notes, together with digital cameras to record them. This is quick and easy, but it has a couple of problems. One is that for complex data and projects that require traceability, such as for product requirements in some regulated industries, such records are difficult to change frequently. It is usually better to invest upfront in building a database for project data.

The other problem is that for dispersed teams, clearly wall charts and sticky notes are not very portable, so team dispersion must shift the documentation balance to more formal means than are needed for a colocated team.

Development Process

The contrast between traditional and flexible approaches carries over into the development process as well. If you ask someone following a traditional approach how they develop products, they are likely to respond with the process they use: Stage-Gate, PACE®[4] (Product And Cycle-time Excellence), or their own proprietary one. That is, the process is the centerpiece of their product development. Those following a more flexible approach might mention a methodology (Extreme Programming or Scrum in agile software development for example), but such methodologies are not centered on the process.

In lack of a process to point to, flexible developers point to a set of values that guide them, such as the *Agile Manifesto* (Beck et al., 2001), or to a set of tools, such as the ones described previously.

It is important to note that the picture is not as black and white as presented. Most developers use a process somewhere between flexible and structured, as Boehm and Turner (2004)

describes, and the balance tends to shift during a project from more flexible in the beginning to more structured at the end. This occurs because uncertainty decreases during the project while the amount invested rises, both of which suggest a more structured approach later.

As we move to a more flexible process, the type and caliber of people on the team will also shift. In a flexible environment, people will have to be comfortable with more ambiguity, and at least some of them will also need skills to adapt and create processes as they go, as Cockburn (2002, pp. 14-18) describes.

A flexible process is likely to be heavily dependent on experimentation. If so, particular attention should be paid to the capacity to experiment: testing laboratories, model shops, rapid prototyping machines, and analysis software. This is especially challenging for a dispersed team, because replicating such facilities in multiple locations is costly. Experimentation capacity is critical because if it is not sufficient, experiments will wait in queue for completion. Studies of queues show that time in queue increases dramatically long before one reaches the rated capacity. This understanding is vital for using experimentation effectively. The learning type of experimentation discussed here loses its value if people have to wait to receive the learning. They will just have to proceed in making decisions without it, and then the learning will not support their decisions.

Finally, if you are building a flexible development process, build it up, as Boehm and Turner (2004) recommends, rather than starting with a process and trying to remove items. Although the latter seems attractive and easier, what happens is that, to be safe, people will be conservative in removing something that has had value in the past. Also, it takes a seasoned practitioner to be capable of judging that an item will not be needed. The beauty of the flexible approach is that you can always add later what you didn't notice you needed today!

ASSEMBLING A KIT OF FLEXIBILITY TOOLS

Please reread the section Using Flexibility Tools. You are likely to gain additional insights from it now that you understand each of the tools, and it will be helpful as you assemble the tools to use on a specific project.

Remember that each project is different and thus will require a different combination of the tools. In some cases, a tool may not apply to your project. For instance, project architecture generally is not useful with homogeneous products like paints or plastics. On the other hand, be careful about excluding a tool just because it may be difficult to apply. For example, members of a global product development team located remotely from their customers could easily dismiss customer visits as impractical. However, Morgan and Liker (2006, p. 30) report that a Toyota chief engineer (in Japan) found it so important to experience his customer situation in North America that he explored 50,000 miles of highways in the United States, Canada, and Mexico, and this gave him a great deal of understanding to make trade-offs and changes as development of a new Toyota model proceeded.

These tools generally have costs or other undesirable side effects associated with them, so they must be applied selectively. Use them more on projects where change is likely and the benefits of change will pay off. Identify the portions of a product that are most likely to change and apply them there rather than broadly across the product. As a project moves from its beginning toward market introduction, project complexity and investment increase while uncertainty should decrease, all of which suggest that you should reduce the amount of flexibility as the project progresses.

Be forewarned that simply putting these tools in place is the easy part. More difficult and more critical to long-term success is cultivating the underlying values and culture that support flexibility.

People naturally gravitate to what is comfortable, and uncertainty is uncomfortable. Managers in particular, like to know what is going to happen, even if they have to make up a story to satisfy their need for certainty (Smith, 2005). Consequently, as much as you might wish to enjoy the benefits of flexibility quickly, you are more likely to be effective by starting with a manageable pilot project using some of your most capable, flexible people and expanding slowly as your people and management gain experience with the flexible approach (Smith & Reinertsen, 1998, Chap. 15).

By nurturing the adoption of these tools and approaches, you will develop a greater ability to make changes during development, and this will, in turn, provide a supportive environment for the types of iteration, trials, and exploration that are necessary for creativity to flourish.

REFERENCES

Adams, J. L. (1974). *Conceptual blockbusting.* Stanford, CA: Stanford Alumni Association.

Adams, J. L. (1986). *The care and feeding of ideas.* Reading, MA: Addison-Wesley.

Beck, K. (2000). *Extreme programming explained.* Boston: Addison-Wesley.

Beck, K., et al. (2001). *Manifesto for agile software development.* Retrieved April 16, 2006, from http://agilemanifesto.org

Boehm, B., & Turner, R. (2004). *Balancing agility and discipline.* Boston: Addison-Wesley.

Brown, S. L., & Eisenhardt, K. M. (1998). *Competing on the edge.* Boston: Harvard Business School Press.

Christensen, C. M., & Raynor, M. E. (2003). *The innovator's solution.* Boston: Harvard Business School Press.

Christensen, C. M., Anthony, S. D., & Roth, E. A. (2004). *Seeing what's next*. Boston: Harvard Business School Press.

Clark, K. B., & Fujimoto, T. (1990). The power of product integrity. *Harvard Business Review, 68*(6), 107-118.

Cockburn, A. (2000). *Writing effective use cases*. Boston: Addison-Wesley.

Cockburn, A. (2002). *Agile software development*. Boston: Addison-Wesley.

Cooper, A. (1999). *The inmates are running the asylum*. Indianapolis, IN: SAMS/Macmillan.

Cooper, R. G. (2001). *Winning at new products*. Cambridge, MA: Perseus.

Cooper, R. G. (2005). Your NPD portfolio may be harmful to your business's health. *Visions, 29*(2), 22-26.

Deck, M. J. (2002). Decision making: The overlooked competency in product development. In P. Belliveau, A. Griffin, & S. Somermeyer (Eds.), *The PDMA toolbook for new product development* (pp. 165-185). Hoboken, NJ: John Wiley.

Eckes, G. (2003). *Six sigma for everyone*. Hoboken, NJ: John Wiley.

Githens, G. D. (1998, October). *Rolling wave project planning*. The 29th Annual PMI Seminars & Symposium, Long Beach, CA.

Kelley, T., & Littman, J. (2001). *The art of innovation*. New York: Doubleday.

Larman, C. (2004). *Agile and iterative development*. Boston: Addison-Wesley.

Loch, C. K., DeMeyer, A., & Pich, M. T. (2006). *Managing the unknown*. Hoboken, NJ: John Wiley.

Mascitelli, R. (2004). *The lean design guidebook*. Northridge, CA: Technology Perspectives.

Merriam-Webster. (2000). *Merriam-Webster's Collegiate Dictionary* (software ed., Version 2.5). Springfield, MA: Merriam-Webster, Inc.

Morgan, J. M., & Liker, J. K. (2006). *The Toyota product development system*. New York: Productivity Press.

PMI (2004). *A guide to the project management body of knowledge* (PMBOK® Guide, 3rd ed.). Newtown Square, PA: Project Management Institute.

Savage, S. L. (2003). *Decision making with insight*. Belmont, CA: Brooks/Cole.

Smith, P. G. (2001). Using conceptual modelers for business advantage. *Time-Compression Technologies, 6*(3), 18-24.

Smith, P. G. (2005). Why is agile development so scary? *Agile Project Management Advisory Service* (Cutter Consortium), *6*(9), 1-3.

Smith, P. G., & Merritt, G. M. (2002). *Proactive risk management*. New York: Productivity Press.

Smith, P. G., & Reinertsen, D. G. (1998). *Developing products in half the time*. Hoboken, NJ: John Wiley.

Sobek, D. K., II, Ward, A. C., & Liker, J. K. (1999). Toyota's principles of set-based concurrent engineering. *Sloan Management Review, 40*(2), 67-83.

Thomke, S. H. (2003). *Experimentation matters*. Boston: Harvard Business School Press.

von Hippel, E. (1994). *The sources of innovation*. New York: Oxford University Press.

ENDNOTES

[1]   This author believes that *virtual,* in the context of teams, is poor terminology, because

virtual means, "being such in essence or effect though not formally recognized or admitted." (Merriam-Webster, 2000) Teams are all about performance, and such cloudy terminology weakens teams' performance orientation. Therefore, *dispersed* is used in place of *virtual* in this chapter.

[2] Stage-Gate is a registered trademark of the Product Development Institute.

[3] Microsoft and Outlook are registered trademarks of Microsoft Corporation.

[4] PACE is a registered trademark of PRTM.

Chapter XIII
A Spatial Environment for Design Dialogue

Thomas Leerberg
Designkolen Kolding, Denmark

ABSTRACT

This chapter offers a spatial concept of the way virtual design team work. It is concerned with two problems that face creative teams today: (1) that the design process is carried out through a diverse range of digital media, which are not or only poorly integrated and (2) that the digital tools used by virtual teams are not designed for virtual team work but used in a very pragmatic way, which often limits the creative efficiency. The chapter argues that space has a structure and that we can use that structure to navigate and place information in space and thereby create a design space with the virtuality and creativity of an open 'reflection-in-action.' Further, it argues that we have to develop concepts of team setting, team solving, substituted process paths, and supplemented process paths to expand our understanding of these issues. This will be demonstrated through two constructions for virtual teams: virtual platform and topos.

INTRODUCTION

In 1990, the First International Conference on Cyberspace was held at The University of Texas in Austin. At the conference, a small group of people was standing in front of the unknown frontier to what later turned out to be an entirely new reality. The architect Michael Benedikt (1991) described this vast landscape, while emphasizing the potential of space:

In cyberspace, information-intensive institutions and businesses have a form, identity, and working reality—in a word and quite literally, an architecture—that is counterpart and different to the form, identity, and working reality they have in the physical world. The ordinary physical reality of these institutions, businesses, etc., are seen as surface phenomena, as husks, their true energy coursing in architectures unseen except in cyberspace. (p. 123)

Benedikt saw then, what we see today. That the potential of institutions and businesses is determined by their ability to work together and prosper in the virtual space, which has been developed parallel to the physical reality. He described how the inhabitants of this space made sense of their surroundings by mapping the space from within—as isovists (Benedikt, 1979). They gained the ability to navigate through and manipulate a space filled by information—and in the end to construct a spatial architecture that served their specific needs. What Benedikt and others in 1990 saw in the distance, has now formed a new spatial reality with the potential to become a new virtual workspace side by side the 'brick and mortar' reality of traditional organizations.

This potential of parallel realities in space is also one of the key issues of virtual teams as described by Kimble, Li and Barlow in their paper from 2000:

An essential aspect of virtual teams is to exploit the features of electronic space. ... To survive in the information economy organizations must not only exploit geographical differences and overcome geographical constraints in the physical world, but they also have to exploit opportunities and face threats in the new electronic space. (p. 4)

There should be a realization of the great opportunity and tool at our disposal. It is a tool for more than just bridging geographical differences in an effort to prosper and develop new markets. It is also a way to create new spatial environments and define the new identities and energies needed to progress as creative cultures. It is a new way to control space and time, substitute the lack of presence or supplement the presence already shared with new layers of reality.

The thesis presented here is that to fully understand virtual teams, there must be a more explicit acknowledgement that they operate in both real and virtual spaces, and that these spaces do have a structure and architecture, which need to be understood even further. Virtual teams are much more than just a clever way to optimize the distribution of resources—it is the creation of a new reality, where the focus must be the construc-

tion of new informed spaces for working and how these define and support the progress of virtual teams and creativity.

In the following, an examination is presented of how designers act in virtual teams and how they may benefit from an active approach to the space they work in. Three constructions of the integration of virtual teams in spatial environments for creative success are presented. These constructions are essentially specification elements for virtual environments, where virtuality, as a tool for bridging degrees of separation, has become an integrated part of current design methods and practices. In the first construction the argument presented is that team setting is just as important as problem solving in the case of virtual teams (Schön, 1983). The second construction argues that the process paths of virtual teams can either substitute the lack of presence or supplement the traditional tools of the designer. In the third and last construction the point put forward is that virtual teams can be situated in a design space together with a representation of the design problem for greater creative success.

SPACE AND VIRTUALITY

The space that Michael Benedikt described above clearly had a structure—even an architecture. It was an environment that a designer could enter and move across in an instant without much effort—where he or she could construct spatial relations, meet other people, exchange information, and leave again. Nevertheless, how do people operate in such informed virtual spaces?

One way is to address how they are put to use—their performative character—as a metaphorical model for spatial organization of information (Fabrikant, 2000) or as a perceptual model (Bois, 1991) that mimes the way we perceive physical space. Space as a metaphorical model has often been used to organize information, from simple spatial diagrams that show numeric trends to very complex relations of mapping networks or natural phenomena (Tufte, 1997). Space as a perceptual model has been used to convey information all the way back to the political propaganda of the nation state in the panorama invented by Robert Barker in 1787 (Crary, 1990; Comment, 1999). Both of these performative characters are essential for the construction and use of virtual workspaces and thereby for virtual teams.

The geographer Sara Fabrikant has used space, both as a metaphorical model to construct landscapes of information and as a perceptual model for the communication of information. As a metaphorical model, space does not have a 'voice' of its own. It is merely a medium used to position and contain information—and thus become an informed space. We may add spatial properties to information that previously were without such properties, and arrange information in a spatial constellation defined by a specific set of parameters. Fabrikant calls this process spatialization (Fabrikant, 2000) with a reference to the cognitive scientist George Lakoff. He suggested a metaphorical transformation from physical space to conceptual space by embedding objects with few or no spatial attributes into spatial constellations with structures of compatible spatial attributes. Fabrikant (2000) describes it as:

Spatialization, which combines powerful visualization techniques with spatial metaphors, has a great potential to overcome current impediments in information access and retrieval. Spatialization is utilized to create lower-dimensional digital representations of higher-dimensional data sets, whose characteristics are often quite complex. These digital data sets may not be spatial in nature. Common spatial concepts such as distance, direction, scale and arrangement which are part of the human's experience in everyday life are applied, to construct abstract information spaces. Spatialization offers the field of geography, which investigates space and spatial relations, oppor-

tunities to apply the body of knowledge to other nonspatial domains. (pp. 69-70)

Fabrikant (2000) can construct a correlation between space and information, by using a spatial metaphor. It is similar to the construction of place and space—the situating of events—in architecture (Tschumi, 1990; Bachelard, 1994). The scenarios she describes are primarily related to information retrieval, where the construction and logic of the library becomes the model for the space in which information is contained and organized.

By following the suggestions of Fabrikant, we could place virtual teams together with the information they use, in a virtual space by using the metaphorical and the perceptual potential of space. Such an understanding of space could nurture the technological skills needed to surmount the barriers of space and time we meet in a day-to-day design practice.

Just as the understanding of space is vital for placing virtual teams in virtual spaces, so is the understanding of virtuality. Since 'virtual team' is an elusive and broad concept, we must ask what constitutes a virtual team? If two designers are sitting across from each other, using text or video-chat in their design process, is it then a virtual team? Is it the technology they use, that defines their status as a virtual team or is it that they find a solution to their separation in time and space?

To the design theorist Donald Schön (1983) the virtual space or world of the designer, is the place where he can unfold his creativity:

In his virtual world, the practitioner can manage some of the constraints to hypothesis-testing experiment which are inherent in the world of his practice. Hence his ability to construct and manipulate virtual worlds is a crucial component of his ability not only to perform artistically but to experiment rigorously. (p. 157)

Schön (1983) continues:

Virtual worlds are contexts for experiment within which practitioners can suspend or control some of the everyday impediments to rigorous reflection-in-action. They are representative worlds of practice in the double sense of 'practice.' And practice in the construction, maintenance, and use of virtual worlds develops the capacity for reflection-in-action which we call artistry. (p. 162)

The virtual space that Schön describes is a free space of opportunities, ideas and abstraction that belongs to the individual designer. In the case of designers, they may be separated in space, just by the table in between, the wall to the next room down the hall or by thousands of miles to the other side of the planet. As for time, they may be separated by many time zones but working simultaneously or working in the same time zone at different hours of the day. This means that designing tools for virtual teams is no simple matter. There is no standard scenario of how, where and when designers work, just the idea that through a diverse range of technologies we may bridge some degree of separation—big or small, local or global—and thereby facilitate continued cooperation.

CONSTRUCTION 1: DESIGN, FROM TEAM SETTING TO PROBLEM SOLVING

As we enter design from the space and virtuality of virtual teams, we could observe design[1] and the designer from different points of view. From a critique of technical rationality, Schön (1983) describes the designer as a person framed in a process of constant setting and solving—reflection in action—where new problems seem similar but are always solved anew. A lack of this understanding has led to the failure of professionals' ability to solve society's problems, mainly because of the categorical separation of researcher and practitioner in the paradigm of technical rationality.

Donald Schön (1983) writes:

From the perspective of Technical Rationality, professional practice is a process of problem solving ... But with this emphasis on problem solving, we ignore problem setting, the process by which we define the decision to be made, the ends to be achieved, the means which may be chosen. ... Problem setting is a process in which, interactively, we name the things to which we will attend and frame the context in which we will attend to them. (pp. 39-40)

However, if we apply Schön's description of the design process to that of virtual teams in an informed space, we end up with a rather near-sighted view on design. Schön's account of the design process is observed from the point of view of the individual designer—from the interiority (Eisenman, 1999) of design so to speak—and not from that of the team—the exteriority of design. We may end up with the impression that the designer is working alone and the challenge is to distance the designer from the standardized chain of production. Nevertheless, I will argue that the point of view of the team of designers is just as essential to the success of the design process. The importance of the exteriority of the design process is nowhere more visible than in the work of virtual teams. In many ways, we could argue that Schön understands design as the effect of an individual reflection rather than the result of dynamic team collaboration.

Therefore, we have to add another dimension to Schön's account of the designer, namely that of the team—the dimension in which the designer is no longer alone. Just as problem setting was introduced as an activity of same importance as problem solving, we have to introduce team setting and team solving as disciplines, with just as much importance as the setting and solving of problems. We have to afford just as much attention to the team, which the designer is a part of, as to the problem he is about to solve. This realization could lead to another view on virtual teams, with less focus on the organization of resources and more focus on providing tools for design dialogues. In other words—the virtual team is defined by how it works rather than who the members are. To paraphrase Jon Katzenbach and Douglas Smith in their book from 1994, the performance challenge is team setting, not convincing people to be a team (Katzenbach & Smith, 1994).

An important issue is whether activities like team setting, team solving, problem setting, and problem solving belong to a specific place on the process path. At first glance, one could argue that "good practice" is to do the setting before the solving. However, if we go along with Schön's argument that we constantly frame and reframe our projects as designers, then there will be a constant setting of teams and problems going on, all the way through the process-path—as a partner to the team and problem solving.

CONSTRUCTION 2: SUBSTITUTED AND SUPPLEMENTED PROCESS PATHS

We are today faced with a situation, where what before was an oddity, has now become a normality—where the constant design dialogue not only is a normal occurrence but also a clear expectation. Virtual teams have become a daily practice more than a special event, which eventually must lead to another view on how we work.

So, how can we create an integrated position for virtual teams in the design process? Which activities of the design team do we aid by introducing group-ware tools and technologies? How do we embed virtual teams in a spatial environment with a structure that may include all the participants and parameters of that workspace?

At one level we can construct a substitution for the clear lack of shared physical presence,

shared language, shared time, shared culture, and so forth; and on another level we can supplement our ordinary workspace with new possibilities. This means that the group-ware may be useful to designers whether they are separated or not.

The first level is a substituted process path, where degrees of separation are substituted through a range of tools, which together aspire to reach a certain degree of normality. Below this level, the crisis of separation is so profound that cooperating in virtual teams is impossible.

The second level is the supplemented process path, where designers who are sitting across from each other use a similar range of tools as in the substituted process-path to gain new possibilities and reach a new level of extranormality. In this way, virtual teams may develop skills of concurrence, documentation and creativity beyond normal aspiration.

By constructing an extra level of virtual teams, we could expand the repertoire (Schön, 1983) of these teams to make new understandings and actions accessible through a supplemented process path. If we relate such an expansion to the level of saturation, by communication and information technologies and the ever increasing need for professional mobility, it is hard to imagine that the individual designer would not have virtual tools in his repertoire and use them even though he was at the same place, at the same time as the people he cooperated with.

In their article, "Effective Virtual Teams Through Communities of Practice," Kimble, Li, and Barlow (2000) have suggested that time, space, and organization can either be 'same' or 'different' and thus describe a spatial matrix of eight possible situations or scenarios of virtual teams. The matrix can be read as a dynamic sliding bar from the 'same' situation (supplemented process path) to the 'different' situation (substituted process path). If we accept the limited set of parameters or dimensions used to describe the configuration of the virtual teams, it shows two interesting characteristics in the extreme ends of the scale. The teams could share the same time, same place and same organization, or they could have different time, different place and different organizations. The 'same' situation could be seen as traditional and normal while the 'different' situation suffers a so profound crisis of separation that cooperation is hardly possible.[2] The more parameters that are different for the teams the more fragile the cooperation will be.

So groupware technologies for virtual teams could not only solve teams in the 'different' situation, they could just as well be applied to the 'same' situation. This means of course that methodological tools developed for substituted process paths could be used for supplemented process paths and have a positive spin-off for design methods in general.

CONSTRUCTION 3: DESIGN SPACE

Rikard Stankiewicz, professor at the Research Policy Institute, School of Economics and Management at Lund University, offers two concepts that are directly related to the construction of a spatial context for virtual teams—namely that of evolutionary regimes of technology and the construction of design spaces. Stankiewicz' argument begins as a critique of how the evolutionary process of technology has been the succession of revolutionary paradigms, which do not have the ability to accumulate knowledge, techniques and information, but instead separate design into discrete design regimes that had very little exchange with other regimes, and therefore wasted valuable time and information (Stankiewicz, 2000). This should be seen as a direct challenge to the setting of virtual teams and the way they perform.

Figure 1. Different levels of separation: Substituted and supplemented process path, levels of normality and crisis below which the separation is impossible

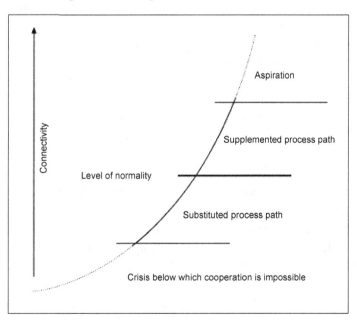

Stankiewicz (2000) subscribes to the idea that design is the act of combining discrete elements—'operands' in his terminology—but combined through multiple dimensions, and not just as a one-dimensional chain or sequence. In this way, the operands themselves are spatialized to form a network of interconnected elements, where each one is more than just a single procedure. Such operands could define the process path for team setting, team solving, problem setting, and problem solving. So, instead of seeing the design task as a diffuse cloud of issues, Stankiewicz' concept creates a clear structure, where the single operand can be addressed and solved. Stankiewicz then combines the operands with the environment or structure of the design space, making the structure of the space itself the actual design. In this way, the solution to a given design problem becomes a question of selecting the right operands and combining them in the right way—in other words, to construct the right design space for the specific virtual team and the specific task at hand.

In his approach, Stankiewicz (2000) is close to Donald Schön's concept of problem setting, reflection-in-action and repertoire. According to Stankiewicz, the designer is embedded in an acquired design space as a technological community or culture, and the design space is embedded in the artifact because of the designer's combination of the operands in his or her particular design space.[3]

Stankiewicz (2000) writes:

An engineer is a person who has mastered a particular design space. Normally that space is not his personal invention. He acquired it, both in its soft- and hardware aspects, from his predecessors ... [and further that] ... operands can be embodied in artifacts and transferred in that form. (pp. 3-4)

The concept of design space must be seen more as an analytical tool, than as a performative tool for the production of design. Therefore, we could argue that this concept has to be challenged and developed further, to become an active design tool, by developing group-ware and methods for virtual teams.

A CASE OF DIALOGUES: VIRTUAL PLATFORM

In the autumn of 2005, Designskolen Kolding took the first step to create a virtual platform for design dialogue and virtual teams by launching a three-phased research and development project with close ties to the education and practice of designers. The overall aim of the project was to facilitate cooperation and cultural exchange between designers, first by providing a virtual infrastructure between students at cooperating schools worldwide, and later to include an exchange with professional practice.

The project was realized by research and education resources of Designskolen Kolding with funding from The Danish Center for Design Research (CDF). It was carried out in cooperation with Lena Merhej at American University of Beirut, Lebanon (AUB), Tarek Al-Ghoussein at The American University of Sharjah, UAE (AUS) and Olga Shustrova at Saint-Petersburg State University, Russia. The construction of the platform was done by Thomas Leerberg, Damion Bailey, Jens Paldam, and Lars Lyngstadaas at Designskolen Kolding.

Aims and Concerns

Dialogue, traveling workshops and cultural exchange has long been an integrated part of Designskolen Kolding's activities and teaching evidenced by projects in China, England, Holland, India, USA, and the other Nordic countries. Thus design dialogue is taught throughout the school from BA and MA levels, to PhD and has become one of the most important qualifications students bring with them to their professional life, thus redefining the role of the designer as a networked practitioner. In the beginning, the dialogue was carried out via fax-machines, mail, and telephones. Later, it moved on to use e-mails, videos and instant messaging, but it was always a kind of 'exquisite corps' where the students would add to or transform what other students abroad had already done. It was only a real dialogue when it was set up as a traveling workshop that physically brought the students to another location.

With the project 'Virtual Platform,' the aim was to change all this by constructing just that—a virtual platform for cooperation and exchange between students of design without them ever having to meet in the real world. This required the development of new virtual design tool that would make it possible for designers to work together across borders, time zones, cultures, languages, and economies. Such a broad tool should consist of a design method, a shared terminology, a range of solid design tools, and a distributed network-based environment.

At present, designers use a wide range of media and technologies, few of which are designed for, or by designers. Most of them lack a shared concept; so the challenge was to provide the look and feel of an informal design method, where the designer could feel the materials, have favorite tools and spontaneous inspiration.

The project was concerned with three problems that face virtual teams today:

- The creative process is carried out through a diverse range of digital media and technologies, which are not or only poorly integrated.
- The digital tools used by virtual teams are not designed for the specific purpose they serve, but often used in a very pragmatic way with limited creative efficiency as a result.
- The virtual teams need a shared terminology to communicate and reach a sufficient level of team setting.

The two primary focal points of the project were therefore the integration of technologies (mobile phones, laptops, PDAs, workstations, etc.) and the construction of a shared design space. Other focal points were the notification to users of events in their shared design space, the recording of project history and the possibility of displaying a public design process—a 'reality process.'

Development

Virtual Platform is a complex construction with a wide range of modules, domains and design spaces, which all together assist the flow of the process path needed by virtual teams. The platform is constructed around four main modules:

- A dynamic php-database containing user-names, passwords, profile data, user specific uploads, and administrative settings. This allows users to create profiles, leave small notes to other users for initial contact before setting up a project, and configure their own design space.
- A dynamic ftp-database containing uploaded files and other data that is created in specific projects. This allows multiple users to share references and products, and to keep track of the projects' progression.
- An html-interface containing the first information the user will meet as the designer arrives at the platform—user-guides and FAQ about the platform, a public gallery where users may post the finished work, pre-recorded lectures, and other shared information of broad interest. This offers an open end to the platform for all levels of users and technologies.
- A Flash-interface containing the work environment with all the tools, live streaming lectures, pre-recorded lectures, profile management, and project management. This offers a high quality interactive design space with easy access to the design tools.

The html and Flash interfaces act as a bridge between the users and the projects, and have been chosen to ensure the highest level of cross-platform usability on the client side. The live interaction and communication between users—the spatial arrangement of objects in the design space, the exchange of text messages, the use of web-cams, the simultaneous sharing of drawings, and the audio conversations—are carried through a Flash media server as shared objects and streams, which enables the creative process between the clients. This choice turned out to be optimal in terms of fast programming, predefined modules, server plug-ins, flexibility in use, and usability in an environment of mixed operating systems. As the Flash media server was hosted remotely, it could be scaled to fit specific events and workshops. During the development, the platform was tested on mobile phones and PDA's using Flash version 7 and on laptops and workstations using Flash version 8.

Domains

The use of Virtual Platform is further divided into private, shared, and public domains. The domains specify the distribution of rights between users. In the private domain, the user has full control of his process path through specific user-settings and a private sketchpad. Files, information, and users can then move from the private to the shared domain at users will, for instance if a private sketch is moved to the shared domain as part of a discussion. In the shared domain, members of that particular design space can manipulate the shared information. This can be in the form of arranging images in a specific order as a storyboard or sketching on top of uploaded images. In the public domain nonregistered users and visitors can observe the design process, for instance in the galleries containing the process history and the final products. The public domain is thus open to all and not restricted in any way. The members

of a virtual team 'sign-off' at the end of a project, by posting material in the public galleries.

Since there is a constant flow of files, information and users between the three domains, it is crucial to inform the user where he or she is, and who has the right to be in that location. A private sketch should remain private until the author of that sketch chooses to share it with his virtual team or with the greater public. A shared design space should in the same way, remain a domain of that particular virtual team unless they choose to invite other users. The consistent use of domains will also ensure a sufficient level of security on the platform, distribution of rights, avoid abuse, and afford the user a high level of control over his particular design space.

Design Spaces

As the user arrives at the Virtual Platform for the first time he is asked to create a profile, which will let him move on to the design space, to be contacted by other users, and to setup teams and projects. Without a profile, the user only has access to the public domain.

The user enters setting space, where one can create and manage their profile and do the team setting as described above. Users have to provide a valid e-mail address and will then receive a password with a link to the login page. In the setting space, the user is able to:

- Receive a password by mail and login to the platform
- Create a personal profile with data, images of own works and opinions on future projects
- Browse other users' profiles
- Comment on other users' profiles
- Establish contact with other users
- Set up a team, agree on the task, establish leadership and proceed to a shared session
- Post thoughts and ideas that would facilitate the formation of thematic teams

- Be appointed/create a session in the solving space
- Invite other users to join that session
- Finalize a session and sign-off

A single user or a group of users can enter solving space, where each project will be appointed a specific session. This session holds all the data and tools that are shared within the virtual team connected to that particular project. In the solving space, users are able to:

- Establish a design dialogue with other users

Figure 2. The usability flow of Virtual Platform

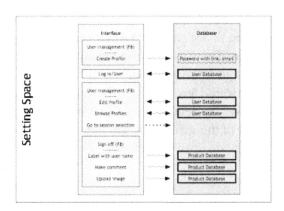

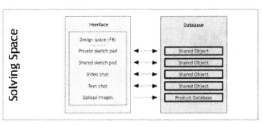

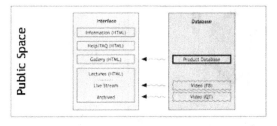

- Sketch ideas and share them with others
- Communicate through different means respective of bandwidth/technology
- Share digital work created outside the platform
- Invite input from other users or keep the session private
- Create an overview of the design process in time
- Show nonverbal emotions to other users work

When a project is finished, the user will sign-off in the setting space and post material in the public space. The uploaded material is labeled by the authors' usernames to facilitate future contacts. In the public space, users are able to:

- Browse the products that the users choose to publish
- Upload documentation of the final product
- Comment on the process

Scenarios

As the process path moves across the three domains, through the three design spaces and makes use of the four database/interface-modules as described above, there are two main scenarios that illustrate the potential of the platform.

A scenario for a substituted process path could be that two designers are separated by physical location and time. They have both created profiles with description, thematic interest and images on the platform and received passwords. Because they do not know anybody on the platform, they would browse the final work in the gallery space and browse other users' profiles in the profile space. By leaving notes to each other, they would get in touch, agree on a project, and create a session. As the project proceeds, they would be present in the same session through simultaneous actions—drawing, uploading images, text, or video chatting. If they are not working at the same time, they can leave messages to each other as text-chat, which will also serve as a history of their notes. When the project is finished, they will agree on what to publish in the public space. This use of the platform would first be a mix of social construction and team setting, and then a substitution for the presence that the users do not share. The simultaneous activity, while being a temporal feature, seems to be the benchmark of remote presence.

A scenario for a supplemented process path could be that a group of designers are well accustomed to working together but need a new way to record and document their work process. They would quickly create profiles and move on to create a session for their shared project. The solving space of their session would function as a shared consciousness of the project, containing all the files they use, all correspondence, and notes. If some of them decide to work at home or do field work, the platform moves with them. Since it runs on mobile phones and PDAs the virtual team can still keep in touch and have access to all the material, live video-chat, interactive sketching and uploading of images even though some of them are at a construction site, a factory, or visit-

ing a client. In this way, the platform becomes a supplement to the ordinary tools of the designer, providing him or her with a way to keep track of the design process in real-time and bring his work environment with him.

Both of these scenarios have been used in student-work at Designskolen Kolding.

Evaluation

Tests and evaluations were an integrated part of constructing the project. Two usability tests with approximately 70 students working in teams were carried out during the development phase and gave us invaluable knowledge and feedback on the use and construction of the platform. This made us improve the interaction between users and adjust the flow of the process path. After the platform was constructed, another and longer test was done in a real-world situation. It was a workshop on the theme 'space' involving American University of Beirut, The American University of Sharjah, and Designskolen Kolding.

The overall feedback from the tests and evaluations was concentrated on issues of informing the user of the spatial configuration he is in and

Figure 3. The graphical user interface of Virtual Platform

how he navigates in that space, general usability, hardware issues and the ability to customize particular sessions and design spaces. Some of the responses asked for:

- A better division between public and private areas of the platform, which could give better control of how sketches, and so forth would be shared and made public
- A more intuitive use of the tool, which comes even closer to collocated work
- An even faster flow of data between client and server
- The possibility to change session
- Information on who is in a particular session
- A clearer definition of rights and ownership of the shared objects

The feedback also touched upon the use of the tool as a substituted process path versus a supplemented process path as described above. Some students expected a tool that could supplement all of their ordinary tools while the tools they were presented in the test, merely substituted the presence of their teammates. The real world test that was carried out as a workshop was a mix between these two ways of using the platform. The members of a group at one location would leave messages on the platform for each other to ensure a continued work process with the members of a group at another location. In this workshop, we had virtual teams working together on the platform, while the members were physically located in Kolding, Beirut, Sharjah, Saint Petersburg, and Tokyo.

The space of Virtual Platform must be seen at a conceptual level—as a design space for exchange and communication. So in essence the spatial environment was created to provide the users and teams with an ability to qualify their presence and related artifacts, and thus create both a formal and informal environment for greater creativity. These point in at least two important directions:

(a) giving the user the ability to customize the specific workspace and thereby qualify an individual view on other team members to get a more personal feel of the interaction and (b) to provide the users in general with more ways to organize and structure their process-path.

As the concept of design is expanding from a traditional view of an aesthetic preparation of industrial production to entail a wide range of structuring and planning activities in anthropology, economics and human resource management, it defines a new therapeutic role for the designer. He has to 'go-between' other vocations and make the whole integration work. In this way, we could see virtual teams in the spatial construct of operands as described above, even as an economy of information—as an intricate exchange of information, experience, expertise, opinions, and ideas to serve the higher purpose of adding value to a shared enterprise.

A CASE OF SPACE: TOPOS

The application topos was one of the results of the research project 'WorkSpace.' It was a joint group of The Aarhus School of Architecture, The Department of Experimental Computer science at University of Aarhus, and Department of Sociological Studies at Lancaster University.

Topos can be seen as a parametric workspace, or as a representation of a design process. Topos has the ability to place a wide range of documents in the same context—a metaphorical and perceptual space—and to manipulate these documents. As the user is located 'within' the model in Topos, different workspaces can be selected corresponding to different 'setups' or manifestations of information objects. These can be virtual models, where corresponding information can be displayed as the different parts of the model is selected and displayed. This function will expand the traditional selection of layers in CAD applications, since the interface is in the same 'space' as the objects themselves, and that the content of the different workspaces may consist of a diverse range of text-documents, Web pages, images, cameras, and so forth.

Space is primarily a metaphor for the average user in Topos—an easily comprehensible way to arrange, visualize and manipulate documents, as argued by Sara Fabrikant. However, this metaphorical use of the workspace is changed as architects and designers place spatial objects in the workspace metaphor—adding 'real' spatial dimensions to the arrangement of hyper textual proxies in the metaphorical space. In this way, Topos can be seen as a hybrid between a simulated real space and a metaphorical space.

The workspace is collaborative and may be shared with multiple users. Each user may see a different manifestation of the information that is placed in the workspace.

Scenarios

The use of this cumulative design space is two-fold. In a design situation the external references may be present in the same space as the objects that are being designed, which is usually not the case in common CAD applications. In an investigative situation, it means that one may build a diagrammatic space, while investigating how it was realized in a final building through photographs, synthetic models, archive material, and so forth. In other words, the use of a cumulative space is both found at the very beginning of a design process, when only data from a site or a program is present, and at the very end, when the final product will be evaluated or studied further. Overall, it makes it easier for the designer to control all the materials that are involved in the design process through an active use of the space in which, the design process takes place.

A scenario, which was tested during the development of Topos, was the dynamic interaction within a team of architects, where one group was at the construction site while the other group stayed in the office. Before one group left, the team agreed on what material was needed and placed that in the workspace. This included descriptions of the building, a spatial model of the building and the landscape surrounding the building, and general reference material. As one group was inspect-

Figure 4. The graphical user interface of Topos with a spatial model placed in the workspace together with images, movies and Web pages

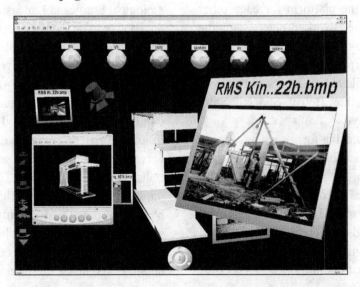

ing the building site, their location was mapped through GPS on to the spatial model of the building site in the shared workspace. When the group in the field uploaded images to the designspace, these images were positioned in a spatial constellation relative to the spatial model of the building site. In this way, both groups could get an easy overview of the design problems at hand, which facilitated faster and better decision-making.

Evaluation

The cumulative space builds on well-known procedures of spatial manipulation, while it also adds entirely new potential. The manipulation of spatial properties of the design space is similar to that of common 3D design applications; location, rotation, scale, transparency, and to some extent, color. The spatial organization is also similar to the use of classes, layers, and groups and parents in common CAD applications, even though the Topos terminology of proxies and workspaces is more precise, regarding object structure. However, what sets the cumulative space apart from common CAD applications is the ability to cumulate a wide range of data objects in one space and to have a live update of these data objects by proxies. The design space may even be distributed among an unlimited range of users who will all have the ability to analyze and discuss its content.

CONCLUSION

It should now be clear that space has a structure (Benedikt, 1991) and that we can spatialize (Fabrikant, 2000) both the navigation and the information of that space to construct a design space (Stankiewicz, 2000) with the virtuality of an open reflection-in-action (Schön, 1983). It should also be clear that we need to develop a more precise vocabulary to describe what goes on within virtual teams and how these teams do design.

These requirements have been addressed in this chapter—by describing team setting, substituted process paths, and supplemented process paths. Conclusion are therefore (a) that we focus just as much on the team setting as on the problem solving, as we strive for a higher efficiency of virtual teams, (b) that we plan for both substituted and supplemented process paths to reach the highest creativity of virtual teams, and (c) that we are very specific in the way we construct design spaces and what metaphors we use to do so.

From the constructed design spaces for virtual teams—virtual platform and topos—we have learned how valuable the spatial approach can be. Space has a great potential, both as a shared terminology for virtual teams and as a way to navigate through, and structure, information.

The two cases presented above were both constructed in, and aimed for an academic context with students as the main user group. If virtual platform or topos were to be transferred to professional use, they would both have to adjust to the habits and environments of new users. However, the fundamental terminology and spatial metaphors would remain the same, as would the structure of databases, domains, and design spaces.

For both academic and professional applications, there will be a demand for appeal and convenience. Since the market today is saturated with services that all contain a small part of what platforms for virtual teams may offer, changing the habits of designers will be a very real challenge. The integration of cooperative tools must demonstrate a significant improvement over traditional nonintegrated ways of working in order to succeed.

There is no doubt that we have moved a long way from the first definitions of cyberspace and virtuality in 1990. Today mixed reality, virtual teams and remote presence is something we meet every day, often without noticing it. However, there is not yet a seamless integration in daily work practice. The substitution of physical presence is still far from carrying all the human information and exchange that goes on when sitting across from another person—although development such as that shown in this volume show we are moving closer

We are at the brink of constructing an entirely new reality that can both substitute and supplement the process paths of designers. Therefore, it seems that we are, just as Michael Benedikt was at the first conference on cyberspace in 1990, still standing in front of a vast unknown landscape—not just of virtual opportunities, but also of very real possibilities.

REFERENCES

Bachelard, G. (1994). *The poetics of space*. Boston: Beacon Press.

Benedikt, M. (1979). *An introduction to isovists*. Austin, TX: UT Austin School of Architecture Working Paper Series, University of Texas.

Benedikt, M. (1991). Cyberspace: Some proposals. In B. Michael (Ed.), *Cyberspace: First steps* (pp. 119-224). Cambridge, MA: The MIT Press.

Bois, Y-A. (1991). *Painting as model*. Cambridge, MA: The MIT Press.

Comment, B. (1999). *The panorama*. London: Reaktion Books. Translated from B. Comment (1993). *Le XIXe siècle des panoramas*.

Crary, J. (1990). *Techniques of the observer*. Cambridge, MA: The MIT Press.

Eisenman, Peter (1999). *Diagram diaries*. London: Thames & Hudson.

Fabrikant, S. (2000). Spatialized browsing in large data archives. *Transactions in GIS, 4*(1), 65-78.

Katzenbach, J. R., & Smith, D. K. (1994). *The wisdom of teams: Creating the high-performance organization*. New York: Harper Business.

Kimble, C.s, Li, F. & Barlow, A. (2000). *Effective virtual teams through communities of practice* (Research Paper No. 2000/9). Glasgow: Strathclyde Business School.

Schön, D. (1983). *The reflective practitioner*. Paperback edition (1991). Aldershot, UK: Ashgate.

Stankiewicz, R. (2000). *The concept of 'design space.'* Retrieved November, 15, 2006, from http://www.lri.lu.se/pdf/Crafoord00/rsws.pdf. Modified version published in J. Ziman, (Ed.) (2000), *Technological innovation as an evolutionary process*. Cambridge, MA: Cambridge University Press.

Tschumi, B. (1990). *Questions of space*. London: AA Publications.

Tufte, E. (1997). *Visual explanations: Images and quantities, evidence and narrative*. Cheshire, CT: Graphics Press.

ENDNOTES

[1] The term 'design' is primarily understood as a verb and not as the stylistic label or stigmata of an object. It is neither a normative judgment of, what makes good or bad design, nor is 'design' limited to traditional industrial design.

[2] In practice there would be many other factors or parameters, which the team could either share or differ. It could be language, cultural codes, ethics, censorship, supervision, technologies, or bandwidth.

[3] We could also say that the designer has the role of the initiator or decision-maker of a design process that will manifest the design space in a series of artifacts through the addition of material—real or virtual.

Chapter XIV
iCE:
Interactive Coinnovation Environment

Terry Rosenberg
Goldsmiths, University of London, UK

Mike Waller
Goldsmiths, University of London, UK

ABSTRACT

As it becomes increasingly important to work in new sociotechnological formations such as the virtual spaces across networks, so does the requirement to build new tools to furnish this emergent landscape. This chapter looks at the way a virtual space may be built and used to facilitate group, team and individual thinking in developing projects and also shaping practice in organizations where innovation is an important focus. The chapter describes the work being done to produce an interactive networked based 'coinnovation' environment (iCE); where members of an organization, individually and variously, may contribute their thoughts to help innovate—develop 'prospects'—for the organization's projects.

INTRODUCTION

Adopting a culture of innovation is a huge step for many companies, but it is clear that those that are able to make the step usually reap huge rewards. The Design Council (2006) in the UK reports that 80% of the Fortune 500 companies have listed innovation as one of their top priorities. This comes as no surprise. The move from the identification of the need for innovation to the implementation of stratagems to educe innovation is for most companies/organizations rather tricky, however. There is an innate difficulty, a kind of schizophrenia in organizations, where on one hand, they are looking to a logic of efficiency, low or justified risk, and clear and assured targets and on the other, they are looking for innovation, which requires flights of imagination, risk-taking, speculation, and experimentation; contradictory in every sense to the first position.

Design programs may help to alleviate the tensions between the two positions—stripping away the fear often associated with creative work by demystifying the processes of innovation. As stated by Stamm (2003) 'design as a profession holds some of the answers to integrating innovation into the culture of business' (p. 3). Increasingly, design is becoming involved in business; producing innovative designs for businesses and, at the business end of businesses, using design thinking to facilitate innovative business practices (designs of business).

At Goldsmiths College we are currently designing an interactive coinnovation environment (through the rest of this chapter abbreviated to iCE) for organizations of various kinds. The environment is designed to help produce innovative designs for business but may also help produce innovative designs of a business. The core around which the iCE is conceived, is being designed so as to be able to make visible the flights of imagination, the process of speculation and programmes of experimentation, and, through this visualization, to some extent, implicitly, map risk through the course of an innovation process. This core is, in essence, the visualization of design thinking—virtual creativity made explicit.

BACKGROUND

Renaissance figures like Da Vinci and Galileo looked to diagrams to explore problems and conceive ideas; circumventing words and numbers

Figure 1. Diagram of Einstein's sketch showing a space of speculation or hunch

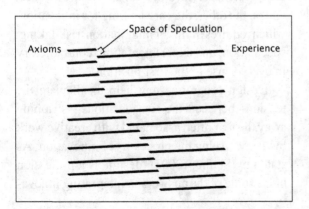

to work in images of, and for, thought. Through drawing they made their thought process visible, considering connections and relationships between things. Working through homologies; for instance, observing connections in the spirals of a whirlpool vortex and the spiral growth of plants (Da Vinci)—they were able to understand something of the nature of things as they exist. They were also able to take these observations and extrapolate from them so as to make conjecture as to how things may be.

The iCE is particularly focused on how things may be. The roots of the iCE lie in earlier research of ours into a particular cognitive act; an act of thinking that makes a jump into what is not yet known or in existence—namely, the 'hunch.' Einstein (1949) wrote in his scientific papers, that the two postulates of relativity were no more than 'hunches'. In perhaps the most significant advance in science in history, rigorous scientific method was accorded no part by Einstein. And, the workings of the imagination were relegated to a point on the horizon of practice, where innovatory thinking disappeared as mere 'hunch'. He evolved his hunches into the postulates about time and space, which we now know as relativity, without recourse to experiment or testing. Instead, there is only the necessary mathematics built on an instantaneous thought; the hunch. In fact we may think of the mathematics as merely illustrations of those remarkable hunches. Mathematics that was valued for its aesthetic of sense; as it was only some time later that it was 'proven.'

The idea that the imaginative leap, the hunch, is dimensionless is of course absurd. Einstein is disingenuous and self effacing when he presents it as such. The hunch has thickness in his thinking. It is clear from the traces of his thinking (Einstein has left jottings and diagrams) that there is indeed more to his 'hunches' than he admits. He knows, understands, and destabilizes past practice and asserts new ways of thinking, connecting until then unconnected ideas and images; all the time hypostatizing his thinking through representation—thus, constructing a scaffold for his hunches.

In Figure 1, one may see how Einstein 'pictures thinking' and thinks in pictures. The speculative (hunch) is built using visual, spatial, and schematic representations which allow him through his illustration to engage in the trajectories and particular landmarks in his thinking. The iCE at its core is essentially focused on building a shared representation of and for innovatory thinking, having the same kind of sense as Einstein's diagram.

THE SPACES OF THE ICE

The architecture of the iCE is based on four interconnected spaces which form the environment. There is a space geared to team formation, one for idea evaluation and an archive space. But central to the iCE and the space in the environment that is most evolved in our designing is the ideational space; a tool for innovative thinking (see Figure 2).

The 'ideational space' is the space described in some detail in this chapter; the other spaces being in their conceptual infancy. Requirements of the other spaces as opposed to their design will be described, so that we may articulate the way in which a team may use the iCE. The ideational

Figure 2. Architecture of the iCE

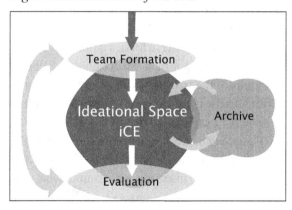

space is the operational key to the iCE and the other three spaces augment this core.

The Ideational Space

The ideational space is built on two notions: First, on a supposition that there are patterns of innovatory thinking that are shared and these may be represented and thus communicated. These we refer to as 'plottings.' Second, that all innovatory programs (across numerous practices) may be mapped using a key of generic landmarks; the key, the landmarks, being the same across all projects even though the map is detailed specific to individual project use.

The ideational space of the iCE provides maps, with prompts and plottings, to support individuals, but especially groups and teams, develop and apply various stratagems to promote innovative thinking (new imaginings, or what we call 'prospects'—explained later).

Innovative thinking is considered to be both new ways of thinking and also thinking that is directed towards gaining the 'new.' To some extent this doubled reading is codependant. To think the new, one in most instances needs to think anew; find disruptive strategies to break with old, ingrained and habitual thinking and find new trajectories of thought. The environment helps in this process.

Although the early maps and plottings on which the design of the iCE is based were directed to individual use, it became increasingly apparent that when transcribed to a space that could be shared, the digital space of the iCE, the maps and plottings would also be useful in connecting together different individual thinking, imaginations, in and across groups. In the due course of the chapter we will expand on the way one can create an environment (virtual and indeed actual) where one can connect and directly communicate the connection of individual thinking, to support team or group work.

The iCE provides the potential to map an 'interplexus'—where the threads of individual thinking/imagining may be connected to one another but also to other networks of thought, activity, and production..

PLOTTING TYPES OF THINKING

The plottings are derived from earlier research into the hunch (the 'naked hunch'—apologies to William Burroughs), as indicated earlier in the chapter. In the earlier research, in order to explore possibilities of a technicity of the hunch—the speculative program of thinking—we built what we called a *reservoir* (for ideas).

The reservoir used spatial, temporal, and material metaphors to help plot what is known (or knowable) and what is not-known (or not knowable) in a creative enterprise. We used the idea of ground to depict what we know and water to depict what is not known. The notion that what we know is solid ground is embedded in the everyday language we use (i.e., 'What are the grounds for saying that?'). Ground is the base from which the speculative flight takes place. The liquidity of speculative thinking—open to constant change, flow ... provisional, uncertain—was best suited to images of water. The idea of surface and depth oceanic thinking (Ehrenzweig, 1971), of currents and flows seemed to suit the idea of the speculative. Precedence for this mapping of uncertain thought as water was found in the work of that great philosopher of the 'material imagination' (Bachelard, 1983).The different natures of bodies of water in movement suited the idea of different kinds of imaginative thinking; the idea of water as both a reflective and transparent surface also seemed to have resonance with what we observed of the speculative dimension of innovatory thinking.

To know the different natures of engagement with the two elements—ground and water—as research and search, a review of Rosenberg (2000) is useful:

The paradigm for (re)search on the ground is supported in the images of excavation and construction. (Re)search in open water may be imagined as swimming and diving. In open water the swimmer or diver is immersed and at the mercy of the element, water—whereas, on land, the element lies outside the person digging or building and is very much controlled by them.

These ideas about ground and water and their different terms of engagement are early references on which the iCE is overwritten. In the Reservoir we also described two tendencies or forces moving between ground and water. The first force, the centripetal is a force that moves back (poesy) to what is known: "The centripetal impulse pulls inwards trying to make coherent with what we already know. The programme of the centripetal is to make fast, secure and stabilize; this force tries to ground what we know in already established fact knowledge" (ibid.). The opposing force (centrifugal) draws thought into fluid and open spaces (water), where things are not formed and not knowable (at least until the project is complete): "The centrifugal impulse draws out possibilities beyond, and creates deviations from programmes to normalise. Its pull is to expand and develop opportunities. It rattles the movement to substantiate. The impulse is not towards certainty but to escape from it" (ibid.).

These forces are ever present in a creative (especially innovatory) project working in creative thinking simultaneously; the centripetal and the centrifugal working together to create a dialectical tension between the drive for substantiation (knowing) and the drive for deviation (not-knowing). Different topographical details and different strengths of the two forces allow the mapping of different patterns of creative/innovative thinking. A series of examples is illustrated in Figure 3.

Figure 3 shows how linear thinking gathers the centrifugal drive (the errant line in the diagram) in a channel of intention set around what one knows. The thinking is conservative driven to find a solution to a problem which in its determination sets limited scope for solutions. The errant line of discovery, the centrifugal force, is guided in a channel of intention.

In lateral thinking there is a step aside. It starts with a determined and determining problem which sets out the thinking space in much the same manner as the linear thinking example. But then one steps laterally from the ground of the problem set to another ground so as to deal with the problem in another context. One then steps back in one's thinking into the original focal channel of the original problem set, with insights from the step aside that will help solve the problem.

Combinatory thinking is a kind of dream thinking where the focus is determined after the lines of discovery have interconnected. There is still ground in sight and the lines of discovery are connected and substantiated by a centripetal pull back to ground. Combinatory thinking works in the surprise of connections.

One kind of thinking is not prioritized over another; each has their occasion for use. Indeed they may be used alternatively on the same project. But even as described here the categories and types of thinking are broad in category and in the brush of description. We have moved on in the iCE to create a more sophisticated breakdown of types based on what we call 'prospecting'. These 'prospects,' described next, may still be seen as movements across knowing and not-knowing, across water and ground. They may indeed, be gathered into the broad brackets of the categories of linear, lateral, and combinatory thinking but the prospect has a finer grain of detail.

PROSPECTS

Innovative thinking is thinking as a form of prospecting. We use 'prospect'—in its multiple definitions of expectation, yield, and view.

Figure 3. Types of thinking

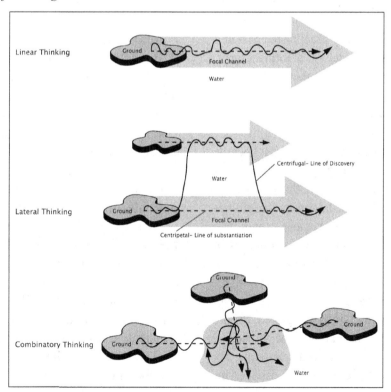

To elaborate, a 'prospect' is:

- An expectation of what is yet to happen
- Poiesis (poetic process) that yields futures
- A view, not only into, but on the possibilities of that future, its practices, its spaces and objects (a critical view onto not only the future sense of what is proposed but, also, a critical purchase on its wider repercussions)

So we understand the 'prospect' as the key to innovation, as a manifestation of the practices of 'constructed speculation'. The prospect is an attempt to uncover what is there and is not yet uncovered (like prospecting for gold) and at the same time, trying to realize a future possibility (as in trying to realize one's job prospects). Innovatory thinking (design) is an expectation of what is yet to happen and an attempt to bring about desired futures. But in order to make this future it needs to dig into past and current forms, technologies, practices, events and so on. Prospecting is an attempt to uncover what is still to be found in the past, present, and future. But in terms of design/innovatory practice the past and the present are used to deliver a future object, event, system, experience, or other output.

Plotting Prospects

As research and designing progressed it became increasingly apparent that the prospect was a key concept. With the background of the diagrams of types of thinking (linear, lateral and combinatory thinking, Figure 3), we began to appreciate the need for more specificity to create maps of 'prospecting'—in response developing maps of movements in knowing and not knowing, focused on time and spatial movements. Although in many ways they are tightly integrated, for the sake of organizing and mapping the 'prospect' time and space were considered separately. By using 'timing' and 'spacing' as processes of in-

novatory thinking we were able to create a quite comprehensive set of plottings of patterns for prospects. We were able to extend our research from illustrations of types of thinking to a point where we could build a portfolio of patterns (of thinking) that could be used to explain, communicate and, indeed, be used for idea generation itself. These patterns are the ideational generator of what has become the iCE.

Timings

The temporal or historical dimension of thinking calls for the consideration of patterns, pulses, and beats of change over time. These may be regular and predictable (or at least thought to be) as in, for example, trend analysis, or, they may be irregular, as in the fore and back projections illustrated in Figure 4.

In trend analysis/prediction one looks at the changes of a design (it could be any 'object'—business practice, product, system, management structure and so on) over a period of time. Through marking progressive difference as regular movement, one can infer a tendency of change and make a prediction as to how the 'object' may be in the near future (if change happens in the regular way it can be seen to be doing). This produces a novelty of the same; the beat goes on.

Back casting too works on a regular pulse. But in back casting the regular pulse moves backward from the future. In back casting one needs to appreciate the developments that have led to the 'object of consideration' being what it is (context changes, 'object' changes, etc.) but one takes a 'flier' and has a surmise as to how the 'object' may be in a far flung future. One then works backward from the object to the near future and ultimately directs one's attention to realizing that near future. Back casting although fairly radical thinking (prospecting) is also based on a regular beat.

The two other 'timings' depicted in Figure 4 work on the idea of irregularity, of disrupting the beat of change. Fore-projection works on the idea of lost or forgotten 'objects', or can even relate to beat erasure. In other words the object has been held up in development in the past or one intentionally goes back to a particular point in past development and brings this old idea of the 'object' up to contemporary technologies and practices, in order to see how this leap over the beats of change may spawn an object of the near future. For example one may browse the shopping catalogues of the 1800's and find Victorian products that have no contemporary equivalent and use these as points of departure for contemporary product design.

In back-projection one takes a leap to the future 'object', appreciating its future context. One may appreciate the way the future scene conditions the object. We have, with our students and in our workshops with industry, used scenarios from science fiction—literature and film, to set the scene for evolving the 'object'. Again, an example from product development, we used films like *Blade Runner* and *Minority Report* to set the scene to evolve domestic products that were not featured in the movie (e.g., a child's buggy, a toaster, etc.). The new objects are designed for the future scene.

Forecasting, back casting, fore- and back-projection are the four fundamental movements or 'timings' along the timeline. There are inflections and nuances in movement that we have not described here. But, essentially one may move the 'object' of concern, its contexts (the landscape that holds it, political, economic, social or technological), or the subjects which interact with it and the practico-material spaces in which it operates along the timeline to direct and orchestrate innovatory thinking, or, what we have called 'prospects.'

Figure 4. Timings

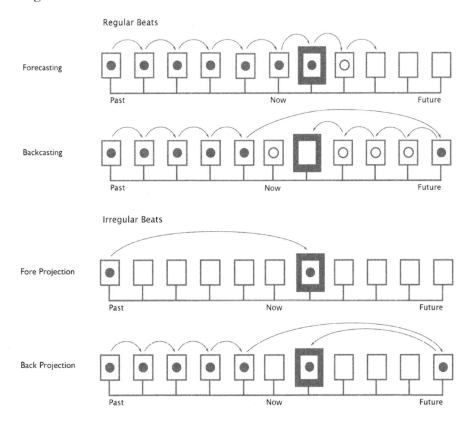

Spacings

To a large extent 'timings' frame the prospect linearly; they are after all tied to a time line. There is no chance to contrast and combine different 'objects', contexts, scenarios, and so on. This requires a laterality of thought to encounter other such 'objects'—in similarity (synectics), (Jones, 1992) or difference (antonymics). In synectics one thinks of a parallel situation to solve a problem, whereas, in an antonymic relationship one is consciously seeking out the tensions caused by difference across two dissimilar spaces.

We may think of moving an element (syntagm shift) from one context to another or one context (in toto) shifted so as to be overlaid over a new context (paradigm shift). An example of a syntagm shift would be, for instance, to move domestic lighting (typologies) into the public space of a square or street to provide one with stimulus to conceive a new generation of urban lighting; lighting that a passerby may switch on or off like they would their standing lamp in the living room. A paradigm shift is typically used by architects where they may overlay the context of one site over another; for example, designing a bank as though it was a street market. The social interactions of the market

would provide a new way of thinking for a way of organizing the architectural spaces of the bank so that its transactions may be reconsidered within the sociality of the street market.

We have considered different kinds and natures of movements across space from a flow, a movement that embraces contiguity and contingency, to bounds where there is rupture in the flow—a contiguous connection—between spaces (paradigm and syntagm shifts are of this kind). A typical example of a contiguous flow would be a spiral dynamic. Two forms of spiral have been conceived, a two-dimensional static spiral and a three-dimensional spiral (which takes the two dimensional spiral on a spatial journey).

A spiral will have at its center an 'object,' say a pen. The pen is thought of in a specific place, perhaps a study. The spiral maps the connective chain from the pen to the thing next to it and then the thing next to that thing and so on. For instance, next to the pen may be a pencil, then next to that a pot, a pad, a computer, a file, a desk, a carpet, walls, a room, a building, and so on. Through a set of contiguous relationship one may move from the object, the pen, into larger and larger spaces. One may then design from the outer spaces of the spiral back in to the pen; in regular or irregular movement (see Figure 5).

Three-dimensional spirals (see Figure 6), create dynamic in space. These also begin with an 'object' in the center of the spiral. But this time it is not thought to be still in a specific place the spiral itself moves through spaces.

We have also looked to investigate space as plastic (in the sense of being malleable) and have thought about folding space to connect points, lines, and spaces in new and unexpected ways.

These processes, spacings, can be used in combination with each other or indeed with the timings to provide an extended repertoire of innovatory thinking processes. These spacings are also in the idea generator of the iCE.[1]

Figure 5. Static spiral

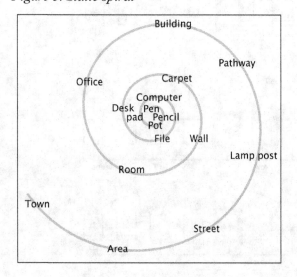

Figure 6. Dynamic spiral

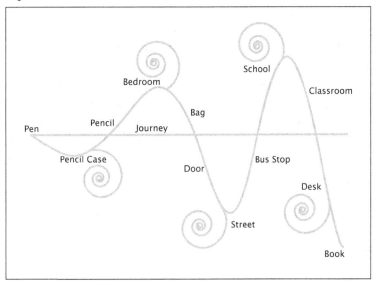

MAPPING THE SPACES OF PRACTICE

We have written about how one may move in the tensions that link knowing to not knowing, and produced patterns and processes of innovatory thinking that are finely detailed. With these however, there is no way of locating the 'prospecting' in practice. To this end, a map to allow the placing of loci for specific practices and their prospects has been developed. Of course, the particularities of every practice cannot be known yet we can provide the opportunity for teams and individuals to produce the specificity of their own 'practice' maps.

The map therefore provided in the iCE is keyed with a set of demarcated spaces in which one can map the practice. There are zones that are universal to every practice that need to be filled with the particular 'tokens' and 'nodes' of each. In the iCE, the rudimentary space is provided, into which the particular practice can be mapped.

The rudiments of the map mark out three zones, into which one can act to organize the particular loci of practice. There are zones of production, reception or consumption and a mediating zone—perceptual mediation. This perceptual zone mediates the 'gaze' in practice from production to reception/consumption and vice versa. One may place filters, philosophic, political (like Marxism), or poetic, to lens the 'gaze' from one zone to another (this is explained in the walkthrough of the software that follows).

But these zones need articulating. The zones need to be filled with at first general features which later can be built to higher specification. Until the prospecting starts, one merely works from the legend or key provided to build general features and relationships in the map.

To elucidate further one may think of it in this way: in a map of a physical terrain one would know the ways in which elements relate. If one has a legend of a map that lists roads, bridges, mountains, streams, tunnels, and so on they would know the way things go together. One may easily conjecture that a bridge would go over a stream or span a gorge in the mountains in order to build a road that connects one place to another on the map. A tunnel would probably run through the mountains, but may in some instances run under the stream.

Similarly, relationships may be mapped in the spaces of business/design practice—the kind of way things go together. A legend for a practice may supply us with elements (tokens and nodes) such as 'product,' 'user,' 'designer' and/or 'producer,' 'site,' and so on to be dropped into the generic zones of the map. The key elements begin as tokens, but once placed in the map they become loci in the articulated practice. They become points of departure and references for prospecting as well as information posts (access to research), when specificity is written in to them. One may easily fathom the relationship between these elements, as general tokens, and place them in the space of the map—in particular related to the different universal zones. They become specific through research.

We have also thought of externalities—influences—almost like winds that will ventilate the spaces of practice. In particular we have thought of A.L.F.E. and S.T.E.E.P. influences. A.L.F.E. is an acronym that stands for *art, literature, film* and *event* and S.T.E.E.P. stands for *social, technological, economic, environmental* and *political*. These winds blow into both the zones of production and consumption and one can trace their potential influence there.

The way the map may be used to shape the prospect is described in the walkthrough below.

WALKTHROUGH OF iCE SOFTWARE

The software program opens to a menu. Included in the menu is a user's guide which will detail ways in which the iCE may be used. There will also be a button which links to a page with a list of project maps within the organization as well as links to live projects and to completed projects housed in the archive space. The completed projects, in conjunction with the guide are useful in understanding and illustrating how the iCE map may be specified in order to propagate innova-

tive ideas. At a later stage the projects may also be searched in the archive so as to access different information gained during each project. For instance, in a new product development project one may search past projects to access research into a user group that may be equally relevant to the current project.

Any new project will need to be registered and a project file opened. Project members will also need to register. Once the users of the iCE are familiar with the basic functions of the iCE they can move to the team formation space. At this stage it is possible to set the access to the iCE for other stakeholders who are not members of the innovation team, allowing external onlookers (clients) to watch as the project unfolds, or indeed, to participate, as desired. It is also possible to invite other teams—global, on the other side of the world, or, local, within the same building to participate at times or during the whole of the project, as desired.

The Team Formation Space

The team formation space performs a number of functions. Firstly it allows the team members to introduce themselves to each other. In some cases, members of the team may not have encountered each other before and may not ever do so, apart from in the virtual space of the iCE.

We are developing 'profiling' questions to elicit information from participants that may be used to short-cut introductions and allow for accelerated social and professional interaction. The profiling will also be used to help build the team. Most profiling (Belbin®'s team role inventory[2]) fixes character and aptitude and sets these characters to fixed roles within a team. We are working on 'profiling' and team formation support, acknowledging that some individuals may have more aptitude for certain roles than others and therefore incline to certain tasks, but, and this is crucial: we believe for a creative productive team, also acknowledging that characters and abilities of different kinds may bring different things to different roles. The iCE is designed to allow a group of individuals to organize themselves as a team—considering not only the tasks and concomitant roles that members of the team need to take on, but also the way team spirit may be forged; the team not only forms around capabilities but also character and relationships.

The team formation space we are designing therefore, allows for flexibility in assignment and adoption of roles and tasks. Using systems like De Bono's 'six thinking hats,'[3] roles can be assigned and exchanged at any time through the duration of a project. As is inferred above, it is important to stress that not only do hats, like the 'cautious' black hat (one of De Bono's thinking hats) conform to the shape of their wearers head but that heads also shape hats! Furthermore, roles should not be stifling and fixed as new insights and creative opportunities will come to light in role exchange.

Each participant of the team will be represented in the spaces of the iCE by an avatar. The team formation space is where the avatar is given definition. A series of templates will be used initially to define an individual member's role, capabilities, and tasks. Within each avatar, this information is stored for reference, while links to individuals

work on past projects will also be available. The avatar will be composed to reflect the spirit or character of the team member it represents. Each member of the team is able to communicate with, and have insight into the other members within the space by simply selecting their avatar. We envisage the avatar and associated content shifting during the course of a project, with roles being fluid, and task assignment changing during a project and from project to project.

Briefing for Project

The iCE specification currently has a briefing space housed in the team formation space, since briefing affects team formation. We envisage that the project brief will be received in this team formation space, as it is important that the roles and tasks are driven by the requirements of the brief, and can be set up (even in a fluid way would be desirable) at the moment of the briefing. At least the kind of tasks/roles that will be required through the course of the project should be laid out with an understanding that they are not necessarily set for the full duration.

The iCE will provide a series of prompts and aids to unpick the brief, helping to reveal its 'ur-

Figure 7. The three zones of the ideational space of the iCE

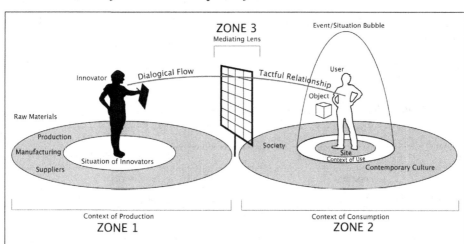

brief' (i.e., the set of forces and influences that give rise to the brief) to the newly formed team. There will be links or possible bolt-ons, of other software, that will allow the users of the iCE to access other tools to help unpick the brief and find relevant references and connections for the project (see Malins, Watt, Liapis and McKillop, "Tools and Technology to Support Creativity in Virtual Teams, Chapter XI in this book). The key word search described in the Malins chapter would have particular relevance.

The team can also use the iCE's archive as a resource to inform and build reference for their project. The research done in previous projects can be used, where relevant, to support the new project. A search engine will allow the new team to draw up information on anything from user behavior to the behavior of material (in product development, for instance) from previous project research. The research methodologies and creative stratagems of previous projects can also inform the new project.

The unpicking of the brief encourages the team to identify the project loci which informs the preliminary ideational mapping that happens in the ideational space of the iCE.

IDEATIONAL SPACE: THE THREE ZONES

The ideational space, as mentioned earlier in the chapter, has three zones in which the loci of a project can be mapped. The way a team may engage with and use the three zones, of production, reception/consumption, and perceptual mediation, is described in Figure 7.

Zone One: Context of Production

The 'zone of production' may be understood in a general sense as a space of business, commerce, manufacture, and anything relating to production. Within this zone lies the subzone, the 'situation of the innovators.' The avatars of individuals in the team will appear in the subzone as it is important that members of the team are able to locate themselves within the map (see Figure 7) and appreciate that they are implicated in the innovation process and don't just preside over it.

Moving away from the central core of the innovation team, indeed beyond the company, are situated the suppliers and services that support the company. In order to make an innovation breakthrough, the focus for creative input may well be directed to re-organizing the relationships or indeed redesigning particular elements represented in the zone of production. The team may redesign the way in which the company is (re)sourced, using the spatial and temporal patterns of thinking described in this chapter. They may also re-design the innovation team itself and its activities. Using fictional characters would allow thinking to be textured by the attributes of the fantasy character adopted. A student at Goldsmiths once designed a product while taking

Table 1. Tripartite relationship of object, user and context

Object	User	Context
1. possession	person/individual	biography, personal experience
2. tool	operator	system/interface
3. artifact (socio-cultural)	group (social)	society/culture
4. product	consumer (individual or consumer group)	market

on the persona of Cyrano de Bergerac. The radio he designed had the romanticism and bravado of de Bergerac and carried an inventiveness that could not have otherwise been gained.

Zone Two: Context of Consumption

Opposite the zone of production is the zone of consumption. At the center of the consumption zone is the locus of use. The locus is a compound relationship. The user is located in relationship to an 'object' of use (this 'object' can be a service, a product, perception and so on) and a site of use (see Figure 8). The relationship of the three (user, object, and site) gathers in a situation or event space, and this in turn is encompassed in what is called the context of use. The event of use may be regarded at different scales and inflected in different contexts. Table 1 gives examples of some of the different scales and inflections of a contingent tripartite relationship of object, user, and context.

There may well be other ways of conceiving this locus of use. The way the context of use/consumption is scaled and considered will clearly lead to different directions for innovative

Figure 8. Object, user and context

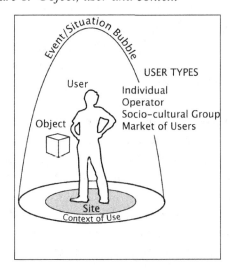

thinking. It is in most cases worth thinking in multiple; considering and working through and testing ideas of the intended 'object' on a number of scales and inflected contexts (more later in the section "Specifying the Map").

Zone Three: The Mediating Lens

Between the zone of production and zone of consumption (Figure 6) there is a mediating space which mediates the 'gaze' from production to consumption and vice versa. It may be considered as a lens with a way of coloring or tinting the view from one zone to the other.

There are changes of perception which are brought about through movement of ideas and data across the mediating space/lens, from one zone to the other. In design thinking the flow is two way, a 'dialogical flow'. In art it is more often than not one way, rhetorical; the artist expresses what they think without hearing and responding to the views received. In designing there is dialogue, something like a conversation, across this space. The designers/innovators need to consider what the 'user' will say about what is innovated. They therefore need to proceed tactfully. The word 'tact' is used pointedly, described by Tact De Certeau (2002). " ... the apprehension and creation of a "harmony" among particular practices ... [through] ... , the ethical and poetic gesture of religare (tying together)" (p. 74). What we are proposing is tying together the activities of production and consumption through this mediating space. From the designer/innovators point of view, tact can be taken in two registers: first, 'empathetic tact' where the producer steps into the shoes of the consumer to identify with them, and, second, 'sympathetic tact' which seeks to understand or be sensitive to the consumer without identifying oneself with their situation. An example: if one is looking at the plight of the homeless and needs information one may actually sleep on the streets for a month in order to 'empathize' with their situation, which a student of ours did (much to our alarm!) or, one may research data on the homeless, elicit information from them through questionnaires and so on and have 'sympathy' with their circumstance.

In some projects one may consider how the construction of the perceptual tint in direct alignment with the project (e.g., company brand in relation to a product development) or one can use this zone to produce a conceptual texture as creative provocation, by dropping in suggestive features that may guide the project. Into the lens one can drop theories, articles, ethical principles, company missions, and poetry so that they/it may color the view and shape, shift, motivate, influence, and direct[4] the creative process in different ways.

PRIMING THE MAP

The map as stated earlier is not yet detailed. There are merely three zones and an expectation that particular features will be placed in the map. These features exist as 'tokens' of likely and perhaps key elements in a brief to innovate.

The team should work together in priming and then specifying the map. To some extent, the unpicking of the brief is a prelude to priming the map. During the briefing, the team needs to work out not only the forces that give rise to the brief (ur-brief) but also the locating and located elements of the project. The team may work with the map to clarify the loci of the project. They may also open up the map in the ideational space and then click and drag the 'tokens' from the key into the zones of the map; thereby using the mapping to discuss and agree the key loci of the project. The map can of course be added to or modified at any time during the course of the project—but it is primed in and for discussion about the project at the start. Later it is used to stimulate and make visible the team's 'prospecting'.

Once the key elements have been placed into the map one may add a calculus of references;

the forces that gave rise to the brief and a set of references that may influence the brief (ready to be dropped into the mediating space). These include the A.L.F.E. and S.T.E.E.P. nodes referred to earlier. Bringing these nodes to the mediating lens or up to each token directly will shape and shift different creative agendas for the team. When A.L.F.E. or S.T.E.E.P. nodes are clicked on they unfold allowing the team (or individuals) to enter or access any information they want to store or retrieve; words, images, video, sounds, and so forth (Figure 9). To place a node a user double clicks on the iCE mapping area and a node descriptor box appears allowing the individual team member to place a node title.

Specifying the Map

The specifics of each token (specific to the project) need to be written into the map. Each token is a repository for detail and information about that element or feature of the project. The primed map allows the team to plot the relevant information and, in a way, catalogue information in the spaces represented. For instance, what is known about a user can be stored in the user repository, information about the site in the site repository, and so on. The nodes are similarly loaded with information. In accessing information members of the team just need to select a node or token and click and scroll through information, holding and raising it to the map surface as needed.

The priming of the map also gives clues to the focus and form of the research that may be needed to give 'ground' to the project. The map gives the team a way of organizing what is known and what needs to be known at various stages of the project. It stimulates 'knowing' as a complex and rich activity, running in tandem with the ideational strategies, together making up the prospecting.

One may 'know' the element or token in different ways and contexts, for instance, if we consider the tri-partite relationship of the table in Figure

Figure 9. A populated map

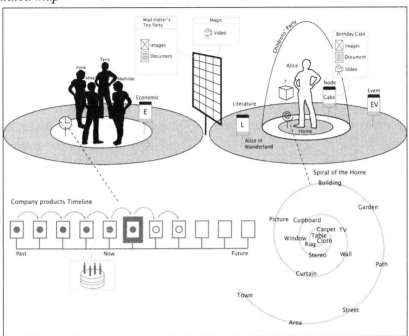

8. Possession and individual circumstance may be researched using personal or psychological profiling, object biographies, and personal histories. The tool, operator, and operating context may be researched through the study of anatomy, particularly postural analysis, the object through research foci like performance analysis and material testing. One may also understand the context through operational and system analysis. Similarly the other two sets of relationships would ask for different kinds of research; for row 3 on the table, discourse analysis, cultural readings, social survey, and so forth, and, for row 4 consumer profiling, market survey, trend analysis and so on. These may well be layered in the depth of the tokens and in the spaces of the map of a project.

The research conducted to look at, for example, the way a human form may ergonomically fit comfortably and be supported in a classroom chair will be different to the research done in understanding the way the culture of the class-room (and classrooms in different cultures) condition the use of the chair. It is clearly a far more rounded project to consider both. In addition, the chair designer may try and understand the chair from the teacher's perspective or the child's, or the education authority's, and so on. Through substituting different users a team will appreciate different requirements for the chair.

One of the ideational strategies the team may use is scenarios, where the real user is substituted for a fantasy user and a fantasy site. One may not know the 'object' to be designed or at least suspend knowing it in the new scenario. For example, the fantasy substitution may have been a result of placing 'children's literature' and/or 'magic' in the mediating lens and the team may lock onto the book Alice in Wonderland and decide to consider designing for Wonderland. The user may then be Alice and the site/situation, the place and occasion of the Mad Hatter's tea party. One would then need to know Alice and the circumstances of the tea party.

If 'Wonderland' was brought to the example of the classroom chair the team would be designing a new kind of object (not a chair perhaps) influenced by shifts in scale and the logic of nonsense given by the story. This would allow for a free play of the imagination. At some stage, the fantasy scenario could be contrasted with more prosaic interpretations of the brief to see what new ideas emerge.

Plottings: Innovating in Space and Time

Once the map is primed the team may wish to use the 'spacings' and 'timings' templates to help generate new thinking. These templates are pulled into the space of the map from the menu. The map will shift upward and the template will appear immediately below the primed map. Although, the menu will be pre-loaded with numerous thinking patterns, some described here, new patterns can be added. We envisage that there will be new patterns using space and/or time given the way these are stretched but others may emerge. The 'patterns' may be used to activate any, some, or all elements of the map. For example, the team may wish to build a temporal map of a company and all its products; first of all mapping its history and then using various 'beats' to gain notional futures. Likewise, we could map the changing user over time and even speculate about a future user. The plotting, in this case a timeline, will appear below the map. We can open and close multiple timelines in order to compare and contrast them, or, if they are used for different elements see how the different timelines work together.

The spatial patterns may also be selected from the menu and dropped into the map space. The tokens/elements may be copied to the pattern (which also holds with the timelines). Once a pattern has been used it is labeled with a titled icon and stored and accessed from a file where the explored patterns are stored.

Methods and Processes File

We are developing a reference of research methodologies and creative stratagems that may be accessed through the iCE software. We will list and place brief descriptions of the methodologies and stratagems in the file, while there will also be hyperlinks so that relevant urls may be accessed to inform the team further. A list of research methodologies are quoted in the section "Specifying the Map." These will be listed and described in a research methodology subfile. The notion of a fantasy scenario (e.g., the Mad Hatter's tea party) would be found in a file on creative processes and stratagems. The list of these methods and processes is there for referral but will also prompt different ideas about ways to activate the map.

Leaving Traces

One of the main aims of the iCE is to make visible the imagining/thinking of the team and, especially of individuals in the team. We are in some way critical of brainstorming because what is made visible is the suggestion thrown out and not what gives rise to them. The iCE not only tries to stimulate innovative thinking but importantly for team work provides a means of communicating the thinking. The iCE makes visible 'innovation trajectories' as 'strings' of connection on the map. The thinking of each individual on the team may be made visible to the others by stringing together the connections in their thinking through phases of the project. The strings may be traced from the individual's avatar in the context of production space and move into various spaces of the iCE and connect to different tokens and pattern templates. The path of the string is determined by the individual innovator looking for potential opportunities to connect aspects of the iCE to innovate (see Figure 10). The string might be a single strand or a multiple series of branches, but what is important is that when they end they form an

Figure 10. Innovation string and knot

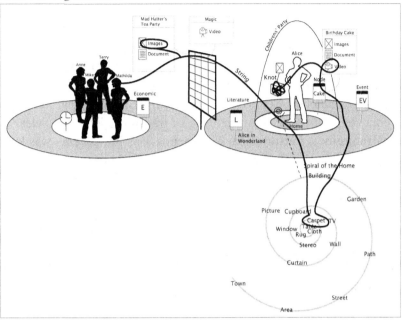

'innovation knot.' These knots hold the individual innovator's generative work, acting as a record of the ideas generated. Each innovation journey is expressed as a string and knot. Some strings pass through other knots to further develop particular ideas. A range of examples follow to illustrate a small number of the possible strings and journeys an innovation team might create. These examples are from a wide range of projects and have been simplified for the purpose of illustration. It is also worth emphasizing that the aim of the iCE is to remain adaptable to a wide range of approaches and will undoubtedly evolve in new ways through the course of its use.

Example 1. Children's Party

The first string example is drawn from a project that explored the context of the children's party to invent new objects. The string begins at the innovator's avatar, travels through the lens, where it connects with the poetic inspiration of 'The Mad Hatter's Tea Party.' It then travels to the site. In this example the site is the domestic home,

entering a spiral dynamic diagram that explores the various spaces and objects of the home. The string then passes through a cultural 'event' node in the situation space within the context of consumption, which is labeled 'your experiences of children's' parties. This holds all of the participant's experiences of the children's party in images, words and film, and some children's first hand experiences as interviews. The string then passes back to the object space where it forms an innovation knot. The string draws on a particular feature of the research in the 'event' node that children are obsessed with fair measurement of cake and sweets, and therefore the objects that were developed focused on measurement whilst being inspired by the fantasy of the Mad Hatter's Tea Party.

Example 2. Back Casting Future Technologies

The second example of an innovation string is from a project exploring the future of domestic cleaning. The string again begins at the innovator's avatar and moves directly to a timeline that grew out of the 'object space' in the context of consumption. This timeline showed the progressive history of devices and technologies used for domestic cleaning, from brushes to current vacuum cleaners, and then projected into the long-term future, researching nanotechnology where nanobots would deep clean your home on a constant basis. From this seemingly fantastical future the string travels back towards the current vacuum cleaner, back casting to identify intermediary phases of development, asking the question what would have to happen between now and this long term future. What are the intermediary steps? The string forms a knot at this intermediate point on the time line where the innovator generated concepts around ultrasonic cleaning technology. Further strings moved from the timeline into the site and situation spaces to project possible applications and concepts for these new objects.

Example 3. An Office Tent

This example is of a project to design an office space for an architect, a space for working together with clients to explore, generate, and reflect on ideas. The string moves from the avatar to the lens which holds some ideas about playfulness and a poem about the wonders of the circus. It then passes into the context of use: situation/event space, identifying the activities of generating ideas and meetings. The string then moves to the object space where it breaks into a spiral dynamic of the office space, starting with the architect's sketchbook. A parallel inspirational situation/event space has been made of the circus which is projected below the main iCE. A spiral dynamic exploring the space and objects of the circus is grown out of this inspirational situation space. The two spirals, one of the office and the other of the circus, are shown side by side. The string passes from the big top tent in the circus to the meeting room in the office spiral forming a knot between the two spaces. Within the knot is the

concept of a tent meeting room, developed in an effort to capture some of the magic and theatre of the circus in the office.

Example 4. Social influence

In exploring the social and environmental trends of transportation it was clear that lowering the emissions in new cars was key to a sustainable future. The string in this example passes from an S.T.E.E.P political node within the context of production, through an ecological and ethical manifesto in the lens through to the object space in the context of consumption. The object node in this case represented transportation and had a timeline attached and opened below the main iCE. The timeline explored the development of the car from its invention, through to safety developments into efficiency, and then as a future prospect where the innovation knot lay. This knot holds ideas about the environmentally sensitive automobile as a logical progression of the timeline. This logical progression could be described as a natural step in the evolution of the car. Drawn out of the knot was another string that knotted again, but this time it suggested a public transport system in a future where no cars featured. This is a complete radical shift from the pulse of the car timeline.

The Active Map and Evaluating Ideas

We are proposing an evaluation space in the complete software version. This is the most under-developed space of the iCE to date. We recognize evaluation of ideas as a significant activity in innovation, and hence it will be an important feature of the iCE. A space to pick up and evaluate the different strings and knots that will have been developed in the projects will be implemented. Teams and other parties with vested interests would use the evaluation space of the iCE to set out strategies for weighing up ideas and working out the next phases of implementing or realizing them. The evaluation space will be explored in the next phase of the development of the iCE.

CONCLUSION

The aim of the iCE project is to produce a virtual interactive coinnovation environment (iCE) for organizations to support group, team and individual thinking in developing innovation projects. The iCE aims to provide prompts for team building and aims to provide participants with a set of referents: thinking types, patterns for prospects and a map of practice(s) to enable them to share and participate in processes of innovative thinking. It also will provide a prop, an axiological tool, for evaluating ideas. The archive space will also provide a space to record processes and house the research findings that lay ground to a project and may be useful in other projects.

What is described in this chapter is the conceptual underpinnings, the aims and to some extent the design of this environment. The iCE is still under construction, so we haven't yet had the opportunity to evaluate it in use. We have used the various tools, the plottings and mapping, with our students and in workshops with various organizations in 'actual' space. Here, it has been greeted positively. It has helped students generate and communicate their ideas and reflect on their processes (across a range of design disciplines including graphics, product, system, and service design). The workshops have had success with various organizations, helping with new product development, marketing and branding. We also believe the ideational tools can be applied to designing management systems—although to date this hasn't been tested.

The iCE will create opportunities in practice that may not yet be considered in a particular organization; obviously, new innovatory processes, shaping teams in various ways (the inclusion of different stakeholders into the innovatory process), setting new ways of placing targets for projects

and so on. The tools may be consciously applied to reshaping an organization, but we also believe the iCE by merely being there will have a positive effect on the practices and shape of an organization as a whole. The concomitance of such a resource may lead to a re-consideration of the enterprise of the organization and stimulate a change in its practices generally as well as specifically.

REFERENCES

Bachelard, G. (1983). *Water and dreams*. Dallas, TX: The Dallas Institute Publications.

Bono, De E. (1990). *Six thinking hats*. London: Penguin.

Certeau, De M. (2002). *The practice of everyday life*. Berkeley: California University Press.

Design Council. (2006). *Encouraging creativity*. Retrieved November 30, 2006, from http://www.designcouncil.org.uk/ (Public Sector link).

Ehrenzweig, A. (1971). *The hidden order of art*. Berkeley: University of California Press.

Einstein. A. (1949). Autobiographical notes. Retrieved November 15, 2006, from http://www.alberteinstein.info/manuscripts

Jones, J. C. (1992). *Design methods*. London: John Wiley & Sons.

Rosenberg, T. E. (2000, July). The *Reservoir: Towards a poetic model of research in design*. Research into Practice Conference. Hatfield, UK. Retrieved November 15, 2006, from http://www.herts.ac.uk/artdes1/research/papers/wpades/vol1/rosenberg2.html

Stamm, Von B. (2003). *Managing innovation, design and creativity*. Chichester, West Sussex: John Wiley & Sons.

ENDNOTES

[1] As a note, lateral thinking uses a spatial side-step to gain a new purchase on a problem. Combinatory thinking makes connections across spaces; its operational processes may include the paradigm and syntagm shifts described, or indeed what we have conceived as a folded spiral dynamic. The temporalizing and spatializing of thinking, as is evidenced, has allowed us to conceive more sophisticated and more finely conceived thinking models than the rather generic descriptions of linear, lateral, and combinatory thought. Although, perhaps, the different thinking patterns we are describing may be bracketed in these categories.

[2] See Belbin® Team Role Profiling Options at http://www.btinternet.com/~cert/belbin_profiling_options.htm and Belbin® Team Role information site http://www.belbin.info/

[3] A decision making tool devised by de Bono to look at things from different perspectives. The six hats represent six attitudes to thinking. For example white hat thinking deals with facts whereas red hat is emotional. The other hats represent other thinking attitudes. The hats are intended to be passed round so that individuals in the team may shift and change their viewpoint.

[4] We have thought of categories of influence based on, 'shapers,' 'shifters,' 'motivatiors,' and 'directors'.

Chapter XV
A Virtual Environment to Support the Distributed Design of Large Made–to–Order Products

Robert Ian Whitfield
CAD Centre, University of Strathclyde, UK

Alex H.B. Duffy
CAD Centre, University of Strathclyde, UK

Alastair Conway
CAD Centre, University of Strathclyde, UK

Zhichao Wu
CAD Centre, University of Strathclyde, UK

Joanne Meehan
CAD Centre, University of Strathclyde, UK

ABSTRACT

An overview of a virtual design environment (virtual platform) developed as part of the European Commission funded VRShips-ROPAX (VRS) project is presented. The main objectives for the development of the virtual platform are described, followed by the discussion of the techniques chosen to address the objectives, and finally a description of a use-case for the platform. Whilst the focus of the VRS virtual platform was to facilitate the design of ROPAX (roll-on passengers and cargo) vessels, the components within the platform are entirely generic and may be applied to the distributed design of any type of vessel, or other complex made-to-order products.

INTRODUCTION

Despite being faced with a situation where computers were generally being used for the processing of data, Mann and Coons identified the possibility of using computers as "partners in the creative process" to facilitate the hypothesis exploration process and consequently produce an escalation of "scientific creativity" (Mann & Coons, 1965). They stated:

It is clear that what is needed if the computer is to be of greater use in the creative process, is a more intimate and continuous interchange between man and machine. This interchange must be of such a nature that all forms of thought that are congenial to man, whether verbal, symbolic, numerical, or even graphical are also understood by the machine and are acted upon by the machine in ways that are appropriate to man's purpose. (Mann & Coons, 1965, p. 3)

To achieve Mann and Coons' vision requires a fundamental understanding of the creative process as well as being able to develop computer tools to attain human and computer symbiosis.

Whilst the vision of a shared understanding between man and machine of all forms of thought has not yet been realised, Cummings discussed the degree to which automation (provided by intelligent decision support systems) could be introduced within the decision process, indicating where computers may be utilised in facilitating this shared understanding (Cummings, 2004). Cummings cites Fitts' list (Chapanis et al., 1951) as representing the respective strengths of humans and computers within the decision making process. Humans are regarded as being better at: perceiving patterns, improvising and using flexible procedures, recalling relevant facts, reasoning inductively, and exercising judgement, whereas computers are regarded as being better at: responding quickly to control tasks, repetitive and routine tasks, reasoning deductively, and

handling many complex tasks simultaneously (Chapanis et al., 1951).

Despite not being included within Fitts' list, Cummings acknowledges an increasing need for the use of computational decision support to help humans navigate complex decision problems.

The CAD Centre was established in 1986 as a research and postgraduate unit within the Department of Design Manufacture and Engineering Management at the University of Strathclyde. The aims of the Centre are to develop the computing technology to support a creative design partnership between man and machine, and to deliver the underlying technology, techniques, and approaches to industry. To achieve these aims, the CAD Centre has evolved research education and technology transfer programmes.

This paper briefly discusses one of the initial visions of the CAD Centre: the intelligent design assistant (IDA) which addresses both the views of Mann and Coons whilst considering how to leverage the benefits of both human and computer within this partnership. The third section discusses how the IDA vision has been realised within a virtual design environment that provides management support for the life-phase design of ships—the VRS virtual platform. The development challenges are discussed within the fourth section, and it's use within the context of the design of a ROPAX vessel is described within the fifth section.

THE INTELLIGENT DESIGN ASSISTANT PHILOSOPHY

A characterisation of Mann and Coons' design assistance philosophy is that of the intelligent design assistant. Figure 1 illustrates some key complementary roles that a designer and an IDA are proposed to play within the scenario of intelligent CAD.

In this scenario, designers are initiators of a discourse; they retain authority and control over

Figure 1. Intelligent design assistant (Copyright University of Strathclyde)

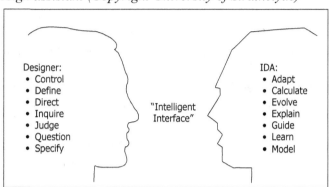

the progress of the interaction with the IDA, and have ultimate responsibility for the correctness of results. They are able to express the nature of the problem, to describe concepts to be explored, and to justify their judgements. In addition, they hypothesise, refer to past experience, and apply a range of modeling tools. In contrast, the IDA is the active partner to the designer. It is a source of design expertise and past experience that complements a designer's memory. It is able to develop an understanding of a problem and description of concepts, assess the feasibility of concepts, identify the implications of concept changes, suggest possible solution paths, and can assume much of the burden of mundane and repetitive analysis tasks. The strengths indicated within Fitts' list of the human are represented within the designer: perceiving patterns to express the nature of the problem; recalling relevant facts to describe concepts to be explored; and exercising judgement and reasoning inductively to justify their judgements. The strengths of the computer are represented within the IDA: reasoning deductively to identify the implications of concept changes; responding quickly to control tasks to suggest possible solution paths; and assuming the burden of repetitive and mundane analysis tasks.

Various implementations of aspects of the IDA vision have been produced that represent different combinations of interactions between the designer and the IDA (Zhang et al., 1997; Yan et al., 2002; Guan et al., 1997; Manfaat, 1998). These implementations have in general had specific applications for the focus of interaction between the designer and the IDA. The IDA vision has been implemented within a virtual design environment that provides management support for the life-phase design of ships—the VRS virtual platform. Whilst the focus for implementation of this platform was ship design, the platform has however been developed to be applicable to any domain where the management of complexity is an issue such as design within the made-to-order sector. The issue of complexity within the coordination of distributed design for example has been considered by Duffy, to consist of complexity of the following elements: the artefact being designed, the design activity itself, the actors involved, the design decision making process, the considerations impinging on design, and the knowledge and sources used and generated (Duffy, 1995). The VRS virtual platform aims to provide some level of support for all of these different types of complexity.

VRSHIPS-ROPAX (VRS) AND THE VRS VIRTUAL PLATFORM

VRShips-ROPAX (VRS) was a pan European maritime project funded under the 'competitive and sustainable growth' theme of the 5th framework in European research. The strategic objective of VRS was to integrate information technology into the life cycle of a product, to sustain competitiveness through improving knowledge and technological skills, thus, following the previously successful pattern of other European industries (e.g., aerospace industry). The project focused upon integrating current effort dispersed throughout Europe to provide a standardised platform upon which a variety of maritime industries could function. Its aim was to support European maritime industries to:

- Maintain and improve their position against worldwide competition by improving their knowledge and technological skills.
- Combine competitiveness/profitability with safety and environmental protection.
- Look at technology and innovation as the main way to survive in the global international market.

The project was based on an industry partnership of 36 different groups within 34 different organisations from academic institutes, marine consultancies, marine research organisations, naval architects, ship builders and operators, port authorities, and a standards organisation. Thus, the constituency supported and represented the requirements of the European maritime spectrum. The two main deliverables were a 'generic virtual platform' and a 'ship platform of critical technologies.'

Whilst the focus here is towards the virtual platform, it is worth briefly mentioning the ship platform. A number of demanding and conflicting requirements were established for the design of the ship platform. Whilst the requirements were not as extensive as would be expected from a shipowner, the requirements were chosen to push the boundaries of conventional ROPAX vessel design, with the resulting design representing an innovative leap. One aim within the VRShips-ROPAX project was to use conventional design tools to

generate a design that satisfied the requirements, and subsequently repeat the process using the same tools within the context of the virtual platform to compare both the process of creating the design, and the design itself. The requirements for the design were: 2000 passengers, 400 cabins, 1.5 kilometres of vehicle lanes, 2000 nautical mile range, and 38 knot service speed. Individually, these requirements do not represent a difficult design problem; however the combination of passengers, cabins and vehicle lanes (which would normally result with a conventional hull shape), and the service speed (which would normally result with a slender hull shape—typically seen within warships) presented a situation where creativity was needed in order satisfy all requirements.

As well as providing a comparison between the conventional design approach and the integrated design approach, the design would be used to produce a $^1/_{20}$ scale model of the ROPAX vessel for testing, evaluation and comparison with the computational models used to simulate the performance, as well as to allow the testing of ship critical technologies, such as different propulsion systems for example.

VRS Project Structure

In order to understand the challenges associated with the development of the VRS virtual platform it is necessary to provide an overview of the individual components of the platform and how they fit together.

Platform Overview

The approach adopted within the design of the virtual platform was to carry out an iterative process of development, test, implementation, and evaluation leading towards the production of a complete virtual platform. The platform consisted of: tools and techniques to facilitate integration, a common model database for the storage of ship-product data, a "virtual" interface to the platform, the product and the process, an inference engine for the management of data dependency information, a process control tool for the co-ordination of process, activities and resources, and a "simulation engine" representing the design and simulation tools being integrated. The relationships between the components of the virtual platform can be seen within Figure 2.

"Wrapping" was required for existing and new design and simulation tools in order to interface with the integration framework and cater for platform (hardware and software) independence. A common model containing consistent ship product data was developed to capture the main knowledge, information and geometry of the virtual ship. The interaction between the tools, their local models, and the common model was managed through version control, consistency/constraint based management, and conflict resolution techniques. The application of life-phases process knowledge/approaches upon the virtual model was investigated through the development of a process control tool, which provides a means

to control and evaluate the "behaviour" of the integrated platform as well as providing support for the life-phases of a ship. The interaction with the platform was realised through a virtual environment, which concentrates upon techniques and approaches to develop real time, virtual interaction. The performance data generated from the simulation engine tools was analysed to provide a means to determine and optimise the overall performance and uncertainty of the virtual ship. Since the performance-modeling tool is not fundamental to the operation of the platform, further discussion of the development of the tool is omitted. All development within the project was generic in nature (other than the ship product data within the common model, and the knowledge within the simulation engine) so that the results can be applied to any industrial domain or discipline. The virtual platform therefore enables extensive simulations, real time virtual interactions, performance analysis, and life-phase support to be undertaken irrespective of the application domain or ship type.

Figure 2. VRS virtual platform components (Copyright University of Strathclyde)

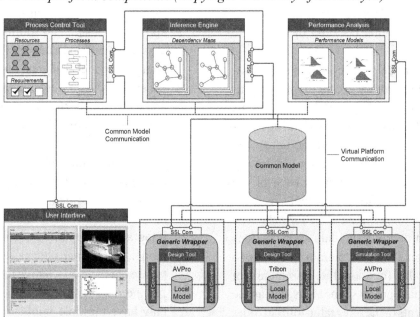

Virtual Platform Objectives

The functionality and objectives of the main components within the VRS virtual platform were as follows:

- **Integration:** The integration aim was to deliver a strategy and architecture to guide the integration activities of the common model, virtual interaction, inference engine, process modeling and control, simulation engine and performance analysis, and reliability components. The main objective of the integration framework is therefore to deliver a flexible protocol and communication mechanism that enables these disparate systems to integrate and coordinate their functionality. To achieve these objectives consideration therefore needs to be given to the platforms and programming languages that both the individual platform components and the integrated design and simulation tools use with the aim of developing a specification for the integration that was platform and programming language independent. Since the platform is distributed, consideration needs to be made to ensure efficient and effective communication of design information between the disparate entities.

- **Common model:** The common model is a database that provides a consistent representation of the data defining the ship systems (ship product model) and external environment (sea state, routes, port facilities), and holds the basic (and common) geometry and information required by each of the integrated simulation engine tools irrespective of the tools' native data formats. The aim when defining the data specifications and schemas for the common model is to consider the functional requirements of the life-phase process models as well as the requirements of the integrated tools in order

to ensure that the common model supports the design requirements of the user, as well as facilitating data transfer within simulation and real-time rendering programs developed within the virtual interaction component for example. Cover for the whole lifecycle of the vessel should be provided, from initial design to disposal; hence the data contained within it should be applicable across life-phases.

- **Virtual interaction:** The common model allows distributed manipulation of the ship product model as well as enabling the virtual environment by allowing the development of the product model using the tools within the simulation engine. The virtual environment is the interface that the users utilise in order to interact with the virtual platform. Since the project was EU funded, the partners and hence users of the platform were distributed across Europe. Providing access to the platform via the virtual interaction component however should be extendable such that it may be implemented either within an organisation, across stakeholder organisations, across partner organisations within Europe, or globally. The virtual environment should provide functionality to enable: multiple users, configuration and use of design and simulation tools, access to the common model, visualisation of common model contents, querying of data consistency status, enactment of processes, and use of the performance modeling tool.

- **Inference engine:** The virtual environment enables users to communicate and share product data and information through the ability to remotely access, query and modify the data contained within the common model. The design or simulation tools being integrated commonly have their own local model, represented either as local files or databases in their own native formats. Changing the data within one tool's local model may have multiple implications or effects on other tools' models. The main objective of the inference engine is to maintain the consistency between these various models through the management of change propagation and conflict resolution between multiple users irrespective of the native formats that the individual design and simulation tools use. The inference engine must manage: dynamic modification to common and local model data, the propagation of changes made to either common or local data throughout the data dependency network, the variation in information requirements, a mapping of the dependencies and relationships between data within the common model, and consistency management and conflict resolution.

- **Process modeling and control:** The process control tool is a planning and enactment environment for the coordination of activities within life-phase process models. This process control tool is used to define an initial sequence of activities, to determine an optimum process schedule, to manage the enactment of the tools within the virtual platform, and to manage the processes under real-time conditions. Since the main objective of the process control tool is to demonstrate how distributed activities within a virtual platform can be managed and coordinated, there is also a requirement that the process control tool manages the resources that are capable of performing the activities, as well as coordinating when and why they should be undertaken.

- **Simulation engine:** The simulation engine represents the integrated design and simulation tools within the virtual platform. These tools enable the design of the hull, general arrangement, propulsion plant, subsystems, and simulation of the operating environment, operations, supply chain, and production. The simulation engine is capable of allowing a through life assessment, ranging from

concept development to performance trials and operational scenarios. The tools are "wrapped" in order to enable communication with the rest of the virtual platform.

DEVELOPMENT OF THE VRS VIRTUAL PLATFORM

This section describes the components that combine to make the virtual platform. A prototype virtual platform was developed in order to determine the most appropriate technologies, to establish the mode of operation of the platform with respect to usability, and determine any shortcomings of the technologies used. Each subsection describes the results from the prototype development where applicable along with the lessons learned from the prototype in order to develop the next stage of the virtual platform.

Integration Component

Rather than focus on the development of the communication mechanism and protocols, the prototype integration component focussed towards the use of an existing adapter to manage the operation of the design and simulation tools within the simulation engine. The design and simulation tools were distributed across a network with each tool individually managed by an adapter. The tools were mapped directly to activities within the process control tool, hence when a process was due to be undertaken, the process control tool would communicate with the appropriate adapter for the mapped activity to start the tool. The mapping of an activity to a tool limited the tool's application to single activities whereas a number of the tools were capable of performing many design activities. The adapter was only capable of managing the start and completion of the tool, and provided no functionality to access the common model for example, and therefore restricted the overall integrated functionality of the platform. A bespoke wrapper was later developed specifically designed to address the integrated management of the design and simulation tools. From the perspective of Fitts' list, the integration framework aimed to respond quickly to integration control tasks. These integration control tasks may for example be the process control tool allocating a conceptual design activity to a designer with the integration component providing a quick response between process control tool and designer. The prototype integration framework did however enable three key requirements to be identified with respect to the communication of data between the components:

- **Message security:** Secure socket layer (SSL) communication should be implemented to utilise public/private key encryption, source authentication and data integrity for the transfer of data between virtual platform components.

Figure 3. XML-RPC functional protocol (Copyright University of Strathclyde)

```
<?xml version="1.0" encoding="UTF-8"?>
<VRSMethod>
    <sender>Sender</sender>
    <receiver>Receiver</receiver>
    <functionName>FunctionName</functionName>
    <params>
        <param>
            <title>Title1</title>
            <value>
                <string>String</string>
            </value>
        </param>
        <param>
            <title>Title2</title>
            <value>
                <struct>
                    <member>
                        <name>Name21</name>
                        <value>
                            <int>42</int>
                        </value>
                    </member>
                    <member>
                        <name>Name22</name>
                        <value>
                            <double>3.14159</double>
                        </value>
                    </member>
                </struct>
            </value>
        </param>
    </params>
</VRSMethod>
```

- **XML message format:** XML should be used as the underlying language for communication of data between virtual platform components due to its inherent extensibility and support throughout the IT community.
- **Message Validation:** XML schemas should be used to automatically check that the messages received by any of the virtual platform components conform to a defined standard.

Existing and well-established integration technologies such as the common object request brokerage architecture (CORBA) were considered for the development of the integration framework. Within this context however, CORBA would have been implemented to facilitate the transfer of objects between the tools to be integrated, rather than enabling the insertion of the tools within the integrated platform.

The aim of the integration framework was to create an open architecture that would enable new simulation engine tools to be easily integrated into the platform with a minimum of development to the tool provider (and modification to the platform) when they become available. In order to achieve this, consideration was given for the types of data to be communicated between the virtual platform components, the frequency of communication, and the type of communication (synchronous/asynchronous) when designing the protocol and communication mechanism. A functional protocol was defined based upon the remote procedure call specification of XML (XML-RPC), unifying all of the protocols within the virtual platform into a single "generic" communication protocol—Figure 3. The protocol has elements to indicate the "sender" and "receiver" components in order that the receiver can check that it is a valid functional request from a valid sending component. The "functionName" element within the protocol is used to define the function (that is mapped to some functionality that the receiving component will perform) using the information contained within the "params" element.

An example of the use of the protocol would be a request from the generic wrapper to the inference engine to perform a status check on a piece of data before modification. A mapping would exist between the requested function and functionality encoded within the inference engine. Any number of parameters may be included within the protocol to enable the enactment of the function by the receiver. Both the sending and receiving components must agree in advance to the structure of the parameters; however the protocol is entirely neutral to the programming languages and the structure of the objects that are used by each component to represent the data.

Software was developed to enable the secure sending and receiving of XML-based communication between virtual platform components. An application programme interface (API) was designed within the software to enable it to be integrated within each of the necessary components within Figure 2. Due to the dynamic nature of the communication within the virtual platform, it is difficult to predict when each component will be required to process communication, or whether the component will be sending and receiving multiple simultaneous communications. The communication software was therefore developed using a multithreaded architecture to queue and sequentially process out-going communication, whilst allowing simultaneous prioritised processing of incoming communication.

Common Model

The common model is a repository for the data that is used by the design and simulation tools as well as for the storage of virtual platform coordination and management data from the inference engine (dependency maps), process control tool (process models) and the performance analysis, and reliability tool (performance models). Three issues required consideration within the design of the common model: storage (how to store the data), structure (how to format the data), and coverage (what data to store). Since the common model, may in principle be used to store and manage large amounts of complex data, to be interactively viewed, added to and modified by a number of distributed users, the common model component addresses Fitts' issue of handling many complex tasks simultaneously.

These issues are however related since the selection of the storage mechanism depends upon the structure of the data to be stored (binary, XML, object-oriented). In addition, the structure of the data is influenced by the requirements of the tools to be integrated as well as the requirements of the users of the platform, and therefore influences and is influenced by the coverage. The current practices and standards used in formatting and structuring engineering data were investigated, including the initial graphical exchange specification (IGES) and the standard for the exchange of product model data (STEP—ISO 10303), and the amount of data to be modeled (complete product information models for ships have been estimated by Catley to be of the order of between two and ten Gigabytes of data (Catley, 1999)). Considerable effort has been thrust towards the development of ISO 10303 STEP application protocols (APs) for ship arrangements (AP215) (2004a), ship moulded forms (AP216) (2003), ship structures (AP218) (2004b), ship mechanical systems (AP226 which has since been withdrawn), and Piping (AP227) (2001)—Grau (1999). A number of occasions have arisen however when attempts have been made to adhere to these APs with the result that "flavours" of the standard have been required in order to utilise the structured, well-defined and standardised data within the legacy applications (Whitfield, 2003a). The focus when defining the coverage of the common model was therefore directed towards "the minimum amount of information that would enable the integrated tools to share an accurate representation of the product." ISO 10303 Part 203 is used to define the 3D design of mechanical parts and was used within the common model as the basis upon which to define the geometry of any aspect of the ship product model. The selection of Part 203 also influenced the structure of the data to be contained within the common model.

Conversion of data to and from the common to native formats was also a significant issue that needed to be addressed, which would influence the structure of the data within the common model as well as how easily and successfully design and simulation tools could be integrated within the virtual platform. Having chosen to base the geometrical data within the common model on Part 203, the focus was then to complete the definition of the structure of the data, through the selection of an appropriate language that would facilitate conversion. EXPRESS (ISO 10303 Part 11 and 12) was developed as a language for the definition of STEP data. Major shortcomings of the EXPRESS reference language from a conversion viewpoint were that it was difficult to decompose EXPRESS-based models into more manageable chunks, and it was difficult for a human to interpret what the data within an EXPRESS file represented. Whilst human readability is not an issue during the process of converting data, it is certainly useful if the conversion algorithm developer can understand the concepts that are being converted whilst producing the algorithms. Attempts to undertake the conversion between formats have in the past faced difficulties due to the complexity and formatting of the data, and have in certain cases required a degree of human interaction (Rando, 2001). Research had been successfully conducted to produce a binding between STEP and XML (ISO 10303 Part 28) and has been applied within the shipbuilding industry (Rando, 2001) with the aim of facilitating the conversion process between the neutral STEP format and the native tool format. It was therefore concluded that an XML mapping of STEP data provided the most appropriate language upon which to base the storage of all data within the VRS platform due

to its extensible nature, support for conversion, and the increasing support within the IT industry. Choosing to manage the data within the common model using XML, facilitated the selection of a storage mechanism.

The XML:DB initiative provides standardisation for the development of specifications for the querying, manipulation and management of data stored within XML databases. This initiative enabled the database to be de-coupled from the rest of the virtual platform, such that the database may be exchanged with alternative XML databases without impacting any of the software that communicates with the database. Documents are then managed within the database in hierarchical collections, similar to the directories within a file system.

Virtual Interaction

The virtual environment represents the "window" to the VRS virtual platform. It is intended to provide functionality to enable communication between, and use by multiple users, configuration and use of design and simulation tools, access to the common model, visualisation of common model contents, querying of data consistency status, enactment of processes, and use of the performance modeling tool. The focus during the development of the prototype virtual environment was towards the production of an open architecture that would enable the configuration and remote use of design and simulation tools, and the visualisation of common model contents. A number of the design and simulation tools to be integrated into the platform had the ability to visually display the data in their local models whilst the user was operating the tool. Rather than developing and producing a new visualisation of the common model data within the virtual environment, the prototype environment initially attempted to enable the user interfaces of the remotely distributed tools to be exported to the virtual environment via the Internet using virtual network computing (VNC) software. VNC enables the viewing and interaction of the desktop of a remote machine within a window of the local machine. The use of this approach meant that design and simulation tools could be "hosted" on remote machines, providing the facility for users to log onto the machine through the virtual environment and interact with the tool whenever required. New tools could be registered and integrated within the platform, and the functionality and visualisation aspects of the tools, utilised irrespective of where either the tool or user were geographically located, and without the need to generate any code to enable this integration—Figure 4. The display of one of these remote machines could in principal be exported to a number of other machines, facilitating the collaborative work of multiple users on the same design problem using the same design or simulation tools.

The network bandwidth required to support this seamless visualisation of remote tools was however demonstrated to be in excess of the bandwidth that was available. Various optimisation algorithms were used within the VNC software in order to reduce the amount of data transferred by sending regions of the display that were changing and by limiting the number of colours that are repainted on the client display. Where this may have been adequate for design situations, where the display does not generally rapidly change, within a simulation situation, it was apparent that the network bandwidth could not support the refresh rates that were required for a smooth transition between frames.

Whilst there is currently VNC software available to support the secure communication of the encoded visualisation data, the security issues relating to the fact that the user has access to the entire desktop of the remote machine were considered to be unsatisfactory. The approach also raised issues relating to licensing of software—not only that used within the platform, but of all other tools available on the desktop of the remote machine, since tools would be available to all partners regardless of whether the user or partner has bought a license for it.

The virtual environment was therefore developed to enable tools that each individual user has available to them locally, to be used within the virtual platform, and for these tools to be available to the users that have registered the tool and not throughout the platform. This change in

Figure 4. Remote export of visualization (Copyright University of Strathclyde)

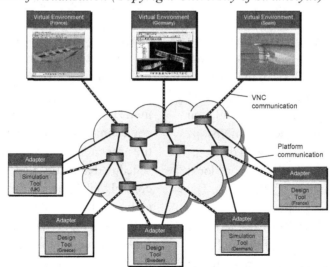

operation and use of the design and simulation tools, had a significant impact on the rest of the platform: the virtual environment was developed to support the use of the tool to perform particular activities rather than as a means for distributed visualisation and collaboration, which impacted the process control tool with respect to the management of the users and the activities that they can perform, and not the tools that they use to perform them with.

The virtual interaction environment was developed to allow the user to log onto the platform, through interaction with the process control tool. Support was provided to integrate design and simulation tools into the virtual platform through the use of the generic wrapper configuration element. Textual communication between users of the platform was provided, as well as interaction with the inference engine and process control tool to determine the consistency status of data within the dependency maps and start processes for example. Distributed collaborative design was thus facilitated by the virtual interaction component and through the provision of interfaces to each of the individual components of the virtual platform provided an "intelligent interface" between the designer and the platform in a similar manner as that depicted within Figure 1.

Inference Engine

The aim of the inference engine is to manage and maintain the consistency of the data within the common model through analysis of the relationships between the data. Data that resides within the local models of the design and simulation tools have inherent dependency relationships with the models of other tools and with the common model. Modifying the data within one local model may impact the models of other tools. The inference engine manages these relationships and ensures consistency between the tools by tracking the data usage of each of the tools and activities that are configured for integration into the virtual platform. Since the virtual platform enables multiple users to simultaneously conduct design and simulation activities, the inference engine also controls data access.

The inference engine automatically creates data dependency maps representing the relationships between data within the common and local models—Figure 5. The inference engine does not store any information relating to the values of the data items—it is only concerned with the state of the data. Data items within the inference engine are modelled in a hierarchical level representing the hierarchical structure of the data within the common and local models and may therefore also be used to represent different levels of abstraction. This hierarchical structure does not however contain any relationships across hierarchies to represent that a change in one piece of data (the hull-form) may affect another piece of data (the sea-keeping of the vessel). Relationships across hierarchies may be established either manually via the virtual environment or the inference engine, or automatically during tool integration. When a design or simulation tool is configured within the virtual platform, the tool's configuration contains information relating to the local and common data that will be used as input and output to the tool. The inference engine uses this configuration information to create a relationship between the input and output data that is used as input. In this way, a network of relationships representing a data dependency map may be created automatically.

The inference engine has two modes of operation: an active mode through automatic interaction with the generic wrapper, and a passive mode through manual interaction via the virtual environment. The active mode is used whenever the user chooses to start an activity that has been scheduled and allocated to them via the process control tool. Functionality is provided within the active mode: for checking the status of the required data before the activity is started to determine if it is already locked for use by another user, locking the data if it is not already locked, automatically

Figure 5. Inference engine: Server side (Copyright University of Strathclyde)

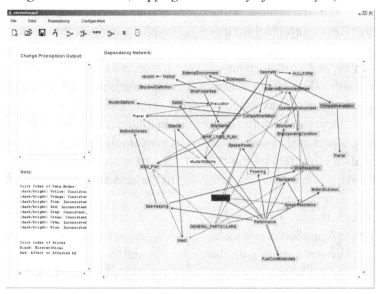

notifying other users of the change of the lock status of data that they may wish to use, and the management of potential conflicts that may arise as a result of multiple users modifying separate but related pieces of data.

The inference engine also provides passive functionality, acting as a server and interacting with the virtual environment to enable the users to query the locked or working status of data, facilitate co-operation between users operating on related pieces of data to avoid conflicts, attach notification triggers to data to inform the user when the state of the data changes, as well as modification of the data dependency network.

Process Control Tool

The prototype process control tool was developed to manage and enact processes through the communication with the adapters developed within the integration work package in order to start a design tool whenever a hull-form design activity requires enactment for example. Processes within the prototype process control tool consisted of activities that were directly mapped to tools that

were capable of performing the activity. Due to tool management limitations of the adapter, it was not possible to provide any additional information to the tool regarding the rationale for undertaking the activity. In addition, each tool that was integrated within the virtual platform was mapped to an activity within a process of the process controller. From a process perspective; the tool could only be used to perform a single activity, whereas in reality a number of the tools were capable of performing a number of different activities. The prototype process control tool also had no formalised modeling of the capability of the resources that were logged onto a platform.

A resource model was created within the process control tool to enable the management of user information and enable them to log onto the virtual platform using the virtual environment in order to be allocated design activities—Figure 6. Resources were modelled within the process control tool as having capability (the measured ability to perform an activity), and commitments (information related to which activities they are currently undertaking, and have undertaken in the past). Information is also modelled with respect to the resource's IP address, as well as other contact details. Within the context of the virtual platform, the process control tool regards a resource as being an autonomous agent capable of performing an activity, and as such manages either human or computational resources. Whenever a tool is integrated, the user is expected to define the activity that they will perform with the tool. This mapping is provided as part of the configuration information of the tool within the virtual environment and not in the process control tool. Processes can therefore be managed and coordinated incorporating activities at any level of abstraction. Once the configuration is complete, the virtual environment communicates with the process control tool to update the resource's details with information regarding this additional capability.

The process control tool can manage and enact simultaneous processes consisting of any number of interconnected activities—Figure 7. Since the process controller is capable of managing and enacting multiple processes simultaneously, in terms of activity allocation to resources, it addresses a number of strengths within Fitts' list: responding quickly to control tasks, repetitive and routine tasks, and handling many complex tasks simultaneously. The activities (and the process control tool) were developed using object-oriented design procedures and are therefore not limited to the activity types defined below:

- **Start activity:** The process control tool uses the start activity to determine the starting point for the process as well as the activities that follow. Each process has exactly one start activity that is included within each process by default and cannot be removed.

Figure 6. Process controller: Resource model view (Copyright University of Strathclyde)

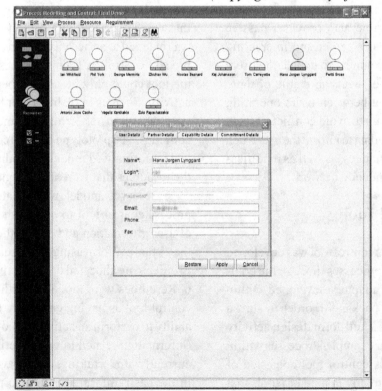

- **Design activity:** The design activity is used to define the nature of any activity that would be allocated to a resource. Additional information is provided to the resource regarding a description of the activity, as well as an optional list of requirements that the resource will be expected to check to determine whether they have been satisfied once the design activity has been completed.

- **Process activities:** The process control activities can be embedded within processes to change the state (start, stop, pause, continue) of any of the other processes.

- **AND activity:** Each of the activities defined above can only have one connection either leading into or out of the activity. The AND activity enables multiple activities to be conducted in parallel by dividing the flow within the process, or waiting for multiple activities to be completed by joining the flow within the process.

- **OR activity:** The OR activity is used in conjunction with a conditional activity, to indicate that the process flow will continue when any of the preceding activities are completed.

- **XOR activity:** The process control tool can manage conditions that return a logical (true/false) result to indicate whether the condition has been satisfied such as the requirement for example which has its status set by a resource when it is associated with a design activity. The XOR activity checks the status of the condition that has been used to define it, and directs the process flow on the basis of the outcome. Conditional connections

Figure 7. Process controller: Process view (Copyright University of Strathclyde)

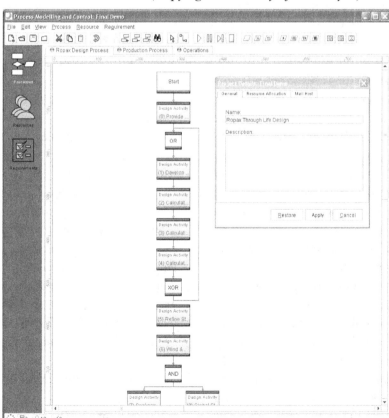

313

are used to connect the XOR conditional activity to other activities, to indicate the process flow that would be undertaken for each outcome.

Two approaches are available to determine the most appropriate resource to perform an activity: single activity and multiprocess scheduling. Single activity scheduling considers the request for a resource on an activity-by-activity basis. When a user configures a tool to be integrated within the virtual platform, the virtual environment communicates with the process control tool to register the user's new capability. When an activity is due to be performed using single activity scheduling, the process control tool firstly generates a list of the resources that are capable of performing the activity. This list is then filtered to determine which of these user are currently online, as well as which are the most efficient at performing the activity. Single activity scheduling selects the most appropriate resource for each individual activity, without considering the process as a whole and hence cannot guarantee that the process lead times will be optimum.

Multiprocess scheduling uses an optimisation algorithm to simultaneously consider all of the activities within all of the active processes that require resources. Using multiprocess scheduling, the process control tool will automatically generate a schedule whenever it attempts to start an activity that has not previously had a resource scheduled for it. Using this approach the scheduling becomes dynamic, reacting to the changing process demands, as well as simultaneously considering the most appropriate resources in order to minimise the lead-times of all of the active processes. Whenever an activity is completed, the associated scheduled resource is removed from the schedule, such that if the activity were to be repeated due to iteration for example, the scheduling procedure would be repeated and therefore not use the same previously scheduled resource. A shortcoming of this approach is that

the scheduling algorithm does not consider the availability of resources during working hours, which is compounded by the fact that the resources may be distributed across various time-zones, as well as the possible variation in the schedule and potential unavailability of a scheduled resource some time the future. These issues could however be addressed by continually assessing the deviation from the schedule and re-scheduling when the deviation exceeds pre-defined limits (Whitfield et al., 2003b).

Simulation Engine

The simulation engine represents all of the design and simulation tools that are integrated into the virtual platform. These tools represent the functionality that is required to design the ROPAX vessel from concept to detail, and simulate the performance of the ROPAX vessel with respect to the environment, operations, supply chain, and production. In order to enable this design, the associated design and simulation tools require integration within the virtual platform. Additional management functionality was however required within this wrapping in order that the tool usage could be coordinated. This functionality was provided in the form of a generic wrapper, consisting of two separate modules, which would be used to integrate any of the simulation engine tools within the platform.

The focus when developing the generic wrapper was on facilitating the open architecture and providing support for any tool irrespective of the function that the tool provides, the programming language that it was written in, or the platform that it operates on. The configuration module is a graphical interface that enables the generation of tool integration information, relating to the management of input and output data, data conversion algorithms, and design and simulation tools.

Once the configuration of the tool is complete, the associated activity becomes available for enactment within the interface of the user's virtual environment. Information is also sent to the process control tool to inform it that the user is now capable of performing the configured activity.

When an activity within a process has been scheduled to a resource, the process control tool communicates with the virtual environment of the resource informing it that the activity needs to be performed. The enactment module downloads the data from the common model, converts the input data to the native format, runs the design and/or simulation tools, converts the output data to the neutral format once the tool use is complete, and uploads the data to the common model in accordance with the rules defined within the configuration. The enactment module also manages communication with the inference engine to check the lock status of any of the data that it will be using. A dialog is displayed if the required data is already in use (and therefore locked). Alternatively, the inference engine will lock the data for the user during the enactment of the activity.

USE OF THE VRS VIRTUAL PLATFORM

When the user starts the virtual environment component, they are presented with a login dialog to control access to the virtual platform. The user is expected to provide information relating to their username and password. The process control tool prohibits further access to the platform if the details do not match those contained within an encrypted database. Once the username and password have been validated, the process control tool registers the details to indicate that the user is online in order that activities may be scheduled and allocated to the user in the future.

The first time the user logs onto the platform, the virtual environment will create a new profile, hence the user is expected to use the configuration module of the generic wrapper in order to define

the activities that the user can perform—see the section "Simulation Engine." Once the user has completed the configuration procedure, the associated activities that have been mapped are registered with the process control tool as new capability.

The user can visually interact with the data within the common model by selecting the element to view (such as the general layout of the decks for example). This visual representation of the common model data is available to all of the users of the platform in order that every user can visualise the progress of the design irrespective of their expertise or available tools. This representation does not however allow modification of the data in the same way that the design and simulation tools would. The virtual environment also allows manipulation of the data dependency maps within the inference engine, and starting of processes within the process control tool.

When a process is started, the process control tool will firstly attempt to allocate resources to the activities within the process that require resources using either single activity or multiprocess scheduling—see the section on process control tool. Once a resource has been identified, the process control tool will communicate with the virtual environment of the resource and allocate the activity to them. When the activity is started, the configuration information is loaded into the generic wrapper enactment module, which will extract the information relating to the input and output data that the associated tool will use. The enactment module will then communicate with the inference engine in order to establish the status of the data. If a different user has already locked the data, the inference engine will inform the user that they may only use a copy of the data, or alternatively defer the activity until later. If a copy of the data is used, any data that is generated from the copy cannot be uploaded to the common model. This limitation is made to prevent inconsistencies arising from multiple users simultaneously accessing and modifying the same piece of data. If the data is locked, the user may interact with the inference engine via the virtual environment to either: request notification when the lock is released; establish which resource has locked the data and communicate with the resource in order to collaboratively work on the data. If the data is not locked when the user starts the activity, the inference engine will automatically lock the data, and allow the user to modify it in accordance with the configuration. The inference engine will also check to see if any other user has currently locked (and is therefore working on) any related data through analysis of its data dependency maps. For example, user A may currently be using the hull-form of the ship to conduct a damage stability analysis, whilst user Z is allocated an activity to modify the hull-form. A relationship would exist within the inference engine between the hull-form and the damage stability performance through the configuration of the damage stability analysis tool by user Z. If user A makes a modification to the hull-form, it could impact the simulation activities of user Z. The inference engine would therefore communicate with both users and provide notification that the activities that they are performing could potentially be in conflict with each other. Given this notification of a potential conflict, it is left up to the associated users to ensure that the actions that they undertake do not result with an actual conflict.

Once it has been established that the data either is not locked, or is locked and therefore copied, the generic wrapper enactment module will download the data from the common model, store it in the defined locations on the user's local machine, run the conversion algorithms and the pass the converted input data to the tool which is then started. The design or simulation tool may then be used in a manner according to the requirements of the activity. Given the nature of the VRS design problem, many of the design tools require a significant amount (days, weeks, or months) of effort in order to generate the required

output. Hence provision is provided within both the virtual environment and the generic wrapper to enable the activity to be stopped, and restarted any number of times, without repeating the process of checking for data locks, and downloading the data. The data that is associated with the activity remains locked until the activity is completed.

Once the user completes the activity, the generic wrapper uploads the generated output data to the common model, communicates with inference engine in order to release the data locks, and informs the inference engine that the output data that the user has created has changed. The inference engine uses this information to manage the consistency of the data within the common model, to ensure that any changes that are made to the model are correctly propagated, and to communicate with the process control tool to undertake appropriate activity. The virtual environment displays a dialog to the user showing the requirements that have been associated with the design activity by the process control tool. The user can use this dialog to select which of the requirements that have been satisfied as a result of performing the activity and may be used by the process control tool to take alternative action. The virtual environment communicates with the process control tool to inform it that the activity is now complete, as well as providing information relating to the state of the requirements. If a requirement is not satisfied, the process control tool may either: re-direct the process to activities that are known to affect the requirement, or ignore the failed requirement and direct the process as planned with the knowledge that the requirement will be satisfied later.

The process control tool also has functionality to enable users of the virtual platform to attach notes to the details of an activity once the activity is completed. This functionality enables a user to provide precise details of the activity that they have performed. For example, it may be necessary to modify the general arrangement if it is established that the evacuation time for the vessel is not appropriate, and in doing so, the user responsible for modifying the general arrangement has repositioned a bulkhead. The user can therefore attach a note to state that the bulkhead has been repositioned, in order that any subsequent activities can consider the new bulkhead position. Alternatively, the user may attach a note to state the reason why a certain requirement was not satisfied. These notes are propagated throughout the processes by the process control tool and may be added to or removed when appropriate by the allocated resources and provide a means of directing design activity towards specific issues.

A number of evaluation scenarios were created in order to test the virtual platform during the development of both the prototype and the current version. The most recent scenario had users distributed across Europe in France, Greece, Sweden, and the UK, logged onto the platform and coordinating their activities to demonstrate the design of a vessel, from a hull-form concept, through to the detail design of the hull including hull-fairing, generation of the general arrangement of the decks within the hull using the hull-form profiles at various sections, and finally generating a simulation of the performance of the vessel with respect to the evacuation of 2000 passengers.

Figure 8. Innovative ROPAX vessel (Copyright VRS & University of Strathclyde)

The focus of these demonstration scenarios was not on the actual design, but on the operation and performance of the virtual platform in supporting the design.

The designers were free to operate with the tools, techniques, and expertise that they would conventionally use. No constraint was placed on the designers in terms of how they would undertake their normal duties through the virtual platform. Decision support was provided to the designers in terms of getting the right information to the right designer at the right time. The designers are otherwise not supported in their decision-making, with the assumption that they are already in possession of the expertise to be able to make the right decisions. The provision of the right information however enables the designers to make informed decisions. The output of the conventional design approach satisfying the design requirements can be seen within Figure 8.

From a creativity viewpoint, the essential difference between the conventional approach and the integrated approach arises as a result of the availability of new types of information. Since the integrated approach allowed the inclusion of previously disparate (simulation) tools that may not have been included within the design process, the output from these tools may be used to influence the design. In certain circumstances this additional information can constrain the solution space by providing a more comprehensive understanding of the viability of the design. In doing so however, it directs the designer towards the solution in a more informed manner. Following the geometric definition of the hull envelope, the general arrangement (GA) may itself be constructed from "modules" from previous vessels. Given the GA, the integrated platform allows the addition of compartmentation representing meta-information of the topological layout of cabins, corridors and stairs for example. The output from this compartmentation would then be automatically transferred to a tool that simulates evacuation of passengers, the result of

Figure 9. Evacuation simulation software (Copyright Safety at Sea Ltd.)

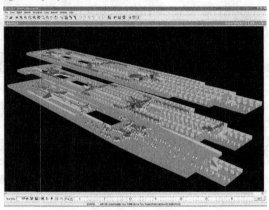

which would be a quantitative estimate of how long it would take passengers to evacuate to the muster stations, as well as a qualitative view of where the evacuation bottlenecks are (typically stairwells)—Figure 9. Whilst these simulations are being undertaken, the conventional design activity using the GA would also be operating in parallel. The output of the evacuation could however be used to modify the GA, when additional design work is usually necessary within further iterative cycles to modify the GA. The platform therefore manages the complexity of the design process integrating simulation wherever it is appropriate, as well as the complexity of the data to enable it to be efficiently transferred between tools, such that the output may be presented to the designer at the right point to inform their decision-making.

FUTURE DEVELOPMENTS AND CHALLENGES

The concept of providing distributed design support has been successfully demonstrated within the VRShips project, and will be further developed within a number of EU-funded projects. These developments aim to enable a more dynamic aspect to this support—creating processes on the fly

and providing support on an ad-hoc basis where required. In addition, support will be provided to processes, tasks and activities irrespective of the life-phase that they represent, with minimal cognitive impact on the user.

One of the shortcomings of VRShips resulted from the way that process models were managed—with the allocation of an activity to a resource (on a one to one basis) that has registered the ability to be able to undertake it. Whilst this approach enabled process planning and design to be undertaken within a formalised manner, activities could only be enacted once the activities that they were dependent upon were complete. Multiple activities could be undertaken in parallel, however no support for overlapping dependent activities was provided.

The consequences of providing this support are however significant and could form the basis for future developments. Assuming that two dependent activities are completely overlapped, and are therefore running in parallel, the two resources performing the activities will be required to be made continuously aware of the actions and outcomes of each other. Changes made to the design for example therefore require continuous broadcast to all the resources that are affected by the change. Similarities may be drawn and techniques adopted within the computer gaming industry whereby servers run environments that contain many users interacting with the environment and with each other. The changes that are made to the environment are continuous and don't rely on a user completing their activities before being broadcast to other users.

Where the VRShips platform was generalized in every aspect other than the data contained within the common model, providing continuous activity support rather than discrete would require a large amount of domain specific knowledge to be supplied to the user. The tools that the user normally operates would require wrapping of source code to enable the dynamic transfer of data during operation to other users. A task or activity level coordination layer would still be necessary to avoid chaotic behaviour, but would provide support for dynamically created processes and would respond to as well as guide the users actions in both a planned and ad-hoc manner. This activity level coordination layer would therefore require domain specific knowledge to be gathered regarding the users actions, to be used as a basis for establishing a new course of action.

The virtual platform developed within the VR-Ships-ROPAX project is currently being exploited within other European Union funded projects within the shipbuilding industry. These projects are aiming to further develop the concepts within different contexts where the long-term strategic focus is towards the production of a commercially viable platform. The success of the platform has been demonstrated within a number of ship design scenarios where the design activity has been predominantly undertaken by designers within the shipbuilding industry. Since the components that manage the complexity of the design process are generic (the integration platform, common model, inference engine, process control tool, and the generic wrapper), the platform is equally applicable to other sectors where complexity within the design process is an issue, such as the large made-to-order industry. Implementing the platform within a different domain would require the definition of a neutral data structure to represent the data being generated and transferred between tools, as well as the production of input/output data converters between the tools. This is perceived to be the minimum development for integration of domain specific design and simulation tools if a standard data representation does not exist. If a standard exists, the platform may be used within the domain without any modification.

ACKNOWLEDGMENT

The authors would like to acknowledge the funding received to enable this research to be undertaken. The VRShips-ROPAX project was funded by the European Commission (grant number G3RD-CT-2001-00506), which is part of the Fifth Framework Programme for Research, Technological Development and Demonstration.

REFERENCES

International Organization for Standardization. (2001). *Industrial automation systems and integration—Product data representation and exchange—Part 227: Application protocol: Plant spatial configuration.*

International Organization for Standardization. (2003). *Industrial automation systems and integration—Product data representation and exchange—Part 216: Application protocol: Ship moulded forms.*

International Organization for Standardization. (2004a). *Industrial automation systems and integration—Product data representation and exchange—Part 215: Application protocol: Ship arrangement.*

International Organization for Standardization. (2004b). *Industrial automation systems and integration—Product data representation and exchange—Part 218: Application protocol: Ship structures.*

Catley, D. (1999). Prototype STEP data exchanges in ship initial design and the provision of an applications programmer interface to "Tribon." In Chryssostomidis, C., Johansson, K. (Ed.), *International Conference on Computer Applications in Shipbuilding.* Massachusetts Institute of Technology.

Chapanis, A., Frick, F. C., Garner, W. R., Gebhard, J. W., Grether, W. F., Henneman, R. H., et al. (1951). Human engineering for an effective air navigation and traffic control system. IN P.M.FITTS (Ed.) Washington, DC, National Research Council.

Cummings, M. L. (2004). Automation bias in intelligent time critical decision support systems. In *Proceedings of the AIAA 1ˢᵗ Intelligent Systems Technical Conference*. Chicago: American Institute of Aeronautics and Astronautics.

Duffy, S. M. (1995). The design complexity map and the design co-ordination framework. In *Proceedings of the 10ᵗʰ Integrated Production Systems Seminar*. Fuglso, Denmark: Insistute of Engineering Design.

Grau, M., & Koch, T. (1999). Applying Step Technology To Shipbuilding. In C. Chryssostomidis & K. Johansson (Ed.), *International Conference on Computer Applications in Shipbuilding*. Massachusetts Institute of Technology.

Guan, X., Duffy, A. H. B., & Maccallum, K. J. (1997). Prototype system for supporting the incremental modelling of vague geometic configurations. *AIEDAM special issue of Geometric Representation and Reasoning in Design, 11,* 287-310.

Manfaat, D., & Duffy, A. H. B. (1998). SPIDA: abstracting and generalising layout design cases. *Artificial Intelligence for Engineering Design, Analysis, and Manufacturing, 12,* 141-159.

Mann, R. W., & Coons, S. A. (1965). Computer-aided design. *McGraw-Hill Yearbook Science and Technology*. New York: McGraw-Hill.

Rando, T. C. (2001). XML-based interoperability in the integrated shipbuilding environment (ISE). *Journal of Ship Production, 17,* 69-75.

Whitfield, R. I., Duffy, A. H. B., Meehan, J., & Wu, Z. (2003a). Ship product modelling. *Journal of Ship Production, 19,* 230-245.

Whitfield, R. I., Duffy, A. H. B., Coates, G., & Hills, W. (2003b). Efficient process optimisation. *International Journal of Concurrent Engineering: Research and Applications, 11,* 83-92.

Yan, X. T., Rehman, F., & Borg, J. (2002). Foreseeing design solution consequences using design context information. *IFIP Working Group 5.2*. Malta.

Zhang, Y., Maccallum, K. J., & Duffy, A. H. B. (1997). Product knowledge modelling and management. In *Proceedings of the 2ⁿᵈ Workshop of Product Structuring—International Society for the Science of Engineering Workshop (WDK)*. Delf, Netherlands, WDFK.

Compilation of References

Adams, J. L. (1974). *Conceptual blockbusting*. Stanford, CA: Stanford Alumni Association.

Adams, J. L. (1986). *The care and feeding of ideas*. Reading, MA: Addison-Wesley.

Agarwal, S. S. (2004). *Supporting collaborative computing and interaction* (No. LBNL-50418): Office of Advanced Computing Research, U.S. Department of Energy.

Agrell, A. & Gustafson, R. (1996). Innovation and creativity in work groups. In M. A.West (Ed.), *Handbook of work group psychology* (pp. 317-343). New York: Wiley.

Albert, R. S., & Runce, M. A. (1999). *A history of research on creativity*. Cambridge: Cambridge University Press.

Allen, T. J. (1977). *Managing the flow of technology*. Boston: MIT Press.

Altshuller, G. (1994). *The art of inventing (and suddenly the inventor appeared)*. Worcester, MA: Technical Innovation Center.

Amabile, T. M. (1979). Effects of external evaluation on artistic creativity. *Journal of Personality and Social Psychology, 37*, 221-233.

Amabile, T. M. (1983). *The social psychology of creativity*. New York: Springer Verlag.

Amabile, T. M. (1983). The social psychology of creativity: A componential conceptualization. *Journal of Personality and Social Psychology, 45*(2), 357-376.

Amabile, T. M. (1988). A model of creativity and innovation in organizations. In B. M. Staw & L. L. Cummings (Eds.), *Research in organizational behavior* (Vol. 10, pp. 123-167). Greenwich, CT: JAI Press.

Amabile, T. M. (1988). Within you, without you: The social psychology of creativity and beyond. In B. M. S. L. L. Cummings (Eds.), *Research in organizational behavior* (pp. 123-167). Greenwich, CT: JAI Press.

Amabile, T. M. (1990). Within you, without you: The social psychology of creativity and beyond. In M. A. Runco & R. S. Albert (Eds.), *Theories of creativity* (pp. 61-91). Newbury Park, CA: Sage Publications.

Amabile, T. M. (1996). *Creativity in context.* New York: Westview Press.

Amabile, T. M., & Gryskiewicz, N. D. (1989). The creative environment scales: Work Environment Inventory. *Creativity Research Journal, 2,* 231-253.

Amabile, T. M., & Gryskiewicz, S. S. (1987). *Creativity in the R&D laboratory* (Tech. Rep. No. 30). Greensboro, NC: Center for Creative Leadership.

Amabile, T. M., Conti, R., Coon, H., Lazenby, J., & Herron, M. (1996). Assessing the work environment for creativity. *Academy of Management Journal, 39*(5), 1154-1184.

Amabile, T. M., Hadley, C. N., & Kramer, S. J. (2002, August). Creativity under the gun. *Harvard Business Review,* 52-61.

Andersen, A. (2001). Implementation of engineering product design using international student teamwork—to comply with future needs. *European Journal of Engineering Education, 26,* 179-186.

Andreasen, M. M., & Hein, L. (2000). *Integrated product development* (reprint). Lyngby: Institute for Product Development, Technical University of Denmark.

Andres, H. P. (2002). A comparison of face-to-face and virtual software development teams. *Team Performance Management, 8*(1/2), 39-48.

Andrews, F. (1975). Social and psychological factors which influence the creative process. In I. Taylor & J. W. Getzels (Eds.), *Perspectives in creativity* (pp. 117-145). Chicago: Aldine Publishing Co.

Apache. (2001-2006). *Maven.* The Apache Foundation. Retrieved from http://maven.apache.org/

Armstrong, D., & Cole, P. (1996). Managing distances and differences in geographically distributed work groups. In S. Jackson & M. Ruderman (Eds.), *Diversity in work teams.* Washington, DC: APA.

Bachelard, G. (1983). *Water and dreams.* Dallas, TX: The Dallas Institute Publications.

Bachelard, G. (1994). *The poetics of space.* Boston: Beacon Press.

Balachandra, R., & Friar, J. H. (1997). Factors for success in R&D projects and new product innovation: A contextual framework. *IEEE Transactions on Engineering Management, 44*(3), 276-287.

Bales, R. F. (1950). *Interaction process analysis: A method for the study of small groups.* Chicago: The University of Chicago Press.

Baran, S., Zandan, P., & Vanston, J. H. (1986, January-February). How effectively are we managing innovation? *Research Management,* 23-25.

Barbiery, T. T. (1999). *Networked virtual environments for the Web: The WebTalk-I & WebTalk-II architectures.* Department of Computer Engineering—Politecnico di Milano. Milano, Italy.

Barlett, C.A., & Ghoshal, S. (2000). *Transnational management: Text, cases and readings in cross-border management.* Boston: McGraw-Hill.

Barron, F. B., & Harrington, D. M. (1981). Creativity, intelligence, and personality. *Annual Review of Psychology, 32,* 439-476.

Basadur, M. (2004). Leading others to think innovatively together: Creative leadership. *The Leadership Quarterly, 15,* 103-121.

Beck, K. (2000). *Extreme programming explained.* Boston: Addison-Wesley.

Beck, K., et al. (2001). *Manifesto for agile software development.* Retrieved April 16, 2006, from http://agilemanifesto.org

Beitz, W., & Helbig, D. (1997, August). The future of education for product developers. In *Proceedings of the 11th International Conference on Engineering Design,* Tampere, Finland (pp. 493-498).

Belbin, R. M. (2003). *Management teams—Why they succeed or fail.* Oxford: Butterworth-Heinemann.

Bell, B. S. (2002). A typology of virtual teams. Implications for effective leadership. *Group & Organization Management, 27*(1), 14-19.

Bell, B. S., & Kozlowski, S. W. J. (2002). A typology of virtual teams. *Group & Organization Management, 27*(1), 14-49.

Benedikt, M. (1979). *An introduction to isovists.* Austin, TX: UT Austin School of Architecture Working Paper Series, University of Texas.

Benedikt, M. (1991). Cyberspace: Some proposals. In B. Michael (Ed.), *Cyberspace: First steps* (pp. 119-224). Cambridge, MA: The MIT Press.

Bernstein, D. (1988). The design mind. In P. Gorb (Ed.), *Design talks!* London: London Business School/Design Council.

Bessant, J., Whyte, J., & Neely, A. (2005). *DTI Think Piece Management of creativity and design within the firm.* Advanced Institute for Management (AIM) and Imperial College.

Beyerlein, M., & Harris, C. (2004). *Guiding the journey to collaborative work systems: A strategic design workbook.* San Francisco: Pfeiffer.

Biggs, M. (2000, September). Assessing risks today will leave corporate leaders well-prepared for the future of work. *InfoWorld,* Retrieved November 3, 2006, from http://www.infoworld.com/

Boden, M. A. (1994). Precis of "the creative mind: Myths and mechanisms." *Behavioral and Brain Sciences, 17*(3), 519-570.

Bodendorf, F., & Swain, P. H., (2001). Virtual universities in engineering education. *International Journal of Engineering Education, 17,* 102-107.

Boehm, B., & Turner, R. (2004). *Balancing agility and discipline.* Boston: Addison-Wesley.

Bois, Y-A. (1991). *Painting as model.* Cambridge, MA: The MIT Press.

Bono, De E. (1990). *Six thinking hats.* London: Penguin.

Bouas, K. S., & Arrow, H. (1996). The development of group identity in computer and face-to-face groups with membership change. *Computer Supported Cooperative Work, 4,* 153-178.

Boutellier, R., Gassman, O., Macho, H., & Roux, M. (1998). Management of dispersed product development teams: The role of information technologies. *R&D Management, 28,* 13-25.

Bradner, E., & Mark, G. (2002, November). Why distance matters: Effects on cooperation, persuasion and deception. In *Proceedings of the ACM Conference on Computer-Supported Cooperative Work (CSCW 2002),* New Orleans (pp. 226-235). New York: ACM Press.

Brandenburger, A. M., & Nalebuff, B. J. (1997). Co-Opetition: *A revolution mindset that combines competition and cooperation: The game theory strategy that's changing the game of business.* New York: Doubleday/Currency.

Breiman, L., Friedman, J. H., Olshen, R. A., & Stone, C. J. (1984). *Classification and regression trees.* Boca Raton, FL: Chapman & Hall.

Broadbent, J. A., & Cross, N. (2003). Design education in the information age. *Journal of Engineering Design, 14*(4), 439-446.

Brown, S. L., & Eisenhardt, K. M. (1998). *Competing on the edge.* Boston: Harvard Business School Press.

Brown, T. M., & Miller, C. E. (2000). Communication networks in task-performing groups: Effects of task complexity, time pressure, and interpersonal dominance. *Small Group Research, 31*(2), 131-157.

Bucciarelli, L. (1984). Reflective practices in engineering design. *Design Studies, 5*(3), 185-190.

Buzan, B. T. B. (1988). *Super creativity.* New York: St. Martin's Press.

Buzan, B. T. B. (2005). *The history of memory techniques leading to mind maps by Tony Buzan.*

Byrne, J. (1993, February 8). The virtual corporation. *Business Week,* 98-102.

Callaway, M. R., Marriott, R. G., & Esser, J. K. (1985). Effects of dominance on group decision-making: Towards a stress-reduction explanation of groupthink. *Journal of Personality and Social Psychology, 49,* 949-952.

Camacho, L. J. (1995). The role of social anxiousness in group brainstorming. *Journal of Personality and Social Psychology, 68*(6), 1071-1080.

Cardoso, H. L., & Oliveira, E. (2005). Virtual enterprise normative framework within electronic institutions. In M. P. Gleizes, A. Omicini, & F. Zambonelli (Eds.), *Engineering societies in the agents world V* (pp. 14-32). Springer.

Cardozo, R. N., Durfee, W. K., Ardichvili, A., Adams, C., Erdman, A. G., Hoey, M., et al. (2002). Perspective: Experiential education in new product design and business development. *The Journal of Product Innovation Management, 19*(1), 4-17.

Catley, D. (1999). Prototype STEP data exchanges in ship initial design and the provision of an applications programmer interface to "Tribon." In Chryssostomidis, C., Johansson, K. (Ed.), *International Conference on Computer Applications in Shipbuilding.* Massachusetts Institute of Technology.

Certeau, De M. (2002). *The practice of everyday life.* Berkeley: California University Press.

Chapanis, A., Frick, F. C., Garner, W. R., Gebhard, J. W., Grether, W. F., Henneman, R. H., et al. (1951). Human engineering for an effective air navigation and traffic control system. IN P.M.FITTS (Ed.) Washington, DC, National Research Council.

Chiaramonte, F. P., & Joshi, J. A. (2004). *Workshop on Critical Issues in Microgravity, Fluids, Transport, and Reaction Processes in Advanced Human Support Technology* (NASA/TM—2004-212940). Retrieved October 30, 2006, from http://peer1.nasaprs.com/peer_review/prog/ahst_2003.pdf

Christensen, C. M., & Raynor, M. E. (2003). *The innovator's solution.* Boston: Harvard Business School Press.

Christensen, C. M., Anthony, S. D., & Roth, E. A. (2004). *Seeing what's next.* Boston: Harvard Business School Press.

Chu, K. C., Urbanik, N., Yip, S. Y., & Cheung, T. W. (1999). The benefit of virtual teaching to engineering education. *International Journal of Engineering Education, 15,* 334-338.

Clark, K. B., & Fujimoto, T. (1990). The power of product integrity. *Harvard Business Review, 68*(6), 107-118.

Clark, L. A., & Pregibon, D. (1992). Tree-based models. In J. M. Chambers & T. J. Hastie (Eds.), *Statistical models* (pp. 377-420). Boca Raton, FL: CRC Press.

Cockburn, A. (2000). *Writing effective use cases.* Boston: Addison-Wesley.

Cockburn, A. (2002). *Agile software development.* Boston: Addison-Wesley.

Cohen, B. P., & Cohen, E. G. (1991). From groupwork among children to innovation teams. *Advances in Group Processes, 8,* 235-251.

Cohen, W.M., & Levinthal, D. A. (1990). A new perspective on learning and innovation. *Administrative Science Quarterly, 35*(1), 128-152.

Collison, C., & Parcell, G. (2001). *Learning to fly: Practical lessons from the world's leading knowledge companies.* Oxford: Capstone Publishing.

Comment, B. (1999). *The panorama.* London: Reaktion Books. Translated from B. Comment (1993). *Le XIXe siècle des panoramas.*

Connelly, T., Jessup, L. M., & Valacich, J. S. (1990). Effects of anonymity and evaluative tone on idea generation in computer-mediated groups. *Management Science, 36*(6), 689-702.

Cooper, A. (1999). *The inmates are running the asylum.* Indianapolis, IN: SAMS/Macmillan.

Cooper, R. G. (2001). *Winning at new products.* Cambridge, MA: Perseus.

Cooper, R. G. (2005). Your NPD portfolio may be harmful to your business's health. *Visions, 29*(2), 22-26.

Costa, P. T., Jr., & McCrae, R. R. (1992). Normal personality assessment in clinical practice: The NEO Personality Inventory. *Psychological Assessment, 4,* 5-13.

Cox, G. (2005). *Cox review of creativity in business: Building on the UK's strengths.* Retrieved November 15, 2006, from http://www.hm-treasury.gov.uk/cox

Crary, J. (1990). *Techniques of the observer.* Cambridge, MA: The MIT Press.

Cross, R., Parker, A., Prusak, L., & Borgatti, S. P. (2001). Knowing what we know: supporting knowledge creation and sharing in social networks. *Organizational Dynamics, 30*(2), 100-120.

Csikszentmihalyi, P., & Sawyer, K. (1995). Shifting the focus from individual to organizational creativity. In C. M. Ford & D. A. Goia (Eds.), *Creative Action in Organizations* (pp. 167-173). Thousand Oaks, CA: Sage.

Cummings, M. L. (2004). Automation bias in intelligent time critical decision support systems. In *Proceedings of the AIAA 1st Intelligent Systems Technical Conference.* Chicago: American Institute of Aeronautics and Astronautics.

Daft, R. L., & Becker, S. W. (1978). *Innovation in organizations.* New York: Elsevier North-Holland, Inc.

Daft, R., & Lengel, R. (1986). Organizational information requirements, media richness, and structural design. *Management Science, 32*(5), 554-571.

Dartnall, T. (1994). *Artificial intelligence and creativity: An interdisciplinary approach.* The Netherlands: Kluwer Academic Publishers.

Davidow, W. & Malone, M. (1992). *The virtual corporation.* New York: HarperCollins.

Deck, M. J. (2002). Decision making: The overlooked competency in product development. In P. Belliveau, A. Griffin, & S. Somermeyer (Eds.), *The PDMA toolbook for new product development* (pp. 165-185). Hoboken, NJ: John Wiley.

DeMeyer, A. C. L. (1985). The flow of technological innovation in an R&D department. *Research Policy, 14,* 315-328.

Design Council. (2006). *Encouraging creativity.* Retrieved November 30, 2006, from http://www.designcouncil.org.uk/ (Public Sector link).

Diehl, M., & Stroebe, W. (1987). Productivity loss in brainstorming groups: Toward the solution of a riddle. *Journal of Personality and Social Psychology, 53*(3), 497-509.

Domeshek, E. A., & Kolodner (1992). A case-based design aid for architecture. In J. Gero (Ed.), *Artificial intelligence in design '92* (pp. 497-516). The Netherlands: Kluwer Academic Publishers.

Drazin, R., Glynn, M. A., & Kazanjian, R. K. (1999). Multilevel theorizing about creativity in organizations: A sensemaking perspective. *Academy of Management Review, 24*(2), 286-307.

Driscoll, M. P. (2000). *Psychology of learning for instruction.* Boston: Allyn and Bacon.

Drucker, P. F. (1988, January-February). The coming of the new organization. *Harvard Business Review, 66*(1), 45-53.

DTI. (2005, November). Economics paper No. 15. Creativity, design and business performance. Department of Trade & Industry, UK.

Duarte, D. L., & Snyder, N. T. (1999). *Mastering virtual teams: Strategies, tools, and techniques that succeed.* San Francisco: Jossey-Bass Publishers.

Dubrovsky, V. J., Kiesler, S., & Sethna, B. N. (1991). The equalization phenomena: Status effects in computer-mediated and face-to-face decision making groups. *Journal of Human-Computer Interaction, 6,* 119-146.

Duffy, S. M. (1995). The design complexity map and the design co-ordination framework. In *Proceedings of the 10ᵗʰ Integrated Production Systems Seminar.* Fuglso, Denmark: Insistute of Engineering Design.

Dym, C. L. (1994). *Engineering design: a synthesis of views.* Cambridge: Cambridge University Press.

Eckes, G. (2003). *Six sigma for everyone.* Hoboken, NJ: John Wiley.

Egan, T. E. (2005). Creativity in the context of team diversity: Team Leader Perspectives. *Advances in Developing Human Resources, 7*(2), 207-225.

Ehrenzweig, A. (1971). *The hidden order of art.* Berkeley: University of California Press.

Einstein. A. (1949). Autobiographical notes. Retrieved November 15, 2006, from http://www.alberteinstein.info/manuscripts

Eisenhardt, K. M. (1989). Building Theories from Case Study Research. *Academy of Management Review, 14*(4), 432-550.

Eisenman, P. (1999). *Diagram diaries.* London: Thames & Hudson.

Ekvall, G. (1983). *Climate, structure, and innovativeness of organizations* (Report 1). Stockholm: Swedish Council for Management and Organizational Behavior.

Ekvall, G. (1997). *Organizational conditions and levels of creativity. Creativity and innovation management, 6*(4), 195-205.

Ekvall, G., Arvonen, J., & Waldenstrom-Lindblad, I. (1983). *Creative organizational climate: Construction and validation of a measuring instrument* (Report 2). Stockholm: Swedish Council for Management and Organizational Behavior.

Eris, O. (2002). *Perceiving, comprehending and measuring design activity through the questions asked while designing.* Doctoral dissertation, Center for Design Research, Stanford University, CA.

Evans, P. (1992). Management development as glue technology. *Human Resource Planning, 15*(1), 85-106.

Fabrikant, S. (2000). Spatialized browsing in large data archives. *Transactions in GIS, 4*(1), 65-78.

Fairbank, F., Spangler, W., & Williams, S. (2003). Motivating creativity through a computer-mediated employee suggestion management system. *Behaviour and Information Technology, 22*(5), 305-314.

Feland, J. M. (2005). *Product capital model: modeling the value of design to corporate performance.* Unpublished doctoral dissertation, Stanford University.

Feland, J. M., Leifer, L. J., & Cockayne, W. R. (2004). Comprehensive design engineering: Designers taking responsibility. *International Journal of Engineering Education, 20*(3), 416-423.

Fischer, S. G. (1997). Computational environments supporting creativity in the context of lifelong learning and design. *Knowledge-Based Systems Journal, 10*(1), 21-28.

Fischer, S. G., Nakakoji, K., Ostwald, J., Stahl, G., & Sumner, T. (1993). Embedding critics in design environments. *The Knowledge Engineering Review, 8*(4). Retrieved October 15, 2006, from http://journals.cambridge.org/action/displayJournal?jid=KER

Frey, C. (2003). The creative thinker's unique approach to mind mapping is a winner. *Innovation Tools.*

Gallivan, M. J., & Benbunan-Fich, R. (2005). A framework for analyzing levels of analysis issues in studies of e-collaboration. *IEEE Transactions on Professional Communication, 48*(1), 87-104.

Gallupe, R. B., Bastianutti, L. M., & Cooper, W. H. (1991). Unblocking brainstorms. *Journal of Applied Psychology, 76*(1), 137-142.

Gallupe, R. B., Dennis, A. R., Cooper, W. H., Valacich, J. S., Bastianutti, L. M., & Nunamaker, J. F. (1992). Electronic brainstorming and group size. *Academy of Management Journal, 35*, 350-369.

Gallupe, R. B., DeSanctis, G., & Dickson, G. W. (1988). Computer-based support for group problem-finding: An experimental investigation. *MIS Quarterly, 12*(2), 277-296.

Gardner, H. (1985). *The mind's new science: A history of the cognitive revolution*. New York: Basic Books, Inc.

George, J. F., Easton, G. K., Nunamaker, J. F., & Northcraft, G. B. (1990). A study of collaborative group work with and without computer-based support. *Information Systems Research, 1*(4), 394-415.

Gero, J., & Maher, M. L (1993). *Creativity and knowledge-based creative design*. Hillsdale, NJ: Lawrence Erlbaum Associations Inc.

Gibson, C., & Cohen, S. (2003). *Virtual teams that work: Creating conditions for virtual team effectiveness*. San Francisco: Jossey-Bass.

Gibson, I. S. (2001). Group project work in engineering design-learning goals and their assessment. *International Journal of Engineering Education, 17*, 261-266.

Gilson, L. L., & Shalley, C. E. (2004). A little creativity goes a long way: An examination of teams' engagement in creative processes. *Journal of Management, 30*(5), 453-470.

Githens, G. D. (1998, October). *Rolling wave project planning*. The 29th Annual PMI Seminars & Symposium, Long Beach, CA.

Glaser, B. & Strauss, A. (1967). *Discovery of grounded theory*. Chicago: Aldine.

Goel, V. P. (1989). Motivating the notion of generic design within information-processing theory: The design problem space. *AI Magazine, 10*(1), 18-35.

Goldberg, L. R. (1993). The structure of personality. *American Psychologist, 48*, 26-34.

Gough, H. G., & Heilbrun, A. B. (1983). *The adjective check list manual*. Palo Alto, CA: Consulting Psychologists Press Inc.

Graen, G. B., & Wakabayashi, M. (1994). Cross-cultural leadership-making: Bridging American and Japanese diversity for team advantage. In H. C. Triandis, M. D. Dunnette, & L. M. Hough (Eds.), *Handbook of industrial and organizational psychology* (Vol. 4, pp. 415-446). New York: Consulting Psychologist Press.

Graen, G. B., & Wakabayashi, M. (1994). Cross-cultural leadership-making: Bridging American & Japanese diversity for team advantage. In H. C. Triandis, M. D. Dunnette, & L. M. Hough (Eds.), *Handbook of industrial and organizational psychology* (Vol. 4, pp. 415-446). New York: Consulting Psychologist Press.

Grau, M., & Koch, T. (1999). Applying Step Technology To Shipbuilding. In C. Chryssostomidis & K. Johansson (Ed.), *International Conference on Computer Applications in Shipbuilding*. Massachusetts Institute of Technology.

Green, G., & Kennedy, P. (2001). Redefining engineering education—The reflective practice of product engineering. *International Journal of Engineering Education, 17*, 3-9.

Greenberg, M. H. (1993), S real time distributed collaboration. In P. Dasgupta & J. E. Urban (Eds.), *Encyclopedia of distributed computing* (pp. 241-254). Amsterdam: Kluwer Academic Publishers.

Greenberg, S., & Fitchett, C. (2001, November). Phidgets: easy development of physical interfaces through physical widgets. In *Proceedings of the 14th Annual ACM Symposium on User Interface Software and Technology*, Orlando, FL.

Greenhalgh, C. (1997). *Creating large-scale collaborative virtual environments*. Department of Computer Science, University of Nottingham.

Griffin, A. (1997). PDMA Research on new product development practices: Updating trends and benchmarking best practices. *Journal of Product Innovation Management, 14*(6), 429-458.

Griffith, T. L., & Neale, M. (2001). Information processing in traditional, hybrid, and virtual teams: From nascent theory to transactive memory. In R. I. Sutton & B. M. Staw (Eds.), *Research in organizational behavior*. Stamford, CT: JAI Press.

Griffith, T. L., Sawyer, J. E., & Neale, M. A. (2003). Virtualness and knowledge in teams: Managing the love triangle of organizations, individuals, and information technology. *MIS Quarterly, 27*(2), 265-287.

Grimson, J. (2002). Re-engineering the curriculum for the 21st century. *European Journal of Engineering Education, 27*(1), 31-37.

Gross, M. D., & Do, E. (1996, October). *Ambiguous intentions: A paper like interface for creative design.* Paper presented at the ACM Conference on User Interface Software Technology (UIST) '96, Seattle, WA.

Grudin, J. (1994). Groupware and social dynamics: Eight challenges for developers. *Communications of the ACM, 37*(1), 92-105.

Guan, X., Duffy, A. H. B., & Maccallum, K. J. (1997). Prototype system for supporting the incremental modelling of vague geometic configurations. *AIEDAM special issue of Geometric Representation and Reasoning in Design, 11,* 287-310.

Guilford, J. P. (1967). *The nature of human intelligence.* New York: McGraw-Hill.

Guilford, J. P. (1984). Varieties of divergent production. *Journal of Creative Behavior, 18*(1), 1-10.

Gupta, A. K., Ray, S. P., & Wilemon, D. (1985). The R&D marketing interface in high-technology firms. *Journal of Product Innovation Management, 2*(1), 12-24.

Gutwin, C., & Greenberg, S. (2000, June). The mechanics of collaboration: developing low cost usability evaluation methods for shared workspaces. In *Proceedings of the IEEE 9th International Workshop on Enabling Technologies: Infrastructure for Collaborative Enterprises (WET-ICE '00), NIST,* Gaithersburg, MD.

Hackman, J. R. (1987). The design of work teams. In J. Lorsch (Ed.), *Handbook of organizational behavior* (pp. 315-342). Englewood Cliffs, NJ: Prentice Hall.

Hackman, J. R. (1990). *Groups that work and those that don't: Creating conditions for effective teamwork.* San Francisco: Jossey-Bass.

Hackman, J. R., & Morris, C. G. (1975). Group tasks, group interaction processes, and group performance effectiveness, a review and proposed integration. In L. Berkowitz (Ed.), *Advances in experimental social psychology* (pp. 47-99). New York: Academic Press.

Halfhill, T., Sundstrom, E., Lahner, J., Calderone, W., & Nielsen, T. M. (2005). Group personality composition and group effectiveness: An integrative review of empirical research. *Small Group Research, 36*(1), 83-105.

Hamel, G. (2002). *Leading the revolution: How to thrive in turbulent times by making innovation a way of life.* New York: Penguin Putnam.

Hargadon, A., & Sutton, R. I. (1997). Technology brokering and innovation in a product development firm. *Administrative Science Quarterly, 42,* 716-749.

Harmut, D. (2000). *SKETCHAND+: A collaborative augmented reality sketching application.* Retrieved September 20, 2005, from http://www.technotecture. com/media/papers/seichter_caadria03_web.pdf

Harrell, F. E. Jr. (2001). *Regression modeling strategies.* New York: Springer-Verlag.

Hayes, N., & Walsham, G. (2000). Competing interpretations of computer supported cooperative work in organizational contexts. *Organization, 7*(1), 49-67.

Herbsleb, J., Mockus, A, Finholt, T. A., & Grinter, R.E., (2000, December). *Distance, dependencies and delay in a global collaboration.* In *Proceedings of the ACM Conference on Computer-Supported Cooperative Work (CSCW 2000),* Philadelphia (pp. 319-328). New York: ACM Press.

Highsmith, J. (2004). *Agile project management: Creating innovative products.* Boston: Addison-Wesley.

Hiltz, S. R., Johnson, K., & Turoff, M. (1986). Experiments in group decision making, 1: Communications process and outcome in face-to-face vs. computerized conferences. *Human Communication Research, 13*(2), 225-252.

Hiltz, S. R., Johnson, K.D., & Turoff, M. (1986). Experiments in group decision making: Communication process and outcome in face-to-face versus computerized conferences. *Human Communication Research, 13*(2), 225-252.

Hirshberg, J. (1999). *The creative priority.* New York: HarperCollins.

Hoffman, L. R. (1959). Homogeneity of member personality and its effect on group problem-solving. *Journal of Abnormal Social Psychology, 58*, 27-32.

Hoffman, L. R., & Maier, N. R. F. (1961). Quality and acceptance of problem solutions by members of homogeneous and heterogeneous groups. *Journal of Abnormal Social Psychology, 62*, 401-407.

Hoffner, Y., Field, S., Grefen, P., Ludwig; H. (2001). Contract Driven Creation And Operation Of Virtual Enterprises. *Computer Networks—The International Journal of Computer and Telecommunications Networking; 37*(2), 111-136.

Horváth, I., Duhovnik, J., & Xirouckakis, P. (2003). Learning the methods and the skills of global product realization in an academic virtual enterprise. *European Journal of Engineering Education, 28*(1), 83-102.

Horváth, I., van Breemen, E., Dutta, D., Yip-Hoi, D., Kim, J., & Lee, K. (2001, September). Education for global product realization on a global scale. In *Proceedings of DETC01/ASME01 Design Engineering Technical Conferences*, Pittsburg, PA (pp. 1-11).

Horváth, I., Wiersma, M., Duhovnik, J, & Stroud, I. (2004). Navigated active learning in an international scientific academic virtual enterprise. *European Journal of Engineering Education, 29*(4), 505-519.

Horváth, I., Xirouchakis, P. Duhovnik, J., & Wiersma, M. (2004). Reflections of teaching global product realization in academic virtual enterprise. In *Proceedings of DETC04/ASME04 Design Engineering Technical Conferences and Computers and Information in Engineering Conference* (pp. 1-10). New York: ASME.

Hundal, M. S. (1995, August). Engineering design education in the USA: Issues and challenges. In *Proceedings of the 10th International Conference on Engineering Design*, Praha, Czech Republic (pp. 318-323).

IJsendoorf, H. (2002). Application of computer aided systems, PD&E Automotive, E-GPR industrial case study, quote from a class discussion.

Imai, M. (1997). *Gemba Kaizen: A common sense, low cost approach to management.* New York: McGraw-Hill.

Inkpen, A. C., & Dinur, A. (1998). Knowledge management processes and international joint ventures. *Organization Science, 9*(4), 454-468.

International Co-operative Alliance (ICA). (1995). *Statement of co-operative principles.* Retrieved November 15, from http://www.ica.coop/coop/principles.html

International Organization for Standardization. (2001). *Industrial automation systems and integration—Product data representation and exchange—Part 227: Application protocol: Plant spatial configuration.*

International Organization for Standardization. (2003). *Industrial automation systems and integration—Product data representation and exchange—Part 216: Application protocol: Ship moulded forms.*

International Organization for Standardization. (2004a). *Industrial automation systems and integration—Product data representation and exchange—Part 215: Application protocol: Ship arrangement.*

International Organization for Standardization. (2004b). *Industrial automation systems and integration—Product data representation and exchange—Part 218: Application protocol: Ship structures.*

Irandoust, S., & Sjöberg, J. (2001). International dimensions: a challenge for European engineering education. *European Journal of Engineering Education, 26*, 69-75.

Ishii, H., & Kobayashi, M. (1992, May). Clearboard: A seamless medium for shared drawing and conversation with eye contact. In *Proceedings of the ACM CHI'92 Conference on Human Factors in Computing Systems*, Monterrey, CA (pp. 525-532).

Jackson, D. N. (1967). *Personality research form manual.* Goshen, NY: Research Psychologists Press.

Jagodzinski, P., Reid, F., & Culverhouse, P. (2000). A study of electronics engineering design teams. *Design Studies, 21*(4), 375-402.

Jarvenpaa, S. L., & Leidner D. E. (1998). Communication and trust in global virtual teams. *Journal of Computer Mediated Communication, 3*(4). Retrieved November 1, from http://jcmc.indiana.edu/vol3/issue4/

Jarvenpaa, S. L., Knoll, K., & Leidner, D. E. (1998). Is anybody out there? Antecedents of trust in global virtual teams. *Journal of Management Information Systems, 14*, 29-64.

Jarvenpaa, S., & Leidner, D. (1999). Communication and trust in global virtual teams. *Organization Science, 10*(6), 791-815.

Johnston, S. F. (2001). Towards culturally inclusive global engineering? *European Journal of Engineering Education, 26*(1), 77-89.

Jones, J. C. (1992). *Design methods.* London: John Wiley & Sons.

Kahn, W. A. (1990). Psychological conditions of personal engagement and disengagement at work. *Academy of Management Journal, 33*, 692-724.

Kanawattanachaia, P., & Yoob, Y. (2002). Dynamic nature of trust in virtual teams. *Journal of Strategic Information Systems, 11*(3/4), 187-213.

Kanter, R. M. (1983). *The change masters.* New York: Simon & Schuster.

Kasper-Fuehrer, E. C., & Ashkanasy, N. M. (2001) Communicating trustworthiness and building trust in virtual organizations. *Journal of Management Studies, 27*, 235-254.

Katz, R. (1982). The effects of group longevity on project communication and performance. *Administrative Science Quarterly, 27*, 81-104.

Katz, R. (1997). Managing creative performance in R&D teams. In R. Katz (Ed.), *The human side of managing technological innovation* (pp. 177-186). New York: Oxford University Press.

Katzenbach, J. R., & Smith, D. K. (1993). *The wisdom of teams.* Boston: Harvard Business School Press.

Katzenbach, J. R., & Smith, D. K. (1994). *The wisdom of teams: Creating the high-performance organization.* New York: Harper Business.

Kazanjian, R. K., Drazin, R., & Glynn, M. A. (2000). Creativity and technological learning: the roles of organization architecture and crisis in large-scale projects. *Journal of Engineering and Technology Management, 17*(3/4), 273-298.

Kelley, T., & Littman, J. (2001). *The art of innovation.* New York: Doubleday.

Khurana, A., & Rosenthal, S. R. (1997). Integrating the Fuzzy-Front-End of new product development. *Sloan Management Review, 38*(2), 103-120.

Kimble, C.s, Li, F. & Barlow, A. (2000). *Effective virtual teams through communities of practice* (Research Paper No. 2000/9). Glasgow: Strathclyde Business School.

King N., & Anderson, N. (1990). Innovation in working groups. In M. A. West & J. L. Farr, (Eds.), *Innovation and creativity at work: Psychological and organizational strategies* (pp. 81-100). Chichester, UK: Wiley & Sons.

Kirkman, B. L., Rosen, B., Tesluk, P. E., & Gibson, C. B. (2004). The impact of team empowerment on virtual team performance: The moderating role of face-to-face interaction. *Academy of Management Journal, 47*, 175-192.

Kirton, M. (1989). *Adaptors and innovators.* New York: Routledge.

Koberg C. S., Detienne D. R., & Heppard K. A. (2003). An empirical test of environmental, organization, and process factors affecting incremental and radical innovation. *Journal of High Technology Management Research, 14*(1), 3, 21-45.

Koen, P., Ajamian, G., Burkart, R., Clamen A. et al. (2001). Providing clarity and a common language to the "fuzzy front end." *Research and Technology Management, 44*(2), 46-55.

Kratzer, J. (2001). *Communication and performance: An empirical study in innovation teams.* Amsterdam: Tesla Thesis Publishers.

Kratzer, J., Leenders, R. Th. A. J., & Van Engelen, Jo M. L. (2005). Keeping virtual R&D teams creative. *Research Technology Management, 48*(2), 13-16.

Kratzer, J., Leenders, R. Th. A. J., & Van Engelen, Jo M. L. (2006). Managing creative team performance in virtual environments: An empirical study in 44 R&D teams. *Technovation, 26*, 42-49.

Kristof, A., Brown, K., Sims, H., & Smith, K. (1995). The virtual team: A case study and inductive model. In M. Beyerlein & D. Johnson (Eds.), *Advances in interdisciplinary studies of work teams: Knowledge teams the creative edge* (Vol. 2, pp. 229-253). Greenwich, CT: JAI Press.

Kurtzberg, T. R., & Amabile, T. M. (2001). From Guilford to creative synergy: Opening the black box of team-level creativity. *Creativity Research Journal, 13*(3&4), 285-294.

Langer, E. J. (1989). *Mindfulness.* Cambridge, MA: Da Capo Press.

Larman, C. (2004). *Agile and iterative development.* Boston: Addison-Wesley.

Leenders, R. Th. A. J, van Engelen, J. M. L., & Kratzer, J. (2003). Virtuality, communication, and new product team creativity: A social network perspective. *Journal of Engineering and Technology Management, 20*(1/2), 69-92.

Leenders, R. Th. A. J., Kratzer, J., & Van Engelen, J. M. L. (2003). Virtuality, communication, and new product team creativity: A social network perspective. *Journal of Engineering and Technology Management, 20*, 69-92.

Leenders, R. Th. A. J., Kratzer, J., & Van Engelen, J. M. L. (2004). Building creative virtual new product development teams. In P. Belliveau, A. Griffin, & S. Somermeyer (Eds.), *PDMA toolbook for new product development II* (pp. 117-147). New York: John Wiley & Sons.

Leenders, R. Th. A. J., Van Engelen, J. M. L., & Kratzer, J. (2007). Systematic design methods and the creative performance of new product teams: Do they contradict or complement each other? *Journal of Product Innovation Management, 24*, 166-179.

Liker, J. (2004). *The Toyota way.* New York: McGraw-Hill.

Lipnack, J., & Stamps, J. (1997). *Virtual teams: Reaching across space, time and organizations with technology.* New York: John Wiley & Sons.

Lipnack, J., & Stamps, J. (2000). *Virtual teams: People working across boundaries with technology* (2nd ed.). New York: John Wiley.

Loch, C. K., DeMeyer, A., & Pich, M. T. (2006). *Managing the unknown.* Hoboken, NJ: John Wiley.

Lovelace, R. F. (1986). Stimulating creativity through managerial interventions. *R&D Management, 16*, 161-174.

Lurey, J. M., & Raisinghani, M. S. (2001). An empirical study of best practices in virtual teams. *Information & Management, 38*(8), 523-544

Lurey, J. S., & Raisinghani, M. S. (2001). An empirical study of best practices in virtual teams. *International Economic Review, 38*(8), 523-544.

MacGregor, S. P. (2002). *Describing and supporting the distributed workspace: Towards a prescriptive process for design teams.* Doctoral dissertation, DMEM,

University of Strathclyde, Glasgow, UK. Retrieved October 15, 2006, from http://www.design4distribution.com

MacGregor, S. P. (2002). *Describing and supporting the distributed workspace: Towards a prescriptive process for design teams*. Doctoral dissertation, DMEM, University of Strathclyde, Glasgow, UK. Retrieved October 15, 2006, from http://www.design4distribution.com

MacGregor, S. P. (2002a). New perspectives for virtual design support. *Journal of Design Research, 2*(2). Retrieved November 15, 2006, from http://jdr.tudelft.nl/articles/issue2002.02/article2.html

MacGregor, S. P. (2002b). The case study method for detailed industrial descriptions: experiences examining distributed design. In *Proceedings of the International Workshop on the Role of Empirical Studies in Understanding and Supporting Engineering Design Work, NIST*, Gaithersburg, MD.

MacGregor, S. P. (2002c). *Describing and supporting the virtual workspace: Towards a prescriptive process for design teams*. (Doctoral dissertation, DMEM, University of Strathclyde, Glasgow, UK). Retrieved November 15, 2006, from http://www.design4distribution.com

MacGregor, S. P., Arana, J., Parra, I., Lorenzo, M. P. (2006). Supporting new product creation in the Mondragon valley. *European Journal of Innovation Management, 9*(4), 418-443.

MacGregor, S. P., Thomson, A. I., & Juster, N. P. (2001, September). Information sharing within a virtual, collaborative design process: a case study. In Proceedings of the ASME Design Engineering Technical Conferences, Pittsburgh, PA.

MacGregor, S. P.; Thomson, A. I., & Juster, N. P. (2002, July). A multi-level process based investigation of distributed design. In *Proceedings of the Engineering Design Conference 2002 (EDC 2002)*, Kings College London, London.

Malins, J., Gray, C., Pirie, I., Cordiner, S., & McKillop, C. (2003, April). *The virtual design studio: Developing new tools for learning, practice and research in design*. Paper presented at the 5th European Academy of Design Conference. Barcelona, Spain.

Manfaat, D., & Duffy, A. H. B. (1998). SPIDA: abstracting and generalising layout design cases. *Artificial Intelligence for Engineering Design, Analysis, and Manufacturing, 12,* 141-159.

Mann, R. W., & Coons, S. A. (1965). Computer-aided design. *McGraw-Hill Yearbook Science and Technology*. New York: McGraw-Hill.

Marchman, J. F. III. (1998). Multinational, multidisciplinary, vertically integrated team experience in aircraft design. *International Journal of Engineering Education, 14*, 328-34.

Marcus, A. (1997, April). *Metaphor design in user interfaces: how to effectively manage expectation, surprise, comprehension, and delight*. Paper presented at the Conference on Human Factors in Computing Systems (CHI '97), Atlanta, GA. Retrieved November 20, 2005, from http://portal.acm.org/citation.cfm?doid=223355.223728

Marquis, D. G. (1988). The anatomy of successful innovations. In M. L. Tushman & W. L. Moore (Eds.), *Readings in the management of innovation* (pp. 79-87). Boston: Ballinger Publishing Company.

Martins, L. L., Gilson, L. L. & Travis Maynard, M. (2004). Virtual teams: What do we know and where do we go from here? *Journal of Management, 30*(6), 805-835.

Mascitelli, R. (2004). *The lean design guidebook*. Northridge, CA: Technology Perspectives.

Masterton, S. J., & Watt, S. N. K. (2000). Oracles, bards, and village gossips, or, social roles and meta knowledge management. *Information Systems Frontiers, 2*(3/4). Retrieved October 15, 2006, from http://springerlink.metapress.com/content/1572-9419/

May, A., & Carter, C. (2001). A case study of virtual team working in the European automotive industry. *International Journal of Industrial Ergonomics, 27*(3), 171-186.

Maznevski, M. L., & Chudoba, K. M. (2000). Bridging space over time: Global virtual team dynamics and effectiveness. *Organization Science, 11*(5), 473-492.

McCrae, R. R., & Costa, P. T., Jr. (1992). Discriminant validity of NEO-PIR facet scales, *Educational and Psychological Measurement, 52*, 229-237.

McGrath, J. E. (1984). *Groups, interaction and performance.* Englewood Cliffs, NJ: Prentice-Hall.

McLuhan, M. (1964). *Understanding media: The extensions of man.* New York: New American Library.

McLuhan, M., & Fiore, Q. (2005). *The medium is the massage.* Corte Madera: Gingko Press.

Merriam-Webster. (2000). *Merriam-Webster's Collegiate Dictionary* (software ed., Version 2.5). Springfield, MA: Merriam-Webster, Inc.

Meyerson, D., Weick, K. E., & Kramer, R. M. (1996). Swift trust and temporary groups. In R. M. Kramer & T. R. Tyler (Eds.), *Trust in organizations: Frontiers of theory and research* (pp. 166-195). Thousand Oaks, CA: Sage Publications.

Miles, M. B., & Huberman, A. M. (1994). *Qualitative data analysis* (2nd ed.). Thousand Oaks, CA: Sage Publications.

MISQ Discovery, archival version, Retrieved June 1997, from http://www.misq.org/discovery/MISQD_isworld/

MISQ Discovery, updated version as of March 24, 2006.

Moenaert, Rudy K., Caeldries, F., Lievens, A., & Wauters, E. (2000). Communication flows in international product innovation teams. *Journal of Product Innovation Management, 17*, 360-377.

Mohrman, S. A., Cohen, S. G., & Mohrman, A. M. (1995). *Designing team-based organizations: New forms for knowledge work.* San Francisco: Jossey-Bass Publishers.

Montoya-Weiss, M., Massey, A., & Song, M (2001). Getting it together: Temporal coordination and conflict management in global virtual teams. *Academy of Management Journal, 44*(6), 1251-1262.

Moreale, E., & Watt, S. N. K. (2003, March). *An agent-based approach to mailing list knowledge management.* Paper presented at the AAAI Spring Symposium on Agent-Mediated Knowledge Management (AMKM '03), Stanford, CA.

Morgan, J. M., & Liker, J. K. (2006). *The Toyota product development system.* New York: Productivity Press.

Morgan, J. N., & Sonquist, J. A. (1963, June). Problems in the analysis of survey data, and a proposal. *Journal of the American Statistical Association, 58*, 415-435.

Mulder, I., & Swaak, J. (2003). ICT innovation: starting with the team: A collaborative design workshop on selecting technology for collaboration. *Educational Technology & Society, 6*(1). Retrieved October 15, 2006, from http://ifets.ieee.org/periodical/vol_1_2003/v_1_2003.html

Mumford, M. D., & Gustafson, S. B. (1988). Creativity syndrome: integration, application and innovation. *Psychological Bulletin, 103*(1), 27-43.

Myers, M. D. (1997, June). Qualitative research in information systems, *MIS Quarterly, 22*(2), 241-242.

Nakakojin, K. (1999, October). *A framework that supports collective creativity in design using visual images.* Paper presented at the Creativity and Cognition '99 Conference. Loughborough University, UK.

Nardi, B. A., & O'Day, V. L. (1999). *Information ecologies: Using technology with heart.* Cambridge: MIT Press.

Nardi, B. A., & Whittaker, S. (2002). The place of face to face communication in distributed work. In P. Hinds & S. Kiesler (Eds.), *Distributed work* (pp. 83-110). Cambridge, MA: MIT Press.

Nardi, B. A., Whittaker, S., & Bradner, E. (2000, December). Interaction and outeraction: Instant messaging in action. In *Proceedings of the ACM Conference on Computer Supported Cooperative Work (CSCW '00)* (pp. 79-88). Philadelphia; New York: ACM Press.

Nardi, B. A., Whittaker, S., & Schwarz, H. (2002). NetWORKers and their activity in intensional networks. *Computer Supported Cooperative Work, 11*(1/2), 205-242.

Nemiro, J. (1998). *Creativity in virtual teams.* Unpublished dissertation. Claremont Graduate University.

Nemiro, J. (2004). *Creativity in virtual teams: Key components for success.* San Francisco: Pfeiffer.

Nemiro, J. E. (2000). The glue that binds creative virtual teams. In Y. Malhotra (Ed.), *Knowledge management and virtual organizations* (pp. 101-123). Hershey, NJ: Idea Group Publishing.

Nemiro, J. E. (2002). The creative process in virtual teams. *Creativity Research Journal, 14*(1), 69-83.

Nonaka, I., & Konno, N. (1998). The concept of "Ba": Building a foundation for knowledge creation. *California Management Review*, 40(3), 40-54.

Nussbaum, B. (2004, May 17). Power of design. *BusinessWeek*, p. 86.

Obeng, E. (1994). *All Change! The project leader's secret handbook.* London: Pitman. Retrieved January 8, 2006, from http://www.physorg.com/news3210.html

Observatory of European SMEs. (2002). *Enterprise and industry business statistics.* European Union Publications. Retrieved October 20, 2006, from http://ec.europa.eu/enterprise/enterprise_policy/analysis/observatory_en.htm

Ocker, R. J. (1995). *Requirements definition using a distributed asynchronous group support system: Experimental results on quality, creativity and satisfaction.* Unpublished doctoral dissertation, Rutgers University, NJ.

Ocker, R.J. (forthcoming). A balancing act: The interplay of status effects on dominance in virtual teams.

Ocker, R. J. (2001, January). The relationship between interaction, group development, and outcome: A study of virtual communication. In *Proceedings of the Thirty-Fourth Hawaii International Conference on System Sciences (HICSS 34)*, HI (CD ROM). IEEE Computer Society.

Ocker, R. J. (2005). Influences on creativity in asynchronous virtual teams: A qualitative analysis of experimental teams. *IEEE Transactions on Professional Communication, 48*(1), 22-39.

Ocker, R. J., & Fjermestad, J. (1998, January). Web-based computer-mediated communication: An experimental investigation comparing three communication modes for determining software requirements. In *Proceedings of the Thirty-First Hawaii International Conference on System Sciences, (HICSS 31)* (CD ROM). IEEE Computer Society.

Ocker, R. J., Fjermestad, J., Hiltz, S. R., & Johnson, K. (1998). Effects of four modes of group communication on the outcomes of software requirements determination, *Journal of Management Information Systems, 15*(1), 99-118.

Ocker, R. J., Hiltz, S. R., Turoff M., & Fjermestad, J. (1996). The effects of distributed group support and process structuring on software requirements development teams, *Journal of Management Information Systems, 12*(3), 127-154.

Oertig, M., & Buergi, T. (2006). The challenges of managing cross-cultural virtual project teams. *Team Performance Management, 12*(1-2), 23-30.

Olson, J. S., Olson, G. M., & Meader, D. K. (1995, May). What mix of video and audio is useful for small groups doing remote real-time design work? In *Proceedings of the Conference on Human Factors in Computing Systems*, Denver, CO (pp. 362-368).

Olson, J. S., Olson, G. M., Storrosten, M., & Carter, M. (1993). Groupwork close up: A comparison of the group design process with and without a simple group editor. *ACM Transactions on Office Information Systems, 11*, 321-348.

Orlikowski, W. (1992, October-November). *Learning from notes: Organizational issues in groupware implementation*. Paper presented at The Conference on Computer Supported Cooperative Work (CSCW '92), Toronto, Ontario, Canada.

Orlikowski, W. (1993, November). Learning from notes: Organisational issues in groupware implementation. In *Proceedings of the 1992 ACM Conference on Computer-Supported Cooperative Work*, Toronto, Ontario, Canada (pp. 362-369).

Orlikowski, W. J. (1996). Evolving with notes: Organizational change around groupware technology. In C. U. Ciborra (Ed.), *Groupware and teamwork—Invisible aid or technical hindrance?* (pp. 23-59). Chichester, UK: John Wiley & Sons.

Orlikowski, W. J., & Hofman, J. D. (1997, Winter). An improvisational model of change management: The case of groupware technologies. *Sloan Management Review, 32*(2), 11-21.

Ottosson, S. (2004). Dynamic product development (DPD). *Technovation, 24*(3), 207-217.

Pahl, G., & Beitz, W. (1996). *Engineering design—A systematic approach*. London, Springer-Verlag.

Parkinson, C. N. (1958). *Parkinson's Law: The Pursuit of Progress*. London: John Murray.

Parmeter, S. M., & Gaber, J. D. (1971, November). Creative scientists rate creativity factors. *Research Management*, 65-70.

Pasmore, W. A. (1997). Managing organizational deliberations in nonroutine work. In R. Katz (Ed.), *The human side of managing technological innovation* (pp. 413-423). New York: Oxford University Press.

Paul, S., Seetharaman, P., Samarah, I., & Mykytyna, P. P. (2004). Impact of heterogeneity and collaborative conflict management style on the performance of synchronous global virtual teams. *Information and Management, 41*(3), 303-321.

Paulus, P. B. (2000). Groups, teams, and creativity: The creative potential of idea-generating groups. *Applied Psychology, 49*, 237-262.

Paunonen, S. V., & Ashton, M. C. (2001). Big five factors and facets and the prediction of behavior. *Journal of Personality and Social Psychology, 81*(3), 524-539.

Pelz, D. C., & Andrews, F. M. (1966). *Scientists in organizations*. New York: John Wiley & Sons.

Pfister, C. S., & Wessner, M. (1998). *The metaphor of virtual rooms in the cooperative learning environment CLear*. German National Research Center for Information Technology.

Piccoli, G., & Ives, B. (2000). Virtual teams: Managerial behavior control's impact on team effectiveness. In *Proceedings of the 21st International Conference on Information Systems* (pp. 575-580).

Pirola-Merlo, A., & Mann, L. (2004). The relationship between individual creativity and team creativity: Aggregating across people and time. *Journal of Organizational Behavior, 25*, 235-257.

PMI (2004). *A guide to the project management body of knowledge* (PMBOK® Guide, 3rd ed.). Newtown Square, PA: Project Management Institute.

Polzer, J. T., Milton, L. P., & Swann, W. B. (2002). Capitalizing on diversity: Interpersonal congruence in small work groups. *Administrative Science Quarterly, 47*, 296-325.

Poole, M. S., & DeSanctis, G. (1992). Microlevel structuration in computer-supported group decision making. *Human Communication Research, 19*(1), 5-49.

Poskela, J., Berg, P., Pihlajamaa, J., Seppälä, J., & Feland, J. (2004, April). The role of roadmaps in fuzzy-front-end phase of innovation process. In *Proceedings of IAMOT 2004, 13th International Conference on Management of Technology*, Washington, DC.

Powel, A. (2004, October). Virtual rooms, real meetings. *Ariadne*, 41, 9. Retrieved October 15, 2006, from http://www.ariadne.ac.uk/issue41/powell/

Press, M., & Cooper, R. (2003). *The design experience: The role of design and designers in the twenty-first century*. Aldershot: Ashgate.

Proctor, T., Tan K. H., & Fuse K. (2004). Cracking the incremental paradigm of Japanese creativity. *Creativity and Innovation Management, 3*(4), 207-215.

Pugh, S. (1990). *Total design: Integrated methods for successful product engineering*. Wokingham, UK: Addison-Wesley.

Rando, T. C. (2001). XML-based interoperability in the integrated shipbuilding environment (ISE). *Journal of Ship Production, 17,* 69-75.

Reddy, M. J. (1979). The conduit metaphor—A case of frame conflict in our language about language. In A. Ortony (Ed.), *Metaphor and thought* (pp. 284-324). Cambridge: Cambridge University Press.

Reinertsen, D. G. (1999). Taking the fuzziness out of the fuzzy front end. *Research and Technology Management, 42*(6), 25-31.

Rice, R. E. (1984). *The new media*. Beverly Hills: Sage Publications.

Rice, R. E. (1994). Relating electronic mail use and network structure to R&D work networks and performance. *Journal of Management Information Systems, 11*(1), 9-29.

Ridgeway, C. L. (1984). Dominance, performance and status in groups: A theoretical analysis. In E. Lawler (Ed.), *Advances in group processes: Theory and research* (Vol. 1, pp. 59-93). Greenwich, CT: JAI Press.

Riopelle, K., Gluesing, J. C., Alcordo, T. C., Baba, M., Britt, D., McKether, W. et al. (2003). Context, task, and the evolution of technology use in global virtual teams. In C. B. Gibson & S. G. Cohen (Eds.), *Virtual teams that work: Creating conditions for virtual team effectiveness* (pp. 239-264). San Francisco: Jossey-Bass.

Ripley, B. D. (2005). *Tree: Classification and regression trees*. Retrieved September 9, from http://cran.us.r-project.org/doc/packages/tree.pdf

Robinson, A., & Stern, S. (1998). *Corporate creativity: How innovation and improvement actually happen*. San Francisco: Berrett-Koehler.

Rocco, E. (1998, April). Trust breaks down in electronic contexts but can be repaired by some initial face to face contact. In *Proceedings of CHI'98*, Los Angeles, CA (pp. 496-502). New York: ACM Press.

Rogers, C. R. (1954). Towards a theory of creativity. *A Review of General Semantics, 11*(4), 249-260.

Rompelman, O., & de Vries, J. (2002). Practical training and internships in engineering education: Educational goals and assessment. *European Journal of Engineering Education, 27,* 173-180.

Roseman, M. G., & Greenberg, S (1996, November). TeamRooms: Network places for collaboration. In *Proceedings of the ACM CSCW '96 Conference on Computer Supported Cooperative Work*, Boston.

Rosenberg, T. E. (2000, July). The *Reservoir: Towards a poetic model of research in design*. Research into Practice Conference. Hatfield, UK. Retrieved November 15, 2006, from http://www.herts.ac.uk/artdes1/research/papers/wpades/vol1/rosenberg2.html

Runco, M. A. (1994). Creativity and its discontents. In M. P. Shaw & M. A. Runco (Eds.), *Creativity and affect*. Norwood, NJ: Ablex.

Runco, M. A. (1995). The creativity and job satisfaction of artists in organizations. *Empirical Studies of the Arts, 13,* 39-45.

Savage, S. L. (2003). *Decision making with insight*. Belmont, CA: Brooks/Cole.

Schank, R. C., & Cleary, C. (1995). *Engines for education*. Hillsdale, NJ: Lawrence Erlbaum Associates.

Schenkel, A. (2004). Investigating the influence that media richness has on learning in a community of practice. In P. Hildreth & C. Kimble (Eds.), *Knowledge networks* (pp. 47-57). Hershey, PA: Idea Group.

Schneider, S. C., & Barsoux, J. (2003). *Managing across cultures*. Harlow, Essex: Pearson.

Schön, D. (1983). *The reflective practitioner.* Paperback edition (1991). Aldershot, UK: Ashgate.

Sclater, N., Grierson, H., Ion, W. J., & MacGregor, S. P. (2001). Online collaborative design projects: overcoming barriers to communication. *International Journal of Engineering Education, 17*, 189-196.

Segrestin, B. (2005). Partnering to explore: The Renault-Nissan Alliance as a forerunner of new cooperative patterns. *Research Policy, 34*, 657-672.

Seidman, I. E. (1991). *Interviewing as qualitative research*. Columbia University, NY: Teachers College Press.

Sell, J., Lovaglia, M. J., Mannix, E. A., Samuelson, C. D., & Wilson, R. K. (1992). Investigating conflict, power, and status within and among groups. *Small Group Research, 35*(1), 44-72.

Sethia, N. K. (1995). The role of collaboration in creativity. In C. M. Ford & D. A. Goia (Eds.), *Creative action in organization* (pp. 100-105). Thousand Oaks, CA: Sage.

Sewell, W. H., Jr. (1992). A theory of structure: Duality, agency, and transformation. *American Journal of Sociology, 98*, 129.

Shalley, C. E., Zhou, J., & Oldham, G. R. (2004). The effects of personal and contextual characteristics on creativity: Where should we go from here? *Journal of Management, 30*(6), 933-958.

Sharples, M. (1994). Cognitive support and the rhythm of design. In T. Dartnall (Ed.), *Artificial intelligence, and creativity* (pp. 385-402) The Netherlands: Kluwer Academic Publishers.

Sherif, M., White, B. J., & Harvey, O. J. (1955). Status in experimentally produced groups. *American Journal of Sociology, 66*, 370-379.

Short, J., Williams, E., & Chudoba, K. M. (1976). *The social psychology of telecommunications*. New York: John Wiley & Sons.

Siegel, J., Dubrovsky, V., Kiesler, S., & McGuire, T. (1986). Group processes in computer-mediated communication. *Organizational Behavior & Human Decision Processes, 37*, 157-187.

Smith, P. G. (2001). Using conceptual modelers for business advantage. *Time-Compression Technologies, 6*(3), 18-24.

Smith, P. G. (2005). Why is agile development so scary? *Agile Project Management Advisory Service* (Cutter Consortium), *6*(9), 1-3.

Smith, P. G., & Blanck, E. (2002). From experience: Leading dispersed teams. *The Journal of Product Innovation Management, 19*(4), 294-304.

Smith, P. G., & Merritt, G. M. (2002). *Proactive risk management*. New York: Productivity Press.

Smith, P. G., & Reinertsen, D. G. (1998). *Developing products in half the time*. Hoboken, NJ: John Wiley.

Sobek, D. K., II, Ward, A. C., & Liker, J. K. (1999). Toyota's principles of set-based concurrent engineering. *Sloan Management Review, 40*(2), 67-83.

Sonquist, J. A., Laud Baker, E.L., & Morgan, J. N. (1973). *Searching for structure*. Ann Arbor: Institute for Social Research.

Sosik, J. J., Avolio, B. J., & Kahai, S. S. (1998). Inspiring group creativity: Comparing anonymous and identified electronic brainstorming. *Small Group Research, 29*(1), 3-31.

Soyjaudah, K. M. S., & Jahmeerbacus, M. I. (2000). A new digital communication course enhanced by PC-based design projects. *International Journal of Engineering Education, 16*, 553-559.

Spender, J.C. (1996). Organizational knowledge, learning, and memory: Three concepts in search of a theory. *Journal of Organizational Change, 9*, 63-78.

Sproull, L., Kiesler, S. (1991). *Connections: New ways of working in the networked organization.* Cambridge: MIT Press.

Stamm, Von B. (2003). *Managing innovation, design and creativity.* Chichester, West Sussex: John Wiley & Sons.

Stankiewicz, R. (2000). *The concept of 'design space.'* Retrieved November, 15, 2006, from http://www.lri.lu.se/pdf/Crafoord00/rsws.pdf. Modified version published in J. Ziman, (Ed.) (2000), *Technological innovation as an evolutionary process.* Cambridge, MA: Cambridge University Press.

Steiner, G. (1965). *The creative organization.* Chicago: University of Chicago Press.

Strauss, A., & Corbin, J. (1990). *Basics of qualitative research.* Newbury Park, CA: Sage Publications.

Strauss, A., & Corbin, J. (1998). *Basics of qualitative research: Techniques and procedures for developing grounded theory* (2nd ed.). Thousand Oaks, CA: Sage Publications.

Suchman, L. A. (1987). *Plans and situated actions: The problem of human-machine communications.* Cambridge, UK: Cambridge University Press.

Sutton, R. I. (2001). *Weird ideas that work: 11½ practices for promoting, managing, and sustaining innovation.* New York: The Free Press.

Sutton, R. I., & Hargadon, A. (1996). Brainstorming groups in context: Effectiveness in a product design firm. *Administrative Science Quarterly, 41*(4), 685-718.

Swann, P., & Birke, D. (2005). *How do creativity and design enhance business performance? A framework for interpreting the evidence.* DTI Think Piece, University of Nottingham Business School.

Taggar, S. (2002). Individual creativity and group ability to utilize individual creative resources: A multilevel model. *Academy of Management Journal, 45*, 315-330.

Tang, J. C. (1991). Findings from observational studies of collaborative work. *International Journal of Man-Machine Studies, 34*(2), 143-160.

Tavčar, J., & Duhovnik, J. (2005). Engineering change management in individual and mass production. *Robotics and Computer-Integrated Manufacturing, 21*(3), 205-215.

Tavčar, J., Žavbi, R. Verlinden, J. & Duhovnik, J. (2005). Skills for effective communication and work in global product development teams. *Journal of Engineering Design, 16*(6), 557-576.

Taylor, C. W. (1988). Various approaches to and definitions of creativity. In R. J. Sternberg (Ed.), *The nature of creativity: Contemporary psychological perspectives* (pp. 99-121). Cambridge: Cambridge University Press.

Teasley, S., Covi, L, Krishnan, M. S., & Olson, J. S. (2000, December). How does radical colocation help a team succeed? In *Proceedings of the ACM Conference on Computer-Supported Cooperative Work (CSCW 2000)*, Philadelphia (pp. 339-346). New York: ACM Press.

Tether, B. S. (2005). *The role of design in business performance.* DTI Think Piece, CRIC, University of Manchester.

The Networking Institute. (2000). *Virtual teams booklet.* Retrieved September 12, 2006, from http://www.netage.com/learning/mini_book/Mini_book.html

Therneau, T. M., & Atkinson, B. (2005). *The Rpart package.* Retrieved November 15, 2006, from http://cran.us.r-project.org/doc/packages/rpart.pdf

Thomke, S. H. (2003). *Experimentation matters.* Boston: Harvard Business School Press.

Thompson, L. (2003). Improving the creativity of organizational work groups. *Academy of Management Executive, 17*(1), 96-109.

Tigris.org. (2001-2006a). *Scarab.* Retrieved October 15, 2006, from http://scarab.tigris.org/

Toomey, L. A., Adams, L, & Churchill, E. (1998). Meetings in a virtual space: Creating a digital document. In *Proceedings of the Thirty-First Annual Hawaii International Conference on System Sciences (HICSS)* (Vol. 3, p. 236).

Top Gear. (1996, March 7). Ford Motor Company case study. *Computer Weekly.*

Trevino, L., Lengel, R., and Daft, R. (1987). Media symbolism, media richness, and media choice in organizations. *Communication Research, 14*(5), 553-574.

Trygg, L., & Nobelius, d. (2002). Stop chasing the front end process—Management of the early phases in product development projects. *International Journal of Project Management, 20,* 331-340.

Tschumi, B. (1990). *Questions of space.* London: AA Publications.

Tufte, E. (1997). *Visual explanations: Images and quantities, evidence and narrative.* Cheshire, CT: Graphics Press.

Ulrich, K. T., & Eppinger, S. D. (2000). *Product design and development* (2nd ed.). Boston: Irwin/McGraw-Hill.

Van Engelen, Jo M. L., Kiewiet, D. Jan, & Terlouw, P. (2001). Improving performance of product development teams through managing polarity. *International Studies of Management and Organization, 31,* 46-63.

VanGundy, A. (1987). Organizational creativity and innovation. In S. G. Isaksen (Ed.), *Frontiers of creativity research: Beyond the basics* (pp. 358-379). Buffalo, NY: Bearly Limited.

Veryzer, R. W. (1998). Discontinuous innovation and the new product development process. *Journal of Product Innovation Management, 15*(4), 304-321.

VIVACE Project. (2005). *Virtual Enterprise Collaboration Hub—Services description.* Retrieved October 30, 2006, from http://www.vivaceproject.com/content/advanced/vechsd_full.pdf

Volpentesta, A., Frega, N., & Muzzupappa, M. (2001). Models and methodology for simulating virtual enterprises in educational environment. *European Journal of Engineering Education, 26,* 391-405.

Volvo Aero Corporation. (2005). *AERO: News, Views & Interviews.* Number 3.

von Hippel, E. (1994). *The sources of innovation.* New York: Oxford University Press.

Walther, J. (1992). Interpersonal effects in computer-mediated communication. *Communication Research, 19*(1), 52-90.

Walther, J., & Parks, M. (2002). Cues filtered out, cues filtered in: Computer-mediated communication and relationships. In M. Knapp, J. Daly, & G. Miller (Eds.), *The handbook of interpersonal communication* (3rd ed.). Thousand Oaks, CA: Sage.

WebEx Communications, Inc. (2006). *Web conferencing, online meetings, and video conferencing.* Retrieved April 30, 2006, from www.webex.com

Weiss, L., (2002). Developing tangible strategies. *Design Management Journal, 13*(1), 33-38.

West, M. A. (1990). The social psychology of innovation in groups. In M. A. West & J. L. Farr (Eds.), *Innovation and creativity at work: Psychological and organizational strategies* (pp. 309-333). Chichester, UK: Wiley & Sons.

Whitfield, R. I., Duffy, A. H. B., Coates, G., & Hills, W. (2003b). Efficient process optimisation. *International Journal of Concurrent Engineering: Research and Applications, 11,* 83-92.

Whitfield, R. I., Duffy, A. H. B., Meehan, J., & Wu, Z. (2003a). Ship product modelling. *Journal of Ship Production, 19,* 230-245.

Whittaker, S. (2003). Theories and methods in mediated communication. In A. Graeser (Ed.), *The handbook of discourse processes.* Cambridge: Lawrence Erlbaum.

Williams, E. (1977). Experimental comparisons of face to face and mediated communication: A Review. *Psychological Bulletin, 84*(5), 963-976.

Woodman, R., & Schoenfeldt, L. F. (1989). Individual differences in creativity: An interactionist perspective. In J. A. Glover & C. R. Reynolds, (Eds.), *Handbook of Creativity* (pp. 77-92). New York: Plenum Press.

Yan, X. T., Rehman, F., & Borg, J. (2002). Foreseeing design solution consequences using design context information. *IFIP Working Group 5.2.* Malta.

Yin, R. K. (1994). *Case study research: Design methods* (2nd ed.). London: Sage Publications.

Yin, R. K. (1998). An abridged version of case study research: Design and method. *Handbook of applied social research methods* (pp. 229-260). Sage.

Ylinenpää, H., & Nilsson, N. (2000, June). Knowledge transfer and organizational competence building: a case study of two knowledge-intensive firms. In *Proceedings of the 5th Conference on Competence Management*, Helsinki, Finland (pp. 1-17).

Žavbi, R., & Duhovnik, J. (2001). Model of conceptual design phase and its applications in the design of mechanical drive units. In C. T. Leondes (ur.). *The design of manufacturing systems, Vol. 5. Computer aided design, engineering and manufacturing* (pp. 1-38). Boca Raton [etc.]: CRC Press.

Žavbi, R., & Tavčar, J. (2005). Preparing undergraduate students for work in virtual product development teams. *Computers & Education, 44*(4), 357-376.

Zhang, Y., Maccallum, K. J., & Duffy, A. H. B. (1997). Product knowledge modelling and management. In *Proceedings of the 2nd Workshop of Product Structuring—International Society for the Science of Engineering Workshop (WDK)*. Delf, Netherlands, WDFK.

Zheng, J., Veinott, E., Bos, N., Olson, J. S., & Olson, G. M. (2002, April). Trust without touch: jumpstarting long distance trust with initial social activities. In *Proceedings of the Conference on Human Factors in Computing Systems (CHI 2002)*, Minneapolis, MN (pp. 131-146). New York: ACM Press.

Ziegler, R., Diehl, M., & Zijlstra, G. (2000). Idea production in nominal and virtual groups: Does computer-mediated communication improve group brainstorming? *Group Processes & Intergroup Relations, 3*(2), 141-158.

Zigurs, I. (2003). Leadership in virtual teams: oxymoron or opportunity. *Organizational Dynamics, 31*(4), 339-351.

Zigurs, I., Poole, M. S., & DeSanctis, G. L. (1988). A study of influence in computer-mediated group decision making. *MIS Quarterly, 12*(4), 625-644.

Zmud, R., Lind, M., and Young, F. (1990). An attribute space for organizational communication channels. *Information Systems Research, 1*(4), 440-457.

About the Contributors

Steven P. MacGregor is an innovation consultant based in Barcelona and a research fellow at IESE Business School where he works across two research streams—business innovation and business in society. He also teaches at the University of Girona and the European University and is part of various working groups and advisory panels in Brussels, including the European Regions Research and Innovation (ERRIN) network. Dr. MacGregor previously held a Spanish government-funded post-doctoral post within the Mondragón Corporation in the Basque Country, the largest industrial cooperative in the world. He is a visiting professor at ETEO, the Business School of the University of Mondragón. He holds a PhD in engineering design management from the University of Strathclyde in Glasgow and has completed visiting researcher positions within university design, engineering and computer science centres at Stanford, Carnegie-Mellon, and Calgary. He was listed in Marquis *Who's Who in Science & Engineering (2003)* at age 25 and has published in *Business Week*, the *Journal of Product Innovation Management*, and the *European Journal of Innovation Management*. An international level duathlete, he has directs a sports tour company in Girona.

Teresa Torres-Coronas has a bachelor's degree in economics (Barcelona University) and a PhD in management (Rovira i Virgili University). She won first prize in the 2000 edition of EADA related management research. She is the author of the book *Valuing Brands* (Ediciones Gestión 2000, Spain), co-author of the book *Retrieve Your Creativity* (Septem Ediciones, Spain), and co-editor of the books *Changing the Way you Teach: Creative Tools for Management Education* (Septem Ediciones, Spain) and *e-HRM: Managing Knowledge People* (IGI Global, USA). She is the author of many articles and conference papers about intangible management, management education, and applied creativity and IT. She is a management professor at the Universitat Rovira i Virgili, Tarragona, and is one of the researchers of the ELIS group (E-government for Local Integration with Sustainability, Hull University). She is an active member of the Management Education and Development Division (Academy of Management) and the Information Resources Management Association (IRMA).

* * *

Thomas Buergi (Dr. Phil., MA) is a professor of cross-cultural management and marketing at the University of Applied Sciences Northwestern Switzerland (FHNW) and programme director of Edinburgh Business School MBA in Basel. He teaches courses in cross-cultural organisational behaviour, human resource management, mergers and acquisitions as well as consumer behaviour. He has worked as a consultant for major organisations. His research interests are in the areas of cross-cultural team development and international brand development.

Nicklas Bylund started as an industrial PhD student at Volvo Car Corporation in 1999 and graduated in 2004 from Luleå University of Technology, Sweden. His focus was put on simulation support for designers in early and late phases of car body development. Since 2004 he has worked in two platform development projects at Ford in Germany as the Volvo representative for car body issues. The position allows a good insight at different levels of hierarchy and departments in the companies.

Alastair Conway is a full-time research assistant within the University of Strathclyde's Department of Design Manufacture and Engineering Management. He graduated from the University of Strathclyde with a BEng (Hons.) in product design engineering followed by an MSc in integrated product development. He was involved in the large and highly successful "VRShips-RoPax"; an EU funded research and development project spanning 13 different European countries and involving 36 different organisations. Conway is currently working as a researcher on the EPSRC funded Grand Challenge project "Knowledge & Information Management Through Life" as well as studying part-time for his PhD in design information capture.

Alex Duffy is presently a senior lecturer and director of the CAD Centre, as well as a professor of research within the Department of Design Manufacture and Engineering Management at the University of Strathclyde. He lectures in engineering design, design management, product development, knowledge intensive CAD, advanced computational techniques, and databases. His main research interests have been the application of knowledge based techniques in conceptual design, product and domain knowledge modeling, machine learning techniques and design re-use, performance measurement and design productivity, sketching and vague geometric modeling, and design coordination. He has published over 100 papers and is on the board of numerous journals and conferences in engineering design and artificial intelligence in design. He is currently the president of the Design Society, an international body encompassing all aspects and disciplines of design. He was responsible for coordinating the VRS-ROPAX project.

John Feland is the human interface architect for Synaptics, the world leader in capacitive interface solutions. A winner of a 2006 Red Dot Design Concept Award, he leads efforts to understand and address key human interface. Previously, he built the Synaptics Concept Prototyping Team that generates next generation user interface devices. While at Synaptics, he completed his PhD at Stanford University where he developed novel innovation metrics that connect design efforts to corporate performance. He served five years as an officer in the United States Air Force where he architected a multimillion dollar environment to analyze missile warning data and crafted award winning engineering design curriculum at the United States Air Force Academy. Before serving in the Air Force, he was a designer at IDEO. He received his SB in mechanical engineering from the Massachusetts Institute of Technology, and his MS and PhD in mechanical engineering from Stanford University.

Javier Fínez has a degree in computer engineering from ESIDE – Faculty of Engineering at the University of Deusto (Spain) and an MSc in applied artificial intelligence from the University of Aberdeen (Scotland). He is currently studying toward a PhD within the Enterprise Organization Department at the University of Basque Country (Spain). Having completed a two-year research post at Fundación Labein, he currently works as a researcher at MIK (Mondragon Innovation and Knowledge), one of the leading Research Centres of MCC (Mondragon Cooperative Corporation) where he is in charge of new technologies for knowledge management. He has published chapters in various books and several articles at conferences in the areas of the extended enterprise, future of work and social change and technology.

William Ion is the head of department and a senior lecturer in the Department of Design, Manufacture and Engineering Management at the University of Strathclyde. He graduated from the University of Glasgow in 1979 with an Honours degree in mechanical engineering with specialisation in production management. Prior to his appointment to the Department of Design, Manufacture and Engineering Management (DMEM) at the University of Strathclyde in 1985, he spent periods with Barr and Stroud Ltd and Yarrow Shipbuilders Ltd. In both of these positions he was responsible for a wide variety of design projects principally for the MOD. He has been actively involved in the development of design and design management education at secondary school, undergraduate and postgraduate levels. He established the University of Strathclyde Product Design Engineering course in 1991. He has been an investigator on research projects in the areas of design methods, computer supported collaborative working in design, design education, and rapid prototyping.

Ola Isaksson holds a position as senior company specialist in engineering design at Volvo Aero in Sweden. He has an MSc in mechanical engineering and a PhD in computer aided design, both from Luleå University of Technology. He joined Volvo Aero in 1994 and is currently responsible for technology and methods development in the area of engineering and product development.

Jan Kratzer is an assistant professor of business development at the School of Management and Organization of the University of Groningen, The Netherlands. His research is mainly on the communicational patterns within NPD teams, the effects of virtuality, and the development of social network measures. Much of his recent work has been published with Roger Leenders and Jo van Engelen. He has authored one book.

Andreas Larsson earned his PhD in computer aided design at Luleå University of Technology in June 2005. He is currently a researcher and project coordinator with a core competence in interaction design of physical and virtual collaboration environments for globally distributed design teams. He is also heavily involved in projects concerning knowledge engineering. His research is influenced by ethnographic and scenario-based design approaches to better tune technologies and methods to the needs of a global workforce. Studies have mainly been carried out in automotive and aerospace engineering projects in industry, and in global research and education projects between Stanford University and Luleå.

Tobias Larsson is an associate professor at the Division of Computer Aided Design, Luleå University of Technology. His core competence is within engineering product development and knowledge engineering. The focus is on supporting engineering product development processes with tools and methods for knowledge engineering in order to enable faster development of new and innovative solutions to industrial needs and opportunities.

Roger Th.A.J. Leenders is an associate professor of business development at the School of Management and Organization, University of Groningen, The Netherlands. His research focuses on various aspects of the performance of NPD teams. Lately, much of his research focuses on the effects of virtuality on NPD teams. He is a specialist in social network analysis. His recent work has appeared in, among others, *Journal of Product Innovation Management, Creativity and Innovation Management, Journal of Engineering and Technology Management, PDMA Toolbook for New Product Development I and II, Social Networks, Team Performance Management*. He has also co-authored and edited three books.

Thomas Leerberg, PhD, is a trained architect MAA and cand. arch. from the Southern California Institute of Architecture, Los Angeles and Arkitektskolen Aarhus, Denmark (1996). He was awarded a doctoral PhD in architecture on the subject "methodology of spatial design tools" at Arkitektskolen Aarhus, Denmark (2004). Since 2005, he has held the position of associate professor of design theory and method at Designskolen Kolding. He has been a guest lecturer in Finland, Russia, Lebanon, and Dubai, and is affiliated with the University of Copenhagen. He has received two AIA-awards, has won six Danish architectural competitions, and has been published widely in Denmark and abroad.

Aggelos Liapis is currently completing a Ph.D. at the School of Computing and Gray's School of Art at The Robert Gordon University, Aberdeen. His research is concerned with the implementation of computer mediated collaborative design environments to support designers when working in remote collaboration. His research considers the nature of creativity and how the creative process can be supported through the use of dedicated online environments. He holds Masters Degrees in Computer Graphics and Network Systems, and a Bachelors degree in Software Development from the universities of Hull, Sunderland and Lincoln respectively.

Julian Malins is a reader in design and the director of postgraduate studies at Gray's School of Art with responsibility for postgraduate research and master's programmes. He originally trained as a ceramicist and ran his own business for a number of years before returning to higher education. He has undertaken post-doctoral research into integrating and adapting new technologies to support design since completing his PhD at The Robert Gordon University, Aberdeen in 1993. Publication topics include: ceramic technology, practice-based research methodologies for visually based disciplines, and the development of virtual learning environments.

Chris McKillop is a research fellow at Gray's School of Art and the School of Computing. Her research interests lie in the areas of learning technologies, student learning, ambient computing and evaluation, and she has conducted research in a diverse range of disciplines including: art and design, psychology, computing, and management. Her current research includes investigating the role of narrative in learning by using online storytelling to facilitate the reflective process and investigating visual representations of learning. She has degrees in artificial intelligence and human computer interaction and designs and evaluates interactive learning environments.

Joanne Meehan was a research fellow in the CAD Centre, University of Strathclyde. She undertook a master's degree in product design engineering at the University of Strathclyde. Following completion of her first degree, she conducted a PhD research project to establish a methodology and tool for establishing functional, behavioural and structural modularity, and used the methodology to facilitate design re-use. Her research interests included modular design, design re-use, product structuring, knowledge management, and design methodologies. She helped coordinate the VRS-ROPAX project and provided technical input to the development of the virtual platform.

A great friend and respected colleague to several of the authors in this book, Jo is sorely missed.

Jill Nemiro, PhD, is an associate professor in the Psychology and Sociology Department at California State Polytechnic University, Pomona, and an adjunct professor in the Human Resources Design master's program at Claremont Graduate University. Her research interests are in the area of organizational and team creativity, and the virtual workplace. She has published numerous articles and book chapters on the topics of creativity and virtual teams. She recently published the book, *Creativity in Virtual Teams* (Pfeiffer, 2004). Professionally, she worked for 20 years on teams in the entertainment industry. Most recently, Dr. Nemiro has led a series of workshops and telecourses on the topic of creativity in virtual teams to corporations looking to improve the quality of their virtual teams. Dr. Nemiro received her PhD in organizational psychology from Claremont Graduate University.

Rosalie J. Ocker, PhD, is a member of the faculty at The Pennsylvania State University, University Park, USA. She has studied creativity in virtual teams in a series of experiments that span 10 years. Most recently her research is centered on the study of subgroups in partially distributed teams. In particular, she is investigating the impact of various dimensions of distance and leadership configuration on team dynamics and performance outcomes in both domestic and international teams. Dr. Ocker has published in various journals and conference proceedings, including the *Journal of Management Information Systems, IEEE Transactions on Professional Communication, Decision and Group Negotiation*, and Hawaii International Conference on System Sciences (HICSS).

Margaret Oertig, MA, MEd, is a lecturer in the International Business Management programme at the University of Applied Sciences (Fachhochschule Nordwestschweiz) in Basel, Switzerland. Her teaching focus is mainly cross-cultural teams, negotiation and conflict management. She is also a tutor on the Edinburgh Business School MBA programme, teaching negotiation. Her research interests are in the areas of simulation gaming and the interaction of trust and knowledge sharing in cross-cultural virtual collaboration.

Terry Rosenberg MA RCA is currently head of the Design Department at Goldsmiths, University of London. He is a practising artist and design theorist. He has taught design at the Royal College of Art and at Goldsmiths. As an academic, his research pivots around two thematic loci—the "representation of ideas" and "ideation through representation". He is interested in how we model thought (the settled) and how we think (un-settled idea) in representational models. He has been working, in this regard, on the "creative hunch" particularly; and has been seeking to develop a technicity of the "hunch" using the idea of "prospects" as its foundational base. He has worked with industry to develop new applications for emerging technologies and has developed creative innovation workshops for regional and international companies.

Preston G. Smith has specialized in time-to-market issues in product development for over 20 years. He is co-author of the classic, *Developing Products in Half the Time*, and has helped many companies shorten their development cycles by applying its methods. After seeing the great power of co-located teams, he has consulted to companies that wished to retain as much of this power as possible with their dispersed teams. More recently, he has shifted from his emphasis from speed to flexibility as he observed companies hamstrung by rigid development processes, and he is preparing a book on flexible product development to be released in September 2007. He holds a PhD in engineering from Stanford University. He is book review editor of the *Journal of Product Innovation Management*.

Angela Stone has a BEng (Hons.) and PhD in mechanical engineering (Sandwich). Starting work in NPD within Oxford Instruments, she switched to academia in 1996 as a senior lecturer within engineering design at Staffordshire University where she was responsible for Award Tutorship for the Design Technology Stream. During her time at Stafford, she worked on the development of EdNet, an engineering design network. Since 2002 she has been a lecturer at DMEM, University of Strathclyde, where she is active in undergraduate and postgraduate teaching, research and industry-led group projects (including Knowledge Transfer Projects funded by DTI) where students are encouraged to undertake computer-supported cooperative work.

Jože Tavčar has been a quality manager at Iskra Mehanizmi company since 2006. Between 2001 and 2006 he was involved in product development as a project leader at the Domel Electric Motor Company. Tavčar received his MSc and PhD degrees from the University of Ljubljana (1994 and 1999, respectively). His research field was information flow analyses, PDM/PLM systems and concurrent engineering. In 1999 and 2000, he participated in a project applying the eMatrix PLM system. Tavčar works part-time at the Faculty of Mechanical Engineering in Ljubljana, and is a staff member of the international global product realisation (E-GPR) course. His current research activities mainly involve collaboration in virtual teams, process optimisation and quality system.

Avril Thomson earned her PhD in 1997 in the field of representation and processing of design standards. As a research assistant in the Department of DMEM, she developed expertise in CSCW as applied to multidisciplinary design projects through work on the Design Council funded "Integration of Design Specialists Through Shared Workspaces" project. She became a lecturer in the department in September 1998 and has been involved in a number of other projects in this area including: ICON and CVDS funded by SHEFC, the main aim of which was to develop approaches to design based upon virtual environments; VIDEEO, funded by SOCRATES to support the design and development of an environment to support the teaching of the NPD process to engineering and business students through scenario-based collaborative projects; Communicative Constraints Imposed by Video Mediated Communication, EPSRC funded to investigate the psychological effects of adopting video mediated communication within a design environment; Achieving and Maintaining Effective Gateway Working, funded by Teaching Company Scheme.

Jo M. L. Van Engelen is a professor of business development and professor of business research methods, School of Management and Organization of the University of Groningen, The Netherlands. He is also member of the executive board of ANWB (Dutch Automobile Club). His research focuses on the performance of NPD teams, on the implementation of market orientation in companies, and on sustainability in NPD. His latest book is on knowledge creation and sustainable innovation (2004, with René Jorna).

Jouke Verlinden is an assistant professor at the Delft University of Technology. He holds an MSc in computer science (1993) and studied virtual reality at the Georgia institute of Technology (Atlanta). After seven years of working in industry as project manager and interaction designer, he returned to academia. At the Faculty of Industrial Design Engineering, he teaches several courses in design and innovation, while his research focuses on the application of augmented reality and rapid prototyping technologies to support design. He is one of the Delft staff members that are involved with the course on global product realisation since its launch in the year 2000.

Mike Waller, MA, RCA, is a lecturer in design at Goldsmiths, University of London. His career has been as an industrial designer for GEC, a design director of London-based design studio, leading a R&D blue sky products group at NCR's Knowledge Lab, and in academia developing master's level courses in creative technologies. His research work predominately focuses on creative applications of emerging technology, ranging from wearable computing through to interactive intelligent products and furniture. He holds international patents in the area of ubiquitous computing products and context based technologies, and his work has been exhibited at the Science Museum in London and an IEEE wearable technology conference in San Francisco. Waller has also developed technologies that exploit network effects, which includes resource sharing and group cooperation.

Stuart Watt is a reader and research coordinator in the School of Computing at the Robert Gordon University, Aberdeen. He originally trained as a computer scientist and worked in artificial intelligence, both in industry and academia, before returning to academic life and moving into psychology and cognitive science. He is a multidisciplinary researcher at the convergence between computing, cognitive science, and the social sciences, whose work is aimed at using computing and related technologies to improve people's use of knowledge and information. His research topics include technology enhanced learning, ambient computing, text categorisation, organisational learning and knowledge management, and theoretical foundations of cognition.

Robert Ian Whitfield is a senior research fellow at the CAD Centre at the University of Strathclyde. In 1991 he gained a BEng (Hons.) in mechanical engineering from Newcastle upon Tyne Polytechnic. Following graduation he then carried out a PhD research project investigating modes of operation of turbo-generator rotor bearings. He continued working within the fields of hydrodynamics and rotor-dynamics for a further 18 months at Parsons Power Generation Systems. On moving to the CAD Centre, he chaired the technical committee of the VRS platform (on which the chapter is based) that was responsible for the design, development and implementation of the virtual platform. He is currently coordinating and undertaking research within a number of European Union FP6 and EPSRC research projects.

Zhichao Wu is a research fellow in CAD Centre, University of Strathclyde. He holds a BSc in civil engineering and an MSc in project management, and a PhD on AI in design. His research interests include learning in design, distributed design, system integration, and data and information management. His recent publications are on collective learning in design and integrated systems.

Roman Žavbi is an assistant professor at the University of Ljubljana, Faculty of Mechanical Engineering, Ljubljana, where he teaches courses on engineering design methods and computer aided design. He also teaches a course on machine elements at the Faculty of Education. His research focuses on prescriptive models of engineering design, especially use of physical laws and complementary basic schemata in conceptual phase of product design, and collaborative product development. In 2001 he joined the international team, which prepared and taught the course on global product realisation (E-GPR). He is also consultant to various Slovenian companies. He holds PhD in mechanical engineering (1998). He spent sabbatical leave at the Technical University of Denmark, Department of Mechanical Engineering, Engineering Design Section.

Index